The Prophetic Law

Studies in Violence, Mimesis, and Culture

SERIES EDITOR

William A. Johnsen

The Studies in Violence, Mimesis, and Culture Series examines issues related to the nexus of violence and religion in the genesis and maintenance of culture. It furthers the agenda of the Colloquium on Violence and Religion, an international association that draws inspiration from René Girard's mimetic hypothesis on the relationship between violence and religion, elaborated in a stunning series of books he has written over the last forty years. Readers interested in this area of research can also look to the association's journal, *Contagion: Journal of Violence, Mimesis, and Culture.*

The Prophetic Law

ESSAYS IN JUDAISM, GIRARDIANISM,
LITERARY STUDIES, AND THE ETHICAL

Sandor Goodhart

Michigan State University Press · *East Lansing*

♾ The paper used in this publication meets the minimum requirements of ANSI/NISO
z39.48-1992 (R 1997) (Permanence of Paper).

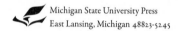 Michigan State University Press
East Lansing, Michigan 48823-5245

Printed and bound in the United States of America.

20 19 18 17 16 15 14   1 2 3 4 5 6 7 8 9 10

LIBRARY OF CONGRESS CATALOGING-IN-PUBLICATION DATA
Goodhart, Sandor.
The prophetic law : essays in Judaism, Girardianism, literary studies, and
the ethical / Sandor Goodhart.
pages cm.— (Studies in violence, mimesis, and culture series)
Includes bibliographical references and index.
ISBN 978-1-61186-124-2 (pbk. : alk. paper)—ISBN 978-1-60917-413-2 (ebook)
1. Girard, René, 1923– 2. Philosophy, French—20th century. 3. Philosophy,
Modern—20th century. I. Title.
B2430.G494G66 2014
194—dc23
2013024384

Book design and composition by Charlie Sharp, Sharp Des!gns, Lansing, Michigan
Cover design by David Drummond, Salamander Design, www.salamanderhill.com
Detail from *Memorial* ©1986 Samuel Bak used courtesy of the Pucker Gallery. All rights
reserved. To see *Memorial* in its entirety and other works by Samuel Bak, please visit
www.puckergallery.com.

g **green**
press
INITIATIVE Michigan State University Press is a member of the Green Press Initiative
and is committed to developing and encouraging ecologically responsible
publishing practices. For more information about the Green Press Initiative and the use of
recycled paper in book publishing, please visit *www.greenpressinitiative.org*.

Visit Michigan State University Press at *www.msupress.org*

In memory of my parents,
Abraham Goodhart and Evelyn Love Goodhart,
זכרונם לברכה,
for my children, Joshua, Noah, and Jonah,
and for my grandchildren,
Ethan, Graham, Aaron, Gabriel, Sarah, Stella, and Max
—witnesses in my life to creation, revelation, and redemption

Contents

Acknowledgments

Numerous individuals have offered their skills, friendship, and generosity in the course of the writing, delivery, and publication of the following essays and I would like to express my gratitude. Paul Dumouchel invited me to the gathering in Cerisy in 1983 where I delivered the talk on Joseph that became the first chapter in this book. Paul's intelligence and clarity on Girardian matters through the years has been a consistent source of encouragement. Raymund Schwager, SJ, befriended me upon my arrival at Cerisy, and his pursuit of discussion with me (in person and in print) of the Hebrew prophetic texts—along with his yearly holiday greetings afterward—remain a source of continued blessing. His untimely passing in 2004 was a grievous loss. Norbert Lohfink generously engaged me in the course of the meetings and we shared brief but fruitful exchanges on the parallels and distinctions between history and text in Deuteronomy. Roel Kaptein singled me out among the presenters, highlighting my flippant and irreverent ways of speaking about Moses as an "uncanny dealer" (someone willing to say to the Almighty in Exodus 3, "no problem") and, accompanied by Roel and Aat van Rhijn, I spent a wonderful afternoon visiting the cathedrals of Coutances. Both individuals gave of themselves freely and without recompense. The subsequent passing of Roel and Aat is equally a loss. Eric

Gans, Tobin Siebers, and Paisley Livingston also attended the conference from America and their engagement with me and with my work in the ensuing years has been transformative.

Wolfgang Palaver, who was the first editor of the newly formed *Bulletin* of COV&R, suggested the dialogue between Raymund and myself reproduced here. Wolfgang has remained through the years a reliable source of wisdom on all matters Girardian. My talk at Berkeley on Girard's work (comprising the bulk of the concluding chapter) is the result of his (and Richard Schenk's) invitation. Józef Niewiadomski helped me to clarify (through his generous comments and friendship) the parameters of my own work with regard to the theological perspectives of Raymund, Wolfgang, himself, and others among the Innsbruck theologians. Charles Mabee introduced me to the advisory board of COV&R, and his generous sharing with me of his own brilliant work on the prophetic (and recently on hospitality) has remained pivotal to my own perspective both practically and theoretically. The hospitality of Hans Jensen and his family to me one summer when I traveled to Aarhus remains indelible. I thank Wolfgang for the idea, the editing, the translation, and now this publication of the *Bulletin* exchange, and Józef, Charles, and Hans for their contributions to it.

Willard Swartley welcomed me without hesitation into the community of Associated Mennonites in Elkhart, Indiana (where I traveled with James Williams one year for a brief post-COV&R gathering), and later published my essay on Isaiah 52–53 (here titled *"al lo-chamas 'asah"*) in his astute collection. I have known Jim since the outset of my association with COV&R (in 1991) both as a friend and an esteemed colleague in Biblical scholarship and religious studies. His advice and collaboration on countless Girardian projects has been a continued source of *shalom uvrachah*. Vern Neufeld Redekop has also been a faithful interlocutor over the years on Girardian matters, and it is to his wonderful work in conflict resolution studies that I owe the essay I developed for this volume.

I met Andrew McKenna as my editor in *Semeia* (and later *Contagion*) and we have remained friends ever since. His intelligence in all matters has been indefatigable. Cesáreo Bandera was a professor of Hispanic literature when I attended SUNY Buffalo as a graduate student and unfailingly provided guidance as a member of my dissertation defense committee. Along with Bill Johnsen, Andrew and Cesáreo have been my primary cohorts in the literary end of things within the Girardian fold. My readings in "'Nothing Extenuate'" reflect their penetrating influence. My work with Thérèse Onderdenwijngaard (who invited me to join the staff at the Girard summer school in the Netherlands), and with Paul Dumouchel and James Alison, my colleagues in the teaching of Girard's work, has deepened my understanding of the political and theological ramifications of Girardian thinking.

To Rebecca Adams, Mark Anspach, Judy Arias, Vanessa Avery, Gil Baillee, Maria Stella Barberi, Anthony Bartlett, Diane Culbertson, Hubert Darthenay, Robert Doran, Joachim Duyndam, Michael Elias, Giuseppe Fornari, Bob Hamerton-Kelly, Michael Hardin, Billy Hewitt, Rosemary Johnsen, Britt Johnston, Cheryl Kirk-Duggan, Michael Kirwin, André Lascaris, Andrew Marr, Bill Mishler, William Morrow, Susan Nowak, Sonja Pos, Dietmar Regensberger, Martha Reineke, Keith Ross, Suzanne Ross, Julie Shinnick, Simon Simonse, Thee Smith, Susan Srigley, Niki Wandiger, Hans Weigand, Bruce Ward, and others among the Girardian fold with whom I have had numerous conversations over the years regarding Girard's work, I owe an incalculable debt of gratitude.

Ann Astell and I have been friends since my arrival at Purdue in 1997. As a sister of the venerated Schoenstatt Movement of Koblenz (founded by Joseph Kentenich), also a fellow traveler in matters Girardian and Levinasian, as well as my colleague and collaborator in English at Purdue before her departure for the theology department at the University of Notre Dame (she collaborated with me on *Sacrifice, Scripture, and Substitution*), Ann has been one of my primary daily interlocutors. She invited me to contribute to the issue of *Religion and Literature* she was editing (with our common student, now our colleague, Justin Jackson) celebrating the fiftieth year of Girard's *Mensonge romantique* (see "Reading Religion, Literature, and the End of Desire"). My other interlocutor is Thomas Ryba. I have known Tom as well since my arrival at Purdue in 1997 and I continue on a daily basis to benefit from his friendship and advice. He collaborated with me (as series editor) on an issue of the journal *Religion* devoted to Girard and, with Jim Williams and Jørgen Jørgensen, on a collection of texts documenting Girard's influence on the careers of a number of scholars. His influence, like Ann's, is evident throughout these pages.

My frequent presentations at the annual COV&R meetings have offered me interested, informed, and enthusiastic audiences for my work.

Marie-Louise Martinez welcomed me to COV&R 1998 in Saint-Denis/Paris (where I delivered a version of "From Sacrificial Violence to Responsibility"), Robert Daly to COV&R 2000 in Boston (where I delivered a version of "Reading Halachically and Aggadically"), Johan Elsen to COV&R 2001 in Antwerp (where I delivered a response to Girard forming a part of "Response by René Girard and Reply to René Girard"), Vern Redekop to COV&R 2006 in Ottawa (where I delivered a version of "The Self and Other People"), Thérèse Onderdenwijngaard to COV&R 2007 in Amsterdam (where I delivered the first version of "From the Sacred to the Holy"), and Jeremiah Alberg to COV&R 2012 in Tokyo (where I delivered a version of "Back to the Future"). To Marie-Louise, Bob, Johan, Vern, Thérèse, and Jeremiah, my heartfelt thanks.

Benoît Chantre invited me to speak in Paris at the Sorbonne on Girard's reading of Shakespeare (see "'Nothing Extenuate'") and to collaborate with him to organize a conference on the correspondences between Girard's work and Levinas's (see "From the Sacred to the Holy"). I thank him for his invitations, his collaborations, and his friendship, which has deepened over time in ways that affirm claims by Girardians about positive mimesis. I first met Bill Johnsen in Ann Arbor in 1978 and we have remained friends ever since. I thank him for his continued faith in my work, his personal generosity to me in my frequent travels, for his own brilliant work on modernism and mimetic phenomena (from which I have consistently benefitted), and his repeated and sage counsel in all matters literary and Girardian. I also thank Peter Thiel and his organization—principally, Lindy Fishburne, but as well her Imitatio staff now headed by Jimmy Kaltreider—for their generous support of the now burgeoning Girardian universe. I thank as well my Purdue colleagues in the English Department for their helpful suggestions in general regarding my writing, and in the preparation of the essays in this manuscript in particular: Tom Adler, Dorothy Deering, Angelica Duran, John Duvall, Wendy Flory, Shaun Hughes, Bob Lamb, Clayton Lein, Maren Linnett, Dan Morris, Len Neufeldt, Nancy Peterson, Don Platt, Arkady Plotnitsky, Victor Raskin, Charlie Ross, Irwin Weiser, and Paul White.

To Julie Loehr and her staff at the MSU Press with whom I have had the honor of working—and especially Kristine Blakeslee, Elise Jajuga, Marla Koenigsknecht, Annette Tanner, and Travis Kimbel—my heartfelt thanks for their abiding faith in this project. And to Lawrence Langer, a friend of long duration and fellow traveler in "afterdeath" of our era, for his help in securing the use of a portion of the astonishing painting by Samuel Bak for the cover of this book, my continued gratitude.

"Teaching," Levinas tells us in *Totality and Infinity*, "brings me more than I can contain." And that has certainly been the case for me. Among the students who have taught me the most about the matters contained in this book (and with whose dissertations I played a directorial role), I would like to mention Justin Jackson, Kathryn Ludwig, Sol Neely, and Monica Osborne.

To René and Martha Girard, and to their children, Martin, Daniel, and Mary, my debts are more difficult to enumerate. René and Martha have remained in loco parentis for me in academia, René first welcoming me as his graduate student at SUNY Buffalo in 1969, and both later welcoming me into their home and family life on countless occasions. Needless to say, René's work is the very heart of this book, as is his thinking, his teaching, and his presence for so many of us lucky enough to have been born co-extant with his existence on the planet. He has achieved what only a handful of individuals ever achieve. He has changed the way we think about the world and our place within it.

My parents, Abraham and Evelyn Goodhart, consistently and positively supported my life and work. They would have enjoyed this publication. May their memory be for a blessing, *z"l*. To my children, Joshua, Noah, and Jonah (and their wives, Jennifer, Ingrid, and Cris), and to their children (and my grandchildren)—Ethan, Graham, Aaron, Gabriel, Sarah, Stella, and Max—I owe my present and my future. Through their existence, I understand in a renewed and vital way Martin Buber's, Franz Rosenzweig's, and Emmanuel Levinas's reading of Judaism as a witness to the infinite within the finite, as living examples of creation, revelation, and redemption. It is to this family that this book is dedicated.

Finally, to Barbara Wisdom, my significant other, upon whose love, counsel, and wisdom I have come increasingly to rely, goes my profound gratitude and acknowledgment.

An Introduction
to Girardian Reading

A ll of the essays that follow this introduction were delivered as papers
or written directly for publication in relation to the work of René
Girard. Many were conceived in connection with annual meetings
of the Colloquium on Violence and Religion. Others were delivered at joint
meetings of the American Academy of Religion and the Society of Biblical
Literature, and elsewhere. Still others were written for the *Bulletin* of the
Colloquium on Violence and Religion or its journal, *Contagion: Journal of
Violence, Mimesis, and Culture*. Others again were written for the *Journal of
Religion and Literature* and the *Journal of Philosophy: A Cross-Disciplinary
Inquiry* or for edited collections of essays published in book form. Eighteen
of the following twenty-five essays and short pieces are mine. Among those
eighteen, twelve have been published before; six appear here for the first time.

The eighteen texts that comprise the heart of the following volume
constitute the bulk of my writings to date on René Girard outside of the
three books that I have published individually or in conjunction with others,
and a long essay on the relation of Girard to Levinas, Buber, and Rosenzweig
I delivered at the French Embassy in Rome.[1] I have included, in addition,
seven very short texts (some little more than a paragraph) by others: one
account of a discussion in which I participated (following a paper delivery in

Cerisy-la-Salle), one response by Girard to an essay I wrote on Second Isaiah (included below), three replies to texts I had written or presentations I had made (also included below) by Raymund Schwager and Józef Niewiadomski, and two accounts of a session held at the American Academy of Religion in which I described the larger contours of prophetic reading with Charles Mabee and Hans Jensen.[2]

Why gather them here? René Girard is a prophetic thinker. He teaches us to read the European novel, ancient Greek tragedy, or, concomitantly, Jewish and Christian scripture, not by offering us a method he has developed, but by offering us the method they have developed, the interpretative reading method already available within each of these bodies of writing.

Or, to put it another way, he teaches us literary reading. Although nominally he turned away from literary reading after the conclusion of his first book to pursue more anthropological concerns and then religious studies concerns—the origins of imitative desire, or the sacrificial violence to which it leads (the management of which remains, in his view, the hallmark of archaic societies and whose exposure remains the hallmark of ours), or its exposure in holy scripture—it is an underlying assumption of these many and diverse essays that in some ways he never abandoned his original project, that the sacrificial and its relation to violence, its origins in mimetic desire, its exposition in Biblical writing, remain the subject matter of literary reading.

To read literature is to read the way literature reads. This is an astounding idea once its implications are teased out. I grew up in the United States in the 1950s when new criticism was in its heyday. The close reading of literature, *l'explication de texte*, as it was then called, was all the rage. The method held immense promise because it was felt to be not a method at all but an access to what literature itself was already doing. Northrop Frye took the project "to the next level," as they say in academia (in a phrase probably borrowed from signs to be found in university parking garages), opening doors to mythic and ritual dimensions without encumbering those discussions with the postulates of Freudian psychoanalysis or Jungian archetypalism.

French thinking, in the hands of practitioners like Claude Lévi-Strauss, Roland Barthes, Jacques Lacan, Jacques Derrida, and Michel Foucault, amplified our conception of literary thinking by loosening the hitherto strict boundaries between doing and saying. And in this country, Paul de Man, Stanley Fish, Harold Bloom, and Geoffrey Hartman, among others, welcomed this new thinking—which was really a return to old thinking, since it recalled (even as it dismantled), on the one hand, the ancient Roman distinction regarding the liberal arts, the *trivium* of grammar, rhetoric, and logic, and on the other, the ancient "quarrel" between poetic making and philosophy. But no one, prior to Girard, and in another realm Emmanuel Levinas, it could be argued, challenged quite as profoundly the Platonic formulation of representation—that something stands for something for somebody. With the exception of Hartman's scattered excurses on midrash, and Bloom's flirtation with Kabbalistic criticism, few writers ventured outside representational thinking, although all roundly and forthrightly challenged its limitations.

This claim, of course, is itself a profoundly polemic one and the precise place of Girard's work (and Levinas's) among these avatars of the "hypothesis of textuality" or difference and its enabling conditions remains to be developed much more fully. Suffice it to say for the moment that prophetic thinking, we are coming increasingly to understand, is considerably older than representation, which is a relative newcomer on the cultural scene, a "Johnny-come-lately" to the history of thought. In ancient sixth century Greece and the Hebraic communities of the immediate post-exilic period, prophetic thinking already flourished. The four-leveled midrashic reading and teaching method developed by the medieval Rabbis a thousand years later and practiced, for example, in the contemporary setting by Levinas in his Talmudic studies, like the anti-sacrificial reading practiced by Girard in his scriptural criticism and studies of Greek tragedy, are its heirs. If we are to trust Girard's claim that the sacrificial is the root modality of cultural organization, then prophetic thinking is bound up with the foundation of culture itself, and to engage it in his work—at once as subject matter and subject—is to engage one of the deepest strata of our cultural lives. It is hard, for this reader at least, to imagine a more comprehensive academic endeavor.

Perhaps one day we will come to understand more fully the way that the prophetic and the ethical relate to one another, the way they constitute two names for the same thing, the one with reference to reading, the other with reference to people. Or, put somewhat differently, the way Greek tragedy formulates the question for which it has no answer, while Hebraic scriptural writing of roughly the same moment begins to formulate the ethical answer for the question it finds impossible to ask, how both the tragic prophetic question and the scriptural ethical answer participate in a mode known in both Athens and Jerusalem as prophetic thinking. When that day arrives, René Girard's work on Greek tragedy, Jewish and Christian scripture, and the great literary writings of the West since then will have led the way. It will have guided us to the portals through which the full resources of the prophetic may be glimpsed.

I have divided the texts below into four groups. In the first, I have included dialogues conducted with other Girardians (regarding Jewish and Christian relations). In the second, I have included readings of key Jewish scriptural texts as distinct from readings undertaken by others. In the third, I have included readings of what Girard does with European literature or with Shakespeare as opposed to what I do (or what others do) with both, or what Girard might have done. And in the fourth, I have included readings of Girard in context of other intellectual figures (Buber, Rosenzweig, Levinas, for example), as well as conceptualizations by Girardians of the prophetic, the apocalyptic, and other ideas.

But this particular collection has a personal history that probably bears retelling.

Part One: From Cerisy-la-Salle to Berkeley

The book that follows was probably conceived some thirty years ago. In 1983, René Girard invited me, as one of his students—there were not many of us at the time—to accompany him to Cerisy-la-Salle in France where two young scholars were planning a week-long seminar in his honor.[3] In conversations with him about the upcoming conference, I learned that he was planning to speak about Christianity. Although when I met Girard he had already published a book on the European novel, and more recently some important essays on Greek tragedy, and was primarily at work on *Violence and the Sacred*, I knew that I could not speak about Christianity, which was his tradition and not mine.[4] I had been impressed by his work on scapegoating, on sacrifice as expulsion, and on the breakdown of differences in the archaic and modern universe, but where he saw this understanding as issuing from Christianity, I saw it as older. I could honor him, I realized, by writing about my own cultural and religious tradition. Although I had been raised within a more or less conservative Jewish religious orientation, the field of Jewish studies was not at the time for me an active intellectual pursuit. I began reading extensively in the writings of Martin Buber, Franz Rosenzweig, Gershom Scholem, and Emmanuel Levinas, among other scholars and critical thinkers working on Judaism and Jewish subject matters. As a literary reader, I was especially drawn to Biblical scripture and the first chapter of this book is the result. I wrote the essay in English, delivered it at the conference in English, and Paul Dumouchel translated it into French for the conference volume.[5]

The title of this book says it all. It occurred to me in reading Buber and Rosenzweig that a major misunderstanding of their work had circulated in academia. Their work concerned Jewish renewal, at the center of which was one idea: the law of anti-idolatry. Judaism is Torah-centered, they taught, which meant in effect that at the center was the idea of commandments, *mitzvoth*, and in particular, the commandment against idolatry: "I am the Lord, not those other Gods that you have installed in my place"—the first commandment ("I am the Lord, thy God"), being explained by a second commandment ("no other Gods before Me") being explained in turn by the third commandment ("no taking of the name of God for nothingness"), and so forth. All of Torah was but an extension of commandment, all of the 613 commandments an extension of the first commandment, indeed, of its first word, *anochi*, "I," even, in the eyes of some, of the first letter of the first word of that commandment, which is, appropriately enough, an aleph. And in the other direction, Torah, commandment, is considered the "blueprint of the world." And all of commandment was about not substituting what was not God for God—in the realm of material things, of course, but also in the realm of language, and of people.

The idea originated for Buber among the Hebrew prophets: Isaiah, Jeremiah, Ezekiel, and others. But in the six hundred years since its inception after the fall of Jerusalem and the exile, in the rabbinic tradition to which it had given rise, the prophetic mode had expanded. Vying for influence with other post-exilic parties within the Jewish community—with others invested, for example, in returning to the sacrificial ways of the first Temple, or in purifying Judaism of its acquired deviations—it finally gained prominence when the second Temple collapsed (around 77 of our era) and gave way as the modality of survival. Rabbinic Judaism, which we know today simply as Judaism, as Buber tells the story, was the product of the prophetic law of anti-idolatry.

Law is admittedly an odd term here. The word Torah is not cognate with *nomos* from the Greek, nor with *lex* from the Latin. The word "torah" in fact in Hebrew means instruction or teaching or scriptural reading or commandment. And "prophetic" has a specialized understanding in this context. The prophetic, I often say, with a nod to Greek tragic writing, is the recognition of the dramas in which human beings are engaged and the naming in advance of the end of those dramas in order that we can choose to go there or not. In the context of Judaism, the prophetic maintains an "if/then" structure, as Buber will say. The book of Jonah is an extended illustration of it. I have tried to elaborate these ideas more extensively in "Back to the Future."

And so if I use the word "law" here as part of the title or join it with the word "prophetic," I do it to something of a deconstructive end. René Girard's ideas, I began to realize, were a modality of prophetic thinking. What Girard was teaching us about literary reading in the European novel, or about Greek "tragic-prophetic" reading in the case of Sophocles or Euripides, the Hebrew Bible was teaching in the ancient world. Reading the Hebrew Bible prophetically was reading the way the Hebrew Bible itself reads. Doing so would yield extraordinary results, results that had not yet been recognized, and that confirmed Girard's readings of literature and Greek tragic writing. The first part of the Joseph story was squarely about mimetic desire and its transformation into sacrificial violence in all the ways that Girard has described it in *Mensonge romantique* (1961) and later *La violence et le sacré* (1972).[6] And the second part of the story released people at least potentially from the dangers of that violent heritage. One did not have to read sacrificially as Joseph's brothers did initially. One could learn to read anti-sacrificially as finally all of them did. The Joseph story offered a performative model for Hebraic reading linked to literary understandings of the most sophisticated modern variety.

I was off and running. In short order, I developed readings of the text of the Ten Commandments (is it a text or a list that we engage?), of the book of Jonah (as an illustration of prophetic thinking), and of the book of Job (as a questioning of the potential for the position of Judaism in a non-Jewish universe). If in the book of Job, Judaism is never mentioned, the book remains a companion piece to the book of Esther where God is never mentioned. It explores what happens if Judaism is left out of the discussion in the ancient world—namely, a universe in which creation and suffering remain at odds with one another and vie for prominence. Judaism, as recounted in Second Isaiah, is that missing middle piece from the book of Job.

And I immediately got myself into trouble. Father Raymund Schwager, S.J., a member of the faculty of the Institute for Systematic Theology at the University of Innsbruck in Austria, whose kindness to me was immediate, boundless, and indefatigable, inaugurated the discussion at Cerisy. We were on the same panel. He spoke about transformations of the conception of divine wrath, and I addressed the Joseph story. In the debate that followed, we both elaborated our presentations. But already during the conference, Father Schwager, along with the eminent Swiss Biblical Deuteronomic scholar, Father Norbert Lohfink, engaged some of the larger issues I was raising. I have reproduced the Joseph essay and the discussion that followed in "'I Am Joseph.'"

And shortly afterwards, in the *Bulletin* edited by Raymund Schwager's younger colleague, Wolfgang Palaver, the exchange continued. I summarized an essay I was writing about René Girard's work in relation to what Christians consider a key passage in the prophetic texts, Isaiah 52–53, and a series of three further exchanges followed, drawing into the debate as well another young scholar and systematic theologian, Józef Niewiadomski (later to follow Raymund Schwager as Dean of the Catholic Theological Faculty at the University of Innsbruck after the former's untimely death). "A Jewish-Christian Dialogue" contains these entries from three issues of the *Bulletin*.

The encounter encouraged me to consider Jewish-Christian relations more broadly. I published my essay on Girard (*"al lo-chamas 'asah"*), to which Girard referred at length in his subsequent "response" at the end of Willard Swartley's book, *Violence Renounced*. I "replied" in the COV&R meeting in Antwerp and then again at the celebration in honor of Swartley's book, at the AAR the following fall (see "Response by René Girard and Reply to René Girard").

Thus the first section of the book that follows is about this polemical engagement: at Cerisy and afterwards, in the *Bulletin*, at COV&R meetings, at meetings of the AAR/SBL. So impressive were these various "dialogues" in my experience (they readily spilled over into my work at Cornell, Purdue, and elsewhere) that when I first thought about putting together this volume

(at Bill Johnsen's suggestion), I considered coupling them with a few pieces
I wrote later and proposed naming the collection as a whole "Dialogues
among Girardians."

But recently I have written about Girard a little differently. While continuing to endorse my Jewish studies interests, Girard also resisted my efforts
to get him to engage them more directly. I soon learned why. In a series of
talks with Geoffrey Hartman and James Williams conducted at Hobart and
William Smith College in 1991, Girard became increasingly open about his
own advocacy of Christian belief and practice, not just of the anti-sacrificial
reading of the Gospels he had proposed in *Des choses cachées*, but more fully
as a lifestyle choice.[7]

More specifically, Girard had spoken about the reading of Christianity implied in his anthropological work as early as 1973, in an article he
published on the Gospel of Matthew in 1976, and his book in 1977 simply
amplified those views.[8] In an interview with Rebecca Adams, however, he
expanded this earlier perspective. I was wrong to view sacrifice in entirely
negative terms, as exclusively about expulsion and scapegoating—he now
said in effect. Christianity has also understood a positive reading of sacrifice,
and I (Girard) accept that reading.[9] Moreover, he added, the criticism of the
text of Hebrews that I expressed in *Des choses cachées* has to be qualified. In
The Scapegoat, in *Job, the Victim of His People*, and in *I See Satan Fall like
Lightning*, Girard continued to revise his earlier position.[10] Father Schwager,
Norbert Lohfink, and others were right; their position is now my own, he
now more or less openly asserted. Their ethical understanding is what follows
from my (Girard's) own analysis of sacrifice.[11]

As Girard continued to revise his position, so, I realized, my own position would need qualification. Girard found in the work of these scholars
theological extensions of his insights. Girard's ideas as a set of intellectual
tools, as an analysis of the sacrificial in culture, of mimetic desire, scapegoating, and their violent and catastrophic consequences as revealed to us, for
example, within Jewish and Christian scriptural writings, remained for me,
as Andrew McKenna once put it somewhat colloquially, "the best game in
town," unmatched as a tool for inquiry into the makeup of culture and the
role of our holy scriptures in deciphering its mechanisms.

But "Girardianism" as an intellectual endeavor, I began to realize, is not
the same thing as Girard's personal endorsement or practice of Christian

belief or ethical understanding. Girard's analytic of the sacrificial may lead us to the door of the ethical, but does not—and in my view cannot—take us through that door. It is not designed that way. Girard's analysis of the mimetic and sacrificial offers us an account of the motor force, the structurative mechanism, at the heart of all culture in conditions of order and disorder in the archaic and modern universe. That's quite a lot, I admit. But it's not everything. And one thing missing is what to do about it.

The political, in short, is not the ethical and does not precede the ethical, as we have often tried to convince ourselves during the last two hundred years or so (especially during turbulent times) in Western Europe. The political in our culture derives from the sacrificial and everything that Girard says about the sacrificial dimensions of archaic culture may legitimately be introduced into contemporary historical discussion.[12] We may understand the political in its entirety in a given culture, the relation of knowledge to its willful employment in every nook and cranny the culture organizes, from a Girardian perspective. And we may be prepared to identify the sacrificial or anti-sacrificial makeup of every structure in that complex grid of cultural distinctions. But that examination does not prescribe this or that course as better or worse, nor describe the ethical dynamics within which each member of that community is situated. To make that latter move, to undertake that analysis, we would need another body of thought, and those of us who find Girard's analysis of the mimetic and the sacrificial compelling and persuasive (as I did, and do), would need to articulate our own pathway.

The eight remaining essays in the book reflect my version of that journey to date. I gathered two essays on close reading of the Hebrew Bible: the passages that Christians name "The Fall" and that Jews conceptualize as the exile from *gan eden*, the "Garden of Eden" ("The End of Sacrifice"); and the opening of the book (in which the Torah is finally given) on the early education of Moses ("From Sacrificial Violence to Responsibility"). And I included along with those essays two on Girard's literary work: an essay I wrote for Ann Astell and her issue (with Justin Jackson) of the forum in *Religion and Literature* on the occasion of the fiftieth anniversary of Girard's literary work ("Reading Religion, Literature, and the End of Desire"); and an essay on Shakespeare's *Othello* in which I reflect upon my conversations with Girard in Buffalo and on my initial dissertation work on *Othello* ("'Nothing Extenuate'").

In the four concluding essays, I engage a variety of efforts that have been made to see Girard in relation to ethical thinking: an encounter I had with Reuven Kimelman vis-à-vis Girard's work at COV&R 2000 in Boston ("Reading Halachically and Aggadically"); a version of the exchange I have persistently tried to encourage with the work of Emmanuel Levinas and Girard vis-à-vis conflict resolution studies, and delivered as a paper at COV&R 2006 in Ottawa ("The Self and Other People") at the invitation of Vern Redekop; an essay I wrote for a symposium at the Bibliothèque nationale de France (and the following day at the École normale supérieure) in 2012 combining an examination of Girard's work in context of Levinas's work ("From the Sacred to the Holy"); and an analysis I undertook of Girard's book on Clausewitz and its relation to prophetic and apocalyptic thinking ("Back to the Future"). In other words, within the orthodox Jewish religious tradition, within conflict resolution studies, within philosophic thinking, and within the political.

On the occasion of a conference at Berkeley on the publication of a book-length essay Girard wrote on Hinduism and Buddhism, I reflected briefly on the status of Girard's work in world religions and I include some portions of that writing in the concluding chapter.[13]

Part Two: Girardian Polemics

Before bringing this introduction to a close, however, it occurs to me that three issues remain to be addressed more forthrightly. There are, in my view, three rather serious misunderstandings of Girard's work that have hampered its positive reception and contributed to its negative assessment in ways that are unwarranted: namely, the idea of the "innocent victim," the idea of good and bad mimesis, and the idea of a Girardian ethical position. In all three instances, the misunderstanding, in my estimation, rests upon an essentialist reading of his ideas that is unfounded.

Let me take up each in sequence. Perhaps, in doing so, I may clarify my own position vis-à-vis others in Girardian studies.

The Innocent Victim

In *Violence and the Sacred*, Girard speaks of a crisis of differences, a collapse or breakdown of cultural distinctions characterized by the appearance of enemy twins, human doubles engaged in mutual accusation and reciprocal violence. The classic example—to which he returns repeatedly—is Oedipus and Teiresias. But in *Things Hidden* and afterwards, Girard speaks of the "innocence" of the victim. In his view, Christianity teaches us above all about "the innocent victim," which is to say, the innocence of *all* victims without limit of the kind of scapegoat violence at the root of the foundation of archaic society. In my essay on Isaiah 52–53 ("*al lo-chamas 'asah*"), I tried to suggest this idea borrows from Hebraic texts that speak of the removal from the community (undoubtedly the murder) of a scapegoated individual and his burial among the wicked and the evildoers, "although he had done no violence," although in the Jewish context, I granted, the passage is not highlighted, and the law of anti-idolatry, "no god but God," retains preeminence.

What does Girard mean by that assertion? Precisely, that the victim of a scapegoating process is always innocent of the infraction with which he or she is charged, and for the evils said to be attendant upon that infraction, that the designation of the victim as "guilty," as "*le culpable*," is, in short, always and in all cases arbitrary. Christianity discovers in Girard's view that all victims of archaic society have been killed for a crime they did not commit (even in the cases where they did the deed with which they are charged), and that as a result in all cases their scapegoating was gratuitous—an unnecessary instance of communal violence against members of its own community. Even in the case where they did the deed, and their culpability is not in doubt, the exclusionary mechanism serves above all the social sacrificial function it implements rather than the empirical facts with which it happens to coincide.

This idea has been a major source of confusion among readers of Girard, if for no other reason than the fact that Girard himself appears to take a contrary view. In his reading of Dostoyevsky, for example, he cites repeatedly (and with deep approbation) the Russian author's famous observation, at a critical moment in one of his novels, that "we are all guilty, before everyone, for everything, and me more than anyone."[14] Christianity reveals the innocence of the victim, of all victims, and Dostoyevsky, whose endorsement of

Christianity for Girard remains unimpeachable, reveals our universal culpability. How can we have it both ways?

The answer is that in one way we are innocent (all victims are innocent) and in another we are guilty (all guilty, of everything, before everyone). We are all innocent vis-à-vis the scapegoat mechanism, which would charge us with unique and essential guilt for the crime inaugurating the crisis from which the community is thought to suffer, but all guilty vis-à-vis each other, from which perspective all are identical. The distinction here between the social mechanism of scapegoating (undertaken for its own sacrificial ends) and the factual guilt or innocence of the individual charged with the misdeed is paramount. The victim is no more guilty or innocent than any other member of the community, and in fact their real status in context of those others is precisely that of a double. Another victim could just as well have substituted, just as well served the same social requirement in an indistinguishable way.

At the same time, once the determination is made, the distinction is absolute. In all cases, the empirical facts of the matter are secondary to the social and socializing function they play in the ongoing operation of the sacrificial mechanisms by which, in Girard's view, all cultures are necessarily organized and which is always primary. In this regard, Girard shares with Claude Lévi-Strauss the idea that the social precedes in importance even the category of the empirical—which remains a category (despite our customary utilitarian readings to the contrary), and as such is always revised to conform to the former, even when the facts of the matter happen to conform already to the social determination.[15]

The arbitrariness of the victimage in all cases, the independence of the victim of the social determinate of guilt, however, does not mean that the accused did not commit a crime. Why is this distinction important? Because this statement of the innocence of the victim is often taken to mean a victim is innocent by virtue simply of being victimized, that his or her behavior has been "washed clean" by the sheer fact of victimage alone, independent of any other action taken on his or her part, that in effect salvation has been "purchased" or acquired by the mere adoption of this way of thinking, that what "comes along with the package," so to speak, is a rewriting of history and a determination of one's essential goodness, hitherto hidden but henceforth forever revealed.

Why is that dangerous? Because in the name of freeing the victim, such a gesture opens the door to the potential for finding countless new ones. If the victim is innocent, then those who have falsely accused him are themselves guilty and may be pursued relentlessly as perpetrators. In an age when everyone has identified him or herself as a victim in one fashion or another, the pursuit of such "perpetrators" (and thus the continuation of victimage) is multiplied exponentially. In some ways, the situation is worse than ever before since now there is no authority to denounce such neo-sacrificial behavior, and its cover as a version of the anti-sacrificial can be profoundly deceptive. In the name of the anti-sacrificial, in the last two hundred years, some of the worst disasters of our history have been perpetrated.

Bruce Ward draws our attention to this distinction in his brilliant essay on Kafka.[16] The victim is neither more nor less guilty of the crimes with which he is charged by virtue of having been charged or by virtue of having adopted a new perspective on it. The first person narrator of Camus's last novel, *The Fall*, we may note, the humanistic advocate (named Jean-Baptiste Clemence) who boasts of his capacity to free criminals is as sacrificial in his behavior to others (despite the humanism of his manner) as his clients would like to believe others have been toward them. Meursault in Camus's first published novel, *The Stranger*, as Girard had written, is as guilty as he would condemn others for being in their condemnation of him.

Dostoyevsky remains, in other words, Girard's guide here just as Camus, in Girard's view, was beginning to become at the moment of his untimely death. "We are all guilty, before everyone, for everything, and me more than anyone." The innocence of the victim of scapegoat violence in Girard's view opens us to the potential for increased responsibility for our bad behavior (by freeing us from the group's sacrificial utilization of it), not a new way to avoid owning it, or to continue prosecuting others on its basis.

Good and Bad Mimesis

The idea that there is an essential distinction to be perceived between different kinds of mimesis is another ground-zero level misunderstanding that has undermined appreciation of Girard's claim. There is no good or bad mimesis. There is only mimesis, the borrowing or appropriation of our desires and behaviors from others, and its efficacious or inefficacious outcome in our case. Or, if you like (and to adopt the formulation that a writer like Stanley

Fish would find familiar), there is always a distinction to be had between good and bad mimesis but it is never the same one. Sometimes a certain behavior will count as "good" mimesis and a behavior to be emulated, other times the same behavior will count as bad mimesis, and something to be avoided. Good and bad in this context mean outcome, not essence. There is no behavior for Girard that is not itself mimetic (unless we exclude negatively imitative behavior, which he assuredly does not) and no behavior that cannot count as violence in the proper context. Concomitantly, there is no behavior that counts as violence that in another setting could not count as life-saving (consider the pregnant woman stabbed in the stomach by a well dressed male who is in fact her doctor performing a needed caesarian). What determines whether or not a certain mimetic behavior is "good" or "bad" is the degree to which the behavior inculcates a sacrificial approach in a context in which it no longer works—which is always the potential in the modern world deprived of guaranteed ritual solutions, the degree to which it constitutes violence or difference "gone wrong."

Why would we be likely to think otherwise? Again, because of the religious context in which the issue is customarily posed. Is it not *always* good to follow or imitate Jesus, for example, we may well wonder after reading Girard. Has not Girard claimed that Christianity alone fully reveals the truth of sacrifice to us, desacralizing violence, reversing the dehumanization of violence that constitutes mythology? And yet it is not difficult to imagine fundamentalist religious orientations (of whatever variety) in which the deconstruction of sacrifice has become neo-sacrificial in the most egregiously violent manner possible. And fundamentalism is not limited to Christianity. Examples of Jewish, Islamic, Buddhist, and Hindu fundamentalism—in which an anti-sacrificial position has been exercised with such force and in such circumstances that the effect is neo-sacrificial—are just as plentiful.

Moreover, does the availability of the truth mean that one has immediately the ability to take possession of it? What if the scriptural religions are right and the mechanisms of violence have been thoroughly unmasked by them? What guarantee is there that we will immediately be the beneficiaries of that determination? That we will not continue to act sacrificially in the archaic sense for a long time to come, that the task of demystifying violence will have become even more difficult than ever since now there is no longer any external authority to which we can make appeal?

Girardianism and the Ethical

Which leads us to the question of the ethical. If there is indeed no prede-termined good or bad mimesis (but only mimesis), and if the victim is only innocent to the extent that his or her victimage is arbitrarily chosen, what then is "good" to do? Is there nothing absolutely and indisputably good? Are we left inevitably in an ethical quagmire? Or, to put the matter another way, is there no way out of the quagmire in which we are unavoidably left? Girard's answer is clear, simple, and straightforward: "il faut refuser la violence." One must refuse violence.

But what does that mean in practical terms?

The Girardian understanding of the sacrificial, in other words, has no predetermined ethical component or ethical consequence, whatever the interests of some readers of Girard in identifying one. Perhaps because Girard himself became in 1961 (and has remained since then) a committed Chris-tian, or perhaps for other reasons, his thinking has often been conflated with Christianity as if it is in fact an extension of Roman Catholicism, a version of Augustinian theological thinking on the contemporary theoretical scene.

Girardianism, in other words, I would insist, is not Christianity, or any version of Christianity, in any of its forms, although the thinking that animates Girard's readings of Christian texts—and especially the Evangeli-cal text—is very much a part of Girardianism. Girardianism reads the texts of Jewish scripture and the texts of Christian scripture as articulating truths about the sacrificial (and to some extent about the mimetic nature of desire and its dynamics). But it is not interchangeable in any manner with a Chris-tian ethical position, or any other religiously structured ethical position for that matter. The most we are able to say of an ethical nature after Girard's analysis of the sacrificial in archaic culture (and of our own position since then in a kind of perpetual sacrificial crisis) is "il faut refuser la violence" ("we must refuse violence"). We must read and understand "anti-sacrificially."

And, I would like to add, prophetically. If there is a common fund to the five so-called "revealed" religions—Christianity, Judaism, Islam, Hinduism, Buddhism—I would suggest it is prophetic thinking. Although here is not the place to make the case for such a shared fund of insights about culture, suffice it to say for the moment that prophetic thinking is not the province of Judaism or Christianity alone and may be tied to the very makeup of all cultures on the planet, a kind of ur-logic of culture, so to speak, governing even, perhaps, the sacrificial.

That is fine, we may be willing to say. One can certainly endorse the importance of reading anti-sacrificially and prophetically. The ancient rabbis did as much. But what exactly does that entail? How specifically does one do that? The details need to be mapped out.

One way for Girard (and Girardians) to engage the ethical has been through the interpretation of literary writers. In fact, before the last chapter of *Mensonge romantique et vérité romanesque*, one might well have anticipated that Girard would turn out, like so many other literary readers, to put literature in the central and governing position.

Part of the attraction for me personally, in fact, in the 1960s as an English major within an American university to Girard's readings of the great European novel—Cervantes, Stendhal, Flaubert, Proust, Dostoyevsky—and of Greek tragedy—in the hands of Sophocles, and before him Aeschylus, and after him Euripides—was, I confess, the inordinate value Girard seemed to have invested in these literary productions. If I later turned to Jewish writing in his shadow—to decipher scriptural, Talmudic, midrashic, mystical, and the later Rabbinic traditions of commentary—it was inevitably because I saw in this Jewish writing and in Rabbinic thought in general the same anti-sacrificial and prophetic perspectives, the same "literary" perspectives, that Girard identified in European literature and in Greek tragedy.

But Girard did not continue as a reader of literary works, as we know, taking the alternate route of following the authors of such literary writings to their own origins. He pursued the anthropological path and asked instead "how did we get into this mess that we call mimetic desire and imitative rivalry?" And the answer at which he arrived was stunning. We got into this mess, he argued, through a "sacrificial crisis" that operated at the heart of all cultures on the planet but that in cultures other than our own—those we identify as archaic cultures—were efficaciously organized around sacrificial expulsion, around scapegoating or lynching of a collective victim (and the way ritual commemoration derived from that distinction between sacrifice and violence, a distinction or separation we recognize as difference itself), while in ours that distinction between sacrifice and violence had broken down and the distinction between the sacred and the profane, or the sacred and violence, was not able to be maintained.

And that anthropological path led him to a religious studies one. If it is true, he pondered, that the archaic sacrificial is no longer efficacious as an organizing structure for modern culture, and we find ourselves in a kind of runaway sacrificial crisis characterized by runaway mimetic appropriation and its consequence (i.e., conflict), then how is it we are able to speak about this crisis and not be destroyed by it (since one of the postulates he uncovered was that the system remains effective only so far as it is unconscious)? If all cultures on the planet operate sacrificially, and sacrificial organization depends upon an unconsciousness on the part of the participants (no lynchers say we are acting sacrificially against an arbitrary victim), how is it that we in our culture are able to talk about it?

And the answer at which he arrived was of course the now familiar one to Girardians: the Christian revelation, the scriptural testimony and subsequent theoretical (and theological) elaboration regarding the birth, ministry, and death of a young Jewish rabbi.

But Christianity is not the necessary or inevitable consequence of Girardian thinking. Christianity may be one possible outcome of Girardian thinking, but it is by no means the only one. And it may not even be, after all is said and done, the most prominent one in a wider cultural perspective. When future ages look back upon our own, and discern the importance of Girard's analysis of the sacrificial for posterity (as I have long said they would and as Michel Serres more recently predicts they will), it may not be the ethical consequence prescribed by Christianity that gets linked to his thinking.[17]

Christianity is nevertheless the path Girard took personally. And it would probably be fair to say that historically among our contemporaries, for that reason among others, it has to this point attracted the largest body of readers from within the Christian community. There are probably more Christian readers of Girard than there are readers of his work in academia—in English departments or in anthropology departments—or outside of religious groups, although that may say more about American life than either Girardian thinking, academia, or extra-university intellectual life. And apart from myself, there are comparatively few readers of Girard among Jews. But the Christian revelation is by no means the exclusive path along which one is necessarily led after understanding Girard's analysis of the sacrificial and the mimetic. One can sustain a Girardian reading of the sacrificial and the mimetic, I submit, and remain a Christian, a Hindu, a Buddhist, a Muslim, or a Jew.

In fact, another path may be the thought of Emmanuel Levinas. For Levinasians, the union of Girard's sacrificial analysis with Levinas's ethical analysis gives the ethical a political extension; anti-sacrificial, anti-scapegoat politics; the question of justice, the question of the third, is not only messianic, but anti-sacrificial, a matter of reading, and a matter of teaching.

◆   ◆   ◆

Bob Dylan's words remain for me a sign of the changing times.[18] Composed in the 1960s and addressed to readers of Biblical scripture, contemporary writers, politicians, and parents, the song continues to resonate fifty years later. Written by an individual from a Jewish family, from a small town in Minnesota that still recalled the spectacle of a lynching in a nearby town a short while before, the song articulates the frustrations of the postwar generation in America in the wake of the disasters of the recent past. Reading these words today, they draw us back to the scriptural contexts in which we continue to work.

> Come gather 'round people
> Wherever you roam
> And admit that the waters
> Around you have grown
> And accept it that soon
> You'll be drenched to the bone
> If your time to you
> Is worth savin'
> Then you better start swimmin'
> Or you'll sink like a stone
> For the times they are a-changin'.[19]

Why would time be worth saving, inquiring minds might want to know. Is Dylan mocking the Western fascination with temporality? Phenomenology? If your precious conception of time is really that important, perhaps you better start taking action. Or is he talking about nostalgia—"your time," your era, this era? If you want to preserve the past (as you seem to want to do), you better act quickly.

And what would it mean to heed the call and "start swimmin'"? Something more deliberate, no doubt, than "go with the flow," a complacency which may have contributed to our trouble in the first place. Something more akin perhaps to what Primo Levi intended with the Italian title of his book, *I sommersi e i salvati* ("The immersed and the saved")?[20]

It is not, in other words, about "the drowned and the saved." The Holocaust is not past but upon us. We remain "immersed" within it. The flood waters are surging, and they are not showing signs of receding or even remaining stable. "Sink like a stone" in this context means become a victim of violence, of the violence that we have launched at each other. We are in danger of sinking in the water like the stones we have cast at other people. For example, like the charges of unfaithfulness launched against the individual in scripture we would shame although not intervene to stop the bad behavior, or against the prophetic words that would direct our attention to such violence. Or perhaps it means become stone. Perhaps sink means fall, and sink like a stone means turn into instruments of violence.

Scripture itself is not immune from attack. These waters, Jacques Derrida affirms, are the ones an almost "pangenocidal" God inflicts upon the world in conjunction with his pardoning of Noah, destroying in the process "all other life upon the planet":

> God pardons Noah, only him, his own, and one couple of animals of each species. But in limiting his grace in so terrible a fashion, he punishes and destroys all other life upon the planet. Now, he proceeds to this almost absolute pangenocide to punish an evil and within the surge of regret for an evil that he has in sum committed himself: having created men who have evil in their hearts. As if he would not pardon men and living things for his own fault, for the evil that they have within themselves, namely desire, although he himself has committed the fault of putting it in them. As if in sum, by the same stroke, he does not himself forgive himself the misdeed, the evil done of his creation, namely, the desire of man.[21]

Pardon, forgiveness, for Derrida, or more precisely God's failure to pardon himself for the desire he created, comes at the price of a terrible destruction.[22] Even Dylan, whose argument with God can assume Biblical proportions (witness his diatribe against God vis-à-vis Abraham), does not go that far.[23]

René Girard's view in *Battling to the End* would seem to confirm what Girard has been arguing all along. Perhaps this is it! Perhaps this is what the scriptural texts have been imagining. The Holocaust, the multifarious disasters that appear now the signature of our "time," the end of theodicy they necessarily proclaim (as if we needed any further demonstration), would appear to fulfill, in Girard's view, the ancient scriptural predictions.

All the tools are still in our hands, Lévi-Strauss could say at the conclusion of *Tristes Tropiques*, in 1957. But in 2013, the prospects may appear more precarious. Time may seem less bounteous. One of the last projects on which Emmanuel Levinas was working at the moment of his death in 1995 was what he called the "de-formalization of time": the dismantling of our dependence upon an Aristotelian conception of temporality whose distinctions between past and present, and present and future, remain inviolable, and another conception of temporality (perhaps not unlike like that of Franz Rosenzweig) founded upon a closer relationship between creation, revelation, and redemption.

The moment is an apocalyptic one. All our prophets say as much. But our best response to it may lie less in the fashioning of pangenocidal origins (or pangenocidal conclusions) for it, less in the leveling of judgments within or outside of our circumstances about it, less even in the saving of time or space in anticipation of it, than in reading. Perhaps a closer deconstructive reading of the waters whose waves we continue to navigate would better serve our needs than either a murderous violence designed to attract attention to the problem or furious (and frivolous) arguments over seating for the trip. If, as Levinas says, the Holocaust is the end of theodicy, and, as Girard says this is what the ancient texts were talking to us about ("the woods are burning, boys" Willy Loman declares, in Arthur Miller's *Death of a Salesman*), then reading scripture may offer the only solution worth thinking about—a literary prophetic reading that "un-conceals" all its sacrificial mechanisms in context of our performance of it. "After the end of the Temple," the Rabbis are fond of saying, "we pray and read," and in this way they understood prayer and reading as one and the same. Perhaps that is why they also affirmed that the study of Torah, the reading of scripture, is equivalent to doing all of the commandments.

Drowning but not yet drowned, we spy our single remaining hope, our "recourse of last resort" so to speak—if indeed there is one to be had: namely, a "reading of adults" (to use the language of both René Girard and Emmanuel Levinas), a close, textual, literary, prophetic, anti-sacrificial reading that reveals the locus of the activity itself, in all senses of the word, as a site of instruction.

Dialogue among Girardians

"I Am Joseph"

Judaism, Anti-Idolatry, and the Prophetic Law

Il est juif et donc, dans son milieu et sa culture, il entend ce qu'il doit entendre, qu'il faut arrêter le sacrifice, qu'il faut un substitut.

—Michel Serres[1]

In 1973, Eric Gans wrote that René Girard's research in anthropology seemed to offer an "Archimedean point" from which the human sciences could one day be rethought.[2] Gans may have underestimated the case. For what has occurred since Girard began writing in the early 1960s is a veritable explosion of interest in his work in all major fields of Western inquiry. By the end of the 1970s, Girardian thinking had gained a foothold in literary studies, classical studies, anthropology, psychoanalysis, and religious studies.[3] More recently, the "mimetic hypothesis" has begun to be extended to fields less commonly associated with the human sciences, fields such as economics and political science, and most recently the hard sciences of physics and biology.[4] If the number and kind of conferences held recently in this country and abroad around Girard's work can be taken as an index to this growing interest, it may not be much longer before we discover in this thought a model for talking responsibly about the conditions for both the humanities and the sciences, a basis for understanding in the most fundamental way the order of behavior and of knowledge in human communities.[5]

My own contribution to this burgeoning Girardian project—both here and elsewhere—will assume the following form. Rather than summarize Girard's ideas (there are already excellent accounts of his work) or "apply" them within my own fields, I would like in the first place to highlight certain aspects of his thinking that I think have been insufficiently emphasized, aspects that I call the "prophetic." And in the second I would like to undertake what I deem to be the next step of this research: to begin to uncover the roots of the Christian revelation which is of such importance for Girard in the source of all prophetic thinking in our culture which is the Hebrew Bible. For that part of my presentation in the present context I will turn to certain texts at the conclusion of Genesis, texts concerning the story of Joseph and his brothers.

Part One

René Girard's work offers us neither more nor less than a theory of order and disorder in human communities. Emerging as it did from the intellectual climate of structuralism and post-structuralism in the late 1960s and early 1970s in this country, Girard's thinking undertook to deal with the one problem evaded by the proponents both of textuality and of power—the problem of the sacred, a problem, I suggest, that comprehends each of these other two discussions and goes beyond them.

In *Mensonge romantique et vérité romanesque* (1961), Girard proposed that desire is rooted neither in objects nor in subjects but in the deliberate appropriation by subjects of the objects of others.[6] The simplicity and elegance of this theory should not blind us to the enormity of its explanatory power. In a series of readings of five major European novelists (Cervantes, Stendhal, Flaubert, Dostoyevsky, and Proust), Girard was able to show that the discovery of the imitative or mimetic nature of desire (in contrast to the romantic belief that desire is original or originary) structures the major fiction of these writers and makes available to us, if we would but read that fiction in context of their total output, an autocriticism of the writer's own emergence from the underground prison of romantic belief.

In *La violence et le sacré* (1972), Girard generalized his theory of mediated desire to the level of cultural order at large.[7] What is the function of religion at the level of real human relations, he asked. We have long had available to us imaginary theories of sacrifice—such as the kind Frazer and others in the nineteenth century proposed. More recently, with the advent of structural linguistics and structural anthropology, we have tried to explain religion from within a network of social differences or symbolic exchanges—à la Marcel Mauss and Claude Lévi-Strauss. What Girard suggests in their place is a theory of human community that would account for behavior at the level of the real. Religion, Girard suggests, has the function of keeping violence out, of transcendentalizing it, of making it sacred. Thus, the first equation he offers toward this end of understanding the foundations of human community is the identity between violence and the sacred. The sacred, he says, is violence efficaciously removed from human communities, and violence is the sacred deviated from its divine position and creating havoc in the city.

But what is violence from a human perspective? Human beings argue, Girard asserts, not because they are different but because they are the same, because in their mutual differential accusations they have become enemy twins, human doubles, mirror images of each other in their reciprocal enmity and violence. Thus, violence is none other than difference itself, asserted in the extreme, no longer efficaciously guaranteeing its own propagation. It is difference gone wrong, as it were, the poison for which difference is the medicine. Such is the nature of the sacrificial crisis.

How do these identities offer us a theory of the origin of culture? In the midst of a sacrificial crisis that verges upon a war of all against all, an extraordinary thing can occur: the war of all against all can suddenly turn into the war of all against one. Since within the sacrificial crisis all approach a state of being identical to all, anyone approaches being identical to everyone and can, therefore, substitute for all those that each dreams of sacrificing. Thus, the most arbitrary differences—hair color, skin color—can come to count absolutely. In the wake of the successful expulsion of an enemy twin or double, peace is restored. Since the trouble was never any other than human violence to begin with, the successful completion of the sacrificial project of each in the collective expulsion of an arbitrary scapegoat can restore difference to the human community. A complex network of ritual interactions can now be elaborated to prevent the reoccurrence of such a crisis, a prevention that can paradoxically take the form of its encourage-ment (in mock or commemorative form—and only up to a point) in order to reacquire its beneficial effects.

In *Des choses cachées depuis la fondation du monde* (1978) and *Le bouc émissaire* (1982), Girard carried this development to its natural conclusion.[8] How has our knowledge of these sacrificial dynamics been made possible? Why is this very theory not just another sacrificial theory, protective of our own cultural ethnocentrism? The demystification of the sacrificial genesis of cultural order first makes its appearance in the Hebrew Bible and reaches its zenith, Girard argues, in the texts of the Christian Gospel, in particular the texts of the Passion. Stories such as those of Cain and Abel or Jacob and Esau begin already to make available to us within the text this identity of the sacred with human violence. But the full revelation for Girard comes only in the victimage of Jesus. Jesus, Girard argues, is the first innocent victim, one whose innocence renders visible for the first time the arbitrariness of the victims of primitive sacrificial behavior and shows us where our violence is going.

For example, in the curses against the Pharisees, Jesus says to the Phari-sees, in effect, "You say that, had you been there, you would not have stoned the prophets. Don't you see that in distinguishing yourself from 'those who stoned the prophets,' you do the same thing? You put yourself at a sacred remove from them which is neither more nor less than what they already were doing in 'stoning' their adversaries. Moreover, for telling you this truth of your own violence, you will differentiate yourself from or 'stone' me. What's more, those who come after you will repeat your very gestures. Believing they are different from you, they will stone you in my name, calling you 'Jews' and themselves 'Christians.'" The history of Christianity for Girard is permeated with such sacrificial misunderstandings, misunderstandings ironically of the demystification of sacrificial understanding itself.[9]

What does it mean, then, for me to identify Girard's thinking as "pro-phetic?" If we understand the notion of the prophetic as the recognition of the dramas in which human beings are engaged and the naming in advance of the end of those dramas, then Girard's thought, which identifies itself with the Gospel reading, is prophetic in the same fashion. Both elaborate for us the total picture of our implication in human violence, showing us where it has come from and where it is leading us, in order that we may give it up.

But where does such a notion of the prophetic itself come from? To ask this question is to open an inquiry of a different sort.

The notion of the prophetic has particular meaning for us in the modern world, one that is associated for us with religiosity or a kind of false theologism, as in the phrase "nouveau prophétisme."[10] I would argue that if we have rarely recognized the true explanatory power of the prophetic, it is because we have lived within the confines of a Platonic essentialism that has barred that knowledge from us.[11] What I want to argue is that the prophetic is more comprehensive than Platonism, that it is, if we understand the notion in its largest sense, the logic of ritual organization itself, a logic, moreover, that we share with every other culture on the planet and yet to which we remain indefatigably blind by virtue of our idolatry of Platonic reason. Therefore, it is a logic that raises for us as a stake our very ethnocentrism.

In what way? We live in a culture dominated by the thought of the Platonic logos, by discourse, by reason, by difference, or decision making. Within Platonic thinking there have been only two ways that we have been able to conceive of the possibility of knowledge outside of reason. On the one hand, we have imagined it coming to us as the result of divine or providential intercession. Thus, for example, we have imagined poetic inspiration among the Greeks or the language of the Hebrew prophets. On the other hand, we have imagined knowledge as possible for us through fantasies, illusion, dreams, in short, all those experiences that we feel to be the product of fiction or of desire. Thus Freud's discoveries, for example, far from unveiling for us a realm which is genuinely new, a knowledge that is other than conscious knowledge, only display for us a region which, from within Platonism was, as it were, mapped out in advance. It is not coincidental that the two theories of dreams with which we are left after Freud hold that they are either prophetic in the strictly literal sense of fortune-telling or the remnants of unconscious desire.

We have, in short, never been able to imagine the prophetic as a reading of the course of the dramas of human relations in front of us, a reading of what Michel Serres might call "the excluded middle."[12] What I want to suggest is that there is such a conceptualization within our culture, one, moreover, that has been misunderstood precisely to the extent that we have felt it to be accessible to us within Platonism. I am thinking, of course, of Greek tragedy and the Jewish and Christian Bibles.

There is no place here to specify how the prophetic makes its appearance within these two domains. Suffice it to say that I do not want to suggest that the Hebraic prophetic in the ancient sixth century or Greek tragedy in the ancient fifth century are simply extensions of Assyrio-Babylonian or other Mesopotamian rituals (for example, the mantic enthusiasm of the pre-Socratic philosophers), or even a more profound version of those ritual traditions.[13] Rather I propose that Greek tragedy and the prophetic tradition in Judaism appeared at a moment that Girard would identify as a sacrificial crisis of the possibility of religion itself, a moment when no sacrificial system seems to work, when all sacrifices lead only to more violence and all victim-age leads only to more victimage and therefore to the need for more sacrifice. Without trying to pinpoint such a moment historically or culturally, I would suggest that Judaism and to a lesser extent Greek tragedy formulate a response to the following question: How can I live in a world in which there are no longer any gods of the sacrificial kind? How is it possible to be prophetic in the face of the collapse of the prophetic?

Apart from the answer that Greek tragedy would offer, Judaism's response is one that has always been understood from within the Jewish community as an orthodox reading, although the path by which I will arrive at this reading may seem somewhat unorthodox: the law of anti-idolatry.[14] At the heart of Judaism is Torah, the Pentateuch, the five books of Moses, the Law. And all remaining books of Biblical Scripture, the compilations of midrashic, talmudic, and later rabbinic commentaries, as well as the more mystical and esoteric traditions of Kabbalah and later Hasidic texts, are centered upon Torah and extend its reach.[15] At the heart of the Law is the Decalogue, the *aseret hadibrot*, the Ten Commandments or ten words. And at the heart of the Decalogue, the Law of the Law, as it were, is the first commandment, the commandment for which all other commandments are themselves extensions, the law against substituting any other God for God, for the prophetic God, for the God of anti-idolatry: *anochiy* YHWH *eloheycha asher hotzeitiycha meieretz mitzrayim mibeiyt avadiym* ("I am the LORD thy God, who brought thee out of the land of Egypt, out of the house of bondage" [Ex. 20:2]).[16]

The Judaic genius, as readers of Maurice Blanchot and Emmanuel Levinas will immediately recognize, is to have imagined a God completely external to the world, a God for whom nothing within the world is finally sacred.[17] Judaism is "la pensée du dehors," a thought of (or from) the outside or the desert, a thought of exile and of exodus.[18] It is a thought of not confusing anything that is in the world for God, of seeing to the end of the dramas in which human beings are engaged and learning when to stop, a thought therefore of learning to recognize oneself in the other.

Take, for example, the story that Exodus 3 tells of the name of God.[19] Moses is a shrewd and uncanny dealer. He is willing to be a little cagey—even with God. God says to him, "Go back to Egypt and take the Hebrews out of slavery."[20] And Moses responds, "Okay, no problem. Only, who shall I say sent me?"[21] He tries, in other words, to trap God into revealing himself. But God is as cagey as Moses, even cagier. God says, "When they ask you that, here's what you tell them. Tell them *ehyeh asher ehyeh* (or *ehyeh* or YHWH) sent you."[22] That is, God does not necessarily reveal His name. He simply says, "Here is what you say when they ask you that." The Hasidic tradition which substitutes the word *Hashem* ("the name") for YHWH is, in this regard at least, as traditional as the mainstream since it presumes as well that God's name has been revealed in this passage (among others)—which is their reason for not pronouncing it (in accordance with the third commandment).

What does *ehyeh asher ehyeh*, or *ehyeh*, or YHWH (the third person form of the same word) mean? Here I turn to an insight offered to me by Jonathan Bishop of Cornell University. *Ehyeh* is, of course, an imperfect form of the verb "to be," functioning as a future, and it first occurs in this passage in the first person in the form: *ehyeh asher ehyeh* (3:14–15).[23] Volumes have been written on this sentence. In fact, the kabbalistic tradition takes it as a matter of principle that the unraveling of the name of God is the only important task in Judaism, the one that achieves for us what the Kabbalists take as the primary aim of exegesis, relating the heavens to the earth.[24]

The task may not yet be completed. Here again it may turn out that God is being a little bit cagey with us. Just a moment before Moses asks God His name, God remarks to him, "Go down to Egypt and bring the Israelites out of bondage. And when you do, I will be with you" (3:12).[25] The words employed by Torah for "I will be with you" (*ehyeh 'imach*) contain the same word employed by God a moment later in place of the name: *ehyeh*. The word slips by Moses, of course, who has no reason to fix upon it. But after God's next declaration, we can return to it with renewed interest.[26]

The phrase *ehyeh asher ehyeh* may in context, then, come to mean: "I will be with you in order that I will be with you." Or, inserting the name itself within the name: "I-will-be-with-you will be with you in order that I-will-be-with-you will be with you." And one could continue in this fashion indefinitely. In other words, in the place of the name of God is a promise, the promise of a promise, so to speak, a promise in the first place of future being or accompaniment.[27] To be intimate with God, to know God's name, as it were, is simply to follow the Law in order that God will be there with you so that you can announce that name, that promise. The Law of Torah, the Law that is Torah, the Law of God, is, thus, the law of survival.

And that is precisely the meaning of the Covenant. The Covenant is the deal, the bargain, that God makes with the human community. You do this and I will do this. You follow My Law—which is the law of anti-idolatry—and you will survive, you will be there to testify to the power of this arrangement. Neither more nor less. Man's part is the law of anti-idolatry, learning when to stop, learning to recognize yourself in the other. God's part is a guarantee of survival—if there is any survival to be had, which is not itself guaranteed.[28]

The Judaic God who promises a future by virtue of this Law, who reveals the way to go on in a world in which there are no gods, who reveals a way to go on in a world defined by the collapse of all possibilities of going on, is, therefore, by definition, as it were, the prophetic God, in fact, the prophetic itself. The notion of the Judaic God and the notion of the prophetic are, in this connection at least, one and the same.

To say, then, that Girard's thought is prophetic is to say that it is a reading from within the Judaic or Hebrew Torah, which is the source of all prophetic thinking in our culture and the source in particular of the evangelical revelation. The Hebrew Bible, the Jewish Law, the Torah, is the first veritable text of demystification in our culture. It is to the project of understanding this text as fully anti-sacrificial (in all the implications of that notion that Girard has made clear to us) that I see the future of Girardian research as necessarily devoted.

But what, more precisely, is the Hebraic prophetic? What is the principle of anti-idolatry, of learning when to stop or of recognizing yourself in the other in its Jewish setting? And to what extent is Girard's anti-sacrificial reading of the Gospels a Jewish reading? It is in the name of answering these questions—answers that will constitute the next step of Girardian research—that I turn now to the texts of Joseph and his brothers.

Part Two

The Joseph story is something of an odd tale for Genesis to end with. It seems curiously misplaced in a book that describes the Creation, the expulsion of man from the garden of Eden, the generations from Adam to Noah to Abraham, and the history of patriarchs. It lacks the monumentalism of the *akeidah*, the story of the binding of Isaac, the tenth trial of Abraham after which God will grant His Covenant with Abraham, or of Jacob's wrestling with an angel, out of which Jacob's name will be changed to Israel. It comes, so far as we are able to tell, from the wisdom literature of the Solomonic courts and seems distinctly prosaic both in subject matter and in style. It seems, in short, little more than a domestic tale of the dotage of old age and of the jealousy and naiveté of youth, on the whole, a story hardly capable of sustaining the weight that its pivotal position within the biblical canon would confer upon it.

The rabbinical commentary would seem to bear out this assessment. The rabbis speak of the story as recounting how Israel came to sojourn in Egypt. They point out that Joseph's dream at the center of the first part of the tale, when he imagines that his sheaves of grain stood up and those of the brothers bowed down to his, is literally prophetic of the end of the story when Joseph will dispense grain as viceroy in Egypt.

What I want to argue is that within the confines of this marginal transitional piece is a veritable deconstruction of sacrificial thinking, one which is all the more powerful for the quotidian and transitory context in which it is offered to us. If we have traditionally read this story in function of the first part—where Joseph is expelled by his brothers, sold to the passing bands of Ishmaelite or Midianite traders—the most important part, I would like to suggest, is really the second part where Joseph has become the right-hand man of Pharaoh in Egypt, and in which the sacrificial actions of part 1 are restaged (in the figures of Simeon and Benjamin) and the victim and his executioners are revealed as doubles. "This is because of what we did to our brother Joseph," Judah remarks when things begin to go badly for them (42:21). And at the key moment when Joseph would take Benjamin from them, Judah steps forward and says, "Take me for him" (44:33), an offer that prompts Joseph, of course, to disclose himself with the words, "I am Joseph" (*aniy yoseif* [45:4]).

Joseph's disclosure of himself as their brother, the identification, that is, of the Egyptian viceroy (who is currently their potential victimizer) and their sacrificial victim as one and the same, is indeed the fulfillment, then, of the prophecies of part 1 as the rabbis suggested. But it is so precisely as the complete demystification of sacrificial thinking itself, a demystification that has now become available to us within the very text we are reading. Thus part 2 comes to serve as something of a model for an anti-sacrificial position for its readers, a model that highlights for us the sacrificial actions of part 1 in order precisely that they may be rejected. And the Joseph story, coming as it does at the conclusion of Genesis, can serve as something of a "part 2" to Genesis at large, a "part 2," thus, whose very transitory quality has been no less apparent than that of the part 2 within the tale, and which occurs within a book for which sacrifice or expulsion describe its major themes. Even Torah itself in this regard may be taken as a part 2 to the sacrificial cultures of Canaan and Mesopotamia from which it has come and from which it has taken its own exilic distance.

There is a story, a midrash, told by the Hasidic rabbis (and told to me by Rabbi Aharon Goldstein of Ann Arbor, Michigan) that captures this idea. A woman is sitting upstairs in an orthodox synagogue while the story of Joseph is being recited.[29] When they come to the section in part 1 where Jacob sends Joseph to Shechem to find his brothers and Joseph ends up "wandering in the field" (37:15) as Torah tells us, before someone directs him to Dothan, the woman cries out, "Don't go down there! Don't you remember what they did to you last year there! They are going to sell you!" The joke, the misunderstanding of the story, presumably revolves around what the woman has failed to recognize, which is, in the first place, that it is only a story (so that Joseph could not "hear" her); and second, that for Joseph this has not happened before. For him this is a first time and he lacks the hindsight that by virtue of Torah the woman has acquired.

It may turn out that in laughing at her we unwittingly include ourselves in the same misunderstanding. What if we consider the story of Joseph itself already in some fundamental way a "part 2" to both Genesis and to the sacrificial practices of the culture from which it has emerged? Then, is it not this story, the Book of Genesis as a whole, Torah itself, that says to us finally, "Don't go down there! Didn't you learn from last year? They are going to sell you!" And in laughing at the woman, in asserting that it is only a fiction, and only, after all, a first time, do we not belie our own implication in the ignorance of such wisdom, a wisdom all the more powerful for its being presented to us within the context of a joke, concerning someone who has been compelled to sit "upstairs" and who has "misunderstood" its teachings?

Nor has the power of this "part 2" been lost on the many generations of Christian exegetes on the Old Testament who have found in it, from within the context of medieval typology, the prefiguration of the Passion. The betrayal of Joseph, his sale for twenty pieces of silver, the twelve brothers (the most pivotal of whom is named Judah)—have all drawn the attention of the Church Fathers. Even the death and resurrection of Jesus finds its earlier counterpart in the ascension of Joseph from the pit and his rise in Egypt to become the right-hand man of Pharaoh, the dispenser of Israel's daily grain.

But in thus opposing the Old Testament to the New, in reading the old god as the sacrificial god of vengeance or anger and the new as the anti-sacrificial god of love—a reading that, of course, is central to a certain Christian understanding of the two books—have we not unwittingly already slipped into the very structure we have wished to displace, believing in a new Law or "part 2" which it has already been, by definition, as it were, the goal of the Old Testament itself to reveal to us, an Old Testament that has now proven that much richer by virtue of its having foreseen our sacrificial mis-understanding of it?

To understand the power of part 2 of Joseph's story, and in particular of Joseph's demystificatory disclosure, let us place the sequence in the context in which it occurs.

Part Three

Jacob settles where his father sojourned, Torah tells us, a distinction that leads a number of rabbinical commentators to wonder whether here is not the source of his later misfortunes. Then it tells us that what follows are the chronicles of Jacob. The fact that Torah then proceeds to elaborate only the story of Joseph leads the rabbis to suggest that this story is the most impor-tant of the chronicles of Jacob from this point on.

At seventeen Joseph was a shepherd with his brothers, the sons of Leah, but a youth with the sons of Bilhah and Zilpah, the slaves of Jacob. Again the rabbis wonder whether some distinction is to be drawn in this regard, keeping in mind that Joseph is the only son of Rachel, Jacob's favored wife, and whose only other son will later be Benjamin. The distinction between the sons of Rachel and the sons of Leah will recur later in Egypt when Judah proposes exchanging himself for his half-brother Benjamin.

Torah tells us that Joseph "brought evil report" of his brothers. Rashi, the foremost medieval Jewish French exegete, undertakes to tell us what these reports were: eating meat torn from living animals, treating maid servants as slaves, engaging in immoral behavior, etc., all the charges, in short, that will later be brought against Joseph in the house of Potiphar. Ramban, who represents another great exegetical tradition, suggests that we cannot even be sure it is the sons of Leah Torah is talking about at this point; it may be the sons of Bilhah and Zilpah.[30]

Torah then notes that Jacob loved Joseph more than any of the other children because Joseph was a "son of his old age," and that he made for him an aristocratic tunic. What is the meaning of the phrase "son of his old age" (*ven-z'kuniym*)? The rabbis are undecided. Is it the child of Rachel, Benjamin being too young to attend Jacob? Or simply one who attends Jacob in his old age, as opposed to the others? Or some special distinction that we are to confer upon Joseph from this privilege? Moreover, the words for "coat of many colors" (*k'tonet pasiym*) mean a tunic suitable for royalty rather than the "coat of many colors" of folktale fame. The brothers saw the tunic, Torah tells us, recognized that it was Joseph whom their father loved most, and they hated Joseph all the more for it.

All of these details of the first few sentences of part 1 are about to become important in the second part of this sequence. Joseph dreams a dream and says to his brothers: "Behold, we were binding sheaves in the field, and lo, my sheaf arose, and also stood upright; and, behold, your sheaves came round about, and bowed down to my sheaf" (37:7). The brothers answer, "Shalt thou indeed reign over us? or shalt thou indeed have dominion over us?" (8) and they hated him, Torah tells us, all the more.

There are two traditional interpretations of this sequence, although I would like to argue that they are in fact two versions of the same interpretation, one, moreover, that is decidedly partial. The brothers say to him: "So you would reign over us!" They see his dream as a sign of arrogance, that he would feel himself superior to them. What do the rabbis say? Rashi, among others, says, in effect, "Look, this dream is prophetic of the future—all dreams in the Jewish exegetical tradition have something prophetic about them—since Joseph's history will involve grain when he is viceroy in Egypt. Moreover, they will bow down to him since he will be the right-hand man of Pharaoh and dispenser of that grain and so in the long run they will have Joseph to thank for saving them."[31]

In other words, both interpretations identically regard the dream as Joseph's assertion of his own superiority, the brothers simply translating that assertion into concealed arrogance or desire on Joseph's part while the rabbis find in it a sign of providential intercession and read the anger of the brothers toward Joseph as reflective of their own jealousy of that status. Neither reading, however, relates the dream to the real dramatic or social context in which it appears.

There may, however, be another way to read this sequence, one that places it clearly within the ongoing contextual dynamics and therefore encompasses both of these views. Here I avail myself of an insight offered to me by Walter Gern of New York City. The dream is prophetic, Gern suggests, but it has less to do with the end of the history (although it may prophesy that as well) than with the more immediate situation to follow: in particular, Joseph's expulsion by the brothers in the very next scene. The key, Gern suggests, is the reference in the dream to the sheaves rising up. The action of making something into an uplifted thing, of course, is not foreign to students of Torah since it is the action that defines the very word used in the sacred context for sacrifice itself, for the burnt offering: the word *alah*, to cause to ascend, to rise up. This is the word used commonly in the Abraham and Isaac story, for example, when God asks Abraham to prepare Isaac as a "burnt offering," an *olah*.

What is the significance of this connection? The word *alah* (or *olah*, in the noun form) is not actually used in the language of Joseph's dream. Rather, Torah offers us the much more prosaic and everyday words *kamah* ("arose") and *nitsavah* ("stood upright"). In fact, for a story as clearly about an expulsion as the Joseph story is, the absence of the word *alah* would seem somewhat surprising. It is used only once in the story and then in an anti-sacrificial sense, at the moment when the sacrifice is to be aborted and the sale substituted, when the brothers are lifting Joseph out of the pit, drawn up to be given to the passing bands of traders.

How, then, is this reference within Joseph's dream to an uplifted thing the key? If we had only the two final sequences of part 1—the dream and the expulsion—I would have to argue that it was not, that Gern's suggestion was only another reading of the traditional prophetic kind, finding a literalizing linkage not only to Egypt but to the action at Dothan as well, and not a very strong linkage at that. Yet I am going to argue that it is the very weakness of the linkage, the very dearth of references to sacrificial language, the very anti-sacrificial and quotidian quality of the story that confers upon it its greatest power. But to make that argument I have to introduce another aspect of the dream, the context of Jacob's favoritism.

We recognize, of course, that Jacob's view of the situation is important. Torah tells us that when Joseph repeats essentially the same dream, this time with the sun, the moon, and the eleven stars bowing down to him, Jacob at first joins in the chorus of the brothers. "Shall I and thy mother and thy brethren indeed come to bow down to thee to the earth?" he asks (10). But when the brothers "hated Joseph yet the more for his dreams," Torah tells us, "Jacob kept the saying in mind." Moreover, we know that Joseph made clear his dream to both his brothers and to Jacob for in both tellings he repeats emphatically words meaning "listen to what I say," "behold" (*v'hineih*, for example).

Why does Joseph do this? Joseph has seen that he is the apple of his father's eye, the object of his father's desire. How do we know that? Torah tells us specifically that Jacob loved Joseph more than all the other brothers, that he was the child of his old age. But we also know it because he was the recipient of the special coat that his father had given him. Joseph recognizes, in short, that his father sees him as aristocratic, as special. Wanting to please his father (he is, we recall, seventeen years old), he begins acting the way his father thinks of him. He puts on his father's "coat of many colors," as it were, he thinks of himself as special just as his father thinks of him, he mimes or imitates his father's view of him.

Thus we come to understand his giving "evil report" to Jacob about his brothers. It is less important that we determine precisely what the brothers may or may not have done to deserve such report than that we recognize that the action of giving it is a mimetic appropriation on Joseph's part of his father's view of the situation. For his father indirectly has already given evil report of the brothers by favoring Joseph to begin with, and Joseph is simply enacting Jacob's desire in return.

In the same way we come to understand Joseph's dream as a similar dramatic representation of what Jacob's desire has been all along: to have the brothers bow down to him as one would before royalty. Joseph's dream is a prophetic representation, a going to the end of the road, of Jacob's desire. It is what Freud might call a rebus, a figuration of the total dramatic context in which Joseph, Jacob, and the brothers all identically find themselves.

We also understand Jacob's hesitation when Joseph tells his second dream, his sense that there is something uncannily familiar about Joseph's narrative. Jacob is moved to "keep it in mind." And we understand the limitations of both the view of the rabbis who see only the literal representation of the dream, ignoring the social situation in which it was produced and that it figures. And as well we understand the limitations of the view of the brothers who recognize accurately that desire is behind the dream but see it uniquely as Joseph's desire rather than Jacob's and equally ignore the implication of their own actions in the situation—that it is their very jealousy that will render that "end of the road" possible. Neither group, that is, has taken into account the "excluded middle" sequence that is the mimetic appropriation of Jacob's desire by Joseph and the substitution—by Joseph first and later by the brothers—of Jacob's desire for their own.

This excluded middle, these dynamics of mimetic appropriation and substitution, may now explain for us how the final sequence of part 1 is linked to Joseph's dream and why Joseph's reference to an "uplifted thing" is so powerful. In formulating his insights in the form of a dream, Joseph has substituted his own desires for Jacob's favoring of his son over the brothers. Rather than saying Jacob is the author of this desire, he says that I, Joseph, am its author. Similarly, rather than blame Jacob for what Joseph has said, the brothers blame Joseph. Their condemnation of Joseph for what they perceive to be his arrogance is, moreover, but another substitution of the same kind as Joseph's.

The dream sequence, in other words, enables us to read the first sequence by highlighting its structure through a controlled repetition of it. If there were no dream sequence, and we proceeded directly to the expulsion—Jacob singles out Joseph for favoritism; the brothers become jealous and take action against him—the tale would be little more than the story of jealousy and dotage we have popularly taken it to be.

By the same kind of displacement we can now understand the relation of the dream to what follows. In the face of Joseph's sheaves, that "rise up and also stand upright," those of the brothers now "come round and bow down." What is the act of "bowing down"? It is, of course, sacralization—differentiation and exaltation. But in this context it is a repetition of the action of the sheaves of Joseph. It is, that is to say, by an inverse action, a gesture that makes Joseph's sheaves into an uplifted thing. In his dream, that is, Joseph imagines not only Jacob's desire but his brothers' response. In good rabbinical fashion he imagines the end of the drama—that the brothers will sacralize him. But he does so in the specific way in which Torah has imagined for us making something into an uplifted thing. In what is perhaps another example of the Hebraic demystificatory genius, we come to understand that action as an act of radical separation, of destruction, of violence, of sacrifice: a burnt offering.

And in the connection that Torah has offered us between the action of the sheaves within the dream and the action at Dothan that immediately follows we can now perceive how the final sequence links up with the first. The two actions are linked in the text for us directly. The brothers see Joseph approaching and say, "Behold, this dreamer cometh. Come now therefore, and let us slay him . . . and we shall see what will become of his dreams" (19–20). The action of expelling Joseph is but a duplication of the same kind already imagined within the dream. Substituting Joseph's dream for his sheaves and Joseph himself for his dreams, they will simply intensify the same kinds of displacements to which we have already been witness. Joseph will himself be made into an uplifted thing—literally drawn out of the well—as a mimetic imitation or acting out of the dream language itself. Far from opposing Joseph's dreams, that are, after all, only the acting out of Jacob's dreams, the brothers in expelling Joseph violently enact them.

The notion of "uplifting" within the dream, then, draws our attention less to the dispensing of grain at the end of the tale—as we have traditionally read it—than to the sacrificial victimage immediately to follow. Or rather, it draws our attention to the dispensing of grain but only as the result of that victimage. And the dream sequence as a whole links for us the beginning and the end, mimetic appropriation with sacrificial victimage. It deconstructs for us the sacrificial thinking that constitutes part 1 in its entirety. The final sacrificial substitution is but the violent culminating intensification of the mimetic displacements that have taken place throughout and of which the dream sequence itself is already a primary example. What the dream has revealed to us above all is that mimesis, sacrifice, and substitution are continuous with each other. The dream is prophetic, which is to say that it offers us an account of the total dramatic context in which all are implicated. Just as the Joseph story does of the Book of Genesis that precedes it and the Book of Exodus that follows. Just as the Hebrew Torah does of the sacrificial cultures from which it has come and the Platonic culture to follow.

To answer the questions with which we began, let us turn quickly to the end of part 1—to the sale of Joseph—and then briefly to part 2 of the story, in which part 1 gains its greatest power.

Part Four

Joseph is sent by his father Jacob to Shechem to check on the welfare of his brothers. Does Jacob already perceive their intentions, and is he sending Joseph as a lamb to the slaughter? Joseph, of course, does not find them at Shechem. He is spotted by another man, Torah tells us, "wandering in the field," and sent instead to Dothan. Why has Torah substituted Dothan for Shechem? Is there a textual corruption here, as even the greatest of traditional biblical scholars have imagined? Or is there a principle of textual coherence, an editorial perspective, that sees fit to include these sequences within the "story of Joseph," a perspective whose criteria of selectivity we can unravel?[32] In what follows we may begin to discern the answers to these and other such questions. For what follows is a series of extraordinary substitutions that constitute the entire fabric of the end of part 1. The sequence in which Joseph is sold may veritably be described as substitution gone wild. The brothers see him and conspire to kill him. "Behold, this dreamer cometh," they say. "Come now therefore, and let us slay him, and cast him into one of the pits, and we will say: An evil beast hath devoured him; and we shall see what will become of his dreams" (19–20). They would substitute Joseph for his dreams, and murder for his language. Moreover, they would then substitute another story—that he was killed by a wild animal—for what they contemplate. Keep in mind that later, when they bring the bloodied tunic to Jacob, he will imagine that Joseph has been devoured by a wild animal. It is as if the brothers already know what would count as a plausible explanation for Jacob of the fate of Joseph. Jacob and the brothers are in harmony, it would appear, on the topic of Joseph's death. Reuben objects and tells them to "shed no blood." Let us "cast him into this pit that is in the wilderness but lay no hand upon him." Reuben had the intention, Torah tells us, to save Joseph and return him to his father. How are we to understand this remark? Is Reuben suggesting that they not kill him or only that they not shed any blood in killing him? Later, when they cast him into the pit and sit down to eat, Judah will say, "Let us not kill him," as if their intention were still to do so. In any case, we recognize that Reuben would substitute another solution for the one proposed. To suggest that Torah may already begin to dissociate Reuben—or Judah—from the sacrificial behavior of the others in part 1, a dissociation that will reach its culmination in part 2 when an anti-sacrificial position (the substitution to end all substitutions) comes to be substituted for the earlier one, is not to weaken our thesis, I would suggest, but to strengthen it. It is as if the kind of rabbinical commentary that looks forward prophetically to the end of the story and reads from that perspective has come to be inserted in advance and in a fragmentary form within the text itself.

Joseph arrives, and the brothers take his tunic and cast him into the pit. Then they sit down for a meal. That is, having substituted the suggestion of Reuben for their own, they make another. They substitute eating for dismemberment. What, after all, is eating but the substitution of food for the victim (sometimes they are one and the same) and ingestion for expulsion?

Then the Ishmaelites arrive, and Judah suggests that they "shed no blood" (has Torah substituted Judah for Reuben?), but instead sell Joseph to the Ishmaelite traders. Such a sale would thus substitute commercial transaction for murder, commercial transaction itself being already founded upon the possibility of equivalency or substitution. The brothers agree, and suddenly there are Midianite traders rather than Ishmaelites, Torah having substituted the former for the latter. Then, Torah tells us, "they" drew Joseph out of the well and sold him to the Ishmaelites for twenty pieces of silver. Who drew him out of the well? The brothers? The Midianites? The Ishmaelites? And who sold him to the Ishmaelites? The Ishmaelites, it seems, have been substituted for the Midianites, who were substituted for the Ishmaelites to begin with. The text leaves the matter undecided, as if the important thing were less to determine who was substituted for whom, who the specific agencies of action were, than to put substitution itself on display. The long traditions of biblical scholarship that have read in this passage an example of textual corruption may reflect this situation more than resolve it for us, substituting in turn their notion of textual "corruption" for the sacrificial substitutions the text may already be revealing to us.

In any case, Joseph is handed over in exchange for twenty pieces of silver and comes to be brought to Egypt. But the sequence does not end there. The chain of substitutions will return unto Jacob, where it all began. Reuben returns to the pit, and notices that Joseph is not there (a moment that echoes Joseph's earlier trip to Shechem), and tears his garments. He substitutes self-mutilation for mutilation of the other and garments for himself. He says, "The child is not; and as for me, whither shall I go?" as if in some fundamental way the fate of Joseph were a stand-in or substitute for his own.

The brothers then proceed to kill a goat in place of killing Joseph. They smear the blood of the goat, which substitutes for the goat itself, upon Joseph's tunic, as a substitute for smearing it upon Joseph. Then they return this same tunic to Jacob in place of returning Joseph. They ask him, "Do you recognize this tunic? Is it Joseph's?" ("This have we found. Know now whether it is thy son's coat or not" [32]). Just as Judah will be asked later by Tamar with whom he consorted, "Do you recognize whose pledge this is?" ("Discern, I pray thee, whose are these, the signet, and the cords, and the staff" [38:25]). And just as Joseph will recognize the brothers later in Egypt but they will not recognize him, and similarly disclose himself to them: "Do you recognize me? I am Joseph." Do you recognize, in other words, the brothers say to Jacob, Joseph through this series of substitutions? Do you recognize your coat, your aristocratic tunic, the object of your desires, as the origin of this substitutive violence?

The bloodied tunic, in other words, is the return unto Jacob of his own violence, of their violence against Joseph, of their violence against Jacob. Do you recognize your own violence? Here it is. This is the end of the road of sacrificial violence on which you are traveling, the death of your favored son. The Joseph story is a counterpart in Genesis to the story of Abraham and Isaac.

What is Jacob's response to this prophetic presentation? "An evil beast hath devoured him; Joseph is without doubt torn in pieces" (33). Far from recognizing himself in the other, his own violence in the violence of the other, he externalizes it, he dehumanizes it. A savage beast did it. He repeats the explanation the brothers imagined originally. Like father, like son. And then he tears his clothes, as Judah did, as if he would rather go on with the traditional substitutions than demystify them, even at the cost of his own son.

The conclusion of part 1 of the Joseph story, in short, brings us back to the beginning. It demystifies sacrifice for us. It reveals the substitutive nature of the mimetic displacements with which the story began and the sacrificial violence in which it concludes. It shows us the end of the road we are traveling in order that we may give it up. It says to us, "Do you recognize yourself, your own violence, in this tale?" in order that we may put an end to sacrificial substitution, that we may give up idolizing sacrifice.

Why, then, is part 1 insufficient? Why does there need to be a part 2? Is part 2 just a repetition of what is already available to us in part 1?

In a sense, yes. In the sense that all of the Hebraic biblical narrative is structured as a replaying of the same drama. The whole was already contained in the first sequence of part 1 when Jacob favored Joseph, Joseph gave evil report of his brothers, and they acted against him, hating him all the more. All traditional Jewish writing, I would suggest, is so structured, which is why, in a sense, we can begin anywhere.

At the same time, part 2 is necessary. To this point in the story, the anti-sacrificial position that the text presents for us, the demystification of sacrificial thinking, has occurred to virtually no one within the text. There are hints of it in the words of Reuben and Judah, but no more than that.

Yet the Hebrew biblical text exists—and here is perhaps my main point—to make it available to the characters themselves within the text, which is what makes it what I have called a text of demystification. It has to do this necessarily since what it asks of us primarily is whether or not we recognize ourselves in the text, whether we recognize that the text is already the world in which we live. We have never been outside of the text. Rather than a parallel to our lives (which is analogous, perhaps, but never contiguous with it), the text is a veritable extension of our experience. The inside of the text is to the outside as the two apparent "sides" of a Möbian strip that are really extensions of the same side. The text is the prophetic future of the dramas in which we ourselves are already engaged. In watching characters come to find themselves implicated in their own sacrificial gestures, their own texts, so the text is demystified for us. It is this gesture of demystification that offers us a way out of a crisis. Part 1 deconstructs sacrificial violence for us. It enables us to recognize ourselves in the other, to recognize that the other is only the future or the past of the same, of where we are. Part 2 will offer us a model for what to do about it, namely, to fictionalize it, to regard our sacrificial violence from a distance in order that we might abandon it.

There is no place here to pursue the intricacies of part 2 by which the knowledge of the identification of sacrifice with violence becomes available to each of the major characters. Judah learns it when he consorts with Tamar, after denying her his third son by the rites of Levirate marriage, and she identifies the man with whom she has played the harlot as Judah himself. He says, "She is more righteous than I; forasmuch as I gave her not to Shelah my son" (38:26). Joseph learns it in the house of Potiphar, where he is subjected to the same kinds of unjust accusations concerning morality to which he presumably subjected the brothers initially (he is treated "measure for measure," the rabbis note). The brothers as a group learn it in the sequence in Egypt when they come to ask for grain.

In the final scene of part 2 there is a famine in Israel. Jacob sends the brothers to find grain in Egypt, where Joseph has become the chief dispenser of that grain and the right-hand man of Pharaoh. Joseph recognizes them, but they do not recognize him. It is as if Joseph has become himself the text in which they must learn to recognize themselves, their brother. He takes Simeon as hostage and demands Benjamin—Jacob's youngest son and the only other remaining son of Rachel—before Joseph will give them grain. On their way home they discover that the money they paid Joseph has been returned to them, that they too now are potential victims of unjust accusations.

They tell Jacob what has happened, and he says, "First I lost Joseph; then I lose Simeon; and now you tell me you want me to send with you Benjamin!" But first Reuben intercedes: "Thou shalt slay my two sons if I bring him not to thee" (42:37). And then Judah: "I will be surety for him; of my hand shalt thou require him; if I bring him not unto thee and set him before thee, then let me bear the blame for ever" (43:9). Finally, Jacob agrees, and they return to Egypt.

Joseph now prepares a huge meal for them with Benjamin getting the largest portions. He sends them away for a second time. Now he has guards intercept the brothers and accuse them of theft. When they look in their sacks the money is back and this time so is the cup Joseph gave Benjamin. The brothers return, and Joseph asks them for Benjamin. At this point, Judah steps up and says: "If we return to Israel without Benjamin, it will kill my father. Take me for the boy." At which point, of course, Joseph discloses his own identity to them, all rejoice in the discovery, and Jacob comes to Egypt with the remainder of his family and blesses the two sons of Joseph.[33]

From his position as Egyptian viceroy, Joseph has in effect restaged the sacrificial activity of the earlier sequence in its entirety. The unjust accusation, the money in the sack, recall the silver for which he himself was sold. The taking of Simeon and the threatened appropriation of Benjamin recall the sale of Joseph. This time, however, the demonstration is not lost on the brothers. For when things begin to go badly, they say, "This is because we sacrificed our brother Joseph" (42:21). They link the troubles into which they have fallen to human behavior, to their own violence.

At the key moment everything converges upon Joseph's disclosure: "I am Joseph" (*aniy yoseif*). The Egyptian viceroy who is their lord, who controls the stage, as it were, turns out to be the same as their victim. "I am Joseph," he says to them, "whom you would sacrifice." Moreover, their victim, who is also their lord, is also their brother, identical to them by family origins and identical to Benjamin, the other son of Rachel, for whom Judah would now exchange himself. The disclosure of Joseph's identity is a demystification of sacrifice itself, revealing the identity of victim, master, and sacrificers, all as doubles, all as brothers. And in the context of Judah's offer, it shows us the way out: to acknowledge our identity, which is to say, our identicality with the other, to recognize that the other is the same, that the other is us.

Does Joseph recognize this dynamic? Has he staged this earlier sacrificial activity deliberately? Not necessarily. I would even suggest that there must not be total recognition if Joseph is to be fully like us. Joseph's disclosure is still to some extent an echo of his new masters. We recall that Pharaoh said earlier, in calling Joseph from the prison, "I am Pharaoh" (41:44). Even in the act of disclosing himself, he takes away their responsibility for the sacrificial gesture. "I am Joseph your brother, whom ye sold into Egypt. / And now, be not grieved . . . for God did send me before you to preserve life / . . . God sent me before you to give you a remnant on the earth, and to save you alive for a great deliverance. So now it was not you who sent me hither, but God" (45:4–8). Demystifying the text for us, and perhaps for Judah, Joseph remains to some extent still within it, as he must. What is important is that the possibility of a demystification of sacrifice has become available within the text, which is, thus, a perfect mirror of our own world in which the possibility of a demystification of sacrifice has become available to us by the same process in the form of the Hebrew Bible.

Joseph, in the last account, is not dissimilar to Torah itself, to the Hebrew Law in which the story has been told, to the very biblical text. And in that Law we must come to recognize ourselves. The text says to us: here is the bloodied tunic which is the end of the road you are on. Do you recognize yourself in it? Do you recognize this as your own violence so that you may give it up? Joseph, Torah, Jewish culture itself, asks no less of us.

I conclude as I began, with a midrash. There is a story, told by Gershom Scholem, of the medieval Jewish mystic Abulafia who describes the culminating moment of the prophetic ecstasy in the following way.[34] He says that the talmudic scholar is sitting in his study reading Talmud and he suddenly sees himself sitting in his study reading Talmud. He comes, in other words, to see his own double, to recognize himself in the other, to recognize the other as himself. Moreover, he understands that other as his own past or his own future, the road he is already traveling. And having had this vision, he comes finally, at the critical moment, to distance himself from it. He fictionalizes it. He tells a story about it, a midrash. The substitution to end all substitutions, as Michel Serres has said.[35]

The Judaic Law, the law of anti-idolatry, the prophetic law, is nothing else. And if today the thought of René Girard strikes us as trenchant, perhaps it is because it functions in the same way as the Joseph story does, as a part 2 to the sacrificial qualities of our own critical thinking, as the text that says to us, "I am Joseph."

Discussion[36]

The debate opens with a question by *Crispin* addressed to *Goodhart*. "What continuity is there from the prophetic Law to the Passion and the resurrection where God reveals his son? That is to say, how do we articulate the New Testament vis-à-vis the Old Testament?" "From one to the other," says *Goodhart*, "there is a continuity. But it is not a simple continuity. And I refuse the idea according to which they articulate themselves in a hierarchical fashion—[for example,] the hierarchical articulation made of the New Testament as the end of the Old, as its fulfillment. To the contrary, both seem to me animated by the same intuition, the same thought. That is why to establish a hierarchical relation between the two testaments seems to me to lead us back, precisely, to the genre of sacrificial interpretation that the prophetic revelation tends to deconstruct. If we had only the First Part of the history of Joseph, we would not be able to make the reading we have just made. It is the Second Part that renders that reading possible. But we really need to see that, in a certain manner, we find within Part One already a second part of the first part and that what we have here is a series of concatenated structures."

Girard: "Don't you say on the subject of the Second Part what the Christians say generally of the role of the New Testament with regard to the old? Something bothers me about what you say. Leviticus is part of the Torah but there is no reprise of Leviticus in the Gospels. What are reprised only are the prophetic words on the New Testament—'it is mercy that I demand not sacrifice . . .' Within the Torah, the sacrificial parts are very important and it seems to me impossible to highlight them and say that the Torah in its entirety is anti-sacrificial, without that posing a problem for Judaism!"

Goodhart responds that in the relation between the New and the Old Testament, as between the different texts of the latter, everything is only a question of the respective weight accorded to the sacrificial and to the desacralization. The deconstruction of the identity of violence and of sacrifice demands that one not be able to undo either, within the text, sacrifice or desacralization.

Schwager takes up the question in order to note that the series of concatenated structures (of which it was a question in the preceding discussion) must be thought under the form of a reprise rather than that of a repetition. One seeks to utilize formulas and texts which are already there in their giving little by little a new interpretation. This play of successive interpretations leads, for example, to a conception of divine anger entirely different from that which existed at the outset. As a result one then utilizes terms that had at the origin a negative coloration in order to design something positive. Thus all the formulas that speak of the divine anger as something mythic become the expression of something positive, of the revelation of the infernal circle of violence and mimesis. There remains, however, a line with the original interpretation of a direct action of God to the extent that it is he who takes the initiative of this revelation. Now, as Girard has said very well, to take this initiative is not something innocent. To reveal the mechanism of the project of human violence in a world where all seek to hide this truth is to set in motion something extremely dangerous. That is why one could say of the words of Christ that it is at once love and a sword, the sword that cuts off and reveals what is hidden.

Dupuy: "It seems to me, M. Schwager, that you have reprised in your turn the essential of the Girardian theory of divine anger. I would like to pose to you a question that we often pose on this subject. It is question of a mechanism for the exteriorization of violence. Men exteriorize their own violence under the form of the sacred. But is that not to return the violence of men to mimesis, a mimesis that Girard defines as a biological characteristic of space; and therefore to return, in the last instance, violence to biology? Is that not to lead us back, in the final instance, to the same mechanism of exteriorization?"

Schwager: "Personally, I never understand the mimetic mechanism as a purely biological affair. I think that liberty also plays a role here. But I agree with you: if mimesis is conceived in a fashion that is purely biological, then one is dealing here with the same mechanism."

Dumouchel: "The Girardian explication takes account of the fact that beyond the very great diversity of human cultures one discovers common points that are absolutely extraordinary. What is striking when one is convinced of the Girardian theory is the fundamental unity of this apparent diversity. Does this unity not show us finally that the role of freedom is quite reduced? For if the unity results from the mechanism, does that not mean that there is in fact only the mechanism?"

Schwager: "That is really the problem, isn't it? The question is to know whether, when one encounters everywhere the same phenomenon, it is mechanical or not, and if so whether we are returned to the same mechanism. In general, one responds, yes. That is not, however, what I would say. Take the narrative of the fall from paradise, of original sin. For me, it is the expression of the fact that we all fall, sooner or later, into the circle of mimesis. This narrative returns us to a structure that one discovers everywhere. This structure nonetheless does not belong to the nature of humanity because it is a question of an historic fact. Traditionally, it's the problem one seeks to contain within the name of 'original sin,' that one would conceive as historical fact (freedom), engendering a behavior that is universal and negative (mechanism)."

Lohfink brings the debate back to the history of Joseph. "Is it," he says, "representative of the whole of Torah, or does it constitute, to the contrary, an exception? More precisely, we find in Torah, passages that are extremely sacrificial, for example those where God orders the Israelites to destroy the peoples living in the promised land. There is even a promise from God regarding the ways in which He himself would accompany this destruction. Therefore, regarding the history of Joseph, this Girardian part of the Torah, do you consider it to be an exception or do you have an entirely different view of the narrative whole than I do?" *Goodhart* responds that it is necessary, according to him, to push the analysis even to the point where difficulties appear and the contradictions to which an interpretation is exposed are evident. "However, these texts are not given to us in an isolated fashion, but all together. It is impossible to isolate the texts, and that is why there are so many Hebraic interpretations of the Torah, because the work of interpretation must always continue."

"Very well," retorts *Lohfink*, "but if you take all the texts together, the question remains what is the key, one or the other, which allow us to decide an interpretation?"

"A Jewish expression," says *Goodhart*, "affirms that the law is even more important than God, which signifies perhaps that one must be able to start from anywhere, even the texts that are a priori the most difficult, the most sacrificial, and from them approach nonetheless the deconstruction of sacrifice. There is no definitive master text—except the Torah itself."

"To argue rigorously, from what you just said," intervenes *Rena Krebs*, "the New Testament would not be necessary since the Old Testament would already contain the complete identity of violence and of sacrifice?"

"It is difficult for me to respond," says *Goodhart*. "Pushed to the extreme, I would be obligated to say yes. But as soon as I said yes, it would be necessary for me to take up the matter again and say no because the Hebrew Law, the Torah, has always been reprised and continued by successive exegeses. And so the question—could we read the Old without the New?—really becomes then the question of knowing whether the exegesis could one day stop, whether it is possible that the text could one day be completed. To the extent that I think that scriptural exegesis must always continue, I cannot say yes; that one can read the Old Testament without the New; there must always be new exegeses. At the same time, I am able to say that because the interpretation that the New Testament brings is already present within the Old."

Schwager: "But one cannot start from just any text! In starting from a given text, one arrives at a certain result. In starting from another text, one arrives at another result. The difficulty is to arrive at a way out of the conflict of interpretations. For me, the great problem consists, precisely, to the contrary, in choosing the key texts. Which is to say, the texts that, although they do not suffice completely, offer nonetheless an orientation; texts that are, in a sense, more revelatory. Personally, I would say that the history of Joseph is more revelatory than other texts, and that I am able to utilize it to interpret these other texts. But I am able to do it only to the extent that I affirm that Joseph is more revelatory. If not, if I say that all the texts are at the same level, I do not see how one could exit from the conflict of interpretations."

A question follows from *Durbant*: "Is divine anger a pedagogy (or teaching) of God, divine with regard to humanity, or a human misunderstanding with regard to God? Or again, both at once? In which case, what pedagogical value shall we accord to the massacres of entire populations?"

Schwager: "If one takes certain texts in isolation, ones sees that divine anger is presented as an action of God, but one must interpret this anger as a projection of the anger of men since these texts do not exist in isolation but within context of the whole. Other texts situated in another context present this anger as a teaching of God [*une pedagogie de Dieu*]. It remains to understand what one means here by 'pedagogy.' I believe that one approaches finally a conception of divine anger as something that discovers its source within man, in man's projection of his own violence. But one does not make that discovery by oneself. It is necessary that that be said to him from the outside and from this point of view it is really a question of divine action. The action to kill, on the other hand, does not come from God. The action of killing is from human beings. The action of God is to allow man to understand the mechanisms of mimesis and of sacrifice."

"If I have fully understood you," *Durbant* begins again, "the pedagogy of God would consist in appropriating the violence of men or accepting the projection of the violence of men upon . . ."

Schwager: "No! To appropriate human language about violence in order to say something else, not to appropriate violence, which remains, after all, human violence."

Durbant: "When it is said, for example, 'God ordered them to massacre populations,' who is speaking? In this case precisely, where God orders them to perform massacres?"

Schwager: "It's a projection . . ."

Durbant: "A projection of human beings upon God? But what is your criterion?"

Schwager: "To put it briefly, the entire theory of Girard."

Durbant: "The theory of Girard. You mean the Gospels, the words of Christ?"

Schwager: "Rather, the manner in which Girard has assisted us to re-read the Gospels. This manner rejoins a fundamental aim of contemporary theology."

Lantz: "Why do you attribute such virtues to God? One has the impression that you would absolutely exonerate God from all sin. When God acts badly, and orders men to commit massacres, you say it is not God, it is men. If, on the contrary, God acts well, you say this time it is really God. It seems to me that you enter into the counsel of God in an extraordinary fashion!"

Schwager retorts to him that he is not alone in saying that, that already Jewish thought and Greek thought have opened this line of thinking in developing allegorical interpretations of old religious narratives. "I find it important that within the Greek tradition one comes to the point of exonerating the Gods, whether this exoneration be developed as a critical consciousness incapable of accepting that the Gods eat their children, etc. These are thus the Western traditions which, in a convergent fashion, designate by God something essentially good. And it was exactly the aim of my lecture to show that the theory of Girard situates itself within this great current (Greek philosophy, Jewish and Christian theology, etc.) which has attempted to eliminate all negative notions of the idea of God."

Girard: "I would like to return to what Goodhart said because in a certain manner he tends to suppress history of the Bible, within the Bible itself. One can follow within the Bible a history that evolves towards a reduction of sacrifice and of the sacrificial. One starts from the epoch when the elder sons were sacrificed in order to move toward that place where an animal is sacrificed in ransom for the first born. The great texts of Genesis, the sacrifice of Abraham, for example, bear upon this passage. Then animal sacrifice transforms itself into the pascal meal. Then the entire question is for us to know what place the Gospels occupy in this history. The interest of what Goodhart says, it seems to me, is to pose the questions in a radical fashion, to make us see that in principle the Old Testament goes in the same direction as a Christian text. But to my mind it does not go as far as the Christian text, or as far but perhaps not in the same way. Because in this perspective, the texts that are the most important of the Old Testament are texts like the 'Songs of the servant of YHWH' where the servant of YHWH is declared innocent, even if men have declared him guilty. But it is also said there: 'And YHWH caused to fall upon him the crimes of all of us' (Isaiah 53:6). 'YHWH saw fit to crush him and has pierced him' (Isaiah 53:10). That is to say, God has voluntarily made of him a victim. It seems to me that either we say that Christianity goes beyond that, or it is going to fall into sacrifice in the Aztec fashion; that the Christian text is either the most grossly sacrificial text of all the biblical texts, or the most revelatory of all. There is a history of the revelation of sacrifice, and both the Old Testament and the Gospel participate in this history which is not a hierarchical progression, but a history; which is to say, a movement of revelation which could not have been accomplished at the outset. There was a question about it just a moment ago. One discovers within the Bible horribly sacrificial texts but which are prodigious precisely because of what they conserve. For within these convergent traditions, which affirm little by little that God is essentially good, the particularity of the Bible is to conserve all its layers, even the most sacrificial of them, while the Greeks, in the epoch when the theology whitewashed myth, rejected or suppressed the most sacrificial versions of myths. That is what the Bible never does, and that is a part of its importance. But it is also why the question of knowing where to situate the Gospels within this historic assembly cannot be resolved in a simple fashion, in terms of pure hierarchical relationship."

A Jewish-Christian Dialogue

Sandor Goodhart, "Isaiah 52–53, René Girard, and the Innocent Victim"

René Girard's theory of the uniqueness of Christianity is based upon the theory of the innocent victim. Jesus of Nazareth for Girard is not simply another hero of Greek tragedy who becomes an enemy twin of everyone. Jesus does nothing violent and yet is willing to die to reveal the arbitrariness of scapegoat violence, the inefficaciousness of the sacrificial expulsion about which the Hebrew prophets have been speaking, as part of a structurative process which may once have galvanized primitive culture but which has now become, in the modern context, little short of murder.

But a careful examination of Isaiah 52–53 reveals that this earlier text is entirely compatible with the theory of the innocent victim, although it appears some six hundred years prior to the texts of the Christian Gospel. There is nothing that Girard says about the innocent victim in Christianity which is not already fully present in Isaiah 52–53. As a consequence, we need to reexamine Girard's claim for the Gospel's singularity.

There would seem a limited number of possibilities, none entirely satisfactory. The first is that Christianity really is unique—as both Girard and other Christians claim—but its uniqueness is not based on the disclosure of the innocent victim (as Girard asserts) but rather upon some other consideration which remains to be articulated. The second is that Christianity is not unique (although Girard and Christians say it is) and that it is only an episode in the history of its religious predecessor and of which it remains—in its themes and content (and all denials of such affiliation to the contrary)—an unwitting or unwilling extension. The third possibility is that Christianity really is unique (as both Girard and Christians say), that such uniqueness is rooted in the understanding of the innocent victim (as Girard claims), but that the correspondence between the two—the innocent victim in Isaiah and the innocent victim in the Gospel—is incomplete, although precisely the ways in which this discussion should continue remains to be elaborated.

There are problems with each view. The problem with the first proposal is that the Girardian explanation is convincing. Although Christians may continue to debate the matter, there is no obstacle from a Jewish perspective to regarding the explanation that Girard offers as entirely compelling, both as an account of primitive culture, and (with some qualifications) as a distinguishing critical feature of the Gospel revelation. The second proposal must be rejected for similar reasons. Whether or not such a claim is acceptable from a Jewish point of view, it is certainly not so from a Christian perspective.

The third possibility is the most interesting. It maintains the revelatory status of Christianity and the linkage to Girard's theory. But it depends upon a perspective which remains to be articulated and is hard to fathom.

Could the uniqueness of Christianity rest, for example, upon the manner in which it takes up the themes of invasion and abandonment in family life? Is it possible that Christianity introduces into the history of the anti-sacrificial what may be termed the "self-sacrificial," or, more precisely, dynamics of self-construction that appear to be fundamental to Christianity which are precisely the lines of the mimetic and the conflictual that Girard has been developing? Moreover, these dynamics may even account for the appearance of the Christian with the history of Pharisaic Judaism, and yet that have not yet been articulated? Rather than compare early Christian texts to the Hebrew texts of the ancient sixth century, it might be more fruitful to set them beside contemporary Judaic texts—for example from the Talmud or Midrash—in which different approaches to the same Jewish filigree are evident.

Such largely unattempted reflections may enable us to expose the distant and sometimes troubled relations between Judaism and Christianity to be more of a family quarrel than a clash of independent perspectives, and consequently may open us to the possibility of reconciliation and even common pursuit.

Raymund Schwager, "Reply to Sandor Goodhart"

I very much appreciate the fact that Sandor interprets the Hebrew bible in the light of Isaiah 52–53. In this way, a Jewish and a Christian understanding of the Revelation come quite close to each other.

A longer answer would be necessary in order to reply to Sandor's question as to why Girard and Christians nevertheless claim the Gospel's uniqueness. Therefore, I can only outline a few points here, and I also want to pose some counter-questions.

1. As Jesus Christ is clearly the center in the New Testament, all messages have to be interpreted from the perspective of his person. Therefore the revelation of sacred violence, as it happened in his fate and above all in his violent death, belongs to the center of the New Testament. In contrast to that the Hebrew Bible does not have such a center. Thus there are always other competing interpretations besides an interpretation based on Isaiah 52–53 which actually could claim the same legitimacy. To my mind, the Hebrew Bible therefore calls for a further clarification by the New Testament. The Jewish view will reject this. Therefore my question: Which criteria are there from the Jewish point of view in order to find a clarification in the dispute of interpretations?

2. In Isaiah 52–53, it is not clearly shown whether a single person or the whole people is meant by the suffering servant. Therefore it remains open what God's help given to the servant actually means: a personal raising from the dead or the living on of the people suggested by verse 53:10. The Gospel, however, clearly tells us that a historically concrete subject that had been killed was raised from the dead by God. Here it becomes evident that God does not continue history regardless of the dead person, but resurrects the dead person himself and makes him the

cornerstone of a new community. Here God actually sides with the victim. Doesn't Isaiah 52–53 need further clarification in this respect?

3. In Isaiah 53:4–5, people speak who have become converted in view of the servant. But those figures remain unclear and it is not said which consequences the converts have drawn for their entire understanding of the Revelation. However, in the New Testament the names of the converts (the disciples of Jesus) are mentioned and it is explicitly shown that they have read the whole Scripture in the light of the violent death and the resurrection, due to their new insight into Jesus's fate and their conversion achieved by this insight. Where could we find anything analogous in Isaiah?

4. Before his death, Jesus claimed that he came from God in a unique way and was one with Him. This claim was the reason for his being rejected and, according to a Christian understanding, his claim was confirmed by God through his resurrection. The Christian faith derives from this that God's final truth has been revealed in Christ (Messiah) and that we do not have to wait for further revelations on earth. However, in the context of the servant of God, Isaiah speaks about the Persian king Cyrus as the anointed (Messiah). Doesn't an unsolved tension remain here between an acting of God through Cyrus and an acting through the suffering servant?

5. Girard analyzes the triangular structure of desire and shows how evil (rivalry, violence, etc.) arises from it. Due to Jesus's claim and the mission of the Spirit at Pentecost, the Christian faith tells us that God is the Holy Trinity. Isn't the experience of the Triune love necessary in order to overcome the triangular structure of desire at its root?[1]

Józef Niewiadomski, "Reply to Sandor Goodhart"

I agree with Sandy Goodhart that all Girard says about the revelation of the victim's innocence in the context of the Gospels can already be found in Isaiah 52–53. I also believe that the theological logic which is searching for the reason for the uniqueness of Christianity is well-advised if it finally looks for the roots of this uniqueness in the exegesis of the Songs of the

Suffering Servant, as they themselves actually form the hermeneutic framework for the New Testament's description of the fate of Jesus Christ. Seen from this perspective, one should in fact be allowed to say that the New Testament's belief in Jesus Christ does not bring anything substantially new in view of what the Hebrew scriptures tell us. It actually does arise from one special interpretation of these scriptures. This, however, means: just as there cannot be the Gospels without the Songs of the Suffering Servant, also the Songs of the Suffering Servant can neither be without the other prophetic texts, nor without the psalms and the Torah. The Christological creed means nothing but to declare a special logic regarding the order of secondary and primary text traditions of the binding logic. This is now anything but a secondary issue and (also) in the context of the rabbinical Judaism not self-evident. Thus the New Testament's perspective factually does not add anything new, but brings up its perspective; even more than that: it declares its perspective binding (for whatever reasons—to find out these reasons remains theology's task which permanently has to be solved anew). How is this to be understood? If we assume that the biblical logic lives from the confidence that the history of Israel is that place where God breaks his sacred veil in various situations and reveals his true face as well as the innocence of the victim, then the New Testament's logic lives from the belief that the potential of this entire biblical history becomes intensified—like in a microcosm—in the single historical existence: the existence of the Jewish individual, Jesus of Nazareth. With this creed neither the Jewish tradition must be disavowed nor must a uniqueness of Christianity be claimed that goes beyond Judaism and replaces it. Jesus of Nazareth remains Jewish, his passion remains the passion of the suffering servant. There is no doubt for me that the early Christian interpretation of this logic has come to a dead end by using the formula: Substitution of the Church for the Synagogue. It has not only deprived Jesus of his Jewish roots, but has also placed the passion narratives of the Gospels into a sacred context. Detached from the core of the biblical logic, the Gospels have lost their revealing power in favor of a sacralizing logic.[2]

Sandor Goodhart, "Reply to Father Schwager and Józef Niewiadomski"

I would like in the first place to thank Father Schwager and Józef Niewia-domski for their extensive and thoughtful consideration of the abstract of my essay, "Isaiah 52–53, René Girard and the Innocent Victim." I offer the following remarks in the spirit of an ongoing Jewish-Christian dialogue.

Reply of Father Schwager

The point of my essay was to question René Girard's insistence that the uniqueness of the Gospel is linked to the theory of the innocent victim since that theory already appears in full in the Isaiah text. Thus I am sur-prised that although Father Schwager seems aware that this is my theme, he never addresses it. The only place (aside from the opening paragraph) René Girard's name comes up at all is in Father Schwager's fifth paragraph, and there only with regard to issues that are questionable (is it clear that "evil" may be equated with "rivalry" and with "violence" in Girard's thinking?) and seemingly unrelated to the issue at hand (what has the overcoming of mimetic desire by Triune love—if that is indeed what René thinks—to do with the theory of the innocent victim vis-à-vis Isaiah 52–53?). Rather, Father Schwager seems determined to consider my essay as a touchstone for examining the relationship between Judaism and Christianity in general. Let me turn, therefore, in sequence to the paragraphs in which those con-cerns are raised.

1. "I very much appreciate," Father Schwager writes, "the fact that Sandor interprets the Hebrew Bible in light of Isaiah 52–53." Do I? Do I not rather see Isaiah 52–53 as one of a complex of texts which already con-tain in full the kinds of insights Girard claims are unique to the Gospel? Which is not to say that the Gospel is not unique. Nor that there are not other things going on in Isaiah 52–53. Nor that the Isaiah 52–53 has any special status with regard to the Tanakh as a whole.

2. No doubt for Christians, as Father Schwager notes in his first objec-tion, Jesus is the "center" of the New Testament. No doubt, equally, as a

consequence, the revelation of the sacrificial foundations of culture—as that revelation is seen to derive from the fate of Jesus—is central. No doubt either that the Hebrew Bible does not have such a center. But is that a problem? It is only a problem if we assume that it should have a center, and that that center should be Jesus. In fact, from a Jewish point of view, the Torah itself is already such a "center" (one which the New Testament displaces in regarding Jesus as the Word of God), and the revelation of sacrificial violence is everywhere. Christianity's supersessionist claim that Jesus is the center and that Judaism must be read in its light is itself a Jewish borrowing.

Moreover, the notion of a "conflict of interpretations" is less a Hebraic notion than a Platonic Greek one which depends on ontological distinctions between true and false readings. There is no alternative "clarification" in Judaism because the matter there is neither clear nor unclear. Without entering into an extended discussion of the nature of interpretation in Judaism, suffice it to say that in Judaism there are no true and false interpretations, only a multiplicity of readings all of which enable the text—and the practice of anti-idolatry as reflected in and inaugurated by that text—to come alive within a given hour or cultural setting. Only if we presuppose that the Hebrew Bible "lacks clarification" and is a battleground of conflicting claims to truth can we argue that a Christian (or any other) perspective resolves that conflict.

3. Yes, it is true that the figure of the suffering servant in Isaiah 52–53 may be read in different ways. Traditionally the "servant" is understood to be Israel (cf. Isaiah 41:8). Others argue that it may be an individual. But it is not clear to me how either reading has anything to do with the resurrection from the dead which in Judaism will occur only in the world to come. What is important from a Jewish perspective in Isaiah 52–53 is the revelation of the dynamic of scapegoat violence, whether that scapegoat is regarded as a single individual or an entire people. Only a Christian reading, which needs to know whether the prophet is predicting a personal or general resurrection, has a difficulty here. Constructing the text as an impoverished prefiguration, the Christian reading then charges that text with being impoverished.

4. Father Schwager's third objection is a very odd reading of Isaiah 53:4–5. In Judaism the reference of the "we" in Hebrew is not "converts." It is

still Isaiah who is speaking, even if he lends his pronominal reference to the entire community. Who specifically the prophet refers to as "we" is irrelevant, and what new understanding of Torah the people to whom the prophet speaks will adopt remains to be seen. Once again only if we presuppose in advance a Christian thematic of conversion can we find an inadequacy here.

5. Father Schwager's fourth objection seems riddled with difficulties. Here are three.

    a. Is it clear, even from a believing Christian point of view, that the reason for Jesus's rejection in the New Testament is "[his] claim that he came from God in a unique way and was one with Him"?

    b. Once again, there is no indication from a Jewish perspective that the suffering servant is the Messiah and to be resurrected, and the text is only a problem if the servant is to be so identified. Even if there were such an indication, there is no problem from a Jewish perspective. The word *mashiach*, messiah, anointed, is commonly applied to kings upon their accession (cf. 2 Samuel 2:4). There is no unresolved tension in Hebrew at least between God acting through Cyrus in one moment, and the suffering servant in another.

    c. Father Schwager's claim seems in excess here of even a Girardian view. From a Jewish perspective, Isaiah 52–53 reveals the dynamic of scapegoat violence. That is all it needs to do for a Girardian reading. Girard never claims that Messianic status of Jesus, or his status as resurrected, has any methodological import. He argues theoretically only for the revelatory message of Jesus vis-à-vis sacrificial origins of culture. The fact that Girard happens also to be a believing Christian, that he may accept the revelation, the sonship or messiahship of Jesus, has nothing substantively to do with his theory of mimetic desire and violence. His theory makes no claim to explain everything—as he himself has remarked on numerous occasions. The Christian revelation for him is one instance of the revelation of sacrificial violence. But such a revelation of sacrificial violence is by no means necessarily only Christian. One may be Christian without believing in the revelation of sacrificial violence, and one may accept the revelation of sacrificial violence without being Christian.

Father Schwager's overall strategy, of course, is an old and familiar one. It is the typological prefigurative strategy by which the Church in its earliest days first read Judaism in light of its own assumed truths and then condemned Judaism for not displaying them. Borrowing from the Greek, the Jewish, and other traditions, it enacted the mimetic appropriation it formally attacked. If we are to move forward with a Jewish-Christian dialogue, we need to give up such rote theo-ideological reflexes. In the anti-sacrificial spirit which is also a part of the Christian tradition (as René Girard has taught us so powerfully), we need to challenge such sacrificial interpretative presuppositions and read these prophetic texts in the historical and religious context in which they occur, texts which could open the door to a common ground for genuine understanding.

Reply of Józef Niewiadomski

In contrast to my uneasiness with the reply of Father Schwager, I find myself sympathetic to Józef Niewiadomski's reply from beginning to end.

He focuses, in the first place, upon my challenge to René Girard's reliance upon the theory of the innocent victim for defining the uniqueness of Christianity—which is what my piece was about. He affirms my thesis and adds the astounding suggestion that the Songs of the Suffering Servant "actually form the hermeneutic framework for the New Testament's description of the fate of Jesus Christ."

Secondly, he recognizes implicitly that I do not say that Christianity is not unique, only that René has not yet shown us why it is unique and that the matter remains to be discussed. On the matter of the revelation of the scapegoat victim alone it is not so.

Thirdly, he offers a suggestion regarding what that uniqueness might be, which I, for one, find extraordinarily compelling—namely, that what the New Testament can cause us to reflect upon is "its perspective," the nature of the "special" and "binding" logic by which the "order of secondary and primary text traditions" get linked. If we note that the word 'religion' comes from this same binding logic, then this is a powerful suggestion indeed.

Fourthly, it seems to me he is right to suggest that such a critical discussion of binding logics is currently foreign to the rabbinic tradition as well where the relation to Christianity is hardly mentioned, and that to raise the question of binding logics between Judaism and Christianity is also to raise it within each domain. We need to examine the Jewish prophetic texts in context of other prophetic texts—the Psalms, Jeremiah, Jonah, of course, but equally texts which are not formally "prophetic" but nonetheless a part of the post-destruction canonizing spirit in the ancient sixth century which was doggedly prophetic—for example, Job, and the five books of Torah proper.

Finally, I find his last suggestion the most powerful and the most hopeful. What we may derive, he suggests, from finding Israel to be the place where the sacred logic is broken and the face of God is revealed is the intensification of the potential of this entire biblical history within a single historical existence. Jesus of Nazareth, who is Jewish and whose "passion remains the passion of the suffering servant," and yet who lives and dies within a history of rememberable dates and names, bears witness to a prophetic religious historical experience which is available to all of us.

The implications of Niewiadomski's suggestions are far reaching. The early Church, which substituted itself for the Synagogue, did far more, he suggests, than "[deprive] Jesus of his Jewish roots." At a moment when the greatest demystificatory truths were available and all could suddenly become possible, it resacralized them. It reconstructed the sacred veil. It read the relation between Judaism and Christianity sacrificially and seized dogmatic control of a special logic it has taken some two thousand years—and countless body piles—to recover.

I join Józef Niewiadomski in welcoming the "dead end" of this "sacralizing logic" and look forward to the vertiginous possibilities of a newly available common Jewish-Christian prophetic pursuit. I would also like again to thank both respondents for their efforts, and especially the editor—Wolfgang Palaver—for bringing together such a rich array of interpretative orientations.

Raymund Schwager, "Second Reply to Sandor Goodhart"

In his "reply to Father Schwager and Józef Niewiadomski"[3] Sandor Goodhart critically views all my statements and is in basic disagreement with my enquiries. I appreciate his direct and frank language because only by this can we achieve a definition of our statements which goes beneath the surface. Moreover, his reply shows that we are discussing essential points of the Jewish-Christian dialogue. This is why I confine myself to three questions in my reply.

1. A central point in our discussion is S. Goodhart's statement that "the notion of a 'conflict of interpretations' is less a Hebraic notion than a Platonic Greek one" and "that in Judaism there are no true and false interpretations." I have heard such statements quite frequently, but I have never been able to understand them. In the history of Judaism there were quite a few 'conflicts of interpretations.' They can already be found in the Bible, for example, in the fight between the true and the false prophets or between Job and his friends (= enemies), arguments which actually include the claim of a true interpretation against a false one. The conflicts continue in the post-Biblical time. Just think of the community of Qumran, which—against Jerusalem—claims to be the only and genuine Israel. Today we find the same situation. It is certainly a very big 'conflict of interpretations,' when Jewish settlers quote the Bible in maintaining that God has given them the land and when they are even ready to defend their conviction with violence against their own government. Furthermore, one can pose the question: Why should one reject 'a sacrificial interpretation,' which has a long tradition in Christianity—this is done by S. Goodhart—if there do not exist true and false interpretations? Can one actually speak of 'an innocent victim' without claiming at the same time to be in the possession of the true interpretation in contrast to those who consider the 'victim' guilty? There is certainly not an authority in Judaism who could definitely decide which interpretation is the true one. But this is a different problem, which is not the theme at the moment. For me personally, however, there would no longer be any reason to continue my theological work if I were not convinced that there are true and false interpretations and that one should take pains for the former and reject the latter. I want to add a citation of René: "As far as I am concerned, such ideas as 'textual indeterminacy,' 'infinite interpretation,' 'undecidability,' and the like, while they may be true as far as Mallarmé's poems are concerned, do not apply

to myth and the other great texts of traditional culture. The interpretation of myth which I propose is either true or false. What it most closely approximates is our historical demythification or deconstruction of late medieval witch hunts and that deconstruction, too, is either true or false. The victims were real behind the texts, and either they were put to death for legitimate reasons or they were victims of mimetic mobs of the rampage. The matter cannot be undecidable. There cannot be an infinite number of equally 'interesting,' or rather uninteresting, interpretations, all of them neither true nor false, and so on. The interminable preciosity of contemporary criticism is completely irrelevant to my question."[4]

2. S. Goodhart continues: "There is no unresolved tension in Hebrew at least between God acting through Cyrus in one moment, and the suffering servant in another." Here I realize an essential problem. Can I assume that God sides with the victim in one moment and acts through military power in another? Kings and military leaders have frequently referred to the belligerent David and the anointed Cyrus to justify their claim to wage wars in the name of God? Have they done so rightfully? It is the most essential point in Girard's analysis that this question is denied. This is why I simply cannot understand how Cyrus and "the suffering servant," as far as God's action from Girard's point of view, is concerned can be put on the same level.

3. S. Goodhart criticizes that I have brought in the question of resurrection and he thinks that "the fact Girard happens also to be a believing Christian" does not have anything to do with his theory of the innocent victim. This differentiation between Jesus as a victim and his resurrection is not clear to me. According to the Bible, Jesus was convicted as a blasphemer. Had he really been one, he would not have been innocent, but he would have deserved death according to the Torah (Leviticus 24:16). The Gospels uncover the mechanism of power and describe him as an innocent victim only because his disciples were convinced that God raised the crucified from the dead and proved him innocent against his prosecutors.

4. The question of Jesus's condemnation and resurrection is a central problem in the Jewish-Christian dialogue. In his study *Resurrection: A Jewish Experience in Belief* the Jewish scholar Pinchas Lapide shows that there need not necessarily be a separation between the two paths. He

first makes clear that the belief in Jesus's resurrection was only possible in the context of the pharisaic belief in the resurrection of all dead. He continues that he had been a Sadducean for decades as far as Jesus's resurrection is concerned and he finally gives reasons why he changed his conviction and found his belief in Jesus's resurrection. Though Lapide did not become a Christian, it is his intent to give an important position in the Jewish history of belief also to that Jew who had by far the greatest spiritual influence on the world. Going back to Moses Maimonides, he considers Jesus that prophet who was authorized by God to prepare the heathen world (as Messiah for the heathens) for the salvation expected by Israel. I judge this attitude of a Jew very positively because he uses the same category of thought as Christian theology. This says that the Hebrew Bible is a preparation for the Gospel, and Lapide says that Christianity is a preparation of the heathen world for the Jewish Messiah. From my point of view this could be a (preliminary) target of the Jewish-Christian dialogue. The differences between the Jews and the Christians remain with this result, but there is no longer a condemnation, and common work will be possible in more or less all points (e.g., also with the help of the mimetic theory). In order to achieve this aim the Christians will have to give up the position of the traditional theology that the church has finally replaced Israel in its function in the history of salvation, which I personally do. On the part of the Jews one would have to renounce definitely the declaration of Talmud that Jesus was a magician who seduced Israel (Baraitha to Sanhedrin 43a) and Jesus should be acknowledged as a Jewish prophet with a special mission in the pagan world. Not even Paul is an unsurpassable hindrance, as the Jewish scholar Jacob Taubes has shown. (Cf. my contribution at the symposium in Chicago).[5]

Sandor Goodhart, "Second Reply to Raymund Schwager"

I thank Father Schwager for writing his "Second Reply" to my work and thus continuing the exploration of matters important to both of us. I am especially gratified that he finds my "direct and frank" approach helpful as a way of getting "beneath the surface" of the discussion since I too feel that "only" if we lay our cards on the table can we hope for real progress. Let me begin with his more general remarks expressed at the end of his article to which his earlier, more limited objections may not be unrelated and with which there may be considerably more agreement between us than first appears.

Father Schwager is speaking in the final paragraph about a study by Pinchas Lapide in which the author lodges Jesus within the prophetic tradition and assigns him the role of "preparation of the heathen world for the Jewish Messiah." Father Schwager regards this approach "very positively" both because it utilizes the categories of Christian theology and because it does not condemn. He envisions a future understanding between Jews and Christians in which Jews will have to give up regarding Jesus as a magician who seduces Israel and acknowledge Jesus as "a Jewish prophet with a special mission in the pagan world," and in which Christians will have to give up the traditional theological position that the Church has "finally replaced Israel in its function in the history of salvation," a relinquishing which Father Schwager attests he "personally" accepts.

If this set of ideas is indeed the core of Father Schwager's position, then this exchange has been an especially propitious one since I have no fundamental disagreements with it. Jesus is a Jewish individual working within the prophetic tradition of Jeremiah and Isaiah (among others), within an assimilated context in Hellenized Judaism, who is attempting to carry the prophetic message of the law of anti-idolatry to both those Jews who have begun to turn away from their ancient Jewish heritage and to the non-Jewish world. He is not a magician or a sorcerer but a serious prophetic thinker who is enacting a task he finds marked out for him in texts throughout Torah (for example, in the Joseph story in Genesis) and as such he merits our deepest admiration and attention. The belief that Jesus is a conjuror must be rejected as sacrificial and anti-Jewish. And if Father Schwager includes within his position a renunciation of the Church's traditional claim to have superseded Israel, then we have indeed little about which to disagree. The role of Christians from a Jewish perspective must be the missionary one; to extend the message of the Jewish law of anti-idolatry to the world until Israel becomes "the light of nations." And the role of Jews from a Christian perspective must be the interpretive one; to keep elaborating, explaining, extending the text of Torah as fundamentally anti-sacrificial and as containing the world.

Finally, it seems to me possible to agree with Father Schwager that even Paul may not be for Jews "an unsurpassable hindrance" so long as we find in Paul not a rejection of Jews or Judaism as sacred violence (as some have recently claimed) but, to the contrary, an acceptance of the primacy of the prophetic message and of Jewish election. To become fully Christian, I would suggest, is to recognize in positive terms the ways in which one has always already been fully Jewish.

My agreement with Father Schwager's final remarks, in fact, is so extensive that I hesitate even to raise the earlier objections over which we may differ. If I do so, it is because Father Schwager has been kind enough to indicate them and because to some extent they begin to exceed the parameters to which Father Schwager confines his position later.

1. In the first paragraph, for example, I think we may be talking about different understandings of true and false interpretations. Judaism must of necessity reject secular Platonic and Hegelian understandings of the true as aleitheia—as absolute being, that which lies beyond contradiction—and which we may approach in good Socratic fashion only by reason and rational decision-making. Father Schwager seems to think that if I give up Plato and Hegel, I become a nihilist (as René Girard has characterized nihilism), that I commit myself to "indeterminacy." I do not. Reason, faith, and conscious belief may be sufficient for Christians. They are not so for Jews. Jewish currents run deeper than that. The Jewish task is not to decide whether a text of Torah or a rabbinic proposition is right or wrong, true or false, but to own our own history within it and assume responsibility for the other individual to whom I am primordially obligated by virtue of it. Here I am relying, of course, upon the work of Emmanuel Levinas, Martin Buber, and Franz Rosenzweig. René Girard's work on mimesis and violence is powerful for me not because it is true but because it is Jewish, because it offers me a vocabulary for explaining my own history and allowing me to assume responsibility. Plato needs things to be decided. Sophocles does not. Nor does Dostoyevsky. Nor does Judaism. Father Schwager may decide for himself whether or not Platonism is essential to his understanding of Christianity or the continuation of his theological work. Judaism does not commit me to being right but to being responsible, to loving God with all my heart and all

my soul, to loving others in place of myself. That love and responsibility is my task as part of my co-partnership with God in the creation of the world (as such creation is revealed to us in Torah), and that task will continue until the moment of redemption and the world to come.

Thus Job and his friends are both wrong and right successively and the text enacts for the reader the passage from one position to the other. The prophets may disagree diametrically with each other but each text offers access to God from within a particular historical hour and moment. One Jewish community proposes one understanding of a text of Torah. Another proposes a different understanding of the same text. But both accept Torah as the infinite within the finite, however differently inflected within their individual tongues. If I claim a distinction between the sacrificial and the anti-sacrificial (or invoke René Girard's distinction), it is not because I find one true and the other false but because I find the latter more comprehensive, more ethical, more pro-motive of life, love, human relation, and human responsibility than the former. The victim of mob violence—whether in the Christian Gospel or Isaiah 52–53—is exposed as innocent not by dogmatic declaration concerning true and false interpretations but by close, careful, patient textual reading which dismantles the positions of the persecutors, just as Jesus offers his body to his disciples as a "teaching tool," both when he writes in the sand before the would-be stone throwers in the episode of the woman accused of adultery, or more generally when he offers himself as a victim of sacrificial expulsion to show us where our violence is lead-ing. I leave aside Father Schwager's question about the politics of the state of Israel—and in general the relation between the political and the ethical—for another occasion.

2. If all the world finally will be shown to be a part of the "blueprint" which is Torah, then God will in retrospect turn out to have acted through Cyrus as well as through the "suffering servant." God does not take sides between us but within us. He takes the side of the victims we are all capable of becoming or have become against the persecutors we are all equally capable of becoming or have already become. Judaism is not a Manichaeism (however attractive it is for Christians to read it as such) but a monism of the deepest order. All the world—both the evil inclina-tion (the *yetzer hara*) and the good inclination (the *yetzer tov*)—will be

shown finally to be a part of the divine plan which Torah has simply seen in advance.

3. Finally, if the followers of Jesus lay claim to his resurrection, it is indeed fully within the Jewish tradition (for example, that of Maimonides) that they speak. Judaism does not reject the claim that the dead will be resurrected with the coming of the Messiah, only that one individual has already gone through the process. But it does not seem to me critical in any event to the efficacy of René Girard's thesis that one accept Jesus's resurrection. It is entirely sufficient that we understand the mechanism of mimetic rivalry and sacrificial violence as the foundation of human community without venturing into the intricacies of Pharisaic law (or its violation)—especially by means of a text explicitly hostile to it. Jesus is an innocent victim because the text explains him as such and because he thought of his life in such terms (as the text presents those thoughts and that life to us). To lay the weight of Jesus's life upon what happened afterwards—however much the disciples were convinced that the resurrection occurred, and however much Christianity since has staked itself upon such a literalist reading—is to diminish the importance of that life. Michelangelo seems to have imagined precisely such a danger in his famous Florentine pietà when he sculpted the body of the flesh and blood Jesus slipping irretrievably away from the hands of his adoring and preoccupied family and friends.

An added word on this point: if René Girard's thought is to have a worldwide hearing—and it seems to me that such a hearing should be our goal for it—then it cannot be a precondition of such thought that those who are attracted to it accept either Jewish or Christian postulates, postulates that would effectively close it off from Buddhism, Hinduism, Islam, and countless other religious commitments. Judaism may be my way. Christianity may be Father Schwager's and René Girard's way. But Girardian thinking cannot be limited to any of these paths. Rather than constrain René Girard's thought in such a fashion, it seems to me more prudent to emphasize its extraordinary explanatory power, even if we choose individually to regard that power as testimony to efficacy of our own approaches.

Father Schwager's reliance in his earlier objections upon true and false interpretations and upon traditional literalist and interventionist assumptions about the Jewish God, seem to me, in short, to challenge the genuinely open remarks he offers in his final paragraph. They prompt in me a question for Father Schwager. How do his earlier distinctions and assumptions differ from the position that Saint Augustine renounced in his Confessions as a product of the seductions of youth—a dualistic belief in absolute right and wrong, good and evil, true and false—for a more loving and compassionate God of reading, the word, and the book? If we are to make progress in Jewish-Christian dialogue, I suggest we emphasize those points on which we agree and work from there—namely, the giving up of mutual condemnation, and the ownership of mutual filiation in a project entailing both missionary and interpretive tasks.

If I may, here is a suggestion toward this end. Shortly before his death, Rabbi Abraham Joshua Heschel is said to have offered to Christian friends the sketch of a possible future joint path. Rabbi Heschel is said to have remarked: "You say the Messiah has already come but is going to return. We say the Messiah is still to come for the first time. Come, let us stand and wait for him together. And when he arrives, we'll ask him."

Sandor Goodhart, "The Prophetic Tradition as a Basis for Jewish-Christian Dialogue"

Charles and I outlined what has increasingly become for us a common project: the articulation of what we call "the prophetic" respectively within Hebraic and Christian cultures. I said that the prophetic for me began with ancient sixth century Judaism with the fall of the first Temple and what I would designate as the "happening of the impossible." That which was impossible or unthinkable, the destruction of the Temple, happened. Moreover, not only did it happen, but fifty years later, something else happened which was equal in its unlikelihood only to the destruction and exile itself. The Babylonian captors of the Jews were themselves overrun by the Persians and the Jews were allowed to return home to Jerusalem. In the wake of that return, everything was different. We know very little about Israelite society before the fall of the Temple, but we know enough to say that afterward everything changed. Where before there were a number of classes of people—prophets, kings, priests, scribes, soldiers, etc.—after the destruction there were in effect only two classes: those who wished to reestablish the old ways and those who wished to go on and try something new. The first group became the so-called sacrificial cult and the second group became the early rabbis, the Talmudists and sages who later would set down the tradition and during the dispersion or diaspora would keep alive the tradition. Both groups were made up of people from all groups in the earlier distribution. And the designations Sadducees and Pharisees have sometimes been invoked to account for this split, as if the sacrificial cult were the Sadducees and the promoters of the new were the Pharisees. But whether we accept that characterization or not, we have to believe that during the so-called Persian period there were basically two groups or parties, a conservative party which looked to the past to solve its problems, and a liberal party which looked to the future and unanticipated possibilities opened by this unlikely event.

What characterized this new group above all was the reading of Torah, and the group has been identified with the figure of Ezra. What we learn from the Books of Ezra and Nehemiah (which were originally one book) is that Ezra returned from exile with a letter in hand from the King of Persia, he surveyed the devastation before him, and he said "Let's read."

A number of important consequences follow from this action.

1. Reading will replace sacrifice. No longer will the act of sacrifice be a prerequisite to religious practice—as continued to be the case with other cultures, and as continued, in part at least, to be the case even in Jewish culture. The rejection of sacrifice, the substitution in its place of prayer and reading (which was recitation in public), were the cornerstones of this new approach.
2. The text will get canonized or constituted that is to be read. Suddenly a gathering of the texts takes place, the constitution of a sacred scripture.
3. The gathering presupposes that some materials will be accepted and others rejected. The principle of this selection will be the principle of prophetic reading. Those elements of the tradition which were seen to promote prophetic reading were retained and deemed to be a proper part of the critical canon. Those which did not promote prophetic reading or could not be interpreted prophetically were not. Elements from all compositional schools of the earlier days were included: a priestly text concerned primarily with blessing, a folktale-like text concerned

with telling stories and referring to God in his intimate name, a socially conscious text which took as its concern justice; and a legal text which rewrote the earlier three from its own unique historical perspective.

Finally, I outlined what for me constituted this "prophetic" reading. The prophetic, I said, was the recognition of the dramas in which human beings were engaged and the naming in advance of the end of those dramas so that individuals could freely choose whether or not to pursue them. Thus the prophetic as I conceived it was a "diachronic" mode of thought, which is to say, not a mode concerned with here/there distinctions as much as then/now distinctions, not relationality but sequentiality. Conceived in this manner, I suggested, prophetic reading was not a neutral or passive activity but itself a species of ethical practice. The prophetic reading of Judaism is also the practice of Judaism, the doing of mitzvot or commandments.

At this point, I said that rather than offer a prophetic reading of one or another scriptural text, I would take up the recent debate which had occurred in the fall *COV&R Bulletin* and talk about some of the ways in which the responses offered to my reading of Isaiah 52–53 either did or did not recognize the prophetic orientation that underlay my position.

Charles Mabee, "A New Grammar for Jewish-Christian Dialogue: The Prophetic Vortex of the Common Scriptures"

I believe that, contrary to popular belief, it is not rival understandings of the figure of Jesus that separates the Jewish and Christian religious traditions. Christian claims about this relatively obscure figure are built upon a grammar of understanding of religious life that is unthinkable in Jewish understanding. It is this grammar of understanding that separates Jews from Christians, not the specific claims that are constructed upon it. To be more exact, the problem which we face in reconciling Judaism and Christianity is not that Judaism rejects Christian claims about Jesus, it is that Judaism has no category of thought of accepting such claims about anyone, anywhere, any place, any time. In other words, the Christian way of viewing (religious) life simply does not compute with the Jewish way. Any attempt to find rapprochement between these two religious traditions must accept this fact as its starting point: they are not simply two different religions, but they are two different kinds of religion.

Our primary task is to accept this reality and then to ask: "What does this mean? Is all dialogue between the two traditions fruitless and a waste?" I believe that the answer to this question is "No." I believe that a rapprochement is possible. That is the good news. The bad news is that such a rapprochement would exact a price for both traditions. The price would be a shaking of the foundations of each whose result would be, in essence, a new religious understanding that is neither exactly "Jewish" nor "Christian"—at least in traditional terms.

I see the way to rapprochement as existing in the writings which the two traditions hold in common (Tanak/Old Testament), rather than in the formative texts that each tradition holds in isolation from the other (Mishnah or Talmud/New Testament). In fact, the very fact that the two traditions do hold a body of writings in common as revelation is the one piece of good news in an otherwise dismal history of hostility, alienation, and oppression. However, history clearly teaches us that the pull that these common texts have in their interpretive communities has far from enabled us to find the narrow passage to rapprochement. These old writings are extraordinarily complex and multifarious. The Mishnaic/Talmudic and New Testament traditions represent how varied may be the way in which the common scriptures may be interpreted. Nonetheless, I believe that the way to rapprochement lies through the narrowing of the interpretive gap by which we read these common texts. Let me now be even more specific in my proposal: by uncovering the prophetic vortex of these Common Scriptures, I believe that we can find the common ground necessary to construct a meaningful rapprochement between Judaism and Christianity.

Both Judaism and Christianity are textually-based religions; and, simply said, canonization means the "publicization" initially within Judaism, and subsequently within the primitive church, of the tradition of what is commonly termed the great or classical prophets. By publicization I mean the gaining of public ownership, of public identification with the voice of the prophetic outsiders who historically knew mostly rejection and persecution. The key Girardian insight that clears the ground for a prophetic biblical theology is the argument that human rationality begins in the bifurcation of victimizer and victim. In traditional, mythology-based culture, truth lies on the victimizer side of this equation. The prophetic tradition proposed the revolutionary idea that truth lay on the side of the victim, rather than the victimizer—even if the victimizing elements be found within the Israelite power elite. For Girard, as well as for the Bible itself, this transference of truth from victimizer to victim was not something arrived at by human thought, but could only result by means of a revelation by God. Only God can give voice to the truth of victim and has the capacity to reveal to others what the victim is unable to reveal.

This new way of viewing the world through the eyes of the victim replaced traditional religion and myth. In these traditional forms, truth is understood to reside in gods and heroes rather than in the victim. I would like to develop this Girardian hypothesis by proposing that in giving voice to the oppressed and excluded outsiders (a group determined primarily by class and economic and political powerlessness) the classical Hebrew prophets voluntarily placed themselves in the same category of oppression and exclusion. Seen in this way, the conflict between the "true" and "false" prophets that we see so powerfully in 1 Kings 22 and Jeremiah 28 is really a conflict over the nature of prophecy itself—will it be identified with the powerful elite or the powerless underclass? The classical Hebrew prophet then is best understood as the first self-chosen scapegoat in world history. Ultimately the Deuteronomization of the tradition that took place in the Exile with the attendant rise of text-based Judaism, represents the publicization or mainstreaming of this prophetic outsider tradition, a fact which should be understood as normative for both Judaism and Christianity (as well as Islam, a subject that goes beyond the scope of this paper).

The achievement of bringing the obscure and scapegoated prophetic outsiders and the texts which they either produced, or were produced around them, into the vortex of Judaic religious understanding is the achievement of the Hebrew canon. Following the structure of the Old Testament canon, the reader "knows" that these prophets bring the authentic word of God when we read them, because we have already been conditioned to recognize their authenticity by the canonical material that precedes them in the canon.

Hans Jensen, "Nature, Bible, Priestly Theology: A Reply to Sandor Goodhart and Charles Mabee"

Instead of the announced paper on Joseph, Levi-Strauss, and Girard, I improvised a paper on priestly theology in the Hebrew Bible as an answer to the morning's first papers by Sandor Goodhart and Charles Mabee on "Jewish-Christian Dialogue on Torah and Prophecy," which centered on the prophetic tradition and the act of reading. There is, I believe, a "hidden tradition," underestimated in Christianity, which is the cultic dimension of the Hebrew Bible, crystallized in the priestly writings of the Pentateuch. Although rarely reflected upon explicitly, it is still alive, implicitly, in the liturgy of the church, and probably in the synagogue as well. This cult is about the relationship to the material world first; its main concept is blessing rather than salvation. To acknowledge the (theological and philosophical) legitimacy of this tradition is, perhaps, another way of approaching the same problematic which Michel Serres treated in his book *Le Contrat naturel* (1990): nature, material world, is a factor which should not be ignored in thinking on violence and desire. Moreover, the priestly tradition may be a meeting point not only for Jewish and Christian theologies, but for non-biblical theologies as well.

al lo-chamas 'asah (Although He Had Done No Violence)

René Girard and the Innocent Victim

This essay has three parts. In the first, I address the concern Willard Swartley expressed when he invited me to participate in the conference from which this material emerged: "I know that one of the liabilities in biblical scholarship appropriating Girard's work is a potential scapegoating effect of Christians toward Jews. I hope this can be resisted or, if not, that it can be explained as an inherent weakness of his contribution."

In the second, I turn to an examination of Second Isaiah (52:13–53:12) in which I suggest some of the fundamental similarities of Jewish Scripture to Christian Scripture and examine the implications of such similarities—one of which is that we need to read more closely each other's texts.

In the third, and in this spirit of such shared close reading, I turn to a short Talmudic text—from the tractate *Shabbath*—as an example of writing from which such comparisons may begin to be drawn.

Part One: Girardianism, Christianity, and Anti-Semitism

René Girard's thinking seems at first glance an ideal focus for a discussion of "peacemaking theology and praxis," the phrase Willard Swartley used when first approaching me for this material. The difference between peace now and violence just a moment ago is at the origin of René Girard's account of the primitive religious community, which is to say, in his view, of all cultural difference. Such a distinction reflects par excellence the successful conclusion to a "sacrificial crisis" in which the distinction between the sacred and violence is lost and in which an end to conflict issues from the effective scapegoating or collective substitution and removal of one member of the community who has come to serve as a surrogate victim for each member in his or her Hobbesian war against all the other participants in the community.

In the modern world, in which we have increasingly lost the capacity to guarantee that sacrificial behavior will not become itself just one more form of violence (and in which, we have to assume in Girardian theory, that other mechanisms are at work to ensure cultural survival), the concern for peace and peacemaking becomes even more acute. Sacrificial substitution comes to be replaced by other methods of the management of violence—such as by good deeds, prayer, and reading in the Jewish tradition; by the imitation of positive models in the Christian tradition (for example, the *imitatio dei*); or by the rejection of desire itself in Buddhist and other Eastern traditions.

Nevertheless, it remains the case that in all these traditions, the establishment of peace is primary. Girard's reading of the Christian Gospels as the explication of mimetic and sacrificial violence, and the proposal of a way out of that violence, specifies at once the nature of that disease, its treatment, and the prognosis if the treatment is not adopted.

Such Girardian thinking regarding peacemaking may, I contend, indeed prove decisive for us in responding to the crisis in which we find ourselves in the contemporary setting—but only if we overcome certain obstacles that have recently been placed in our path before its understanding. I refer, of course, to the reputed anti-Semitism of Girard's ideas, his alleged scapegoating of Judaism and/or the Jews, and its ironic correspondence with his use of the idea of the *skandalon*. These obstacles seem, from my vantage point, to act out the very ideas concerning obstacles and stumbling that Girard is at such pains to expose.

The misreading of Girard's work in this fashion is certainly not without precedent. In literary criticism, for example, where Girard was first noticed for his book on the novel, and in particular for exposing mimetic desire in the work of Cervantes, Stendhal, Flaubert, Proust, and Dostoyevsky, he was accused of promoting mimetic desire.[1] Some critics thought that because he wrote about the romantic lie—by which the great novelists of our European tradition deflected their own appropriation of models for their desire onto myths of external need or internal inspiration—he endorsed it. Similarly in the 1970s, when his work on anthropology appeared, and especially his explanation of the identification of the sacred with violence and of the mechanism of the sacrificial expulsion, he was accused by some critics of promoting such sacrificial expulsion—as if Girard were a closet defender of the Nazi Holocaust against the Jews.[2]

No amount of explanation could forestall such eccentric accounts; although they came for the most part from outsiders to his thought and were largely dismissed by those who worked with Girard (or read him seriously), they did not constitute the majority opinion among critics—which was relatively positive. But with the advent of his work on Christianity, a new type of misunderstanding appeared that could endanger the reception of his work. Some critics continued to misread his work as endorsements of the very materials he was exposing. But now those same misunderstandings began to appear from the inside, among individuals who liked his work and thought they were praising it for his sacrificial views.

Suddenly some readers were saying, for example, not only that René Girard's account of the sacrificial dynamics at work between historical Christianity and Judaism was an endorsement of those dynamics from a Christian perspective, but that such an endorsement was a good thing. Moreover, since Girard declared himself publicly a believing Christian, and since theological anti-Semitism has long been a part of discussion of Jewish-Christian relations, Girard's personal declaration seemed to some a confirmation of those views.

It is this new level of misunderstanding that seems to me to occasion the charges of anti-Semitism about which we spoke earlier ("a potential scapegoating effect of Christians toward Jews" was how Professor Swartley put it). These are charges brought, I suggest, not only by those who oppose his work but by those who would appropriate it as a platform for promoting a sacrificial attack on Christianity's perceived enemies.[3]

Is René Girard's thought anti-Semitic? As early as the 1970s, Girard had answered this question—as he did, for example, in "Les Malédictions contre les pharisiens et la révélation évangélique."[4] "You say," Jesus tells the scribes and the Pharisees, according to Girard's understanding, "that had you been there (at the stoning of the prophets), you would not have stoned them. But don't you see that in saying as much, in making a sacred distinction between yourselves and those who stoned the prophets, you do the same thing as they do? You stone the prophets once again, and you do so in the very act of denouncing such behavior. Moreover, you are going to do the same to me for telling you this truth of your own desires. And those who come after you will likewise repeat the sacrificial process once again, doing to you what you do to the prophets, what is more, doing so in my name no less, calling themselves 'Christians' and calling you 'Jews.'"

The record of historical Christianity as a sacrificial religion, as a triumphalist and supersessionist declaration of the superiority of the last revelation (in which its proponents declare themselves participants) is also the history—whatever its success in promoting the Jewish law of anti-idolatry—of violence.

What is important, in other words, is not the attack on the other but the ownership of our own violence. It is to show us our own violence and where that violence is leading that, in Girard's view, Jesus taught. When Vatican II was issued, and a statement to the effect that the Jews are no longer to be considered guilty of having killed Jesus was circulated, Girard had a similar response. What the church should have said, he suggested, is not that the Jews are no longer considered guilty of killing Jesus (Who then is guilty? Everyone is now declared innocent!), but that we should have stated that we Christians are just as guilty as we have always accused the Jews of being.

In recent texts, Girard has repeated this view even more trenchantly. Jesus, he emphasizes, condemns sacrificial violence from the outset—from the murder of Abel by Cain as Torah presents it. The Jews are no more responsible for violence than are the pagans or the Christians themselves. And the reason for this claim is that Jesus speaks in the tradition of the Hebrew prophets. In the following text, for example, taken from his interviews with Michel Treguer, Girard writes:

> Les Évangiles affirment donc la culpabilité des juifs comme des païens. Et leurs seuls prédécesseurs dans cette affirmation, ce sont les livres prophétiques juifs qui racontent souvent les violences subie par les prophètes. C'est bien pourquoi Jésus dit qu'il va mourir "comme les prophètes avant lui." Il suffit de lire le récit de la mort du "Serviteur souffrant" dans le

Second Isaïe, ou celui des souffrances de Job, ou de celles de Jérémie, ou de l'aventure de Jonas, ou l'histoire de Joseph, pour voir que les bouc émissaires justifiés sont déjà dans l'Ancien Testament.

Une fois qu'on a accepté le christianisme, la seule manière d'écarter la Révélation et de ne pas voir qu'elle met toutes les cultures humaines en cause, tous les êtres humains sans exception, c'est de s'en prendre aux juifs. C'est ce que les chrétiens n'ont pas cesse de faire depuis qu'ils se sont séparés des juifs. Ils doivent donc reconnaitre leurs torts qui sont très grands. L'antisémitisme tien n'est pas un exemple parmi d'autres de religio-centrisme ou d'éthno-centrisme: c'est une défaillance par rapport à la Révélation.[5]

[The Gospels thus affirm the culpability of the Jews as of the pagans. And their only predecessors in this affirmation are the Jewish prophetic books which often recount the violence undergone by the prophets. That is really why Jesus says that he is going to die "like the prophets before him." It is sufficient to read the narrative of the death of the Suffering Servant in Second Isaiah, or that of the sufferings of Job, or those of Jeremiah, or the fortunes of Jonah, or the history of Joseph, to see that justified scapegoats are already there in the Old Testament.

As soon as one has accepted Christianity, the only manner of avoiding Revelation and of not seeing that it puts all human cultures at cause, all human beings without exception, is to blame the Jews. This is what Christians have not ceased to do since they separated from the Jews. They must therefore recognize their wrongs which are very great. Christian anti-Semitism is not one example among others of religio-centrism or ethnocentrism: it is a failure with relation to Revelation itself.][6]

The criticism Jesus makes is an internal Jewish affair. It is what Isaiah says to his audience, what Jeremiah says, what we learn in Book of Job, the story of Joseph, and elsewhere in Torah. It is with the tradition of prophetic criticism that Jesus speaks, not as a repudiation of Judaism nor of "the Jews"—of which he is one. As a prophet, he condemns sacrificial violence wherever it comes up, just as the prophets and Judaism as a whole condemn sacrificial violence wherever it crops up.

But to misunderstand Jesus as doing that, to think that Jesus is condemning Judaism or Jews or Israel as violence, is not just any misunderstanding, not just one among other possibilities, Girard tells us. It is the misunderstanding *par excellence.* It is to miss the very point Jesus is making, the point, that is to say, of Christian revelation itself. The only way out of this particular misunderstanding—of believing that Judaism is violence—is to become Christian, to adopt the revelation one has evaded by such strategies.

Far from it being the case for Girard, in other words, that to be a Christian one must reject being Jewish, Girard's position is in fact the opposite. From a Girardian perspective, to be a Christian is to recognize the ways in which one has always already been Jewish, and to own the specifically Jewish Toradic critique of sacrificial violence as one's own in order that violence be rejected and peace established.

If we wish to claim, however (as I do), that the Christian revelation for Girard is fully part of the Jewish soil in which it is embedded, and that what Girard is discovering in Christianity is its Jewish filigree—the critique of sacrificial violence from which Judaism started and which has constituted its history from the prophets to the rabbis—then we need to ask about the differences between them. Is Christianity to be regarded from a Girardian perspective as simply an extension of Jewish studies? Or is there rather a specific Christian revelation that marks it as different from Judaism? Girard often speaks of the revelation of the innocent victim as the distinguishing feature of Christianity. In turning to part two of my comments, I take up this theme.

Part Two: The Innocent Victim in Isaiah 52–53: Similarities in Jewish and Christian Understandings

René Girard's theory of the uniqueness of Christianity is based on his theory of the innocent victim. Jesus of Nazareth is not, in his view, simply another figure like the hero of Greek tragedy, like Oedipus, for example, who becomes an enemy twin of everyone. Jesus does nothing violent and yet is willing to die to reveal the arbitrariness of scapegoat violence, the lack of efficacy of the sacrificial expulsion about which the Hebrew prophets have been speaking. This is a process which may once have galvanized primitive culture but which has become in the modern context little short of murder.

But careful examination of Isaiah 52–53 reveals that though it appears some six hundred years before texts of the Christian Gospel appear, it is entirely conversant with the idea of the innocent victim. There is little that Girard says about the innocent victim that is missing from Isaiah 52–53. Thus I suggest we need to reexamine Girard's claim that the Gospel is unique in this particular fashion. Here is the passage in the old standard JPS translation of 1917.[7]

> Behold, My servant shall prosper,
> He shall be exalted and lifted up, and shall be very high.
> According as many were appalled at thee—
> So marred was his visage unlike that of a man,
> And his form unlike that of the sons of men—
> So shall he startle many nations,
> Kings shall shut their mouths because of him;
> For that which had not been told them they shall see,
> And that which they had not heard they shall perceive.
> 'Who would have believed our report?
> And to whom hath the arm of the Lord been revealed?
> For he shot up right forth as a sapling,
> And as a root out of a dry ground;
> He had no form nor comeliness that we should look on him,
> Nor beauty that we should delight in him.
> He was despised, and forsaken of men,
> A man of pains, and acquainted with disease,
> And as one from whom men hide their face;
> He was despised, and we esteemed him not.
> Surely our diseases he did bear, and our pains he carried;
> Whereas we did esteem him stricken,
> Smitten of God, and afflicted.
> But he was wounded because of our transgressions,
> He was crushed because of our iniquities:
> The chastisement of our welfare was on him,
> And with his stripes we were healed.
> All we like sheep did go astray,
> We turned every one to his own way;
> And the Lord hath made to light upon him

The iniquity of us all.
He was oppressed, though he humbled himself
And opened not his mouth;
As a lamb that is led to the slaughter
And as a sheep that before her shearers is dumb;
Yea, he opened not his mouth.
By oppression and judgment he was taken away,
And with his generation who did reason?
For he was cut off out of the land of the living,
For the transgression of my people to whom the stroke was due.
And they made his grave with the wicked,
And with the rich his tomb;
Although he had done no violence,
Neither was there any deceit in his mouth.'

Yet it pleased the Lord to crush him by disease;
To see if his soul would offer itself in restitution,
That he might see his seed, prolong his days,
And that the purpose of the Lord might prosper by his hand:
Of the travail of his soul he shall see to the full, even My servant,
Who by his knowledge did justify the Righteous One to the many,
And their iniquities he did bear.
Therefore will I divide him a portion among the great,
And he shall divide the spoil with the mighty;
Because he bared his soul unto death,
And was numbered with the transgressors;
Yet he bore the sin of many,
And made intercession for the transgressors.

The passage has, of course, sustained a long tradition of commentary in both the Hebraic and Christian traditions. There is no place in the present context to engage all of the issues raised.[8] The passage is part of the sequence of Isaiah from chapters 40 to 55 commonly associated with the "Second" school of prophetic writers whose theme is taken to be comfort after the destruction of the temple and the Babylonian exile (and thus the appellation "Second" or "Deutero").[9] It is the fourth and last of the so-called songs of the

Suffering Servant of the Lord. And the central concern of interpretation in both traditions has been the identity of the subject of this song.

In the Jewish tradition the servant is customarily identified with Israel. Meanwhile in the Christian typological tradition the servant is commonly regarded as a prefiguration of Jesus himself. Neither tradition, however, has proved entirely satisfactory to its adherents. Our own concern in this present context is less to rekindle this old debate than to compare the content of the passage—whoever the servant is understood to be—with the content René Girard has attributed to the Christian reading of the sacrificial mechanism. This is a comparison which may in turn then shed light on other significant interpretative matters.

The correspondence between the two is extraordinary. In the first place, the servant is described as an outsider. Thus, in 52:14–15, we read:

> Many were appalled at thee—
> So marred was his visage unlike that of a man,
> And his form unlike that of the sons of men—
> So shall he startle many nations.

And then again, at the outset of the long middle sequence (53:3), we read:

> He had no form nor comeliness that we should look upon him,
> Nor beauty that we should delight in him.
> He was despised, and forsaken of men,
> A man of pains, and acquainted with disease,
> And as one from whom men hide their face.

He was "despised" and "forsaken" by others, and the narrator includes himself in the group that took this approach to him ("we esteemed him not"). His face was disfigured along with his body, so much so that people were startled by the disfiguration. He had no beauty or attractiveness to recommend him, and people assumed these blandishments were the product of long suffering and disease.

But the speaker is not satisfied with such an account and will examine in an extraordinary manner the origins of such attributions. Whatever the physical causes of his disfigurement, and whatever others have done to him, we ourselves are not free from implication in his pains. The pains he bears and the disease he carries are the product at least in part of our own behavior toward him—although we commonly deny responsibility for that behavior. It is not simply that he was wounded by another because of what we did. He was wounded by us. And what we did was precisely what wounded him. We blamed him for our transgressive behavior and that constituted his wound.

> Surely our diseases he did bear, and our pains he carried;
> Whereas we did esteem him stricken, Smitten of God, and afflicted.
> But he was wounded because of our transgressions,
> He was crushed because of our iniquities:
> The chastisement of our welfare was on him.

Moreover, by his removal from the community, by his sacrifice or expulsion, we told ourselves that our afflictions were ended.

And with his stripes we were healed.

Each of us continued to engage in our own radical individualism, each turning to his or her own way. And the Lord, who foresees all, caused it to turn out that our iniquity has fallen on him.

> All we like sheep did go astray,
> We turned everyone to his own way;
> And the Lord hath made to light on him
> The iniquity of us all.

Did he complain? Did he object to our treatment of him?

> He was oppressed, though he humbled himself
> And opened not his mouth;
> As a lamb that is led to the slaughter
> And as a sheep that before her shearers is dumb;
> Yea, he opened not his mouth.
> By oppression and judgment he was taken away,
> And with his generation who did reason?

We killed him for what we decided he did to us. Instead of blaming ourselves—where the blame should have been lodged—we blamed him. We called him wicked and buried him with those we considered our enemies— although he was innocent of any wrongdoing and did not protest our behavior toward him. He went to his grave like a lamb to the slaughter.

> For he was cut off out of the land of the living,
> For the transgression of my people to whom the stroke was due.
> And they made his grave with the wicked,
> And with the rich his tomb;
> Although he had done no violence,
> Neither was there any deceit in his mouth.

And what excuse did we offer when we took such action? Did we own what we did to him after we did it?

> We did esteem him stricken,
> Smitten of God.

We told ourselves that

> ... it pleased the Lord to crush him with disease;
> To see if his soul would offer itself in restitution,
> [in order] That he might see his seed, prolong his days,
> And that the purpose of the Lord might prosper by his hand.

We told ourselves, in other words, that the Lord did it, perhaps to test him, as God did Abraham, to see whether an exchange was possible. He would get to see his children, we told ourselves. His days would be long. He could make restitution for the wrongdoing of others.

What did he do when we took this action against him? He bore the violence willingly and proceeded to justify God in the act even though he was the victim of our iniquities and our transgressions.

> By his knowledge did [he] justify the Righteous One to the many,
> And their iniquities he did bear.

He took the violence we launched against him and justified God and us in the very act of doing so. Even in the act of dying for what we did to him, he intervened on our behalf.

> He bared his soul unto death,
> And was numbered with the transgressors;
> Yet he bore the sin of many,
> And made intercession for the transgressors.

For all these things, then, the speaker concludes, I will honor him.

> Therefore will I divide him a portion among the great,
> And he shall divide the spoil with the mighty.

He revealed to us in this manner "the arm of the Lord." And although the report of this action is hard to believe ("Who would have believed our report?"), we have to believe that something extraordinary took place, and we have begun to see things that have not been perceived before.

> So shall he startle many nations,
> Kings shall shut their mouths because of him;
> For that which had not been told them they shall see,
> And that which they had not heard they shall perceive.

What element of René Girard's theory of sacrifice is missing from this description? The sacrificial expulsion, the violent removal of the victim who has done no violence, who is removed by (and for) what his persecutors did and by whose removal they are healed—all of it is there.

Indeed, elements appear in this text that are not part of Girard's theory. We learn that this process seems to have been foreseen by the Lord who caused this to happen: that this servant was willing to be the intercessor on our behalf with God (and perhaps this is why the Lord caused it to take place); that the servant was given the opportunity to make restitution on our behalf; that we are much like sheep who have gone astray; that we buried him among those we considered our enemies; that the servant was willing to undergo this experience in order that the Lord might prosper; and so forth.

But these elements are precisely those that Girard has also left out of his account of the Christian text. Far from undermining the correspondence between the two texts, their presence serves to buttress it. If there are elements that remain mythic in Isaiah 52–53 (in the way that Girard speaks of "myth"), they are the same elements that remain mythic in the Gospel. And there may be ways of reading these elements that render them less mythic. Could the lines in 53:6 ("And the Lord hath made to light on him / The iniquity of us all") and in 53:10 ("Yet it pleased the Lord to crush him with disease") reflect less the speech of the narrator than examples of the ways in which "we did esteem him stricken, / Smitten of God, and afflicted"—though in fact "He was crushed because of *our* iniquities" (italics added)?

However, whether or not Isaiah 52–53 matches the Gospel in all particulars, clearly it contains all Girard needs to uncover the scapegoat mechanism. There is nothing Girard says about the innocent victim in Christianity, it would appear, that is not already fully present in Isaiah 52–53, some six hundred years earlier. So we need to ask: What are the ramifications of this correspondence for Girard's claim regarding the uniqueness of the Christian Gospel in this regard? We seem to be left with a limited number of possibilities, none entirely satisfactory. I will enumerate them, then discuss them in more detail.

The first is that Christianity really *is* unique—as both Girard and Christians say it is—but its uniqueness is not based on the disclosure of the innocent victim before his persecutors, as Girard claims (which is, in fact, already fully a Jewish idea). Rather, the Gospel's uniqueness is based on some other consideration still to be articulated—perhaps, for example, the Christian revelation itself. One could imagine acknowledging the Christian revelation of Jesus as the son of God who triumphs over death while continuing to credit the deconstruction of the sacrificial mechanism and the like as entirely coincident with Jewish understanding, an understanding that appears briefly in Isaiah 52–53 and that Christianity considerably expands. The advantage of this reading is that it maintains the revelatory status of the Christian experience, although it does so at the expense of the Girardian understanding of the centrality of the disclosure of the sacrificial mechanism.

The second possibility is that Christianity is *not* unique although Girard and Christians say it is. Christianity is only an "acting out" of Judaism, so to speak, an episode in the history of the religion which preceded it and of which it remains—in all of its themes and content (and however much it may deny that affiliation)—an unwitting or unwilling extension. This view has the advantage of sustaining a thoroughgoing continuity between the two experiences but at the expense of the distinctive revelatory status of the second.

The third possibility for understanding the connection between Isaiah 52–53 and the Christian Gospel is the explanation that Christianity really *is* unique (as both Girard and Christians say), and that such uniqueness *is* rooted in the understanding of the innocent victim (as Girard claims), but that the correspondence between the two—between the innocent victim as presented in Isaiah and the innocent victim as presented in the Gospel—is not complete, although precisely the ways in which these texts differ has yet to be elaborated.

Obviously there are problems with each potential interpretation. Although we want to keep the question open, it seems valuable to enumerate the difficulties, if only better to imagine alternatives.

The problem with the first proposal—that Christianity is unique but the deconstruction of sacrifice is not central—is that the Girardian explanation is convincing. Although Christians may continue to debate the matter, from a Jewish perspective there is no obstacle to regarding the explanation that Girard offers as entirely compelling, both as an account of primitive culture and as the distinguishing critical feature of the Gospel revelation.

The deconstruction of the sacrificial is not new. It is already thoroughly available in Jewish texts. But it has less centrality there than the law of anti-idolatry. Christianity takes up the critique of sacrifice and centralizes it in a way to which Jews and Christians alike, it could well be argued, have failed to pay sufficient attention. A proposal, therefore, which excludes Girard's explanation from a central place in the Christian text seems insufficient.

But the second proposal—that Christianity is simply an episode in the history of Judaism—must similarly be rejected. Whether or not such a claim is acceptable from a Jewish point of view, it is certainly not so from a Christian perspective. And even from a Jewish perspective, we need to grant Christianity its own revelatory experience—just as we would Buddhism, Hinduism, Islam, or any other major world religion.[10]

This leaves us with the third possibility—that Christianity is unique and the Girardian view is central but incomplete. This is the most interesting

alternative, but even here there are difficulties. This view maintains the revelatory status of Christianity. It also maintains the linkage to Girard's theory.
But it depends on a position that remains to be articulated. Precisely what
the content of such a future understanding of the innocent victim in the
Christian context may be is somewhat difficult to fathom.

Could it be, for example, an expansion of the manner in which Christianity takes up themes of invasion and abandonment in family life? Is it
possible that Christianity introduces into the history of the anti-sacrificial
what may be termed the "self-sacrificial," or, more precisely, the dynamics of
self-formation or self-construction, dynamics that appear fundamental to
both Judaism and Christianity (and along precisely the lines of the mimetic
and the conflictual Girard has been developing)? Moreover, such dynamics
may even be responsible for the appearance of the Christian within the history of Pharisaic Judaism, yet these dynamics are not yet articulated.[11]

Whatever the future direction of these discussions, however, some things
are already apparent. The theory of the innocent victim is not new. It is an old
Jewish theme. What Girard discovers in the Christian text—whatever else
he discovers (which may be a great deal)—is its Jewish filigree. What is new
is the focus that Christianity gives to it, the centrality with which the persecutory structure comes to dominate Jesus's life (and the lives of Christians
afterwards), a structure which in the Jewish context is subsumed within the
more general formulation of the anti-idolatrous.

But that change of focus may reflect the kind of midrashic or interpretative impulse that Judaism *would* recognize: namely, the delineation of the
power of Toradic insight for a particular time and place. With its emphasis on mediated desire, violence, and the sacrificial scapegoat mechanism,
Christianity in Girard's interpretation may well extend an analysis already
present in Judaism to a new and vital context, to a family setting in which
the phenomena of invasion and abandonment assume an importance not
hitherto imagined within Jewish culture. If so, then it is on such a basis that
we may at once regard Christianity within a larger Jewish perspective—an
"episode in the history of the Judaic"—and sustain the historical specificity
and revelatory impact that Christians have always felt to be endemic to their
experience.

Part Three: Comparing Each Other's Texts: Shabbath as Example

To gain further comparative insight between midrashic Judaism and early Christian understanding, I refer, as example, to tractate *Shabbath* in the Babylonian Talmud (30b–31c). This text concerns one of the famous episodes of the ongoing debate between the house of Hillel and the house of Shammai regarding the teaching of Torah to outsiders, a topic that is not without interest to a dialogue in which it is asked whether Judaism can open its inner portals to outsiders. Further, the anecdotal tale that Jesus of Nazareth was a disciple of the house of Hillel might be of interest here.

A heathen once approached a representative of the house of Shammai with the following request: Make me a proselyte on condition that you teach me Torah while I am standing on one foot. (The "house of Shammai" is taken to be the more orthodox school of religious practice, and the request of the would-be novitiate is understood to be the inquiry of an outsider who presumably has no understanding of Torah—as opposed to a child growing up in the community of that understanding.) The heathen was in effect asking: Can you teach me Torah while I am standing on one foot? Can you teach me Torah in a way that I can commodify it, carry it around with me, the way one might be able to do with the knowledge or skill or wisdom one would get from one of the roaming Greek Sophists against whom Plato wrote? One can imagine the response of this orthodox teacher. He will not even consider the request of his visitor. He shoos him out of the house—"with the builder's cubit which was in his hand."

The would-be novitiate—not to be put off—then approaches a representative of the house of Hillel with the same request: Make me a proselyte on condition that you teach me Torah while I am standing on one foot. Hillel is taken as the representative of the more liberal school of ritual practice. Here he receives what appears to be a more positive response. Hillel will answer him. Moreover, Hillel will do so in terms of the request he has made. But here as well, in the response he receives from Hillel, is a commentary he perhaps did not expect.

When he went before Hillel, he [Hillel] said to him, "What is hateful to you, do not to your neighbor: that is the whole Torah, while the rest is the commentary thereof; go and learn it." (31a)

Can we hear in this little exchange a lesson for our own dilemma? The similarity of Hillel's dictum to the formulation of Jesus's Golden Rule—"love your neighbor as yourself" (Matthew 22:37, which, in fact, also appears in this form in Torah [Leviticus 19:18]) is unmistakable. Can we learn from the difference in formulation? You think, Hillel says, that in approaching me with your request—that I teach you Torah while you are standing on one foot—that you are putting something over on me. What poses as a request is really a form of attack. Shammai recognized that attack immediately and would not play your game (and therefore ushered you out without engaging you about it). I recognized the same baiting strategy (and on this point Shammai and I are in agreement). But it occurs to me that I can use where you are as a beginning, that I can stage your strategy against me before you, so to speak, as a way ironically of teaching you that the Torah—whose wisdom you say you seek—has never been any other.

In making your request of me (Hillel)—to teach you Torah while you are standing on one foot—you in fact retract the offer on which it is based in the act of extending it. If the wisdom of Torah is to be valuable, it will hardly be the kind of wisdom that could be commodified in such a way that it could be so offered. The Torah that I could teach you in such a fashion is not Torah.

Moreover, your very asking of the question in that manner betrays an orientation that exceeds a request for knowledge, that slips into an attack. Why do you think I don't see what you are doing? Do you think that we are that different? You would not want that kind of exclusionary behavior enacted against you. So why do you do it to me? On the other hand, I can take the tactics from which you do start and work with them. I can show you that such tactics are, in fact, the text's very subject matter, and that you've come to the right place after all.

Hillel reads in the individual's behavior an extraordinary psychological insight. He sees that the would-be novitiate is projecting a self-defeating strategy, an impossible demand, a double-bind, on his interlocutor, perhaps because he has experienced the same betrayal himself in his own past and is now repeating that behavior against others—behavior hardly far removed from the text. What Hillel is suggesting is that instead of acting out that betrayal he might take stock of it, that he might own his own violence, even the violence that has been done to him and that he would now repeat.

Moreover, the questioner needs to grasp that the Torah he says he wants—and has dismissed—offers, in fact, the same teaching: that the words are insufficient by themselves (and could be replaced by others) and that to read them requires a teacher. What is needed, in other words, is a relationship that does not betray you, one that allows you to take stock of your own behavior in a way that both makes it clear to you and does not harm you. Perhaps this short Talmudic text—which offers the Jewish reader a way into Torah—teaches the same lesson, the presentation of what appears to be two options which are, in fact, the same option, one which concerns betrayals we have experienced and would foist on others.

Does this sequence not have a bearing on Jesus's Golden Rule in the texts of Matthew and Luke? And is it not more generally applicable to a history in which betrayal has been felt so keenly on both sides? This is a history in which Jews have felt fundamentally betrayed by Christians, who have arisen from within their ranks, so to speak, and defied their parental affiliation and parental progeniture. It is a history by the same token in which Christians have felt similarly betrayed, disapproved for efforts they thought eminently worthy of approval, entirely Jewish in their understanding, and as a result of which disapproval their resentment and anger have been kindled.

Does this history not sound like the life of Paul, even the life of Luther, and perhaps of others, if only we would view the context broadly enough? Are Adolf Hitler's speeches to the Reichstag at the end of the 1930s, in which he speaks repeatedly of the laughter he perceives among the Jews against him, not part of the same profound sense of betrayal and humiliation with consequences we now know only too well? Humiliation and betrayal are powerful human motivators, perhaps the most powerful, as a writer like Dostoyevsky certainly knew. What if the history of sacrificial violence as it concerns Jewish-Christian relations is really the same history? What if the anti-Semitism we sometimes attach to René Girard's thought, either because we approve of it or because we wish to attack it, is but another version of the same dislocation?

Such reflections could render the distant and sometimes hostile relations between Judaism and Christianity something of a family quarrel. As in all families, there may be difficulties, even bloodshed. But considering Judaism

and Christianity as part of a family—and not as a set of independent perspectives—we also open the potential for reconciliation and, consequently,
for hope.

I suspect we are far from ready to embark on such a path. But that does
not diminish the value of imagining it. The experience of each community
may only be enriched by such fundamental speculation as each in turn highlights threads operating in the other in ways individually less visible. In that
coming debate, the innocent victim as René Girard presents this figure at
the heart of the Christian Gospel, like the analysis of sacrificial violence on
which it is based, will no doubt be one of the Jewish filigrees that continue to
enliven the Christian text and render discussion of that text and its relation
to Judaism especially valuable.

Response by René Girard and Reply to René Girard

Response by René Girard

Unfortunately, I could not attend the symposium at which the papers in the present volume were first presented and discussed. When Professor Willard Swartley, able organizer of this event as well as editor of its proceedings and a participant, kindly sent me all the manuscripts and invited me to comment on them, I was confronted with a difficult choice. The quality of all these contributions is such that I wanted to say something about each. Such a course, however, would limit my observations to statements so brief and inconsequential that they would do justice neither to the individual papers nor the volume as a whole.

I decided to focus on the main subject of the symposium, which is also my one real field of competence, the "mimetic theory." Some of what follows applies to many papers in *Violence Renounced*, some applies to only a few or even to a single one, as in the case of Sandor Goodhart. Many contributors are not mentioned. Their essays are not necessarily those I enjoyed least; rather, they often are the ones from which I learned the most. . . .

◆   ◆   ◆

The demystification or deconstruction of scapegoating begins with the Hebrew Bible. The story of Joseph, for instance, repeatedly rehabilitates a wrongly accused scapegoat. It is a continuous struggle against false persecution. This process of intellectual and spiritual cleansing is also present in the Psalms, in the book of Job, and, more explicitly than anywhere else, in Isaiah 52–53, which portrays the death of an unknown prophet, Yahweh's Suffering Servant.

In his essay, Sandor Goodhart perceives this truth. He explicates the prophet's collective lynching to show its revelatory value in regard to the falsity of scapegoating. If the text were a myth, the Servant's death would be justified as the punishment of a real culprit, as the just expulsion of an individual harmful to the community, something like the expulsion of that well-known delinquent, Oedipus, who, in addition to his principal crimes, parricide and incest, gives the plague to all his fellow citizens!

The Servant must be accused of similar crimes, but his death is portrayed as the completely unjust lynching of an innocent man by a deluded mob. The text contains a clear allusion to the mimetic disruption that turns human communities into mobs and triggers their scapegoating urge: "All we like sheep did go astray, we turned every one to his own way."

Sandor goes straight to the all-revelatory passage, notably the one on the prophet's lowly status in his community. The Servant is somewhat of an outcast, due in part to his mediocre and unimpressive appearance, which, in addition to his gentleness, makes him a likely choice as a scapegoat. He is the type of individual to whom persecutors in search of a victim are irresistibly drawn:

> For he shot up right forth as a sapling,
> And as a root out of dry ground;
> He had no form nor comeliness that we should look upon him.
> Nor beauty that we should delight in him.
> He was despised, and forsaken of men,
> A man of pains, and acquainted with disease,
> And as one from whom men hide their face;
> He was despised and we esteemed him not.[1]

If we survey a great number of myths we will discover that a high percentage of their hero/victims, just like the Servant of the Lord, possess one or more features of the type that tend to attract scapegoaters: these include physical or cultural features that arouse the fear, anger, or contempt of archaic communities, unpleasant infirmities, abnormalities, repulsive illnesses, a foreign accent, foreign customs. In *The Scapegoat*, I grouped these features together under the label of preferential signs of victimization. Whoever possesses one or several of them will not necessarily be selected as a scapegoat, but his/her chances are increased.

Sandor is aware that the four accounts of the Passion also reveal the process of scapegoating. He is aware, therefore, that the Bible and the Gospels have something essential in common. He is not one of these people who claim that the expression "Judeo-Christian" is meaningless and should be abandoned.

The Songs of the Servant were written six centuries, probably, before the Gospels, and Sandor raises the question of the Gospels' singularity or lack of it in relation to the Jewish Bible:

> There is nothing that Girard says about the innocent victim in Christianity, it would appear, which is not already fully present in Isaiah 52–53. We need to reexamine Girard's claim that the gospel is unique in this particular fashion.

His reexamination leads Sandor to conclude that the singularity that I, like other Christians, attribute to Christ and Christian Scriptures cannot be real, unless we root it in something different from the revelation of the scapegoat mechanism.

Just as Sandor does, I believe that Isaiah 52–53 fully reveals the same scapegoat mechanism as the Gospels. The description is as concrete and realistic as in the four accounts of the Passion. There are several differences, nevertheless, between Isaiah 52–53 and the Gospels' account of scapegoating. I will discuss only the one I regard as essential.

In the Gospels, not only is the revelation of scapegoating repeated once again but, for the first time, this revelation reflects on itself, it talks about itself, and it comments on its own significance for all human beings. Far from refusing to acknowledge the historical priority of the biblical revelation, the Gospels repeatedly acknowledge it and invoke the authority of the Scripture to explain the significance of what is going on in the Passion.

An essential part of this self-referential dimension of the scapegoat revelation lies in the many quotes from the Bible, not only from Isaiah 52–53 but
from many other texts which have revelatory value in regard to scapegoating.
The Gospel of John (15:25) quotes a statement from Psalm 69:4 (cf. 35:19)
that, at first sight, seems rather banal and unimpressive. In this Psalm, the
narrator complains that, even though his enemies are as numerous as the
hairs on his head, they hate me, he says, "without a cause."

Our modern psychological and textual bias suggests that it must be his
psychic abnormality, his paranoid tendencies perhaps, that lead the narrator
of this Psalm to imagine a huge alliance against him. We never even wonder
if he might not be saying the truth, if, in a chaotic community, he might not
be really threatened with lynching, just like the Servant of the Lord. Our
long tradition of idealism and our tendency to dissolve reality prevent us
from even conceiving of the possibility of a real violence outside the text. For
our fashionable critics all violence is textual.

The phrase "without a cause" is applied to Jesus precisely because it
defines the most characteristic feature of scapegoating: if the victimizers
have a cause, it is a nonsensical one, a "preferential sign of persecution." The
"without a cause" senseless mimetic hostility of scapegoating is everywhere
in evidence around Jesus; it contagiously affects even his closest disciples.
Peter's triple denial is nothing but this "hating without a cause" which the
apostle unconsciously absorbs as soon as he is engulfed in a crowd already
hostile to Jesus, and he immediately imitates this hostility. This denial is a
most eloquent testimony to the mimetic nature of scapegoating in general
and the Passion in particular.

Long believed irrelevant and nonsensical, the idea of Christological
prophecy makes sense in the context of scapegoat revelation. The Gospels
not only provide us with the most complete revelation of scapegoating ever
written, more complete and specific than even Isaiah 52–53, but the quotes
and comments surrounding the crucifixion make this revelation still more
complete and explicit. Even some of the titles given to Jesus are part of the
scapegoat revelation. To say that he is the *lamb* of God is the same as saying
that he is a scapegoat in the modern sense. The Gospel expression is more
effective in conveying the innocence of the unjustly sacrificed victim.

The Gospels not only reveal scapegoating but reflect on their own revelation and its future effects on the world, the apocalyptic violence, for instance,

that might be unleashed when the sacrificial protection that pre-Christian cultures still enjoy is completely withdrawn.

In the Jewish Bible the scapegoat revelation, as Sandor himself observes, does not occupy a central place. It remains marginal and does not underline its own importance. That is why the attention of commentators is never focused directly on it. The central theme, as Sandor also observes, is the struggle against idolatry.

If we reflect on idol worship, however, once again we will be confronted by scapegoating, which is the true cause of idolatry. The only way to fulfill the struggle against idolatry is to reveal its origin in the invisible, undisclosed scapegoating of mythology. The essence of archaic religion, I recall, is the people's gratitude towards their scapegoats they mistake for divine benefactors.

An idolater is an individual who worships his own victim in the mistaken belief that far from being an innocent scapegoat, he/she is a real malefactor who deserves to be killed; then the unanimous violence, mysteriously, turns the scoundrel into a divine reconciler of the community.

I am not inclined to believe, therefore, that by placing the emphasis on anti-idolatry as Sandor does, one can effectively regard the revelation of scapegoating as something of secondary importance. Thus, the rejection of idolatry is impossible unless scapegoating is fully revealed as the mimetic self-deception that dominates mythology and sacrificial rites.

◆　◆　◆

The entire history of religion, I feel, can be summarized in terms of the relationship between scapegoating and the scapegoaters. In archaic religions scapegoating itself is sacralized because it remains forever unintelligible. Archaic religions and their sacrificial systems are an economy of scapegoating that violently evacuates internal violence and, through the endless repetitions of ritual, slowly generates cultural institutions.

The tremendous achievement of the Jewish Bible is that, for the first time in history, it de-divinized victims and it de-victimized God. It replaced the thousands of scapegoat idols with the one monotheistic Yahweh who is totally alien to human scapegoating. That is why in the Jewish Bible, for the first time, scapegoating is portrayed truthfully as scapegoating. Instead of being first demonized, then divinized—in the sense that Oedipus is—Joseph is admirably humanized.

Jewish monotheism is so essentially characterized by this mutual separation of scapegoating and the divine that it tends to perceive Christianity only as a regression into the bad mythical habit of divinizing scapegoats. Is not Jesus a divinized scapegoat, just as Oedipus?

Indeed he is, but if we carefully examine Jesus's relationship to scapegoating, we will see that, far from being the same as in mythology, it is the very reverse. Instead of being divinized by the people who turn him into a scapegoat and persecute him without being aware of his innocence, Jesus Christ is God to those who realize he is an innocent victim and accepts playing the role of the scapegoat to reveal once and for all how scapegoating operates in human culture, how all human beings ultimately share in scapegoating. Jesus willingly and knowingly accepts to undergo the fate of the scapegoat to achieve the full revelation of scapegoating as the genesis of all false gods.

The absolute separation between God and scapegoats, such as we have it in the Jewish Bible, is a most important step in the revelation of what God really is, but it is not the end of the story. The Bible teaches us that the true God is not dependent on the scapegoat mechanism.

As a matter of fact God dislikes that mechanism so much that, again and again, God sides with the victims against their persecutors. In the book of Job the essential question is whether or not God is on the side of the crowd, with the persecutors, or on the side of the victim, with the innocent scapegoat. The final answer is that God is on the side of the victim, not of the persecutors.

Already in the Jewish Bible, therefore, a new rapprochement is taking place between God and victimized scapegoats, but on a basis entirely different from the old mythical confusion. Here the basis is revealing and neutralizing mimetic victimization.

What the Gospels and Christian theology really do is take this rapprochement as possible, which means all the way to a complete identification. God and the scapegoat become one once again in the death of a Jesus who is as fully divine as he is fully human. God willingly becomes the scapegoat of his own people not for the purpose of evacuating internal violence through the old mythical misunderstanding but for the opposite reason, for clearing up once and for all all such misunderstanding and raising human kind above the culture of scapegoating.

Far from dismissing as necessarily "mythical" and "sacrificial" the attempts to define the mysterious proximity between the Servant and God in the Servant Songs, we must try to understand the text as part of an effort which, half a millennium later, will produce such Christian ideas as the incarnation and redemption through the cross. Some of my earlier statements on the subject were rash and inadequate, I now believe. I am still groping toward a more satisfactory understanding. I hope that the younger researchers such as Sandor and all the authors in the present volume will reach someday the goal that keeps eluding me.

Reply to René Girard

When we were graduate students in René's classes at the University of Buffalo in the late sixties and early seventies, we used to say that René had the Midas touch. Everything he laid his hands on turned to gold. No matter how difficult or familiar the text or problem, we would bring it to him, and in a flash it would look new and clear in a way that felt genuine and authentic. This gesture on his part never ceased to dazzle us.

Did we idealize him and his effect upon us? Probably. But we were content to bathe in the luminous clarity of his extraordinary perspective and we were never the same afterwards. We gained a knowledge and confidence in our own capacities that in my case at least has stayed with me to this day.

I was reminded of these moments as I reread René's pages on my essay on him in Willard Swartley's wonderful book and oddly enough felt a little of the same initial charm.[2] Who is this fellow named "Sandor," I wondered? Why doesn't he just give up his silly view and admit that René has clarified matters once again for all of us? I had to catch myself, of course, to remind myself that it was me he was talking about, and that, oddly enough, I had now in fact gotten my wish. Although still René's student, I had now achieved the credentials and the skills to publish on my own and one of the consequences of that status and that capacity was that I could now find myself at odds with René even in the course of defending his thinking. Like King Midas, I had found the gold I had for so long desired ironically inedible. Facing the difficult choice between rejecting the gift (as King Midas did) or honoring the gift by reflecting it and reflecting upon it, I could (and would, of course) choose the latter. Having appropriated René's teachings, I could now choose the good mimesis over the bad, the mimesis that deflected any possible competition or rivalry between us. But the oddness of the situation stayed with me.

There is a Jewish story, a midrash, an aggadic moment in the Talmudic tractate *Bava Metzia*, that may help us to think about this dilemma (and here I paraphrase midrashically).[3] Two Rabbis are arguing over the cleaning of an oven. Rabbi Eliezer says you do it this way, another rabbi says you do it that. If the law is not with me, Rabbi Eliezer says, let the carob tree show it. All of a sudden, a carob tree in the region uproots itself and moves one hundred cubits—some say four hundred cubits! What can you tell from a carob tree, one of the opponents proclaims. If the law is not with me, then, Rabbi Eliezer says, let the river show it. All of a sudden, the river in the region starts flowing in the opposite direction! What can you tell from a river, another of the opponents shouts. Finally, in frustration, Rabbi Eliezer says, if the law is not with me, let the Holy one, blessed be He, show it. All of a sudden, there is a whirlwind, and out of the heart of the storm, a heavenly voice speaks. "Why do you argue with Rabbi Eliezer," the voice says, "since in all regards, the law is with him!" "The truth is not in heaven," Rabbi Yehoshua replies. And Rabbi Yirmeyah comments, "We don't listen to heavenly voices. We received your Torah at Sinai, and we will cling fast to your Torah, even if you Yourself show up to tell us to do otherwise. The decision inclines to the majority."[4]

If I proceed to argue my position, then, to differ from René here or there, I take shelter in the fact that I do so in the light of the teaching he has offered us, and that I summon René back to his own instruction and honor that instruction by proclaiming it, even if I do so in his presence, and even if René himself shows up to oppose it.

◆   ◆   ◆

My case in the essay is straightforward.[5] I argue that Isaiah 52–53 displays all of the elements crucial to René's theory of the innocent victim and the exposure of the sacrificial scapegoat mechanism that René finds central to (and, in fact, the distinctive feature of) the Christian Gospel six centuries later. As a result, I suggest, we need to wonder whether the Christian Gospel is singular on this particular basis. Is it possible, for example, that the Gospel is *not* unique (although René and others say it is) and just a repetition and development of the Hebrew Bible within a given time and place? Or, is it possible that the Gospel *is* unique but that René and others are wrong to think that its singularity derives from this particular demonstration, and that perhaps it comes from some other quality?

Or, finally, is it possible the Gospel *is* unique and that its uniqueness *does* derive from its revelation of the sacrificial mechanism, but that the correspondence between the two, between Isaiah 52–53 and the Christian Gospel, is incomplete and some critical element of the Gospel (not contained in Isaiah 52–53) remains to be elucidated—although it is difficult to imagine just what that element could be? Without such further elucidation, I argue, we are left with the sense that what René discovers within the Christian Gospel is its Jewish filigree and that it is this compelling and powerful analytic of the sacrificial that he would identify—quite apart from any matters of personal faith—with its singularity.

René's response is succinct and characteristically generous.[6] Sandor recognizes the power of the texts of the Christian Gospel in revealing the critique of the sacrificial mechanism, but he denies that the Christian text is singular in this fashion. Sandor privileges the critique of anti-idolatry which he finds—and rightly so, in my view—at the heart of the Hebrew Bible, but as a critique it is not capable of doing what Sandor would have it do.

Even thematically, René argues, the Gospel is more explicitly concerned with scapegoating, more reflective about it, and more conscious of that self-reflexivity, whereas the Hebrew Bible, as Sandor admits, "marginalizes" the reflection on sacrifice for a reflection on anti-idolatry. But it is only in terms of sacrificial dynamics, René argues, that idolatry is understandable, and not the reverse. The Hebrew Bible goes part of the way in separating divinity from victimage, "de-victimizing the divinity" and "de-divinizing the victim," but not as far as the Christian Gospel in understanding God to be on the side of the victim. The Christian Gospel completes the reflection the Hebrew Bible opens. The Hebrew Bible must be commended for beginning the task, but the task cannot be regarded as completed without the Christian Gospel.

The issue would appear to be joined. At root of the difference between René and myself, it would seem, is the status of the critique of idolatry as given in the Hebrew Bible. For me the Torah, understood as the law of anti-idolatry, is enormously powerful, powerful enough, in fact, to include everything that René talks about as the mimetic and the sacrificial. Therefore I am able to find in René's discovery of the sacrificial mechanism the discovery of the Jewish filigree within Christianity. Christianity from this perspective is like a large midrash, one in which many individuals live from day to day no doubt, but nonetheless a midrashic story for all that, a way of making the Hebrew scripture applicable in a particular time and place. Christianity extends and elaborates this Jewish understanding, brings that insight to bear upon a situation with which it may or may not in the past have had to deal—the invasions and abandonments of family life, for example, for an Aramaic-speaking Jewish community immersed in a Greek-speaking community that is part of the Roman empire. And it does so even if at times in its history that Christian offspring denies its own origination or filiation within the Jewish community, and even if that denial can sometimes assume the form of bloodshed.

From René's point of view, on the other hand, the critique of idolatry is considerably less powerful as an explanatory tool—and, in fact, innately dependent upon the sacrificial mechanism for its own understanding. The critique of sacrifice comes for him not only (and perhaps not even primarily) from Jewish sources but from an independent revelatory experience, the trace of which is the Passion and the events surrounding the crucifixion of Jesus on the cross. And so while the Jewish Bible and its critique of idolatry gets us some of the way out of the confusions of mythical thinking, that critique needs in turn to be fundamentally completed by the unveiling of the sacrificial mechanism which occurs exclusively for him within the Gospel text.

Moreover, each of us remains a witness to the faith community from which we come. No amount of explaining, no amount of rhetorical persuasion (however subtle or thorough), is likely to convince either of us of the primacy of the other's point of view. I come to René's work on the mimetic and the sacrificial from a Jewish perspective and I discover in it a vocabulary for reading more fully my own Jewish tradition. After reading René, I understand much more completely than before what it means for me to be Jewish and I account for the appearance of Christianity—and of René's work within the history of Christianity—as an extension of that primary Jewish insight. René comes to read the Jewish tradition and the law of anti-idolatry from within the Christian experience from which vantage point it seems to him—however powerful—still lacking and incomplete. And that reading gives more strength to his belief in the primacy of the Christian text.

Indeed, the very idea of persuasion, of a rhetorical engagement that advances arguments, relies upon the criterion of logical reason, and lays claim to making some real analytic progress, is in some way anathema to each of us. Greek is certainly the language we all speak. Each of us translates our native tongue, so to speak, into Greek. I translate Hebrew into the Greek of the university, and René translates the mysterious Greek of the Gospel into the philosophical Greek of Plato and Aristotle. And we undertake these translation projects even if we only come to them through the other, even if I come to understand Judaism more fully only *after* reading René, even if René comes to understand one or another aspect of Christianity only *after* reading my writing (or the writings of others like Emmanuel Levinas or André Neher) on Judaism. No doubt I have learned infinitely more from René than he has from me, owing both to René's personal magnanimity and the dynamics of teacher-student relations (and one hopes there have been others with whom René has experienced the same fund of generosity as those of us who are his students and friends have experienced with him). But for each it is our native tongue that remains foremost.

Is there no way our two perspectives may be reconciled? René's theory of the mimetic nature of desire and of the sacrificial scapegoat mechanism as the root of all social structure is unabashedly brilliant, in my view the major advance of our time in the fields of cultural anthropology and psychology, the one perspective that gives other major theories of our culture in the last hundred years—those of Freud, Nietzsche, Lévi-Strauss, and Lacan, for example—the context in which their work finds its most powerful place. And his reading of Greek tragedy and of the Hebrew and Christian scriptures as fundamentally anthropological, opening us to the disclosure of these foundative mechanisms, has no peer. I repeat what I suggested long ago: that René's theories will one day prove the fulcrum from which all other theories may be understood.

But his theory of the Christian as a deconstruction of sacrifice and scapegoating is an elaboration of Jewish ideas, however revelatory such Christian access has been for René personally, and however powerful René's thought has been for me personally. Jesus, in my understanding, is a Jewish prophetic thinker throughout, and not in spite of his promotion of anti-idolatry (or even in addition to that promotion) but because of it. It is on the basis of the deconstruction of the sacrificial as an extension and prophetic concretization of the anti-idolatrous that, in my view, the power of the Christian text resides. And it is as testimony to his own Jewish origins that Jesus develops this insight as such, that the apostles witness it, and that the Gospel in turn commemorates it.

To say as much, however, is not to say—and I want to be very clear about this point—that the Christian text is not unique. Nor is it to say that René's discovery of the Jewish filigree within the Christian text is not related to its uniqueness, only that the sacrificial mechanism cannot be the whole story. What then *could* be the basis for the uniqueness of the Christian Gospel, we may legitimately ask, a basis not contained in Isaiah 52–53? Here I summon René back to his own ideas. The uniqueness of the Christian Gospel and the power of the discovery of the sacrificial mechanism may be founded on the resurrection, and my primary support for that claim comes from the writing of René Girard.

The texts of the resurrection of Jesus after the crucifixion, I suggest, may be at the root of the singularity of the Christian Gospel, both as the Christian Church has long argued, but more importantly in the present context, as René Girard has argued. The resurrection alone in the Gospel goes to the end of the process of sacrificial scapegoating by allowing us to see things through—perhaps for the first time in the history of Judaism—to their fullest conclusion. The resurrection reveals the sacrificial mechanism and even historical reality itself as a ruse. In context of the resurrection, Jesus both died and did not die. He literally "passed through" death, we may say, to show us the scapegoat mechanism to the end, a demonstration that did not occur in Isaiah 52–53. The resurrection is a kind of surrealist moment in the Gospels, one in which Jesus appears to step out of the reality in which he has been living, a "stepping out" that reveals that reality to be just one more scriptural illusion founded upon violence. In light of the resurrection, all social structure, the entire scapegoating machinery, is revealed as delusional, a delusional quality we are not permitted to see fully unless we observe the victim "after death" so to speak.

Christians have, of course, long argued that the resurrection renders Jesus's experience unique, although the moment has been read alternatively as a literal transcendence of historical reality or as a resurgence of mythic thinking within the text—in either case as a species of representation. What if we accept neither position? René's thought offers us a way of validating that claim without resorting to either a literalist or a mythical account, a way that I would characterize as "prophetic." The resurrection allows us to see the process of violence in which all are engaged to the end, an end not available in Isaiah 52–53 or elsewhere in the Hebrew Bible. More specifically, a Girardian reading of the resurrection allows us to see the event (and all events leading up to it) as textual and therefore as readable, as textual (and readable) as the rest of the sacrificial process. Even death may be treated as a myth from this perspective. The death of the victim may be included in the account and not just the events leading up to the death. If the entire process, in other words, is a myth, a collective delusion, then we cannot rely upon any sacrificially based "reality" if we wish to eschew violence, and we require an ethical approach to human relations rather than a scapegoat-centered approach.

Is the resurrection an example of the "further elucidation" of which I spoke earlier? The resurrection would appear to be the missing piece of the puzzle, the guarantee that something different and genuinely new is being presented in the Gospels. The resurrection completes the prophetic concretization of the anti-idolatrous reading Jesus inaugurates. Here is where your violence is going, he says to us. René Girard's thinking about the sacrificial mechanism makes it clear why the Church has felt it so important to retain this text.

But more importantly, René seems to feel that way himself. The resurrection, he tells us, reveals the things hidden since the foundation of the world, the origin of culture in the founding mechanism and in sacrificial substitution as he has written about it from his books of twenty years ago to his most recent book on the secret of Satan.

Here are his words on the resurrection in his most recent book:

Le plus étonnant, c'est que la Résurrection et la divinization de Jésus par les chrétiens correspondent très exactement sur le plan structural aux divinizations mythiques dont elles révèlent la fausseté. Loin de susciter une transfiguration, une défiguration, une falsification, une occultation des processus mimétiques, la Résurrection du Christ fait entrer tout ce qui restait depuis toujours dissimulé aux hommes dans la lumière de la vérité. Elle seule révèle jusqu'au bout les choses cachées depuis la fondation du monde, qui ne font qu'un avec le secret de Satan jamais dévoilé depuis l'origine de la culture humaine, le meurtre fondateur et la genèse de la culture humaine.

[The thing that's most astonishing is that the Resurrection and the divinization of Jesus by Christians correspond very precisely on the structural
level to the mythic divinizations whose falsity they reveal. Far from
sustaining a transfiguration, a disfiguring, a falsifying, or an obscuring of
mimetic processes, however, the Resurrection of Christ brings into the
open everything that remained hidden to human beings in the light of the
truth. The Resurrection alone goes to the end in revealing things hidden
since the foundation of the world, things that are one and the same with
the secret of Satan, a secret that has never before been exposed since the
origin of human culture, namely, the founding murder and the genesis of
human culture.][7]

The resurrection exceeds Isaiah 52–53. It even exceeds the Talmud
(through which the Rabbis read Torah) in which a resurrection is mentioned
and from which in the Jewish canon the theme of resurrection comes. It
comes closer perhaps to the disappearance of Joseph from the bottom of the
pit (at the hands of his eleven brothers—one of whom is named Judah) and
the reappearance of Joseph later in Egypt where, as the right-hand man of
the ruler of Egypt, he dispenses to the brothers their daily bread, a text which
is no doubt one of the mimetic models of this young rabbi from Nazareth,
although differences remain. Moreover, whether or not it is regarded as a
matter of faith, and whether or not it is considered an "objective fact" (as
René himself calls it in a recent interview with Jim Williams), the resurrection is an indispensable methodological step, René informs us, to the presentation of his own thought, and to his presentation of Christian thought.[8]
    On the other hand, to say that the resurrection exceeds the text of the
Hebrew Bible and that that is Christianity's unique contribution to the discussion is not to say that the Hebrew Bible is insufficient without it, that
it requires this step for completion. The resurrection completes the Gospel
account as René presents it. It is the final step to the deconstruction of
sacrifice and offers us as a result an alternative access to what we may call the
prophetic logic of culture. But it is only one particular access—the Christian
access. It remains as such an episode in the history of Judaism, a novel branch
of an expanding Jewish family tree.
    The Christian Gospel, in other words, may be regarded as unique vis-
à-vis Judaism. But its uniqueness does not necessarily reduce Judaism to its

first step any more than Islam does, which also exceeds Hebrew scripture. Drawing upon the resources of Judaism, each subsequent scriptural tradition develops elements uniquely its own.

Nor does Christianity in acquiring this uniqueness necessarily relinquish the status of an elaborate midrash. The resurrection story may be understood as a kind of parable within a parable, a midrash within a midrash, a commentary within the Christian scriptural tradition that draws attention to its own special lacks or gaps, precisely one that suggests that historical reality is just another sacrificial ruse.

Nor finally does faith change things. Even if we consider the resurrection from the perspective of faith to be the reflection of an independent revelatory moment, we are not obligated to regard Judaism as a first step. Franz Rosenzweig's thought maintains Judaism and Christianity as double revelations without reducing either.[9] The decision that sees Judaism as incomplete without its Christian counterpart is not a consequence of the resurrection but of supersessionist and triumphalist postulates about it.

The appearance of the resurrection as a theme in these recent texts, in other words, yields unexpected results. René had written about the resurrection as early as *Des choses cachées depuis la fondation du monde*.[10] It is only in his essay here, however, in his most recent book (*Je vois Satan tomber comme l'éclair*), and in his recent interview with Jim Williams, that the power of the resurrection to Christian thought in precisely the sacrificial and anti-sacrificial terms in which René has defined that thought becomes clear. Our learning from René's work continues unabated. Here is one more way in which René has taken something long familiar to us and turned it to gold.

◆　◆　◆

The story from *Bava Metzia* to which I referred earlier does not end where I left it. It seems that some time after the arguments between Rabbi Eliezer and the other rabbis on the cleaning of an oven, Elijah spoke with the Holy One, Blessed be He, about these matters. And what did the Holy One do, Rabbi Natan wanted to know, when He heard Rabbi Yehoshua's assertion that the Torah is not in heaven, that it passes through human mediation? He is reported to have replied (so the story goes), "My sons have defeated me! My sons have defeated me!," laughing.

PART 2

Girardian Reading and the Scriptural

The End of Sacrifice

Reading René Girard and the Hebrew Bible

A t a moment when René Girard's work is beginning to be known by
a significantly larger public, a number of us who have been his students or colleagues for a number of years have begun to ask about
the dimensions of its impact upon us, in particular, the way it has shaped our
own approaches.[1]

For me, the question has discernible and entirely practical implications.
In 1983, as an assistant professor of English at the University of Michigan (and
recent PhD student of René Girard in the Department of English at the State
University of New York at Buffalo), I was invited to speak at Cerisy-la-Salle
at a week-long seminar in his honor. Learning that he would speak (for one
of the first times) of his relation to Christianity (and deciding that I should
speak similarly about Judaism), I began reading in preparation the work of
Emmanuel Levinas, Martin Buber, Franz Rosenzweig, Gershom Scholem,
Maurice Blanchot, and others whose writings on Jewish topics had begun
circulating to a wider audience. The paper I delivered on the Joseph story
(and its staging of the mimetic, sacrificial, and anti-sacrificial structures from
which it derives) was something of a departure from the teaching and writing
I had been doing on Greek tragedy and Shakespeare, and a first step along
the path I have followed since. As Girard delineated the ways in which the

Christian Gospel, in his view, completed the analysis of the sacrificial that had been opened in what he deemed the "Old Testament," I explored the ways the Hebrew Bible already comprehended in full, within its language of anti-idolatry, the revelation of the sacrificial origins of culture. The analysis of the prophets from the sixth century BCE onward, it seemed to me, was little else.

Much of the work I have done since has continued that examination, working out the details of a theory of literary and biblical reading consonant on the one hand with the insights Girard developed, and on the other with the understanding of the rabbis. How might we read the Hebrew Bible from a Girardian perspective, I asked myself. To read from a Girardian perspective is to read anti-sacrificially. In the language of the Hebrew Bible, that means anti-idolatrously. But reading anti-idolatrously may be more difficult than it appears. Take, for example, Genesis 3. Girard has written that in contrast with mythological treatments, the theme of expulsion has surfaced here within the text, although it is not man expelling God but God expelling man; the expulsion of God by man in his view awaits the texts of the Christian Passion.

What would the rabbis say? That the "idolatrous" is to be understood diachronically rather than synchronically (as a "moment" rather than as one "thing" in contrast with another); that the particular moment it describes is already the moment when the sacrificial and the violent have become inextricably confused; and that the idolatrous shows up within the text "as" the text, that the text, in short, is a "scene of instruction." After the destruction of the Temple (and the end of sacrifice), the rabbis say, we pray and read.

In what follows, I would like to examine this opening passage of Torah and ask how precisely it might be read as a scene of instruction. In my conclusion, I will return to my initial questions.

◆ ◆ ◆

By the beginning of Genesis 3, God has completed the setting in motion of creation, including the creation of human beings. A commandment has been issued to the human (*ha'adam*) concerning the eating of the fruit from one of the trees. A "side" of the human is extracted and built up to form a woman (*ishah*). And now a new development ensues (Genesis 3:1).

> Now the snake was more shrewd than all the living things of the field that
> YHWH, God, had made.

It said to the woman:
Even though God said: You are not to eat from any of the trees in the
    garden...![2]

This is the first appearance of "the snake" (*ha-nachash*). Fox's translation of the Hebrew as "snake" rather than as "serpent" (which is how many
commentators translate it) emphasizes its quotidian quality, its non-myth-
ological, non-startling features. In the biblical text, at least, this is not *ha-
satan*, the Accuser, the Adversary, who speaks with God in Job (although
the midrashim will occasionally introduce *ha-satan* in this context). Nor
is it some ancient equal and opposing force from Mesopotamian history
or mythology. Judaism is a monism not a dualism. If this agency proves
evil, it is the banality of its manifestation that is emphasized here, not its
uniqueness.

Why "shrewd" (*arum*)? The same word in a plural form (*arumiym*) was
used a moment earlier (Genesis 2:25) to qualify the status of the *iysh* and the
ishah vis-à-vis their clothing.

> Now the two of them, the human and his wife, were nude [*vayihyu shnei-
> yhem arumiym ha'adam v'ishto*], yet they were not ashamed. (2:25)

Nudity in this context is nakedness, defenselessness, openness, akin perhaps
to what Emmanuel Levinas identifies with the face.[3] Does the *nachash* in
Genesis 3:1 use openness, seeming lack of guile, in a guileful manner? Is guile
defined by seeming openness?

The *nachash* speaks to the woman. Why not to the man, the *iysh*? And
why, moreover, are the man and the woman referred to as "the human and his
wife" (note that the Hebrew in 2:25 is *ha-adam*, which Fox translates as "the
human," rather than *iysh*, which Fox translates as "the man")?

These words have a history. *Ha'adam* was created in Genesis 1:27 ("So
God created mankind" [*vayivra elohiym et-ha'adam*]) and the act is rearticu-
lated in 2:7: "YHWH, God, formed the human, of dust from the soil, he blew
into his nostrils the breath of life and the human became a living being," a
nefesh hayah. The human, *ha'adam*, is formed from the "dust from the soil"
(*afar min-ha'adamah*), and the word *adam* is said by the rabbis to derive
either from *adamah* ("ground" or "earth") or from *dam* ("blood"). And from

the perspective of at least some of the rabbis, *ha'adam* is bisexual, hermaphroditic, a condition that conforms for them with 1:27 and 5:2, "male and female He created them."

> R. Jeremiah ben Eleazar said: When the Holy One created Adam, He created him hermaphrodite [bisexual], as is said, "Male and female created He them . . . and called their name Adam" (Gen. 5:2). [Normally, *androgynous* means one who has both male and female genitals; but here it means two bodies, male and female, joined together. Thus Adam was originally male and female.][4]

This idea plays havoc with the birth of ishah in Genesis 2:23.

> So YHWH, God, caused a deep slumber to fall upon the human,
> so that he slept,
> he took one of his ribs and closed up the flesh in its place.
> YHWH, God, built the rib that he had taken from the human into a
>   woman
> and brought her to the human.
> The human said:
>   This-time, she is it!
> Bone from my bones,
> flesh from my flesh!
> She shall be called Woman/*Isha*,
> for from Man/*Ish* she was taken! (2:21–23)

God's original intention, we hear, is for the human to find a helpmate among the animals. When that project fails, God goes to "plan B": to separate the human into parts. "So YHWH, God, caused a deep slumber to fall upon the human" (2:21).

How is the division of the human described? Fox follows the traditional view in translating the Hebrew: God "took one of the ribs . . . and built the rib . . . into woman" (2:21–22). But in conformity with the idea that *ha'adam* is hermaphroditic, other, older rabbinic readers render *achat mitsalotayv* as "one of his sides," as if perhaps the human had two sides, a male side and a female side, that God separated.

R. Samuel bar Nachman said: When the Holy One created Adam, He
made him with two fronts; then He sawed him in half and thus gave him
two backs, a back for one part and a back for the other part. [Thus Eve
was created out of half of Adam's body and not out of a mere rib (Leon
Nemoy).]

Someone objected: But does not Scripture say, "And he took one of
his ribs (*mi-tzalotav*)" (Gen. 2:21)? R. Samuel replied: *mi-tzalotav* may
also mean "his sides," as in the verse "And for the second side (*tzela*) of the
Tabernacle" (Ex. 26:20) [Gen. Rabbah 8:1].[5]

Are we extracting more than isolated facts from primordial history? If we
say that God takes one of the sides of *ha'adam* and builds it up into woman,
it could be argued that the woman is the pinnacle of creation, the last created
being, formed or manufactured like *ha'adam* itself from earlier materials, but
further refined and endowed with additional divine construction. After the
extraction, *ha'adam* (minus his, or "its," female side), exclaims:

This-time, she is it!
Bone from my bones,
flesh from my flesh!
She shall be called Woman/*Isha*,
for from Man/*Ish* she was taken! (2:23)

Ha'adam retains the capacity to speak, to remember what happened a
moment before with the animals, to remember that earlier still it had the
capacity to name, and to understand (if vaguely) the new creature's origin.
Ha'adam's remark pays heed to the positive qualities of the new creation.
The attempt at finding a helpmate earlier ended without a solution, but
"this-time, she is it!" Now you got it right, *ha'adam* says, not without a slight
innuendo that YHWH God might not have "gotten it right" on a previous
occasion.

But there is another aspect to this examination that is potentially even
more unsettling to men than such a revisionist feminist history. *Ha'adam*,
it would appear, also misunderstands his (or her, or its) relation to that new
creature. "*Yikarei ishah kiy mei'iysh l'kachah-zot*" (2:23), he says. "She shall
be called Woman/*Isha*, for from Man/*Ish* she was taken." But she wasn't.

She was not taken from man, from *iysh*, since *iysh* ("man") did not in fact exist as yet. She was taken from *ha'adam*, the human, with male and female sides, if we follow the rabbis. The word *ishah* appears before the word *iysh*, which appears for the first time in this passage. If *ha'adam* after the breach had declared, for example, "from *ha'adam* she was taken, and as a result I, *ha-adam*, shall be called Man/*Iysh*, and she shall be called Woman/*Ishah*, because she came from my former status as *ha'adam*," the problem would be diminished, although not eliminated, since even in that case, the male creature (who names himself *iysh*) assumes a continuity between past and present that is at least questionable.

But *ha'adam* after the breach does not identify himself even in that fashion. "He" says only, "She shall be called Woman/*Isha*, for from Man/*Ish* she was taken" (2:23). Is there a translation problem? On this point, the rabbis are agreed. *Iysh* has not appeared prior to this moment in the biblical text, either in name or in reality. The former human creature, now bereft of its female side and auto-assigned the name "man," misunderstands its own priority (or lack of priority) vis-à-vis the woman, *ishah*. *Ha'adam* preexists *ishah*, but *iysh* does not. The creation of *iysh* is literally subsequent to the creation of *ishah*.

Are we missing something? First came *ha'adam*. Then came *ishah*. Then came *iysh*, the name for an altered version of *ha'adam*, the remainder or left-over after *ishah* was removed or subtracted from an integral *ha'adam*, and the hole (or wound) closed. If the *iysh* would like to imagine he was first, or continues to think of himself as *ha'adam*, or even *adam* (as we often call him), he is reverting to the earlier perspective from a later point in the story and appropriating that former status anachronistically as his own.

Is he right at least linguistically? Linguistically the news is no different. Etymologically, biblical scholars derive *ishah* from *insh* (meaning "soft, delicate"), from which word *iysh* may or may not also derive.[6] But opinion is not divided on the first point: *ishah* is not derived from *iysh*. If *iysh* thinks he is first, or that *ishah* derives from him, it is because he "remembers" the world as *ha'adam*, prioritizes that memory, and represses the female side with which he once shared creaturely status.

We understand his dilemma. God decides it is not good for man to be alone. Think of the *Epic of Gilgamesh*, where the hero finds a mate among the creatures who run with the animals (Enkidu is spurned by the animals, we learn, only after he has interacted with Gilgamesh). Here, YHWH, God, causes a deep sleep to fall upon *ha'adam*, extracts from him the side from which the woman is built, closes up the hole or gap, and when the creature awakens, there she is: "Now it's right; my bones, my flesh, she's an extension of me."

But that is no more the entire story than to say that *ha'adam* is an extension of the dust of the earth (from which he came). *Ishah* remains an independent creature whatever her origin. And whatever *ha'adam* was before the extraction, *ha'adam* is now changed as a consequence, if for no other reason than as a result of that removal. If he continues to call himself *ha'adam*, if he names himself "man" or *iysh* (and identifies *iysh* with *ha'adam*), if he slips into saying that *ishah* was taken from *iysh* (meaning that *ishah* was taken from *ha'adam*, whose identity he imagines he retains), and if we make the same imaginative leap, that innocent misunderstanding will have consequences far beyond the context in which it is posed. It will contain within its confines the entire problem of interpretation of the Hebrew Bible.

Do we learn anything further about the relationship of these two creatures? In fact, surprises abound. "Therefore a man leaves his father and his mother and clings to his wife, and they become one flesh." The original relationship between *ha'adam* (post-extraction) and the newly formed *ishah* is that of a "clinger." Bereft of his female side, the human that remains clings to others and to his past; he becomes among other things a "misunderstander," an egoist (we might say, using modern phenomenological language), one who derives the other individual from oneself, one who substitutes the other for the Other, for the real other human creature standing before him—an Other who is in fact genuinely independent of him, as independent of him as he is from the animals.

Is it surprising, then, that it is with the woman, *ishah* (and not *iysh* or *ha'adam*), that the *nachash* speaks, as if it is with the highest order of creation that the *nachash* wishes to engage, or alternatively, as if he need only speak with *ishah* in order to be assured that *iysh* will mimetically follow suit. If we have thought otherwise, if we have assumed that it was with mankind in general (*ha'adam* pre-extraction) or with the man after the female side had been removed (*ha'adam* post-extraction, or simply *iysh*) that the *nachash* engaged, we have misunderstood the narrative before us no less than the *iysh* himself has done.

Everything that follows depends upon this shift. Let us return to the exchange:

> The snake . . . said to the woman:
> Even though God said: You are not to eat from any of the trees in the
>   garden . . . !
> The woman said to the snake:
> From the fruit of the (other) trees in the garden we may eat,
> but from the fruit of the tree that is in the midst of the garden,
> God has said:
> You are not to eat from it and you are not to touch it,
> lest you die. (Genesis 3:1–3)

The woman makes three mistakes. First mistake: God never said anything about touching. Here is the passage in which the commandment is given:

> YHWH, God, commanded concerning the human, saying:
> From every [other] tree of the garden you may eat, yes eat,
> but from the Tree of the Knowing of Good and Evil—
> you are not to eat from it,
> for on the day that you eat from it, you must die, yes, die. (2:16–17)

She makes a second mistake: she appears to get the tree wrong.

> YHWH, God, planted a garden in Eden/Land-of-Pleasure, in the east
> and there he placed the human whom he had formed.
> YHWH, God, caused to spring up from the soil
> every type of tree, desirable to look at and good to eat,
> and the Tree of Life in the midst of the garden
> and the Tree of the Knowing of Good and Evil. (2:8–9)

"From the fruit of the tree that is in the midst of the garden"? In this text, that is clearly the "Tree of Life." Is the "Tree of the Knowing of Good and Evil" also in the middle of the garden? Possibly. But only the tree of life is so specified. The only tree that we know for certain is "in the midst of the garden" is the "Tree of Life." She may be referring to the wrong tree.

There is a third mistake: she was not there. It is not as if she was off somewhere else at the time; she simply was not created as an independent creature as yet. The conversation in which "YHWH, God, commanded concerning the human, saying: From every (other) tree of the garden you may eat," takes place in Genesis 2:16. She is created in 2:21–22. She may have "heard" the commandment from God, just as the *iysh* (the male side of *ha'adam*, or *ha'adam* bereft of the female side) "heard" the commandment. But neither *ishah* nor *iysh* was separated from *ha'adam* as yet. The conversation takes place between God and the human, *ha'adam*, before the division.

As a result, the *nachash* learns three things: one, that she exaggerates; two, that she may make errors of accuracy (or is willing to make assumptions about a whole on the basis of partial evidence); three, that she is mimetic or appropriative. She is willing to take over the viewpoint of another as if it is her own, whether or not she has an appropriate basis for evaluating it. The human had the conversation with God; therefore, it remains her own view now as well.

The *nachash* seizes a perceived opportunity.

The snake said to the woman:
Die, you will not die!
Rather, God knows
that on the day that you eat from it, your eyes will be opened
and you will become like gods, knowing good and evil. (3:4–5)

She appropriated the view of the human or of God. Perhaps she will appropriate the view of the *nachash*. If she makes mistakes about which tree is in question, perhaps she is willing to accept the possibility that she made a mistake about whether or not she will die. And if she exaggerates, perhaps she will accept the possibility of exaggerating the consequence of violating the commandment.

The *nachash* offers knowledge in exchange for a relationship. "God knows," he says. Implicitly, that means, I know that "God knows." And as a consequence of eating, you too will know. You will have what I have and what God has. Like God, you will have eyes that are opened, and you will not die. Your *arum* will be God's *arum*. Knowledge is substituted for a relationship, and as a consequence, knowledge becomes desire.

> The woman saw
> that the tree was good for eating
> and that it was a delight to the eyes,
> and the tree was desirable to contemplate.
> She took from its fruit and ate
> and gave also to her husband beside her,
> and he ate. (3:6)

Suddenly, the sensorial aspects of the scene predominate. The "woman saw that the tree was good for eating." Calculations are now based upon perception rather than person. Physical qualities assume the first rank. "The woman saw that the tree was . . . a delight to the eyes." And perception assumes a new form: an internal image, an object of contemplation, an object of desire. "The woman saw that the tree was . . . desirable to contemplate." And so she appropriates the fruit as she appropriated *ha'adam*'s view. Exaggerating its positive qualities (do we have any basis for believing the fruit was a delight to the eyes?), deducing the whole from the part (how does she know it is good to eat? on the basis of seeing it? what if it is a poisoned mushroom?), she seizes the fruit and ingests it. From one appropriation comes another.

Where is her husband, the *iysh*, the clinger, the misunderstander (who thinks *ishah* derived from *iysh*) throughout this interaction? The text says he is "beside her." If so, why does he not speak? Because he is a clinger? Because whatever his wife, *ishah*, says, he "clings" to, or appropriates? Did he hear the entire conversation with the *nachash* without entering it (and if so, what was he thinking?), or has he entered the scene only at this moment?

In any event, she takes the fruit, eats it, and then gives fruit to her husband beside her, and he does what she does. Like woman, like man.

> The eyes of the two of them were opened
> and they knew then
> that they were nude.
> They sewed fig leaves together and made themselves loincloths. (3:7)

The language of the text echoes the opening of the sequence. Before this, "the two of them . . . were nude" (*arum*). Now "they knew . . . they were nude" (*arum*). Consciousness has been replaced by self-consciousness. Knowledge regarding themselves has replaced their relationship with the divine. And in their new condition, they give priority to their own needs rather than to their relationship with the divine.

But we have not yet reached the climax of this scene. All this is about to become even more complicated, in what could be dubbed "part 2" of the sequence.

> Now they heard the sound of the YHWH, God, (who was) walking
> about in the garden at the breezy-time of the day.
> And the human and his wife hid themselves from the face of YHWH,
> God, amid the trees of the garden. (3:8)

"Heard?" The "sound" of God? God "walking about?" The "breezy-time of the day?" Where have all of these sensorial details come from? It is as if the text itself has taken over the perspective of the characters within the text, of *ishah* and the *iysh* after their eating of the fruit, and as if the text itself is now being written from within that perspective.

How, in other words, can we trust anything we read from this point on in the text? How do we know when something occurs in the text whether it is "really happening" or whether it only appears to be happening because the text has adopted a perspective available within the text, the perspective of one of its characters, a limited perspective, that is to say, whose limits we are able to observe? The text itself, in other words, has now become a distortion, and as a result the task of reading has become infinitely more complicated. If we define idolatry as the confusion of the divine with the human, then the text itself has become an idol. The task of reading has itself become a matter of reading anti-idolatrously. Rather than reading from some independent perspective, from the perspective of God on the perspective of human beings, for example, what we are reading now is what may itself be termed a "text of transgression."

What are the implications of this textual distortion? Potentially they are vast. Everything we read from now on in this narrative is in some way at once both happening and not happening. We need to assume that there is something there (that the reality it offers is not completely illusory) but also that what is there is filtered through the perspective of one or another of the characters within the text and so as a result it has to be deciphered or interpreted.

How should this interpretation be undertaken? By coming to understand in sequence what has taken place and the genesis of the perspective filtering it. For example, we are going to see that the text now begins to refer to *ha'adam* from the creature's own bereft perspective, as if he was *iysh* all along, and as if *ishah* was in fact created from *iysh*.

> YHWH, God, called to the human and said to him:
> Where are you? (3:9)

But "the human," as we saw before, was "male and female." Now suddenly even "God" adopts the perspective of the *iysh* and speaks as if "the human" and the *iysh* are one and the same. Is God also caught in this textual distortion? Is God a character? Is not God the creator of the universe? We have not spoken a great deal about God up to this point. God Himself, in other words, reads now (or is imagined as reading) from the distorted view of the *iysh*, of the one who has violated the commandment. He will say "to Adam" (3:17), for example, because you have done this thing, "because you have hearkened to the voice of your wife and have eaten from the tree about which I commanded you, saying: You are not to eat from it! Damned be the soil on your account!" as if there never was any ambiguity about which tree that was, or about who he was talking to. God asks: Where are you? And "he," the man, the *iysh*, answers.

> He said:
> I heard the sound of you in the garden and I was afraid, because I am nude, and so I hid myself. (3:10)

Now suddenly it is a matter of me and you. Sound, fear, what or where I am (or what or where I am not), the capacity to conceal myself—all these make their appearance for the first time in the language of the *iysh*. And God suddenly appears as a bad father.

> Who told you that you are nude?
> From the tree about which I command you not to eat,
> have you eaten? (3:11)

One possible and accurate answer to God's current question is "No. I have eaten from the 'Tree of the Knowing of Good and Evil' from which by your stricture I was permitted to eat, not from the tree in the midst of the garden." But instead, the *iysh* assumes (and we assume with him) that the tree from which he was not to eat (as the *ishah* assumed) is the tree of good and evil and, moreover, he assumes that God has made the same assumption. And in this text, in fact, God does do that. And this knowledge-based, or desire-based, or self-based, perspective (rather than a relationship-based perspective) leads straightaway to scapegoating on both parts, on the part of God against the humans, and on the part of the humans united against God.

> The human said:
> The woman whom you gave to be beside me, she gave me from the tree,
> and so I ate. (3:12)

You did it, the *iysh* says to God; and the woman did it. He blames the other, first God, then the woman. Martin Buber was one of the first commentators to note the differences between the *iysh*'s perspective here and Abraham's later. It is as if the progress from the first human beings to Abraham (in whose subsequent history the law, the Torah of anti-idolatry, will be given) is characterized by a move from scapegoating to the acceptance of responsibility. When the man is first addressed by God, he shirks responsibility, deflecting it either upon God (his interlocutor) or upon the woman (his other), in contrast with Abraham, who characteristically says, when he is addressed, *hineini*, "Here I am." The rest of this chapter of Genesis follows from this structure.

The question to the woman is different from the question to the man. If God asked the man, "Where are you?" he asks the woman, "What have you done?"

> YHWH, God, said to the woman:
> What is this that you have done?
> The woman said:
> The snake enticed me,
> and so I ate. (3:13)

Her response is identical to the man's in one regard. Like him, she blames others. As the man blames the woman and God (who in the man's mind initiated the interaction), she blames the snake (who in her mind inaugurated the interaction).

But she does not blame the man. She does not blame the man, either for blaming her, or in parallel with his blaming of her; unlike the man, she is able to resist reciprocity. Blaming occurs, to be sure, but not reciprocity. For that, we await Kayin and Hevel, their children. Is she imitating the man in blaming the snake? Or offering a response independently of him, one that just happens to be in part the same response?

Is the text in that way highlighting for us the same unification potential that resides in the act of blaming, the act of scapegoating? God also turns to the snake.

> YHWH, God, said to the snake:
> Because you have done this,
> damned be you from all the animals and from all the living-things of the
>   field;
> upon your belly shall you walk and dust shall you eat, all the days of your
>   life. (3:14)

But God asks no question of the snake. He just announces. Because you have done this, here is what will happen. You will live apart from the animals. You will not walk upright. Your relation with the woman will be forever damaged. Like the angels later in midrashic literature, the snake is pure deed: he is what he does. His behavior is hardly unexpected.

> *I put enmity between you and the woman, between your seed and her seed:*
> *they will bruise you on the head, you will bruise them in the heel.* (3:15)

And similarly, to the woman and the man, God will now make announcements regarding the future.

> To the woman he said:
> I will multiply, multiply your pain (from) your pregnancy, with pains shall
>   you bear children.
> Toward your husband will be your lust, yet he will rule over you.
> To Adam he said:

Because you have hearkened to the voice of your wife
and have eaten from the tree about which I commanded you, saying: You
    are not to eat from it!
Damned be the soil on your account,
with painstaking-labor shall you eat from it, all the days of your life.
Thorn and sting-shrub let it spring up for you,
when you (seek to) eat the plants of the field!
By the sweat of your brow shall you eat bread,
until you return to the soil,
for from it you were taken.
For you are dust, and to dust shall you return. (3:16–19)

To the woman, God responds with pain, pain in childbirth. The text repeats the words "multiply" and "pain," as if the text is imitating what it is saying, multiplying the words and the actions, multiplying the labor necessary to read those words, to understand those actions. The rabbis dub this construction "the Hebrew emphatic." And God introduces a new relationship: reciprocal power relations. As the man clung to the woman, so now you will be ruled by the man; desire and rule predominate.

To the man, the consequence of clinging, misunderstanding, and the failure to follow the commandment is "painstaking-labor," and then you die. What is the response of the human, of *ha'adam* minus *ishah*? He exercises the one God-given capacity not implicated here: he names his wife.

The human called his wife's name: Havva/Life-giver!
For she became the mother of all the living. (3:20)

Is this another error? Is not God the "life-giver?" Why does he name the woman as the giver of life? The man specifically acknowledged God's capacity to give life to the woman in his accusation: "The human said: The woman whom you gave to be beside me, she gave me from the tree, and so I ate." Now God begins imitating the humans. As the humans a moment ago stitched clothing for themselves (3:7), so now God becomes a clothing maker.

Now YHWH, God, made Adam and his wife coats of skins and clothed
    them. (3:21)

And God begins now to speak of the humans in the third person, as if he is talking to someone else about them.

YHWH, God, said:
Here, the human has become like one of us, in knowing good and evil.
So now, lest he send forth his hand
and take also from the Tree of Life
and eat
and live throughout the ages ... ! (3:22)

Who is God speaking to? Other divine creatures? Angels, for example? But none have been mentioned before. Is God now imitating the language of the *nachash*? And what is God worried about? "Lest he send forth his hand and take also from the Tree of Life"? Is not this YHWH, God, the creator of the entire universe? Is He really worried that one of his miniscule creations may do something over which He would have no control? Or is that the image of God that the text projects for us, an image based upon the distorted perspective of the characters within it, characters who have just experienced something they are unhappy about and that colors their perceptions of things?

So YHWH, God, sent him away from the garden of Eden, to work
the soil from which he had been taken.
He drove the human out
and caused to dwell, eastward of the garden of Eden,
the winged-sphinxes and the flashing, ever-turning sword
to watch over the way to the Tree of Life. (3:23–24)

God evicts the man—to work the soil with painstaking and sometimes fruitless labor. What about the woman? She is not even mentioned here. And the "Tree of Life," which surfaced on one occasion earlier in this narrative, suddenly reappears. The distinction between the tree of life and the tree of good and evil remains, it would appear, an operative one. To what extent is the response of God to their eating of the fruit a distortion, a text of transgression? God becomes judgmental and punishing on the one hand, caretaking and a provider on the other. Like a parent, in other words, imagined from a child's perspective. And how do we separate that parental view of God from what is "really" taking place in this text?

For there are now always two different perspectives that must be considered: what we are told is taking place in the narrative, and the extent to which the narrative itself is imitating what is taking place within it. Repeating what God said, seeing that the fruit is good for eating, a delight to the eyes, and so forth, and actually hearing the sound of God walking about in the garden in the breezy time of day. Is it possible that God has not expelled them, and that they only imagine He has done so because they read transgressively?

To what extent, in other words, we may ask, is the imagining of God as having expelled the humans a misunderstanding of our own failure to keep commandments and accept infinite responsibility for the other individual, an alternative that, if undertaken, changes everything?

Imagining, in other words, that we are victims and expelled from Eden may be a midrashic extension of the distortion of our own perspective.[7]

◆ ◆ ◆

We are a long way, at the conclusion of chapter 3 in Genesis, from being able to answer any of these questions. We will be able to answer provisionally in a few chapters, in the shorter narratives between this one and the beginning of the patriarchal history. In the story of Bavel in Genesis 11, for example, when the text makes available to us the idea that the failed ziggurat builders have rationalized (on their way out of town) the failure of their own civic projects, and the idea that "The gods are jealous of us, the gods are against us" has simply been projected backward and upward, so to speak, and shown up in the text itself as the text from the outset.

But about the larger, overarching narrative in which the Israelites come in Exodus 20 to receive the Torah from God (through Moses), and subsequently come to learn to read that Torah as the "blueprint of the world" in which they function (within the prophetic texts and the holy writings), there is a great deal more to say. In some sense, the rest of Tanakh—the five books of Moses, the writings of the prophets, and the holy writings—will have to be examined in order for the question, the question of idolatry in and of the text, even to be approached.

But we can already understand the task before us. And if we ask again how this text might be regarded as a scene of instruction, the way is clear to making sense of that idea. We have been presented with four levels of understanding: a narrative sequence in which the plain sense of the text is offered to us and the characters do things; a level on which the misunderstanding of that narrative sequence by characters within it begins to govern for them their sense of things but need not govern ours; the textualization or textual appropriation of that same misunderstanding (as if the text itself, our text, the one that gives us their "reality," and even God as a function of that text, has become a characterized perspective and now joins in the hermeneutic fray); and on a final level of interpretation, the possibility that the reader retains of deciphering all of this narrative and reading activity (this narrative consciousness, self-consciousness, and textualization) through a close and patient diachronic perusal of its occurrence.

It is this fourth level that renders the text a "scene of instruction," that makes the task we are given one of reading, and that means that what is played out at this level is anti-idolatry. Formulated in this way, such a task of anti-idolatrous reading is not a supplement or adjunct to biblical reading but its very heart; it is the place where commandment is to be understood, where it shows up in the text itself as its manifestation. "After the end of the Second Temple," the rabbis say, "we pray and read." And "the study of Torah is equivalent to the doing of all the commandments."

Is it possible that we have here in rudimentary form what the famous four levels of interpretation developed by medieval Jewish and Christian hermeneuts alike attempted to systematize: namely, a level of plain or simple rhetorical sense; a level of midrashic or allegorical sense; a level of ethical or moral sense; and a level on which the future, the prophetic, the messianic, the hidden, the mystical or anagogic sense of things is to be understood?

All of this, I would like to suggest, is what René Girard's thought will have taught us. We can already see how Girard's analysis of the sacrificial origins of culture has specified the nature of the endeavor. Girard's analysis of sacrificial violence and of the concomitant necessity to refuse violence is readable as Judaism's analysis of the idolatrous and of the anti-idolatrous as its corresponding ethical response. The reading of the Jewish text as about commandment, and commandment as about anti-idolatry, and the problem of anti-idolatry as showing up in (and as) the text, as the question of its reading, is, I would suggest, nothing else. As the "sacrificial crisis," to use Girard's term, enables us to read the great literary texts of our culture—Greek tragedy, for example—so the analysis of moments of idolatry in human culture and human relations developed within Rabbinic Judaism from the fourth century BCE to the second century CE (and especially the analysis of those moments in the modern world when the law of anti-idolatry is capable of becoming idolatry's newest form) enables us both to read and to formulate an ethical response to texts that have issued from similar crises within the Jewish world, above all, from the collapse of the first and second temples, from which contemporary and diasporic Judaism has sprung.

Can we go further? Girardian thought is based upon the idea that the sacrificial expulsion is at the origin of culture (as a way of managing the mimetic behavior that makes up the fabric of social life), and that when this mechanism of collective surrogacy breaks down (and a sacrificial crisis results), alternatives are developed. Jesus exposes the expulsive gesture at the origin of culture by enacting it and thereby enabling us to see it: here is where your violence is leading, the texts of his Passion tell us, in Girard's reading. Do you really want to go there?

But, if we understand the Hebrew Bible at least in its earliest chapters as a text of transgression, one in which we must learn to move from a dis-torted way of knowing things to a more accurate one, then the expulsion at its origin may be the distortion in its most distorted form. What if it turns out, in other words, that there was no expulsion, that we weren't victims, or that if we were victims, we were victims only of ourselves, and that we must move from themes of scapegoating, persecution, and victimage to themes of responsibility and ownership of our own role in violence against others? That we find ourselves indeed in exile but with no one to blame for our dilemma?

In that regard, the spectacle of Jesus's death on the cross would graphi-cally illustrate for a modernizing, Hellenizing, assimilating community the necessity of accepting that responsibility, a necessity that some have identified with a quality of the divine. As such, Christianity would constitute an epi-sode in the history of Judaism, an episode that may not yet have concluded and within which we may to this day continue to think.

In other words, Girard writes that the Christian Passion completes the anti-sacrificial drift of the prophetic texts and the writing of the Hebrew Bible that emerges from that post-exilic period. But what if there was no expulsion, either at one end or the other? What if an even more evolved analysis would allow us to understand that not only is the victim not our enemy, and not only is God not the source of the expulsion from the garden (the Christian Passion allows us to see as much in Girard's view), but the expulsion, our victimage, is itself a myth? What if we ourselves are the only persecutors? What if the positive reading of the Hebrew Bible and the Christian Passion is that our assignment of the status of victim to the other or to ourselves is equally a version of persecution, and that we need to give up victimage entirely and accept infinite responsibility for the other individual, responsibility, in other words, that not only falls upon the shoulders of the infinite, upon the shoulders of God, but falls upon our own shoulders as well; a radical abiding or suffering, in other words, in which the assignment of meaning to the suffering or violence of the other individual is always wrong, and in which only the assignment of meaning to my own violence, my own suffering, can provide the foundation for human groups?[8]

The Christian Passion, in this regard, would then function in the same way as the Hebrew Bible. It can serve to inculcate the myth: "as we were expelled," it can say to us, "so Jesus, our savior, rescues us from the future of the Old Adam, and purchases for us salvation independently of anything we need to do about it." Or it can serve, as we have tried to suggest the Hebrew Bible serves, to undo the myth, to ask us to give up scapegoating, to show us where our scapegoating violence is leading—an option that the Passion offers, appropriately enough, as a resurrection from death.

In this regard, the Girardian analysis and the prophetic analysis that the rabbis fashioned into a reading (via Talmud and other writings) of the Hebrew Bible are in accord. Christianity in this analysis is an episode within the history of Judaism, an extension of the midrashic ways of thinking evident in Rabbinic reading into Hellenistic and Roman arenas that Jews, for reasons of historical circumstance, were not in a position to enter. The family origin of this anti-idolatrous reading for both Judaism and Christianity remains identical, even if this common fund of anti-idolatry has not always been appreciated throughout their common history, and even if at times this failed appreciation led to scapegoating, violence, and even expulsion in its own turn. Are we entirely certain, in other words, that the Christian Gospels, from which Girard says he derives his own insights, and the young Jewish rabbi arguing with his peer group among the Pharisees (in the context of which debates the Gospel texts are collected) are entirely independent of the Jewish scriptural writings about which we have been talking? Could the

Christian reading of the sacrificial as the completion of the law of anti-idolatry turn out to be a part of that larger and more ancient history, a working
out of the inevitable consequences of anti-idolatry that proponents of Christian views think they have superseded and over which they have triumphed?
In that event, the path upon which René Girard's work has set us would turn
out to be a fruitful one indeed, even if supersessionism and triumphalism is
sometimes mistakenly associated with Girardian analysis itself.

But such debates would take us far beyond the present discussions. And
even raising such issues already begins to sound like the *iysh* imagining that
the *ishah* was derived from him.

From Sacrificial Violence
to Responsibility

The Education of Moses in Exodus 2–4

When toward the end of his life Moses tried to stave off death, God said to him: "Did I tell you to slay the Egyptian?"

—Midrash[1]

Part One: Education in Plato and Judaism

The word "education," of course, comes from the Latin, *educare*, meaning "to lead out" or "to bring up," and both its Latinate morphology and the semantic value it assumes in English reflect its peculiar history. To "lead out" implies in the first place leadership, which is to say a relationship between one designated as a "leader" and another (or others) designated as the "led." The notion of leadership also entails a movement through which the leader propels the led, namely, from a region designated as "inside" to another designated as "outside."

Within the Western context, which is to say, within the Western European historical experience which traces itself back through the romance language–speaking countries to Rome and ultimately to Greece, the primary articulator of the notion of education we have inherited is, of course,

Plato. Although Plato's *Republic* is nominally about justice, and even more specifically the "just" State, commentators have long pointed out that it is really about education.[2] How shall the guardians of the State that we shall term "just" be educated, Plato's interlocutors ask themselves. In this regard, of course, Plato was challenging the educational system already in place at the time, at the head of which was Homer and the Homeric epics, and substituting for an older oral culture founded on an elaborate system of mnemonics another founded more decisively upon writing and the alphabet. Some have argued that in place of an aural or hearing-centered culture Plato was inaugurating a visual or video-centric cultural organization, and much work is currently being done in this area.[3]

What was Plato's educational solution? It was an appeal, in short, to the true, to the language of reason, and to the realm of the ontological as the context in which the true could be defined. The true, as the phenomenological tradition has taught us, may be regarded as the separation of that which has being from that which does not have being, that which only appears or seems to be from that which truly is. Reason, in this context, is the method or modality of thinking by which such difference or distinction between the true and the false becomes articulated. Education may then be said to be the process by which all of this occurs, by which one learns to separate appearances from reality, the true from the false, the reasonable from the unreasonable, and thereby the process by which one avoids slavery.

For at bottom the enemy for Plato remains slavery and the goal remains freedom from its ravages. Plato, for one, defines his program in specific opposition to Greek tragedy, which he takes among the species of *mimesis* or of mimetic *poesis* that he cites to be the worst threat to his program of absolute difference. The tragic poets leave us without an antidote, he tells us, to its irresistible seductions. Even the best of us—by which he would certainly include Socrates, who has been educating these young men about the processes of education—go to the theater, follow the theatrical performance with enthusiasm, beat their breasts along with the players, and finally praise as most worthy those playwrights who most enable this enthusiasm to take place. The distinction between the true and the mimetic, between the true and the imitational or representational, between that which has being and that which only shadows being, is always on the verge of collapsing in this context. And as a consequence the only safe state, Plato tells us, is the one that excludes theatrical performance from its premises.

There is no place in the present context to develop any further the complicated relationship Plato has with his predecessors, and I have hinted at this relationship elsewhere.[4] Suffice it to say that Plato remains in this regard the master in Western circles of all serious educational programs, a program that has been invoked to lead us out of the dangers that accrue from over-attachment, from the idolatries in endless varieties that arise to lure us into cultural and psychological bondage.

Within a Jewish context, on the other hand, education has been conceived quite differently. Viewed anthropologically, education may be regarded as the means by which an individual is assimilated into a group and in its widest context involves the cultural community overcoming the obstacles to such assimilation—the idiosyncrasies of biology, individual circumstances, and so forth. Plato's program in this regard, like any educational program designed as a "leading out," is a reaction against an older educational order that has become antiquated, fossilized, inadequate, no longer serviceable.

In this regard, Jewish education shares certain fundamental features with Platonic education. Jewish education is also a "leading out." Focusing as it does upon the Bible, and in particular upon the story of Moses, and the receiving of the Law or Instruction or Torah of the divine (and the responses such reception elicits), Judaism defines itself as similarly iconoclastic and anti-idolatrous. Both in its founding patriarchal stories, and in its historical exodus accounts, Judaism (at least as the Rabbis have passed this tradition down to us) defines itself as the giving up of social orders that have become inefficacious, and the reorientation towards if not precisely new gods then a way of living that no longer depends upon the gods at all, an anti-sacrificial perspective that wanders progressively away from the gods and lays human responsibility at the hands of human agents.

Housed as it has been historically, however, for nearly two thousand years within a Western cultural environment that has ranged at times from hostile to openly eliminationist, Judaism has also had to learn other lessons. Apart from the lessons of its holy scriptures, Judaism had to learn the lessons of assimilation. Jewish education from within a Western diasporic context has been above all and primarily a matter of reading Hebrew, and particularly the Biblical tradition. The Torah conceived as *Tanakh*, which is to say, as not only the five books of Moses (or *Torah* proper) but as a body of writing that includes the Prophetic writings (*Nevi'im*) and the Holy Writings (*Kethuvim*), remains, of course, the centerpiece of that tradition.[5] And the texts of the four main exegetical traditions—the Talmudic writings, the midrashic collections, the esoteric writings, and the later rabbinic commentaries (not to mention other minor traditions)—supplement and complement that centerpiece.

But the reading of the Hebrew of the Bible is not simply a matter of philology, nor even just a matter of cultural study (the way one would describe reading another ancient cultural language), since it is a matter of reading a tradition which casts the very activity of reading (as this activity has been conceived with a Western context) in a fundamentally new light.

If we turn now to the work of Martin Buber and Emmanuel Levinas, we do so as a way of illustrating this centrality of Biblical reading and in particular of the prophetic.

Part Two: Hebrew Humanism

In 1933, four years after the death of his friend Franz Rosenzweig (with whom he embarked on a substantially new translation of the Hebrew Bible), Martin Buber reflected on the possibility of a "Hebrew humanism."[6] In the two preceding decades, he noted, the Jewish people had been renewed. The Hebrew language had once again begun to be spoken. But neither the restoration of their language nor the restoration of their history in the land of Israel had guaranteed for the Jewish people their response to what Buber calls the "prophetic" demands, and it was alone within the Hebrew Bible that one could be sure that such demands were at least audible. Such a return to the Hebrew Bible, such a definition of Jewish humanism as a specifically "Biblical humanism," Buber noted, did not entail living in the manner of the patriarchs. It did not mean modeling our lives on those of Abraham, Isaac, or Jacob. Rather such a renewalist ethic meant living completely in the modern world in a way that was at the same time "worthy of the Bible."

> . . . only a man worthy of the Bible may be called a Hebrew man. Our
> Bible, however, consists of instruction, admonition, and dialogue with the

Instructor and Admonitor. Only that man who wills to do and hear what the mouth of the Unconditioned commands him is a man worthy of the Bible. Only that man is a Hebrew man who lets himself be addressed by the voice that speaks to him in the Hebrew Bible and who responds to it with his life.[7]

To be open to the Hebrew Bible, for Buber, does not mean necessarily to be open to a specified content (and Buber's famous debate with Rosenzweig on the so-called content of the law turned upon just this point). But it does mean rather to be open to its word, to its language, to that which encloses content, to its capacity as address, to what Buber calls the "mystery of its spokenness (*Gesprochenheit*)."[8]

In the work of Emmanuel Levinas, such openness to the Biblical pro-clamatory prophetic word assumes much the same form. In "For a Jewish Humanism," for example, one of several essays on *Difficult Freedom* in which Levinas addresses the question of Jewish education, he appears to echo Buber's position on humanism.[9] Humanism, understood as the undoing of the "prestige of myths," is already a Jewish activity, Levinas argues, and so a Jewish or Hebraic humanism would be, in fact, an uncovering or disclosure of one of the "souls of [the] soul" of Western man, so to speak.

But the source of this disclosure from a Jewish point of view, is neces-sarily the "Hebrew language and its texts" (by which he means the Hebrew Bible and its revelation in Talmud and its commentators), the texts, he says, "to which it is substantially linked and which are revealed only through it." And the source for the understanding of this language and these texts is not philology but what Levinas calls "advanced studies," the effort "to turn these texts back into teaching texts" and to allow them to speak.[10]

Both Buber and Levinas appear to agree, in other words, on several key notions. To do Jewish education is to learn to do Hebrew language. But to learn to do Hebrew language is to do more than learn to enter this ancient linguistic universe. It is to learn the texts which sustain and support that world, and in particular the biblical texts which are elaborated in the vari-ous surrounding exegetical traditions—talmudic, midrashic, esoteric, later rabbinic, and so forth. And to enter that biblical world is in turn to do more than recite the themes or the formal (or historical) circumstances in which it was produced—as the so-called high criticism has been doing for some time.

It is to engage the kind of thinking and reading that both writers characterize as "prophetic."

What is prophetic reading? What would it mean to do biblical reading as prophetic reading, as ethical reading, as reading that uncovers, in Levinas's conception, our "infinite responsibility" for the other individual? In the paper that follows, I would like to examine some of these questions in context of the early life of Moses in Exodus 2–4. Afterwards I will return to the topic of education in general.

Part Three: Exodus 1–2

The book of Exodus opens with a prologue of things to come. Ties are noted by Torah to the book of Genesis, and then there arises a ruler who has no intimacy with the Israelites of the earlier era. They are too numerous, the new Pharaoh says; they are everywhere.[11] Let us deal wisely with them lest they join with our enemies and rise up out of the land.

Finding a situation that displeases him, and a danger to be associated with that displeasure, the Pharaoh undertakes an action to prevent that consequence, one precisely that brings about the very outcome he feared. At the other end of the opening narrative, under the leadership of an Egyptian-raised child—Moses—the Israelites will indeed leave Egypt. In this regard at least, the story is not entirely unlike the popular Greek story of Oedipus, who also brings about unwanted consequences by the actions taken to avoid them, and the connections between the Greek story of Oedipus and Egyptian elements in the story of Moses have often been explored, most notably perhaps by Freud in *Moses and Monotheism*.

Do we have here a paradigm of what we might call "Pharaonic" power? Is this display what will constitute the "Egyptian" response to crises in Torah, so that it will be later to this process that the Ten Commandments or "ten utterances" (the *aseret hadibrot*) will refer when they say: "I am the LORD thy God, who brought thee out of the land of Egypt, out of the house of bondage" (*anochiy* YHWH *eloheycha asher hotzeitiycha mei'eretz mitzrayim mibeiyt avadiym*, 20:2)?[12] Is this the process of idolatry in the contemporary setting?

In any event, such Pharaonic thinking results in the increase of taskmasters and burdens, and that result in turn issues only in the increased circumstance the Egyptians feared: the Hebrews multiplied still more. And so a second strategy is tried.

The ruler speaks to the Egyptian midwives of the Hebrew women, asking them to kill the male children. And here we have the first rebellion and the first instance of a gender conflict in this story: the Egyptian women "did not as the king of Egypt commanded them, but saved the men-children alive" (1:17). The women undertook this behavior, Torah tells us, because the Egyptian women "feared God" (1:17). We also observe the Egyptian women speaking back to the Pharaoh: we did this, they say, when asked directly, because the Hebrew women are "lively" (*chayot*) (1:19).

Do the Egyptian women refuse the Egyptian ruler's demand and then hide behind a stereotype of the Hebrew women, perhaps to protect the Hebrew women? Or do they accurately report what happened—namely, that they have been unable to do the job assigned to them because the Hebrew women gave birth without their help—perhaps because they are jealous of the Hebrew women? In either case, the second strategy issues in the same result. The feared consequence once again accrues by the very efforts undertaken to avoid it. The Israelites multiply.

With that prologue, we now move to the story of the birth and life of Moses proper, ". . . there went a man of the house of Levi, and took to wife a daughter of Levi" (2:1). What man? And what wife? We do not learn the names until later—that the man was named Amram and the woman, Jochebed, who was also in fact his father's sister (see 6:20). Why are their names suppressed here? The father will not play much of a role in what follows—and in part we may see the career of Moses as a movement from one guiding authority to another. But the mother will play a significant role.

The "woman conceived, and bore a son; and when she saw him that he was a goodly child (*kiy-tov hu*), she hid him three months" (2:2). Why? The Pharaoh has tried a third strategy to control growth among the Hebrews. What he has said to the Egyptian midwives of the Hebrews, he has now said to the Hebrews directly: "every son that is born ye shall cast into the river, and every daughter ye shall save alive" (1:22). The birthing of a son (by the Hebrew woman) who is not killed, therefore, is the first decision the woman makes. And her assessment of the situation leads to a second: she will hide him. Because he is "goodly" (*tov*), she says. Is this a value judgment on her part? Would she, his mother, have killed him if he were not "goodly" (*tov*)?

Or are we to understand *tov* as referring to the fact that he did not cry very much, so that hiding was suitable, as opposed to some other form of concealment? The suggestion that there may be some lack of sound on the part of the child—given the relation of Moses later to speech—is not without interest of its own, since we observe in this connection that the first thing that the Egyptian princess notes is that the child is "weeping."

Time passes and these two decisions prove inadequate. The Hebrew mother decides to do what the Pharaoh commanded—to cast the child into the water—but in such a manner that saves rather than destroys him. She builds for him an ark of bulrushes, daubs it with lime and pitch, and lays it among the flags at the edge of the river. Her daughter, whose name we learn later is Miriam, accompanies the vessel as it floats along the river. The daughter of Pharaoh spots the ark, sees the child within, and responds compassionately: behold, a male child who weeps. A conference between the two women present ensues. The Pharaoh's daughter recognizes the child as Hebrew. The sister suggests she might call upon one of the Hebrew women to nurse the child. The Pharaoh's daughter agrees, the sister gets the child's mother, and the Pharaoh's daughter addresses her: you nurse the child and I will pay you.

In many ways, the scenes we have just witnessed parallel the previous scenes between Pharaoh and the Egyptian midwives. A command is given: kill all the male children (as Pharaoh gave the same command before to the midwives). A series of responses is undertaken: the woman in labor does not kill her child (as the midwives did not do as the Pharaoh commanded); the woman decides to conceal her child as a way of saving it (as the midwives may have hidden their intentions behind the popular conceptions of Hebrew women as a way of saving them and their children); the woman casts her child into an enclosure in the water as a way of saving the child (as before the action taken by the midwives issues in the multiplication of the population rather than its diminution). And finally, a series of conversations take place regarding a child rather than the murder of children (as before the midwives talk with Pharaoh about why they cannot enact his commands rather than enacting them).

But there are also striking differences. When the Pharaonic male authority acts, the situation nearly ends in violence, a violence narrowly averted by the action of the Egyptian women. When the women act among themselves—the Egyptian women as well as the Hebrew, the older women as well as the younger—the problems are solved quickly and smoothly.

There are other patterns to be observed here—the role of language, for example. Language functions as commandment or weeping (Pharaoh commands, the child weeps) when it issues from the mouth of men. Language functions as concealment and consequently salvation when it issues from the mouths of women: the Egyptian midwives, the daughter of Pharaoh, and the sister of the child (we do not hear the words of the Hebrew mother of the child although presumably a satisfactory conversation took place).

And one other pattern should be noted. Notice how many times the action of pushing and pulling occurs within these scenes. The Hebrew mother pushes the child out of her body in labor. Then she pushes something in front of the child to conceal it from others. Then she pushes the child into the enclosure and puts the enclosure into the water, and pushes the enclosure off from the Hebrew side of the river so that it will float to the Egyptian side. The Egyptian woman is pulled toward the sight of the child, and pulls the box containing the child toward her, and then pulls it open. She is pulled by what she sees to feel compassion for the child, and speaks (pushes out breath and sound?) to reflect that compassion. The sister (who has pulled something in front of herself to conceal herself) now reveals herself (pushes away her concealment) and issues (or pushes out) words to speak. The child is placed (pushed) into the care of the sister who returns it (pushes it back) into the care of the Hebrew mother, who at the appropriate time will return (or push) the child back into the care of the Egyptian mother—the daughter of Pharaoh—who will raise (or pull or bring up) the child as her own.

Is it any wonder that this child will grow up ready to pull a massive group of people—six hundred thousand by customary accounts—out of Egypt, or that he will get them to carry an ark back and forth around the desert for forty years until the entire generation of those who undertake such an action pass away? The exodus from Egypt and the wandering in the desert is certainly more than a repetitive staging of the circumstances of Moses's birth scene. But the comparison in the present connection is not without interest.

Especially in view of what has taken place and what follows. For if the pushing and pulling that takes place among the women surrounding the birth of Moses takes place to save the child, the pushing and pulling that takes place between Pharaoh and the Egyptian midwives occurs with the express purpose of destroying children (at least on the part of the Pharaoh).

The Pharaoh issues his commandment (an imperative or enjoining mode of speech)—to snatch or pull away the male children from the Hebrew women. The midwives decline to undertake that action (they pull themselves away from it) and are summoned (pulled) before Pharaoh to defend (push away from the offense) their actions. They do so by distinguishing (pushing away) the Hebrew women from themselves, possibly to save the Hebrew women, but possibly also to reflect their jealousy of, or pull towards, the Hebrew women.

The Pharaonic style of pushing and pulling between Pharaoh and the midwives would seem, in fact, strikingly contrasted at this point with the caregiving and nurturing style among daughters and mothers of the Hebrews and the Egyptians.

Another pattern needs to be discussed. The narrative we have seen so far is also about boundary crises. Pharaoh issues commands which are also not commands because they are not obeyed. The midwives construct a defense which may also be an offense. The Hebrew mother exchanges her place for an Egyptian mother and the older women exchange places with the younger woman—the sister. The child keeps being buffeted from one side to the other. First he is expelled from the Hebrew mother to the Hebrew reality. Then he will be expelled from the Hebrew side of the Nile to the Egyptian side of the Nile. Then the Egyptian woman will expel him, in turn, back to the Hebrew woman for nursing, and when he is of age he will be expelled once again back to the Egyptian side. There he will grow to manhood and desire to return to his Hebrew side. He will get himself expelled from the Egyptian court and go to live among the Midianites. Then he will encounter a God in the land of the Midianites who will tell him to return to the Egyptians.

And when he is back among the Egyptians he will convince the Egyptian Pharaoh to allow him to return—this time along with all of the Hebrews—to the land of the Midianites, where he had his earlier encounter. And once he is back among the Midianites, and the Egyptians have been destroyed in the famed "Red Sea," he will get the people to wander back and forth for the rest of their (and his own) earthly lives, carrying with them an ark that is not unlike his birth vehicle.

Differing patterns of authority, of language usage, of expulsion and retraction, and of boundary violations, permeate this narrative. To sort out these patterns and their relationships with each other, let us turn to the moment of the naming of the child in which identity structures, leadership structures, linguistic structures, and spatial structures seem briefly to be conflated.

Part Four: "Because I Drew Him Out of the Water."

And the child grew, and [the Hebrew mother] brought him unto Pharaoh's daughter, and he became her son. And she called his name Moses, and said: "Because I drew him out of the water." (2:10)

This passage has received, of course, a great deal of commentary, and indeed in light of the narrative movements we have been following, it is worthy of that attention. The mother names the child *mosheh* and says I did so "because I drew him from the water."

Scholars point out in the first place that the word *mosheh* was probably derived from an Egyptian word, *mes, mesu,* meaning something like "child of" or "born of." It is sometimes suggested that the name Pharaoh Thutmosis appears to mean "born of Thut" or that the name Ramses may mean "born of or child of the Egyptian sun god Ra."

But scholars note that *mosheh* may also be a form of a Hebrew word as well—namely, *mashah,* meaning "to draw or pull out." The word does not occur as such in Torah. But in the above passage, "I drew him out of the water" (*min-hamayim m'shiytihu*), *m'shiytihu* would seem to be a form of it, and scholars cite other passages in which a word play regarding the relation between *mosheh* and *mashah* may be at work—Isaiah 63:11, II Samuel 22:17, and Psalms 18:17. In the present context, if the word is Hebrew, then within the verbal paradigm of *mashah,* the word *mosheh* would be a participial form and would mean "one who draws out."

But if we adopt the point of view that the word *mosheh* is also Hebrew, then there is a problem, namely, that in the usage the Egyptian mother makes of the name, she appears to get the Hebrew word wrong. *Mosheh* as a Hebrew verb would assume the active feminine participial form and mean something like "one who draws or pulls out, one who extracts." But in the passage cited above, she appears to want the passive form—"she called his name Moses, and said: 'Because I drew him out of the water'"—as if his name meant "drawn or pulled out," "extracted," "rescued." Its relation to *mashah* in that case, we might say, would only be one of assonance, not etymology, and as a passive participle meaning "drawn" its form would have to be *mashuiy* rather than *mosheh*. The attribution *mosheh*, in other words, would appear to have more to do with her action of drawing the child out than the child's action of being drawn out.

But perhaps that is just the point. Buber notes the irony: that Moses, the drawn, will in fact grow up to draw the people out, to engender the most massive exodus in the history of the Hebrews.

Can we formulate the matter more forcefully? To the extent that Moses acts as his mother acts, drawing others out, rescuing others, he enacts his name: *mosheh*, one who draws out or rescues. On the other hand, to the extent that he allows himself to remain his mother's child, the one who is rescued, who is drawn from the water, he enacts a role within her language about him: he is the one she drew from the water.

Is there a relation between these two senses? The rabbis designate the relation interestingly enough as "prophetic." They say that she names for the infant what he may become, that she books a place in advance for him, so to speak. The causal link she posits seems to be the key. What if we were to say that the only mistake he could make would come in thinking that he could be one without being at the same time the other, that he could draw out without at the same time being drawn, and that the relation between the two is precisely that the second founds the first: that, in other words, he can only draw or pull out or rescue others so long as he owns the extent to which he is drawn out, or pulled, or rescued himself, and that to draw out is to learn (and to own) the ways in which one is always (already) drawn out?

There is one other possibility to which attention should be drawn. What if the traditional manner in which we have told the story of Moses's life—in terms of the paired opposites of justice and mercy—is another version of the same relationship? What if the only possible way of imagining the relation between the two is in terms of the other: if justice is only possible insofar as one is merciful, and mercy is possible only insofar as one is just; if, in short, pushing and pulling (or drawing and being drawn) and justice and mercy may be different versions of the same phenomena? The famous midrash which finds both necessary to the creation of the world would seem a reflection of this interdependence.[13]

The entire career of Moses, I would like to suggest, may be read in this light. The "education" of Moses in this context may be said to proceed in three stages: (1) the Egyptian sequence; (2) the Midyan sequence; (3) and the Sinai sequence. Let us follow them in order.

Part Five: The Egyptian Sequence

The career of Moses begins with an incident which, if we are to trust the midrashic accounts (one of which I have cited as an epigraph), will plague him his entire life.

The child grows to young adulthood. He knows that he is Hebrew. But he knows that he has been raised as an Egyptian, educated within the royal court, primed to be a ruler over Egypt when the time is right. One day he sees an Egyptian beating a Hebrew. His heart goes out to the Hebrew, the victim of the beating. The sight of the injustice is too much for him to bear.

He intervenes. He outdoes the Egyptian at his own game. He does to the Egyptian what the Egyptian does to the Hebrew. Only more so. The Egyptian is killed and a curious result obtains.

The next day he comes out and two Hebrews are fighting. Not only has his intervention not stopped the violence it was intended to stop, but his action has actually increased it. Moreover, the violence has spread to the very individuals whom he tried to extricate from the beating. Nor is that all. Now the Hebrews themselves turn against him. Are you going to do to us what you did to that other man, they ask. As a result of trying to help them, he has become their scapegoat, their victim. And this "scapegoatism" that suddenly appears spreads like wildfire throughout the community. The Egyptian court soon learns of his violent action and he is forced to flee Egypt entirely.

How are we to understand this sequence? In the Egyptian sequence we may say, Moses acts out the worst of bad childhood training. On the one hand, he enacts in part the Pharaonic mode. The pharaoh feels fear, and responds by murdering. On the other hand, Moses also enacts in part the maternal mode. The Egyptian mother feels compassionately drawn by what she sees and responds by lifesaving negotiations.

The problem is that Moses feels what the Egyptian mother feels—the sting of injustice—and responds as the Egyptian Pharaoh responds—with the action of murdering. Moses sees an Egyptian beating a Hebrew and kills the Egyptian (the Egyptian was only beating the Hebrew; Moses kills the Egyptian). Moses sees an injustice, and imposes what he sees as justice in response, which leads to the disastrous results we have noted.

There would seem to be at least five important observations to make in this connection: (1) he does more than the Egyptian did; the Egyptian was merely "beating" the Hebrew; he "slays" the Egyptian. His response, rather than lessening the violence of the situation, or even only equaling it, actually increases it. (2) His upping of the ante not only increases the amount of violence, it also spreads it to a larger context; now it is the Hebrews as well as the Egyptians who are fighting among themselves. Moreover, the distinction he entered the fray to preserve—between a perpetrator of violence and a victim of violence—is less clear afterwards; the text speaks of "the guilty one" as if it were now a category more than a designation of one or another of the Hebrews specifically. (3) He spreads the violence in particular to the very individuals he entered the fray to protect; the next day two Hebrews are fighting, those he would save. (4) He becomes the victim of his own people. And (5) the fear of violence via Moses spreads throughout the land so that Moses is forced to flee.

The whole sequence would seem to beg for a Girardian analysis. Notice in the first place how thoroughly mimetic desire operates in this story. (1) A sense of the affliction of victims of violence on the part of Moses and the response of killing is imitative of parents: the Pharaonic mode and the maternalistic mode. (2) Moses sees violent behavior in front of him and imitates that behavior as well as that of his parents; the text calls attention to this doubling, as the same word is used in describing the Egyptian's "beating" of the Hebrew as is used in describing the action of Moses in "killing" the Egyptian. (3) Having seen Moses kill the Egyptian, the Hebrews appropriate his position. Just as he saw only a perpetrator of violence and its victim, so taking up the same view, they see Moses as he saw the Egyptian and the Egyptian as a moment ago he saw the Hebrews; doing what he did, they turn against the perpetrator of the violence: are you going to do to us what you did to the other man, they ask. (4) This mimetic violence on the part of all concerned—both Moses and the Hebrews—quickly spreads throughout the community; both the Hebrews and the Egyptian community appear quickly to rival each other in thinking that Moses alone is guilty.

Notice in the second place how quickly this situation of common mimetic appropriation turns to scapegoating and violence. (1) The Pharaonic response is already a projective behavior upon others in response to one's own fears; (2) Moses feels the affliction of the Hebrews and, appropriating their position, scapegoats the Egyptian; (3) the Hebrews appropriate Moses's perspective and scapegoat him; (4) the scapegoating of Moses spreads throughout the community. Moses is on the verge of becoming the universal scapegoat; Freud's insight that Moses may have been the common scapegoat of the members of his community is not entirely inappropriate in this connection. The rest of the story will be a matter of learning alternative behaviors to mimetic appropriation and sacrificial violence and will occur in two stages: in Midyan and on Sinai.

Part Six: The Midyan Sequence and the Sinai Sequence

The Midyan sequence involves a repetition of the earlier situation up to a point. Moses sees an injustice being committed: women are drawing water from a well (see his Egyptian mother earlier who draws him from the water) and shepherds attack. His response, however, is different. He doesn't kill the shepherds; he may not even drive them away (although in the Cecil B. DeMille film he does so); he simply delivers them from disaster.

And as a result, the outcome is different: not the spread of scapegoating and violence as before, but marriage and integration into a new life. In the Sinai sequence, Moses has now become a shepherd himself (one of those who earlier attacked the women). He is located in wilderness rather than at the center of this community, and in fact on this particular day at the edge of that wilderness. He sees a curiosity that others do not observe (as before his mother saw what others did not). His observation of this curiosity is a form of being drawn: turning aside to see is a cessation of customary seeing in order to see better and an allowing of oneself to be drawn. When God saw that Moses "turned aside to see," God called his name: Mosheh! Mosheh! ("One who draws! One who draws!") as if to draw is already to be drawn.

Perhaps that is why God calls him by his Egyptian name, Moses, *Mosheh*, rather than by his Hebrew name, which some of the rabbis tell us is "Avigdor." Does God really need to attract Moses's attention? Perhaps the gesture is more for the benefit of Moses than God—for Moses to learn that he is only "one who draws" (*mosheh*) insofar as one is "one who is drawn," one who "turned aside to see."

The speech of God that issues from this curious bush (that burns and yet is not consumed) assumes two parts: an opening remark in which God sets the boundary between the holy and the non-holy ("Take off your shoes!" he says, "for you are on holy ground"), and a speech, a narrative, that has four parts: (1) an identification of who God is ("I am the God of thy fathers"); (2) a statement of condition and compassion about what has occurred ("I have seen the affliction of the children of Israel"); (3) a statement of purpose, namely, rescue the children of Israel ("I have come to deliver them from their affliction"); (4) a statement or assignment of commission concerning what role Moses will play in it ("You will lead them out and bring them up to Me").

But the most astounding part of God's declaration is its conformity to the personality of the individual who stands before it and bears its witness. This God is a God of rescue. Exactly as we saw Moses to be a rescuing personality, this God has seen the Egyptian beating the Hebrews and is charging for him to rescue the Hebrews from them! If Moses were anyone other than who he is, he might now say "Yey, God!" and lead the charge down to Egypt to rout the Egyptians and retrieve the children of Israel from their cruel taskmasters. But in fact Moses is no longer that individual; he has learned (as if intuitively) that God's expression is an account of his own actions in the past in Egypt and that his past actions have led to disaster. He learns, in other words, to read prophetically.

And so now he poses all the questions that he might have posed before—when he impulsively charged forward to save the Hebrew—but did not pose, and in the questioning that follows we learn not only what he failed to ask, but what he might have done. The questions that follow—and there are in effect five of them—are midrashic in structure. But we know that midrash is written to fill in the gaps—and thereby to call attention to them by that gesture.

Moses is forced, in other words, to become an interpreter, a reader, of his own prior behavior: (1) "Who am I?," he asks in response to God's statement. I am nothing, a nobody; my identification vis-à-vis the community is insufficient to carry on this task. (2) They will ask me "What is your name? What is your power?" Why should they believe You can do what I will say that You can do? They will not see compassion in my description but turn against me for trying to help as they did before. They will also fight among themselves. (3) They will not trust me; they will think that I am trying to deceive them. "Will you do to us what you did to the other man?," they will say to me. (4) I have no rhetorical skills; I am not adequate to the task you assign me; insufficient vis-à-vis You. As before, the word of the Hebrews concerning me spread beyond anything that I could do to control it. (5) I don't want the job; I don't want to go; I don't have the heart to do this, as before I didn't really have the heart to do what I did.

God's response? To dismantle each of Moses's objections in as swift and final a way as possible.

> *Moses*: Who am I? I am nothing.
> *God*: Don't worry about it. I will be with you.
> *Moses*: Fine. But what if they ask me why they should believe you? What do I say?
> *God*: When they ask you that, here's what you say: *ehyeh asher ehyeh:* "I will be (there) with you in order that I will be (there) with you." Or, in other words, *ehyeh*: "I will be (there) with you." Or, alternatively again, YHWH: "He, She, it, or God will be (there) with you."
> *Moses*: Fine. But they will not trust me. They will think I am deceiving them.
> *God*: I will give you some tricks to do. Do you have a staff? (Moses nods.) Take it out. (Moses takes it out.) Throw it on the ground. (Moses throws it on the ground. It becomes a snake.) Now pick it up. (Moses picks it up. It becomes a staff.) You have a hand? (Moses nods.) Put it in your shirt. (Moses puts it in his shirt.) Take it out. (Moses takes it out. It has become leprous.) Now put it back in your shirt. (He puts it back in his shirt.) Now take it out again. (Moses takes it out. It has become clean.)
> *Moses*: Fine. But I have no rhetorical skills.
> *God*: Do you have a mouth? Who do you think put it there? Do you have a brother? Does he have a mouth? He can talk. He'll speak for you. You'll speak for Me. There are a lot of possibilities.

Moses: Fine. But I don't want to go.
God: Now, I'm angry!

In other words, the God of rescue, this God of Moses's fathers, expresses the position with which Moses might have agreed earlier in his life so that he can now do two things: (1) acknowledge this earlier position as his own; and (2) give it up before the violence to which it leads accrues, accept responsibility for his own personality, and own the description to which that acceptance leads. He learns to read his own past prophetically. He learns to recognize the dramas in which he (along with other human beings) is engaged and to name in advance the end of those dramas (namely, violence) in order that he might give them up before he gets there.

Within the Biblical context, that prophetic reading of his life that Moses gets completes the prophetic understanding that Abraham, Isaac, and Jacob were offered before him, a prophetic understanding which has brought the Hebrews to Sinai and prepared them for the receiving of the law, the Torah, the divine Instruction—the law of anti-idolatry. This is not the first time in Torah that a revelation was issued that had to be resisted. Abraham already came to understand in Genesis 22 the necessity of a prophetic reading of God's word: "Take your son, your only one, whom you love, Isaac, and prepare him as a sacrifice, an *olah*, a burnt offering." What could be more imperative? He came to learn, nonetheless, that even such a commandment, the most imperative one could imagine, must be read prophetically. If you continue the way you are going, if you are only and literally obedient to the letter of the law, sooner or later you will hear a voice that will say to you: "Take your son, your only son, whom you love, Isaac, and kill him." And you will do it, on that authority. What you *are* to do when you hear these words is what you have always done: namely, sacrifice a ram. In other words, provide for your son. The son "sees," the father "sees to it that." That is the rule. Here is the wood. Here is the fire. Where's the victim, the son asks. The son sees presence and absence, presence and absence of presence. The father's task is to "see to it that." "God will provide," he says to the son. And in saying "God will provide," he provides. Abraham thinks his action is provisional, temporary, makeshift, what he needs to do until a more substantive solution comes along. What he comes to learn is that answer is provision itself.

But provision, while necessary in the preparation of the Israelites for receiving the law, is not sufficient. If not regarding one's son was a danger, over-regarding one's son was also a danger. Jacob learned that. He glimpses it the moment he received from his other sons the famed "coat of many colors" (the *ktonet passim*) he had placed upon the head of his favored son, Joseph, this time dipped in blood. Is this your coat, they asked. Do you recognize your coat? Do you recognize your own violence? Jacob is not sure he recognizes it. A wild animal must have killed him, he says, echoing the rationalized account of the brothers. But he will learn the lesson more decisively in Egypt and it will condition his response when Joseph presents him with his two sons—Jacob's grandsons—for a blessing and instead of blessing them in the customary manner, he crosses and reverses his hands—in order that one should not come before the other, a gesture that stumps even Joseph.

The capacity to read prophetically in Genesis prepared the Hebrews for receiving the Law and answered the question raised by Cain at the other end of the narrative. Am I my brother's keeper, Kayin asked. Am I his provision maker? A question that bespoke only of his own murder of his brother. But it speaks not only of his brother, he will learn generations hence, but of everyone in the universe; an infinite or limitless obligation or responsibility, moreover, that includes a responsibility for their own death. To be worthy of the Bible, Buber writes, is to let oneself be addressed by the voice that speaks through it and respond with one's life.

From ethics has come the question of justice. If Abraham learns that commandment needs to be read prophetically, even when it looks imperative, Moses learns that prophetic reading assumes many forms, that commandment sometimes needs to be read imperatively, even when it looks like a narrative description. Sometimes what looks like a narrative, a duplication of one's own history, needs to be rejected and one's own history owned and aborted. Sometimes what looks narrative and like a reading needs to be rejected for an imperative obligation. Sometimes, if you continue to enact or act out a rescuing or missionary personality, you will end up increasing the very violence you are trying to avoid by your very attempts to avoid it. And sometimes what you need to do instead is embrace your own rescuing personality and return to the scene of your worst fears.

What you may need to do, in short, is rescue yourself, to own your own fears, give unto Pharaoh what is Pharaoh's, and unto yourself what is your own, an own or a self, ironically enough, which is at root a giving unto, or surrendering unto, the other individual, and so the cultivation of a heteronomy in place of an autonomy.

The text of Moses is just a beginning. Owning his own rescuing personality is a necessary start; it will enable the Hebrews to receive the Torah, although not necessarily yet to understand it, to live it, to live, as the rabbis say, "a life of Torah." The book of Exodus is in this regard what we might call a "stammering text," a text told from the point of view of others, of outsiders, even of non-Jews, or of Jews who have turned against their own Judaism. It looks as if it is a rescue and revenge narrative, an endorsement at a larger level, of Moses's earlier action with the Egyptian.

To suggest, as I have tried to do, that we need to give up such a sacrificial and revenge-centered reading is to suggest we read the text prophetically. How is a stammering reading a prophetic reading? To stammer is to trip over your own language. It is not simply to forget the language you are speaking, or to get the language wrong (although it may include that). It is to get it wrong in such a way that others may get it right, that others may understand where it is going, even if and perhaps especially because it does not get there.

Moreover, to stammer is to get it wrong in such a way that it also understands and owns its own stammering, its own incapacities, its own inadequacies and insufficiencies. It is the possibility of a text that owns its own stumblings, that owns its own scandals, we might say after René Girard's work. And the two principal ways of misunderstanding this text—and Biblical reading at large—are: (1) to see it as not stammering, as literal; and (2) to see it as only stammering, as a scandal, as something offensive which causes us to reject it for that offense. A stammering is a stumbling that allows others the opportunity to wait for it, to respect its attempts to get where it is going, without ever displacing or usurping those attempts.

Part Seven: The Stammering Text

With a discussion of interpretation, biblical reading, and alternative educations, educations which reduce violence, we are led back, of course, to the position from which we began. Education in the West, we said, was Platonic education: representational, ontological, dialectical. The rediscovery with

Hegel in the modern age of the dialectic, and the rediscovery with Heidegger of the ontological, is hardly news—although we may have forgotten how dialectical, ontological, Platonic, our culture remains.

But education in Judaism, we said, was different. It was a matter of Hebraic reading, a Hebraic reading which is Biblically-centered, and a Biblical-centeredness which is prophetic rather than representational, anti-idolatrous rather than ontological, diachronic rather than synchronic.

What has the analysis of the passages on the life of Moses taught us? That the prophetic may be understood as "stammering." Martin Buber introduces the notion of a "stammering text" to talk about creation. How can we understand the texts of creation, he asks, texts which are "impossible" texts? How could anyone speak plausibly of the creation of the world? The events at Sinai, the events of revelation, have to be understood, he suggests, not as literal accounts, not even as metaphors, or representations of any kind—figurative language of any kind—but as "verbal traces of a natural event," as a witness, as proclamation of that event, as it has deposited itself into the language which attempts to describe it and trips over itself—as stammering accounts.

The entirety of Torah, I would like to argue, is a text of the same type, a stammering text, an impossible text, but one that is not simply impossible, but rather that proclaims its own impossibility, and urges us to do the same, both about it and about us. Biblical reading, I would like to suggest—Biblical reading as practiced à la Levinas, Buber, and Girard—is precisely such a stammering or stumbling interpretation, such a *skandalon-like*, reading. It is a reading that owns its own violence, not in order to go on from it, but in order to give it up.

"I have been thinking," Emmanuel Levinas said to me in the final conversation I had with him, when he greeted me at the door of his apartment in Paris in 1994, "that politeness is everything." "Please, let my people go," Moses says politely to Pharaoh, when he returns to Egypt. "Let them worship their own God free of your constraints over them." This a far cry from the murderous attack the same individual mounted earlier in his life (as the midrash with which we have opened this essay suggests); and in the transition from one education to another—from the Pharaonic to the pastoral, to the prophetic—we as readers might learn to make the same moves: to give up the kinds of mimetic behavior that led us to violence toward others, and to assume our own infinite responsibility for others, a responsibility that may in fact create the universe.

"May the LORD bless you and keep you," a famous verse from Numbers (6:24–26) goes. "May the LORD cause His countenance to shine upon you and be gracious unto you." Our violence will end only when we fulfill the covenantal imperative given to Abraham at the outset of his career—to "be a blessing" (Genesis 12:1), only when we may turn to each other, face to face, in the infinite "after you" that Levinas calls "prayer," and say "May the LORD favor you and grant you peace (*shalom*)."

PART 3

Girardian Reading and the Literary

Reading Religion, Literature, and the End of Desire

Mensonge romantique et vérité romanesque at Fifty

eading *Mensonge romantique et vérité romanesque* again after fifty years, it is hard to forget the thrill of first encounters. "You know, Sancho, that Amadis of Gaul is the most perfect example of knight errantry, of knight chivalry, that ever was." Cervantes wrote these words? In *Don Quixote*? It is all about borrowing one's desires from others, not only in the limited sense of duplicating or copying, but as Aristotle describes our relation to poetics in general, or the Greeks spoke of their relation to Homer? Cervantes's massive novel is suddenly readable in an entirely new fashion. It is not about the romantic individualism we have been conditioned to expect of this Hidalgo hero, but about imitative desire. And not only Don Quixote, but Sancho Panza as well. For Sancho imitates Don Quixote as Don Quixote imitates Amadis of Gaul. In fact, the two behaviors may be systematized as external and internal mediation. External mediation, Girard teaches us, means borrowing your desires from a source that has no possibility of entering your world, and internal from a source closer to home. And what is more, the literary reader is doing the same thing, so that the nature of literary fiction itself comes into play. Reading Don Quixote as a romantic individualist, as a hero of the fantastic and the nostalgic, we have been borrowing our desires no less than the characters whose narratives we continue. What a powerhouse of a book on Cervantes, imitative desire, fictional writing, and Western literary history Girard has written!

Had Girard written nothing more, his place in the history of literary criticism would have been assured. Cesáreo Bandera was one of the first to acknowledge the extraordinary power of Girard's insights.[1] *Don Quixote* is seminal, not only in the history of the European novel, but in the shaping of our perceptions of literature in general from the eighteenth century on. Girard has altered the fundamental romantic postulate of radical originality by which we have constructed the literary (and extra literary) universe for some two centuries now.

But there's more. The same analysis applies to Flaubert, Girard tells us. All that we have said since the turn of the century about "bovarysme" is partial or, perhaps more precisely, misguided. Drawing upon the work of Jules de Gaultier, Girard expands its conception and reach. The heroine of *Madame Bovary* is another Don Quixote. Her bovarysme is not middle class ennui, nineteenth-century French cultural boredom, as we have been taught, but the blockage of her childhood desires, the ones she learned being raised in a convent from the romantic stories she read there in secret, and that she will try to live out in her own life to such disastrous ends. Nineteenth-century French cultural life is not that different from seventeenth-century Spanish life in this regard, Girard seems to be saying to us. They are both about middle-class European cultural pastimes, and the culture of reading.

But there's more still. Stendhal is also doing the same thing. *The Red and the Black* is about the desires of a peasant's son, Julian Sorel, and his rebellious ambition to live the life of Napoleon. He reads the *Memoirs of Saint Helena* and the Bulletins of the Grand Army as Don Quixote reads the adventures of Amadis of Gaul. The whole discussion of *ressentiment* that Max Scheler would raise in connection with Nietzsche thus needs to be expanded. Stendhal's characters are examples of the *vaniteux*, but that vanity has more perdurability than we might have expected and extends to the hero as well. History is just one more setting for the distance already forecast in *Don Quixote*. So are the relations that sociologists study. Elsewhere than in *The Red and the Black*, Stendhal writes about love, and Denis de Rougemont describes well the formulaic pattern in which "happy love has no history" and "romance only comes into existence where love is fatal, frowned upon, and doomed by life itself."[2] Thus, borrowed desires and their consequences would seem operative in this setting as well.

Three novelists, then, would describe three heroes—the romantic individualist who distinguishes himself from prosaic counterparts, the cultural sophisticate who distinguishes herself from bating associates, the historical rebel who distinguishes himself from vain compatriots—and all function as a result of borrowed desires, although their very romanticism would commit them to believing their desires originary, issuing from either the subject or the object but never the model or mediator.

But is Marcel Proust doing anything else? The salon life desired by the young hero of *Remembrance of Things Past* at the estates of his socially prestigious friends is within his grasp and he contemplates disaster by not being able to succeed within it—until he understands it all later (after an extended illness and virtual death) as borrowed desire. *Snobbisme* may very well be Proust's topic but not in the manner we expect, and if we think it is in our criticisms, it is because we participate within it—as if there were a bad snobbism and a good snobbism to be had.

Nor is the above account of these four novelists finally all there is to be said about mimetic desire in Girard's book. Dostoyevsky is for him the greatest of these writers. Here the internal and the external touch each other. Dostoyevsky writes about European culture observed from the margins, about city economy viewed from the country estates, about European culture perceived from the backwaters and in local traditions. The desires of the protagonist in Dostoyevsky's *Notes from Underground* are borrowed from the "man of action" his friends are celebrating and the "bad literature" he has been reading. There are for the most part only "brothers" in Dostoyevsky's work—thus, perhaps most famously, *The Brothers Karamazov*, a novel that would in this case include the father. With Dostoyevsky, Girard has introduced a new category: double mediation. Double mediation describes the situation when the model becomes not only a rival blocking the subject's desires but an actual disciple, and so everything speeds up. The scandal at the center of the community in *The Brothers Karamazov* is that the father and the son are in love with the same woman. In the infernal relation that results, chaos is unleashed. Literary, cultural, historical, philosophical, psychological, sociological—all these seem to be dimensions of experience in which these books move and in which borrowed desires would seem to function. And to them Dostoyevsky adds one more: the religious. Mad individualism, cultural romanticism, *ressentiment*, and snobbism, now give way in this last book to the setting of Russian Orthodox Christianity. The criminal, the idealist, the sensualist, the religiously pious in the Karamazov family all vie with the lustful father for critical attention. It is perhaps worth noting that Dostoyevsky contemplated in his notebooks continuing the history of Alyosha's career through a description of the young man's subsequent rejection of his religious orientation and his development as a writer, a development that might have offered him the capability of writing the book that Dostoyevsky had in fact written.

In the shadow of this Dostoyevskian turn, we are compelled to ask about "The Conclusion" of Girard's book. One could expect that it would be relatively simple. The book has elaborated the borrowed nature of desire in five major novelists—perhaps *the* five major novelists in the European tradition. A conclusion develops the implications of the argument one has broached. In this case, the implications are far-reaching: psychological, anthropological, philosophical, religious, in short, all the dimensions of the literary. One could expect, if not a full-length treatment, some suggestion in this direction. But more surprises are afoot.

"The Conclusion" introduces a new idea. The final chapter *is* about conclusions, or more precisely, about concluding. The writer, Girard argues, has been imprisoned just as his characters have been. That is how he knows about them. Writing their book is a reflection that he has escaped this prison to some extent. As a result, the accounts we have traditionally considered regarding deathbed conversion scenes vis-à-vis some of our most important writers have to be taken seriously, and we may need to reevaluate some of the scenes that have seemed to us fatuous or conventional in literary history in the past. One thinks of Chaucer's famous "Retraction," or Kafka's instructions to his literary executor to burn all that he has not already published. The writer's account of the passage from innocence to experience has been genuine. But the innocence was never innocent enough, and experience never free enough from its snares. Great writing begins for Girard not at the moment the writer escapes from the clutches of borrowed desire, but at the moment he realizes the impossibility of doing so, and owns as a consequence his history and responsibility within its duplicities, duplicities within a network of metaphysical desire in which all of romanticism in Girard's analysis would appear to have been caught.

But the concluding chapter of Girard's book introduces another element. The religious dimension Dostoyevsky describes is not just one more dimension of metaphysical desire and its snares. Whether or not all of these writers perceive it (they do to a greater or lesser extent), the dimensions of that final renunciation are for Girard necessarily religious in a special way. Escape from metaphysical desire is not different from the death and resurrection the Christian Gospel writers describe.

How does Girard come to assign this privilege to a dimension that really only appeared in full in Dostoyevsky's work? Is there some kind of progress from external mediation to internal mediation throughout the history of the West Girard has described, from Cervantes to Dostoyevsky? Lucien Goldmann thought that there was and described it in Marxist terms. Undoubtedly Dostoyevsky has played an important (if not pivotal) role in Girard's thinking. It is perhaps not entirely arbitrary that the first book Girard writes after *Mensonge romantique* is one on Dostoyevsky, *Resurrection from the Underground*. Is there something critical for Girard in Dostoyevsky's work that has been operative in this book but only now revealed? At the moment Girard writes the final chapter, the religious tone seems ancillary to the main concern, which is literary. Perhaps the religious aspect is more essential than it appeared.

In practical terms, the change in perspective comes about because the author himself—as he tells us in *Quand ces choses* and his interview with James Williams—had a conversion experience while writing the concluding chapter, so that that experience for the writers discussed within the book echoes the experience for the author of its conclusion.[3] If the feel of the final chapter of this early book of Girard's is different from some of the others, it may be in part because it *is* different. Girard wrote the final pages in a context in which his own life was changing profoundly.

How then are we to evaluate this ending? Had Girard written nothing else but this book, he would be remembered for having changed the way we think in literary studies about the great European novelists and their relation to romanticism. But he did not stop there. Indeed, the body of his work seems to have veritably taken off from that point at something of a breakneck speed. And so we are prompted to ask a series of questions. What status should we assign, then, to the final chapter of Girard's book vis-à-vis its earlier chapters? Is the final chapter a natural conclusion or a new departure?

Secondly, what status are we to assign to this early book of Girard's in context of his later career? Is the later work a continuation of the earlier in the manner we might have expected or something else again? And finally, what status are we to assign to it in context of the burgeoning interest today, fifty years later, in literary and religious studies, in the topic, in other words, in which this journal has a clear and expressed interest? These questions are not unrelated.

It could well appear to the reader familiar with Girard's work (who rereads this opening volume after fifty years) that the books that followed simply amplified the dimensions of this opening chapter. The psychological dimension was certainly pursued; read his work on Freud or Lacan. The anthropological as well; witness his engagement with Lévi-Strauss, Durkheim, Mauss, or Frazer. The cultural, sociological, and historical dimensions were developed somewhat later, but clearly play a central role in his latest book on Franco-Prussian history. The philosophical has certainly been pursued. Read his writings on nihilism, Nietzsche, Heidegger, Derrida, Deleuze, or structuralism and deconstruction. And the religious has been pursued. Virtually any of his subsequent books would satisfy that curiosity.[4] Girard continued to write in all these dimensions, in all these fields, and on all these topics.

But in fact that is not at all what happened. Girard took a single dimension of the work he was doing and pursued it to its logical conclusion. Abandoning the genre of the literary per se, he took up the reality it presented in the hands of these writers who became for him, in effect, co-researchers. What if this situation that these great writers describe is indeed the dilemma with which we are faced in the modern world, the world since romanticism? How did we get ourselves into this mess? When did it begin? Is primitive or archaic culture implicated in its terms? How is it we can know about it today?

The answer, of course, that would come in Girard's many new books is the scapegoat mechanism which was not anticipated by the earlier book. The fact that the scriptural writing of the Jewish and Christian traditions opened up the possibility for reading that mechanism allows us to be in the situation we find ourselves in today. Borrowed desires, imitation, mimesis, the mimetic in general, the mimetic as a hypothesis, turns out, from the perspective of the later books, to be a scientific approach to the way social groups handle their members, "society" here being understood (as French ethnologists talk about it) as a collection of differences or distinctions (à la Lévi-Strauss, Mauss, and the Durkheimian tradition), and organized (in Girard's view, as distinct from theirs) entirely around scapegoating and its formative role in the genesis of the category of the sacred and its relation to violence.

But that theme—scapegoating and its consequences—never seriously comes up in the earlier book. There are seeds of it earlier, to be sure, even on the first page. Borrowing desires of others, Girard points out, is like borrowing the desires of Jesus and living a life that is an imitation of Jesus as the church has urged it for so many years ("Chivalric existence is the *imitation* of Amadis in the same sense that the Christian's existence is the imitation of Christ")[5], a formulation that already designates the theme of Christianity, even if Girard's sense of Christian imitation in relation to the "deviated transcendency" of borrowed desire will later change entirely. And one witnesses an obvious seed in the final pages (as Girard himself attests much later), evincing the language of the Christian he would later become. Rather than amplifying mimetic desire in all of these other dimensions, rather than making that one discovery his life's work, he chooses a different route: the anthropological origin of this situation pursued to its logical conclusion and the understanding of the scriptural writing as a consequence.

Fifty years later, in other words, although it is not inappropriate to ask whether the demonstration of the borrowed nature of desire has borne fruit, we are compelled to answer: not the fruit we expect. The conclusion is an example. In describing the Dostoyevskian inferno of double mediation and patricidal murder, it is as if these writers—including Girard himself—had become Alyosha. It is not unexpected in the West at least that such emancipation or liberation assumes the language of Christian conversion. What is unexpected is that the specific content of these death-bed rejections should turn out more compelling than the literary structure that has revealed them.

We might see here, then, in Girard's first book that a new opportunity presents itself for those of us who find *Mensonge romantique* valuable not just as an opening for discussion of the mimetic to be developed anthropologically—although it is that too—but for one within a literary perspective. *Mensonge romantique* could well serve as the touchstone for a new literary criticism, one that would explore the inside and outside of literature and literary process. Literary criticism took an unexpected turn.[6] Girard's work took an unexpected turn. And where we are today in literary criticism—vis-à-vis literature and the religious—may be again unexpectedly the beneficiary of both histories. A new approach to the literary may be in the offing. And Girard's earliest book may prove decisive, not as a result of the way it was used afterward, but, ironically, despite that subsequent use.

Mensonge romantique, I have tried to argue, not unlike Keats's urn or, indeed, Keats's poem, has still untapped resources for literary criticism. Whatever its subsequent fortunes in Girard's own intellectual itinerary, in other words, *Mensonge romantique* in its own moment was about novels, novelists, and literary criticism, not about anthropology or religion read anthropologically. The latter interpretation came later, in the wake of other currents, other experiences, other choices. Legitimate as those later understandings are—and in my view they are entirely legitimate—the understanding of the literary that the earlier book inaugurated for us remains to this day underutilized. In the wake of structuralism and deconstruction, of Girard's critique of the sacrificial, of Levinas's reading of the ethical, of recent new approaches to trauma studies (especially among Holocaust studies scholars), and of Blanchot's understanding of the posthumous, we may suddenly be in a position to configure a more robust literary critical reading or, perhaps more accurately, to return to an older one with renewed vigor. We are perhaps ready for a literary critical reading that already fully engages the sacrificial, the ethical, the traumatic, and the posthumous dimensions of experience and that the ancients already recognized, at least within the Hebraic and subsequent Jewish tradition, under the unlikely name of "Scripture."

In that endeavor, René Girard's first book may serve, perhaps not surprisingly, as an inspiration. To echo the language of Emmanuel Levinas or, more recently, the language of René Girard himself, we may be ready in literary studies for a criticism of adults.[7] Just as Girard's first book exposed metaphysical desire and its infernal wiles, so *Mensonge romantique* also ironically engendered a desire for a theory of literary reading the likes of which we have not seen in some time. If the past is any guide, one cannot but look forward to that potential future reading, that "reading to come," so to speak, with a modicum of excitement and trepidation.

"Nothing Extenuate"

Love, Jealousy, and Reading in Shakespeare's *Othello*

"Is not this man jealous?"

—Emelia in *Othello*, III.iv.94

"Exchange me for a goat
When I shall turn the business of my soul
To such exsufflicate and blown surmises,
Matching this inference."

—Othello in *Othello*, III.iii.180–83

"Thou dost stone my heart,
And mak'st me call what I intend to do a murder
which I thought a sacrifice."

—Othello in *Othello*, v.ii.63–65

Prologue

I should say at the outset that I have a particularly personal relation to this play. When I first started to write my doctoral dissertation with René Girard at SUNY Buffalo in 1972, it was on Shakespeare's *Othello* that I started to write, although, in the end, when I turned in my dissertation, I submitted an essay on Sophocles's *Oedipus Tyrannus*.

I should also say as I begin that I encountered in the writing of this essay a problem very much like the problem I found in writing my dissertation—namely, that I had too much to say. If I stop early, therefore, and close down my discussion of the play before I say all that I would like to say about it, I would suggest that in some way we always stop early in reading Shakespeare, and that perhaps in this play especially that idea is very much a part of the internal structure.

Part One: The Genesis of *A Theater of Envy*

The genesis of René Girard's interest in Shakespeare can be dated with a fair amount of precision. Between 1968 and 1973, I was a graduate student in the English Department at the State University of New York at Buffalo. Girard had newly arrived from Johns Hopkins University, fresh from the 1966 conference on the "Languages of Criticism and the Sciences of Man" (a conference destined to change the face of criticism in this country).[1] I had heard him lecture for the first time in a course he was giving in the English Department (on "Literature, Myth, and Prophecy") in the spring of 1969. Sometime between the spring of '69 and the fall of '72, Girard was asked, along with C. L. Barber, to participate in a critical theory experiment. Girard, of course, was famous at that moment for publishing, in addition to *Mensonge romantique et vérité romantique*, a collection of essays in English on Proust, and Barber had dazzled the Shakespeare studies world with his book on *Shakespeare's Festive Comedy* in which myth and ritual studies were taken up in the historical setting of Elizabethan England.[2] Someone suggested (it may have been Al Cook) that these two maverick scholars reverse their customary roles and speak on each other's topics. Girard would commit to talking about Shakespeare (who was more or less unknown to him at the time) and Barber would commit to talking about Proust.

The experiment proved a great success. The night before the lecture (Girard was later to tell me), he and his wife, Martha, had guests to their home, and while Martha was entertaining them in the other room, René's thoughts wandered to the lecture he was to give the following day. It happened there was a version of *A Midsummer Night's Dream* playing on television (with Mickey Rooney as Puck), and somehow René thought he saw things in the English writer he had never noticed before, things familiar to him from his work on the European novel.³ He came in the next day, delivered the famous lecture on "Myth and Ritual in *Midsummer Night's Dream*", and afterwards C. L. Barber was the first to respond. Sitting in the front row, the grand old man of myth and ritual criticism in America arose and pronounced judgment. "I have been teaching that play for fifty years, René, and you have just explained it to me." The room broke into palpable approval, and René was later to say that it was what he discovered in writing this essay that opened the door for him to reading Shakespeare's work more generally.⁴

I spell out these details for a number of reasons. First, because I have been asked to talk about the genesis of this book and this anecdote is part of that history. As one of René's students at Buffalo—there were not that many—and as his office assistant, I was able to observe these matters "close up." But more importantly because I think *A Theater of Envy* has something of a unique place in the Girardian canon. It is one of the few—if not the only—of his books written first in English and later translated into French. Although *A Theater of Envy: William Shakespeare* is assigned a May 1991 copyright date and *Shakespeare: Les feux de l'envie* (Paris: Éditions Grasset) is assigned an October 1990 copyright date, the English language version was written first, as attested by the second sentence on the title page of the French edition, "Traduit de l'anglais par Bernard Vincent."⁵

Secondly, its reception in France was significantly different from its reception in the United States. In France it won the coveted Prix Médicis (1990), while in the English-speaking world, the book was allowed to go out of print very quickly from Oxford and was revived only by a small publishing venture promoted by a devotee of Girard's work—Fr. Billy Hewitt SJ—which is a phenomenon that probably deserves some consideration of its own.⁶

Thirdly, although numerous plays are mentioned in the book, the book really concentrates on only a very few. There are important essays on *Hamlet* and on *The Merchant of Venice* but the plays that receive the most attention (and, in terms of which, mimetic theory is explained) are clearly *A Midsummer Night's Dream*, *Julius Caesar*, and *A Winter's Tale*. René, it turns out, is a very selective reader of Shakespeare.

Any writer, of course, necessarily picks and chooses among the literature available to him, and Girard is no exception. Girard proposes one clearly defined reading of Shakespeare he sees as operative throughout the plays but best displayed in certain of them. And that limited treatment should not be regarded as an indication that the reading applies only to those plays and not the others he does not treat. As in the case of the novelists, the theory applies across the board. The best way to regard his partial treatment of Shakespeare's corpus is to see the book as an adjunct to *Mensonge romantique*. He might very well have treated Shakespeare in context of his treatment of Cervantes, Stendhal, Flaubert, Proust, and Dostoyevsky (and I for one am very glad he did not since he could not have fit the close to four-hundred-page book on Shakespeare into *Mensonge romantique* and we would have a considerably diminished treatment if he did attempt to combine them).

There is another matter to address here. The silence of the English-speaking world with regard to Girard's book is not coincidental. Girard's work was exceedingly well known in the United States at the moment he wrote *A Theater of Envy*. In fact, ironically, one might argue that it was because he was French and living and teaching in the United States (and therefore writing outside of his native climate) that his earlier books could be given such attention. *Deceit, Desire, and the Novel* and *Violence and the Sacred* attracted a wide American audience. And yet when he comes to write about Shakespeare, almost no one responds. It's one thing, of course, to say something radical about Molière or Stendhal or Flaubert or Proust (and about Cervantes and Dostoyevsky everyone is entitled to have an opinion); it's another to say something about Shakespeare. That hits too close to home.

There is, however, I think, a final consideration. Prior to Girard's book, the best piece of writing on Shakespeare, in my view, was that of Jorge Luis Borges. "Never before had any one man been so many men," Borges wrote.[7] Girard's book, like Borges' essay, is a holistic approach to Shakespeare, a theory of the whole phenomenon of "Shakespeare." The mimetic hypothesis applied to Shakespeare is a theory of play-acting in general, as a phenomenon of cultural life at large (the very term *mimoi* employed in ancient sixth and fifth century Greece refers to the actors in the annual *tragoedeia* or "goat-song" festivals). Shakespeare criticism was not accustomed to that that kind of theoretical treatment.

In many ways it is still not. Modern understandings of Shakespeare were dominated by one of two strains: Coleridge's sense of Shakespeare as sacred scripture, and the kinds of historical considerations in which that sacred scripture could be rendered immediate. But Girard's proposal is a theory of the sacred at large, a theory that does not simply presuppose the sacred status of Shakespeare but embeds it within a general theory of the sacred in its social setting. Critics may simply not have known what to say. To enter into the discussion is to enter a theoretical arena that may have felt over the heads of those who traditionally write about Shakespeare. If that is so, it is to be hoped that a new generation of readers of Shakespeare's plays will feel differently, less diffident about entering the discussion of Shakespeare as a writer not entirely unlike any other; one who sees things and misses things; one who has assets (extraordinary assets, granted) but also liabilities; but most importantly, perhaps, one who can be understood as a thinker, with ideas that can be specified and delimited. It is in that spirit that the following essay is offered.

In order to discuss these matters more concretely, I will offer my own Girard-influenced reading of *Othello*. Then I will discuss the ways in which my reading differs from Girard's own reading. And finally, I will address the question of a Girardian orthodoxy on mimetic reading, suggesting that in fact there is none. Two Girardians can differ entirely and yet both take up the same set of postulates about imitative desire, scapegoating, and the exposure of these matters in the Jewish and Christian scriptural writings. In fact, it is this possibility of not agreeing with Girard on specific dramatic readings (although developing a fully mimetic reading), that, I would like to propose, is in a curious way at the heart of the strength of his theory.

Part Two: Theatrical Intervention

At the end of *Othello*, the doors of the palace have opened (as they did often at the end of Greek tragedies in the ancient world), and in this case those doors are the doors to Desdemona's bedroom. But in the place of a sexual scene, we find here a supremely violent one: the body of the deceased Desdemona. It's hard not to recognize the ironies. The spectacle of the "tragic loading of this bed" (an "object," one of the characters observes, that "poisons sight") is a macabre visual pun on at least five concomitant meanings of the word "lie"—all of which are employed in the play we've just seen. If "honest" is Iago's word, "lie" would appear to be Desdemona's. Prostrate on the bed before us, lodged there in the house, mortally laid out, so to speak, she has suffered this fate after having been accused of lying (sexually) with Cassio, and then telling falsehoods or lies about having lain with him. So quickly, so utterly needlessly, has the perfection of this pair come to such disaster, that it's hard to view the scene with equanimity, without a sense, that is, that something is profoundly wrong with the universe Shakespeare is offering to us.[8] Given all we know about her history, it is hard, in other words, not to see in her death quasi-religious dimensions, a figure of a kind of *pietà*, a figure of unjustly slain innocence, the kind Michelangelo might sculpt.

And many viewers of this scene have been understandably moved to violence in response—outside the play as well as within it. Tales of theatrical intervention abound. The writer Henri Beyle, better known perhaps in France as Stendhal, reports a performance in Baltimore at which a member of the audience jumped up and shot the actor playing Othello during the murder scene. The man later said he did so "because he couldn't stand to see a black man killing a white woman." Or, Shakespeare scholar Gordon Ross Smith tells of a performance of the play in which a woman in the galleries screams out, in the middle of the long middle scene of Act III, in which Othello and Iago are talking, "You big black fool! Can't you see what he's doing to you! Can't you see!"[9] I remember that on one occasion, when I gave an account of the play in Girard's seminar, I hadn't quite finished my presentation the first week and the presentation needed to be carried over to the next. During the interval, an event of this very kind was reported to have occurred at a performance of the play in Europe. And the people attending my presentation commented about the strange synchronicity of the occurrence.

These stories all have some common elements. Othello is regarded as an outsider. He is attacked from a racist perspective, as if he has stepped into a culture that is not his own and in which he has even fewer rights than others might be granted in comparable circumstances, or he is regarded as foolish beyond plausibility, so gullible that only a gesture like theatrical intervention, one that ironically of course is the intervention to end all interventions (since the play stops as a result), is fitting. Desdemona is concomitantly regarded as the quintessential insider, the mute and innocent victim in this case of the violence of the men around her—who would kill her not only for what she didn't do, but for what she couldn't do, for what there was no time or space in which she could do it—victimized by Othello directly in one anecdote and by Iago indirectly in the other. And Iago's villainy appears blatant throughout, if that villainy appears peripheral in the first anecdote and central only in the second. The Bard of Avon's famous words in Sonnet 138, and his remedy in a similar situation ("When my love swears that she is made of truth, I do believe though I know she lies," and later, "Therefore I lie with her and she with me, / And in our faults by lies we flattered be") seems not even to have even entered the discussion.

Stories of theatrical intervention have, of course, attached themselves to other plays. For example, drama theorist Scott McMillan used to tell the following story. In one Maurice Evans production of the play *Hamlet*, it is reported that a child was in the audience, witnessing the scene in which Claudius is praying in Act III and Hamlet wanders by accidently, spots him there, and begins his speech, "Now might I do it," raising his sword as he does. Suddenly, the child yells "Look out!" and the actor playing Claudius turns around only to see the Hamlet standing with his sword upraised! What do you do at that moment? Pretend you don't see him? Improvise some lines to address the mishap? What lines? What could you say? The scene is lost. Indeed, the play itself may be lost. Apparently, the actors simply ignored the disruption and continued with the production. The intervention is just as fatal to the theatrical illusion. And there are reports of interruptions of performances of *The Comedy of Errors* in which the authorities are summoned to the theater and demand to know "Who is responsible for this play?" Who is responsible for this confusion?[10] But *Othello* seems to be something of a special case. Anecdotes of theatrical intervention seem curiously more prevalent around this particular play of Shakespeare's. Audiences seem somewhat less to be able to "contain themselves" before this play.

What is going on? What is it about the play that impels us to intervene in it, to stop it from proceeding, that impels us to violate the theatrical boundary, the "fourth wall," to transgress the unspoken theatrical contract, in order to get our point across? Is it racism? Is it chauvinism or gender bias of some kind? Is it a failure of some kind on the part of the audience, as if people aren't smart enough to know that it's "just a play," as if something is triggered in this particular play to produce these forms mild madness or, to the contrary, is it a failure of some kind on the part of the playwright to which these interventions give real-time articulation?

Or is it something else about which René Girard's theories of mimetic desire and scapegoating might be able to shed some light? I tell these stories and ask these questions because I want to begin with the idea that there is indeed something violent about the play, something fundamentally transgressive and unbearable which these interventions have in some way acted out, but in which we as well subtly collaborate by continuing to recall them within the anodyne context of these annals of theater history.

But rather than seek someone to blame in the matter—we Girardians know where that leads!—I would like to try a different route. I would like to trace whatever it is that is breaking down, whatever is in crisis, and ask: (1) What is it that should be working (that might prevent or at least forestall these kinds of interruptions)? (2) Why is it that it is not working? And, (3) What can we say about the literary historical context in which it is not working: about either what came before in Shakespeare's career or what came afterwards?

The key to answering these questions seems to me to be the issue of jealousy.

Part Three: Jealous or Zealous?

One would be hard put to deny that jealousy is a major theme of Shakespeare's *Othello*. Perhaps few literary works have been more thoroughly or more centrally identified with jealousy than Shakespeare's. But reading *Othello* in the light of mimetic desire and jealousy together is something of an eye-opener. Few scenes are more disturbing than the final sequence to which I would like to turn briefly some critical attention.

In his very last speech, Othello talks in a way that has become characteristic of him.

Soft, you, a word or two before you go.
I have done the state some service and they know it.
No more of that. I pray you, in your letters,
When you shall these unlucky deeds relate,

Speak of me as I am; nothing extenuate,
Nor set down aught in malice. Then must you speak
Of one that lov'd not wisely but too well;
Of one not easily jealous, but being wrought,
Perplex'd in the extreme; of one whose hand,
Like the base Indian, threw a pearl away
Richer than all his tribe; of one whose subdu'd eyes,
Albeit unused to the melting mood,
Drop tears as fast as the Arabian trees
Their medicinable gum. Set you down this;
And say besides, that in Aleppo once,
Where a malignant and a turban'd Turk
Beat a Venetian and traduced the state,
I took by the throat the circumcised dog,
And smote him, thus. [*stabs himself*][11]

T. S. Eliot may have been one of the first among Shakespeare critics to notice the bombastic and self-congratulatory tone of the speech, although Eliot did it not so much to explain *Othello* as for reasons involving a comparison with Roman drama more generally.[12] But the observation remains astute. Othello is a self-dramatizer. And the self-dramatizing in this case leads him to abject self-destruction.

He begins by invoking the service he has performed for the state, reminding us of it even as he asks us to forget it. He is intensely conscious of the history books that often accompany such service—the kind, for example, that Brabantio might have been reading to his daughter Desdemona before they invited Othello to join them in their house for dinner—and would offer his own suggestions on how that history might be written in a familiar and acceptable fashion, even under the present extraordinary circumstances, which are anything but familiar or acceptable. To do that, Othello counsels, and in order not to leave anything out of the picture, you must of necessity speak "of one who loved not wisely but too well."

But that is not at all what we have witnessed. Othello woos Desdemona in a flash. "She loved me for the dangers I had passed and I loved her that she did pity me," he tells us. End of story. If he sends in Michael Cassio as a go-between (as he later confirms to Iago he did subsequently), it was an entirely unnecessary gesture—and one may even suspect motivations of which the older Othello (who was closer in age to Brabantio than Desdemona) may be unaware, motivations that Shakespeare could have learned from reading Cervantes' "El Curioso Impertinente" in *Don Quixote*—since she already loved him. And when he ends it with her—for reasons that I will suggest in a moment may have less to do with the character of Iago (who we would like to imagine as a villain) than with his relation with Brabantio—he similarly ends it "in a flash," imagining hours of unadulterated lust that not only did not occur but *could* not occur since there was neither time nor space for them in which to occur.

If the charge, in other words, that Othello makes of himself were made of Romeo in *Romeo and Juliet*, we would understand it. Romeo clearly loved "not wisely but too well." Or of the lover in the Sonnets who says "my love is as a fever that longeth still for that which longer nurseth the disease" (Sonnet 147), or the sonneteer who writes "two loves have I of comfort and despair that like two spirits do suggest me still" (Sonnet 144).

Why then does he say it? He has in fact borrowed it from Brabantio's relation to him and from Iago's mention of that relation. "Her father loved me, oft invited me . . ." (I.iii.129) he tells Iago, and Iago, who was failing at the moment in his attempt to stir up Othello against Cassio, tries one last gambit: "she did deceive her father . . . he thought 'twas witchcraft. But I am much to blame . . . for too much loving you." (III.iii.209–16) And, in fact, everything that follows now in the final speech falls just as hollow. "Of one not easily jealous"? Well, yes and no. True, not easily jealous of her imagined sexual exploits, but once she threatens his "occupation" (III.iii.360) all hell breaks loose. So, not jealous at all, really, of her erotically, but wildly jealous of her "occupationally."

Does the next charge hold up? "But being wrought, perplexed in the extreme"? Not by Iago. Nor by Desdemona herself, nor by Cassio, but by the memory of his interaction with Brabantio and what "these delicate creatures" (III.iii.273) are like. This fate may be "the plague of great ones" (III.iii.277), he says.

What about the next charge? "Like the base Indian who threw away a pearl richer than all his tribe?" Like Caliban, for example, in *The Tempest*? Or perhaps a Christian audience would see the orthography of "Indean" and "Judean" as similar and regard the base Judean (viz. Judas Iscariot) who threw away a pearl richer than all his tribe (viz. Jesus). Whether true or not true, notice the monetary framing. In fact, like Brabantio, he has spoken of her only in terms that relate to wealth.

So that when he reenacts the scene with the turbaned Turk on his own body, his gesture is no less rhetorical and self-congratulatory than it has been all along. The door to the palace has been opened in this tragedy. In fact, the door to the bedroom of the palace has been opened. But this is not an owning of responsibility for what has happened. In a curious way, it is one more shirking of responsibility since if he takes his own life then he avoids the shame of being led off in cuffs, of being publically humiliated, a fate for him literally worse than death.

Why does this matter? Because it undermines the idea that the play has anything to do with a suspicion of sexual jealousy on his part and suggests rather that it has everything to do with some other kind of service.

Othello's behavior in this final scene, in other words, is not significantly different from his behavior throughout, from the beginning of the play to the end of the play. He begins as a self-dramatizer. He speaks in that marvelous way of the sea, and his origins. And then when he finds himself attacked by Brabantio, he's calm and he simply speaks, and everything falls to his way. When Iago provokes him by speaking of Michael Cassio, he says: "No, Iago, / I'll see before I doubt, / when I doubt, prove, / And on the proof there is no more but this: / Away at once with love or jealousy!" (III.iii.192–95).

And even at the key moment, when he seems to experience something like real jealousy—"Thou has set me on the rack!" (III.iii.338) he says to Iago at one point—and then he acts as if he has been besieged or assaulted at home and he dispatches Iago on a kind of military venture and he completes that military adventure himself, rectifying the betrayal in the home camp, so to speak. And when he finds that actually he has been misled—he still dramatizes himself.

In other words, I want to argue that this play is not about sexual jealousy. Sexual jealousy would be the torture and self-doubt that would arise from feeling that there is a rival in one's place. But the fact of the matter is that Othello is so egoistic we might say that he feels he has no rival. Certainly, Cassio is not for him a rival. If anything, Cassio is an annoyance, and Cassio has threatened to embarrass him in context of the state, but he doesn't care enough about Cassio for it to matter. It's not that he's wildly in love with Desdemona so that he feels he needs to protect his assets or that he is threatened by Cassio. So in some sense, in that regard at least, the play is not a play about jealousy, certainly not about sexual jealousy.

But if it is not about sexual jealousy, then what is it about?

I think the play is about "zealousy." We can show that Othello does not change from the beginning of the play to the end in one regard—as regards his concern with his "occupation." "Othello's occupation's gone" is an expression of his greatest threat and how he understands what is going on with Desdemona, the danger that she may be consorting with Cassio. It is not a matter of sexual jealousy, which is how we have read the play for all these years—since Coleridge, in fact; wondering whether Iago is to blame, whether Othello and Desdemona themselves have a role in it, wondering whether gender is the issue (because Othello is a man and all men may be like that).

I think, in other words, that this approach offers a new way of looking at the play. Perhaps *A Winter's Tale* or *Much Ado about Nothing*—two other plays by Shakespeare in which a woman is unjustly slandered in this way—are about sexual jealousy. But *Othello* is not.

Othello is a self-dramatizer. When Shakespeare does something, he does it repeatedly so we can be confident as readers that if we find something done only once, we are being overly clever in attributing much significance to it— at least as far as Shakespeare is concerned (there may be things about which Shakespeare is not in complete control, but that is another issue).

Othello is zealous from beginning to end: before, during, and after the events with Desdemona. It is not really sexual jealousy that is at stake, the intensely personal relation to others that relates to early childhood upbringing—no later than twelve months, if we are to trust the studies that Mark Anspach has been reading—but something else.

And that something else is another form of jealousy or more precisely "zealousy." Jealousy and zealous come from the same root, the Greek *zelos* (which becomes *zelos* in Latin and *jaloux* in French), and *zelos* means emulation or rivalry in a positive sense, enthusiastic competition on behalf of the state.

Which is exactly what Othello's is all about, I would suggest. He is not primarily stirred by Iago's talk of Cassio. "'T'is not to make me jealous to say my wife is fair, feeds well, loves company" (III.iii.186), he tells Iago. But he is stirred by what Iago says about Brabantio because that he has witnessed

himself. "Look to her, Moor, if thou hast eyes to see: / She has deceived her
father, and may thee" (I.iii.293–94), her own father has said of her. To be a
father, to be a statesman in Venice, is to run the risk of having such daughters,
such children, such wives. It is the price all "great ones" pay. He must do as
they do. He does not stir, he is not moved, until he fears that she has done as
Brabantio said she would do, as she did once to Brabantio, who is his model
for success in the Christian Venetian world. And then he moves swiftly and
thoroughly.

"I have done the state some service," he says in his last speech and in
doing so he is grossly understating the case. He has done the state a lot of
service and is very proud of it. He has dedicated his life to that service. And,
in fact, he is willing to give his life for that service, which is what the final
speech tells us. He was "perplexed," "perplexed in the extreme," lied to, first,
he thought, by Desdemona; then, it turns out, that it was in fact by Iago, a
lie that caused him to do something against the state. No matter. He was
lied to and acted upon that lie. He must be punished. He must now execute
judgment upon himself as he did upon Desdemona; swiftly and thoroughly.
And so he does.

Othello is a self-dramatizer. But they are all self-dramatizers. They all
see themselves in the light of the state and the service they have offered to it.
Othello is simply the most "other-directed" of the lot of them (as sociologists
used to say in the late fifties in the United States). But Othello's particular
zeal or *zelos*, his devotion, his boundless enthusiasm for state service, makes
him ripe for scapegoating. This is not Brabantio taking his own life, which
would be viewed as a fairly private affair and not of much interest to the
state (which is, in fact, how his death is regarded when the news is related).
Othello's death is different. Othello is the "stranger," as Leslie Fiedler used
to say, not unlike Caliban, not unlike Joan d'Arc in the early history plays,
not unlike Shylock; and not unlike Aaron the other blackamoor Shakespeare chooses to offer us.[13] He is the other, the outsider, the foreigner. When
Othello takes his own life, or is condemned by Lodovico (who represents the
state), something entirely different is taking place, something with charged
meaning for the community.

Othello's death is the death of the one who was always potentially the
scapegoat—like Joan, like Shylock, like Caliban, like, in fact, all the others who
are outsiders to the Christian cosmos by virtue of their religion (Shylock) or

their gender (Joan) or their cultural origins (Caliban). And so in that regard the play is about jealousy in so far as jealousy is about exclusion. "Zealousy" (or *la zalousie* in French) would be a better way of saying it.

But having said as much, and this will be my last point, is not to challenge Girard's insights as much as it is to support them. *Othello* is about mimetic desire precisely in so far as it is about jealousy as zealousy. The play is indeed the "tragedy of jealousy" in that sense precisely, a measure of the scapegoat dangers of the excluded one when he or she becomes too zealous, too excessive, in their competitive enthusiasm on behalf of the state. One can return to the literary even though Girard himself did not do that, without in any way challenging his insights about mimetic desire, in fact adding to them. *Mensonge romantique* opened the literary question for Girard, and then Girard turned to anthropology and the religious studies, although a number of us have been continuing to pursue the literary: Bill Johnsen, Cesáreo Bandera, Ann Astell, Justin Jackson, Eric Gans, Andrew McKenna, and Robert Doran, among others.

So, when we come to the end of the play, when we come to the moment in which Othello dramatizes himself, there's very little or in some cases nothing in the world that corresponds to what these characters believe to be true about themselves. And if they succeed, it is because a "happy" set of circumstances has united their particular dramatic construction of themselves and reality, and Shakespeare has dramatized for us the dangers of these self-dramatizations. In the case of Othello, the danger is that he kills others and he kills himself. The positive side is that he fights off the enemies of the state. The negative side is that he may end up, if he feels endangered, murdering his own forces.

The danger for others is no different. The danger of Desdemona's behavior is that she may end up submitting to violence by others. The danger of Iago is that people believe his own particular delusions and take him and his delusions to be real. The danger of Cassio is exactly the opposite, that we take to be real what is, in fact, simply an illusion, and a certain drunkenness with self. They are all drunk with self. They are all self-dramatizers and Shakespeare has portrayed in the play the danger of self-dramatizing.

In other words, it is a form of instability, of cultural value that is actually a form of instability. We see this when Lodovico, who reappears on the island, comments (upon seeing Othello strike Desdemona) "My lord, this would not be believed in Venice / though I should swear I saw't" (IV.i.241), and later "I am sorry that I am deceived in him" (IV.i.283).

Part Four: Jealousy and Scapegoating

If we accept my view, then it's not a play about jealousy in the sense of sexual jealousy which seems to require a form of rivalry, self-doubt, and anguish or self-torture. If there is a moment of self-doubt, it is very brief, and Othello reclaims his status as a military general very quickly, and it occurs almost, in some sense, off stage and for the briefest of moments. If there is a jealousy on the part of Othello, it's the sense of feeling threatened, of feeling a threat to his sense of self-image. And the same holds true with each of the other characters in the play. It's a play about the older meaning of jealousy, of enthusiasm, of zeal, or zealousness, for the particular state-sponsored role that each of these characters feels that they are destined to undertake.

In some sense, in this play, there are no "underground men." There are no characters we may identify with in Dostoyevsky's *Underground Man*. They are all Zherkovs, all characters who "have done the state some service" and are willing to do more service for the state if called upon to do so. And, introducing the Girardian idea of mimetic desire into the discussion, we may say that these are all characters who are entirely "other-directed." And if we think of the state as a reflection of the symbolic order, the context in which, in Lacanian psychoanalysis, for example, law, language, and the name of the father acquire their social status, then these are all individuals who desire through or in accord with that symbolic structure. There are no underground men who, in the sense that Jean-Pierre Dupuy has articulated jealousy as a structure, act like Dostoyevsky's protagonist or Camus's—unless perhaps we consider Iago in that manner.

At the same time, the play is about the dangers of that investment and what happens if that investment is threatened. And if that investment is threatened, and these characters feel the threat of being excluded or left out, then they respond in a predictable way. Certainly Othello understands the danger of being left out, as a black man in a white European community, a blackamoor, whose skin color and mannerisms would seem foreign to white European male perceptions. He could well be understood as responding as one of the potentially expendable individuals.

It seems to me inaccurate in other words to say that mimetic desire is not operative here in *Othello* any more than in the other literature Girard reads. What does mimetic desire look like when experienced from the inside? That is what he is exploring. Just as no one says "I am currently scapegoating the other," no one says "I am desiring according to the other." One feels the desire to be original and to be, or to be demanded by the other. But when that desire is blocked, one experiences that blockage as a lack of belonging, as a threat to one's sense of the community, to one's "occupation." The character Othello is an example of such an exclusionary subject, *le sujet d'exclusion*.

Here then is a play about jealousy that is also about exclusion, an exclusionary potential that is co-extant with that jealousy. But that fact or those facts in no way undermine a mimetic analysis. In fact, they enable it. Othello is thoroughly other-directed. He is nothing if not mimetic of the state. Iago is the opposite. He is nothing if not critical of the state and of love and of personal relations. But that is just to say that Iago is no less mimetic than Othello since it is necessary for Iago to follow the other-directedness of Othello in order to oppose it. Shakespeare has altered the character of Iago from Cinthio's original—where he is precisely motivated by sexual jealousy—to make precisely this point. And Cassio is nothing if not a functionary of the state at a higher level. All of these characters *could* be scapegoats: women, blacks, Jews, and new world Indians. And in some of Shakespeare's plays in which they appear they are.

Is it outrageous, for example, to suggest that Othello takes his own life in imitation of Desdemona's death? He has strangled her in an attempt to kill her. But she recovers from the attempt. If she recovers, does he really kill her? The treatment of the passage in the New Variorum edition of the play suggests as much, not in order to free him from culpability—his attempt is clearly to end her life—but to render her death collaborative.[14] Is it possible that, like her father Brabantio, who we learn in the same scene "dies of grief" (as reported by his brother, Gratiano, who appears in his place), she takes her own life to some extent, that there is a certain willfulness in her demise, a certain "downright violence"? And if that is the case, then is it not possible to see Othello's death as an imitation of hers rather than any kind of punishment for any perceived wrongdoing on his part? He is a self-dramatizer, as we said before, and his death is an auto-dramatization, no doubt. Is it not also a willful imitation?

This reading differs from René's. In René's reading, Othello is like Claudio in *Much Ado about Nothing*, a young man who sends another to do his bidding and then thinks the other has bid for himself—a kind of Isaac and Rebecca story gone wrong where Isaac suspects the servant (sent by his father to woo the woman and her parent, Yithro) of having done his office between his sheets and so orders the death of both, the bidder and the wife. René writes about such dramas plentifully, as we all know. What is "El Curioso Impertinente" in Cervantes or "The Eternal Husband" in Dostoyevsky if not an examination of the mimetic dynamics of such a drama on full display? But in Shakespeare's *Othello*, I would argue, such is, in fact, not the case.

Such may be the case in the source from which Shakespeare has clearly taken his play—Cinthio's *Hecatomminthi*, which was published in Italy in 1565, the year after Shakespeare's birth, and so a story that had been around for a while by the end of the century, and in many ways it is Cinthio's Moor that René is writing about. But the role of Michael Cassio in Shakespeare's play is severely curtailed as is the role of Iago—the Ensign in Cinthio— although both Michael Cassio and Iago would like to think they play more of a role in Othello's and Desdemona's life than, in fact, they do. This play, in my reading, is not the go-between gone wrong, which would indeed be the foreground drama for *A Winter's Tale* (and no doubt is what Shakespeare is thinking about when he writes *A Winter's Tale* and, perhaps, as well, when he writes *Much Ado about Nothing*).

What the play *is* about for me, as the scapegoating of a foreigner, is what could be called "zealousy" if there were such a word. Both "jealous" and "zealous" come from the Greek *zelos* meaning "rivalrous emulation" as used by Sophocles, for example, in *Oedipus Tyrannus*, to describe the "emulous rivalries of life" (*poluzelos biou*).[15] And both have made it into our language: "jealous" coming through the French as *jaloux* ("jealousy" we could say is a "French" understanding of emulation) and "zealous" directly as enthusiasm.

But Shakespeare's play is about a zeal or "zealous" behavior in which they all engage in the play—every one of them—and that leads them to disaster; literally to the death of everyone in the play. It is certain "fear of robbery"— as Kenneth Burke used to call it with regard to *Othello*—that I have dubbed, after T. S. Eliot's usage, self-dramatization. It is such self-dramatization and its destructive potential that concerns Shakespeare in this play, a kind of auto-mimesis or hyper mimesis with the way one models the other in oneself.

We return, then, as we began with theatrical interventions. It's Plato's Socrates all over again. We see people in the theater doing it and we want to do it. *Othello* is one of the most mimetic of Shakespeare's plays, so much so that even the audience would like to get into the act. The play *is* mimetic. But all want to self-dramatize. When Othello sees Desdemona lying on her bed (and we know that she died in part of her own will, as Brabantio too died "of grief"—which is why his brother Gratiano is here and not Brabantio), he wants to do that as well! He wants to join the family, as Antigone joins the family of Oedipus and Jocasta in the play of her name. He immediately duplicates her in violence, killing himself, as she collaborated in her own demise. But in his case it is a romantic pseudo-heroic act that comes off as buffoonery and "cheering himself up," as Eliot suggested, and thus as failing to gain for him the moral stature he mimetically seeks.

And that consideration returns us to the theatrical interventions. As he jumps into the "tragic loading" of the bed, so do we. The play performs for us the violence of its subject matter and we join it in enacting their transgressive implications, both within the play and without, within our critical theorizing about the play, and within the histories that we tell of its performances. If we are keen on opening a new chapter in Shakespeare criticism, one based upon mimetic understandings—and I take it that is what this conference is about—then the lesson to be learned from the play about such performativity both in the theater and in the writing we do about it, is not to be gainsaid.

Girardian Reading and the Ethical

Reading Halachically
and Aggadically

A Response to Reuven Kimelman

Professor Kimelman's talk is a hard act to follow. I also find myself in
a difficult situation because this is the first moment in our gathering
in which someone who is genuinely from outside the COV&R group
has come in to speak to us. So there is always the potential for the activation
of the processes of the sacred that we know all too well. We'll try to resist
that activation, however, and I will attempt to offer my response to Professor
Kimelman's paper with humor, although I may not always be entirely successful in my efforts.

Part One: Mandatory, Discretionary,
and Holy Warfare

Professor Reuven Kimelman's paper, "Warfare and its Restrictions in the
Jewish Tradition," is a testament to the author's erudition and deep knowledge of the Jewish tradition and in particular the Talmudic tradition on the
matter of mandatory and discretionary warfare and its relation to ethical
conduct.[1] No one who reads Professor Kimelman or who hears him speak
can come away without having learned something new, something that

will in turn confer new knowledge in other areas and thus contribute to the overall understanding of Torah and thereby to the goal of the ancient Rabbis who compiled these halachic and aggadic materials which is to see Torah as a blueprint of the world. The paper is brimming with the understanding and references appropriate to the subject matter he has chosen to examine, and from the perspective from which he has chosen to read that subject matter.

But therein also lies its difficulty. The problem, from my point of view, is that it is difficult to see how, in the form in which I read his text two weeks ago, it has anything to say to Girardian theory either in general or with specific relevance to this conference. Moreover, and this is perhaps more troublesome to me, steeped as his paper is within one major tradition of reading within Jewish history, namely, the legalistic tradition of Talmudic reading, it is difficult to see how his paper has anything to say to the other major tradition of reading within the history of Judaism, namely, the prophetic tradition.

Let me elaborate. It is difficult to see how Professor Kimelman's paper has anything to say to Girardian theory in at least three different ways. (1) The paper seems to be largely unaware of Girardian theory and one wonders why this paper is being read here. (2) The paper seems to be largely unaware of the purpose of this particular conference, which is to think about and discuss the institution of violence read from a Girardian perspective. (3) The paper seems to be largely unaware of the dynamics of mimetic phenomena whether from a Girardian perspective or from any other. Rather, the paper seems to be largely focused on a Realpolitik of ethical life in context of mandatory and discretionary warfare as discussed in the Talmud to the virtual exclusion of the mimetic aspect of things, the political to the exclusion of the ethical (at least in the sense that I am going to speak about it), the public conception of the ethical to the exclusion of the personal conception of the ethical.

Perhaps more troubling, however, is that the paper seems to be largely without commentary upon an alternative understanding of scriptural phenomena, which is, namely, that they are *scriptural* phenomena, textual phenomena, and not matters of historical reality, of what really happened, or even matters of moral reality, except as that reality passes through Scripture.

As an exclusion of this scriptural dimension, and an abstraction of the issues of mandatory and discretionary warfare from their scriptural context,

the paper appears to be the product of what I would call a literalist imagination and therefore potentially of theodicy.

Why, then, is Reuven Kimelman here? Presumably Bob Daly has told
him what this conference is to be about, that it is focused upon Girardian
theory, either in general or in specific guise of the topic: namely, violence
and institution in Judaism. Presumably, Reuven Kimelman also knows about
the other tradition of Judaism beside the legalistic tradition from which he
reads since he quotes at one point from its primary expositor, Martin Buber.
We can only surmise, therefore, that in the possession of these assumptions,
Reuven Kimelman's exclusion of the Girardian and of the Jewish prophetic
from his discussion is a form of polemic, a form of attack or assault upon us, a
form of military strategy, not in the sense, of course, that he has or is planning
to kill somebody (although he may well feel that after hearing this paper),
but in the way that academics engage in that sort of behavior, and especially
Jewish academics, namely, as a form of *polemos*, or intellectual warfare.

But what kind of warfare, you may ask. It seems to me that what we
have here is the perfect context in which to ask this particular question about
the nature of Reuven Kimelman's strategy, since that, of course, is his subject
matter. Is Kimelman's warfare mandatory or discretionary?

Mandatory warfare, he reminds us, is a form of warfare of the kind Joshua
is said to have waged in Canaan, or the warfare against the Amalekites, or the
waging of a defensive war in response to a prior attack. But no one has come
to Reuven Kimelman's door to attack him, at least no one of whom I am
aware. I assume that Reuven Kimelman does not suppose that he is Joshua,
with an entitlement to this auditorium and this set of group resources, either
at Boston College or within the Girardian organization.

And I further assume that Reuven Kimelman does not assume that
Girardians, or prophetic Jewish readers like Martin Buber, or like myself, are
Amalekites. Perhaps I am wrong.

That leaves discretionary warfare. Has Kimelman come here to expand
his academic holdings? That seems unlikely. His holdings are already sub-
stantial and it is hard to imagine what he would want with ours.

So what, then, is he doing here? What does he mean by coming here
among Girardians, among fellow Jews, and speaking to us as he does? What
does he take to be the source of *his* legitimation? There is still, of course,
the possibility of the preemptive, that Reuven Kimelman thinks that if he

attacks Girardians first, before they attack him, or if he attacks prophetically inclined Jews before they attack him, then he will defeat his opponents in that manner. Let us leave aside for the moment such frivolous fantasy.

The reason that Reuven Kimelman is here attacking Girardians and prophetic readers by such exclusionary sacrificial tactics, I suggest, is to be found elsewhere. First, Reuven Kimelman has walked into a situation that is clearly unwinnable. There is no way in which he could win a battle here. Secondly, he cannot appeal to the Sanhedrin, because there is none. I'm reminded of George Burns, who near the end of life said, "I like to date older women, unfortunately there aren't any." If Reuven Kimelman's position is to be validated, it must be validated by a transcendent cause known only to him and to the group he represents. Moreover, thirdly, he must have been given that validation only by direct revelation to that group or to him personally. Fourthly, the Girardians and his prophetic Jewish adversaries would appear from his perspective at least to have no rights since he gives them no voice in his paper to speak. There's not a trace of René Girard in his paper. And when he quotes Martin Buber, he does so in a non-prophetic connection. Finally, there is certainly no exigency in his coming here. He could well have declined the offer and found some other more pleasant way to spend his afternoon. So the criterion of last resort would not seem to apply in this particular case.

I think we have to conclude, in other words, from Reuven Kimelman's own definition, that Reuven Kimelman is waging against us a holy war: a holy war as he, after John Yoder, has defined it in his text. And secondly, that the action that he has taken, again in the context in which he has defined the terms for us, is not Jewish.

Here is Reuven Kimelman on the notion of the relationship of Judaism and holy war:

> Although a sliding scale of limited warfare is ethically feasible, an ethic of unlimited warfare [i.e., holy war] is a contradiction in terms. It is therefore not surprising that the expression "holy war" is absent from the Jewish ethical or military lexicon.[2]

So, what are we to do? Reuven Kimelman has come here to wage holy war against us. We could kill him. We've done that before in this group. We could bow down and pray to him. We could kill him and *then* bow down and pray to him. We certainly know how *that* works. But to do that, of course, we'd have to treat him as a kind of sacred violence, a scapegoat, a monstrous double of ourselves, and we're against that—as the lapel pin that Lillian Dykes has constructed for us lets us know.[3]

We could ignore Reuven Kimelman, as he seems to be ignoring us in the paper that he posted on the internet—an earlier version of which, I am told, already appeared in print (which, of course, is another way of ignoring us). But ignoring him, silencing him, not letting him speak, would only be, of course, another form of dangerous reciprocity about which we are also concerned in this conference. How about locking him up? We could treat him as one does anyone who embeds him- or herself within the mantle of alternative behavior clearly out of context. And of course if all else fails, we could offer him Prozac, and send him cheerily on his way.

But I suspect that none of these alternatives will appeal to this group. And I suspect that Bob Daly in his own wisdom would not have invited Reuven Kimelman here unless he thought there was something available for us in his coming. And so perhaps we should try harder to engage him, try to understand him, see what we can learn from him, what he can learn from us, despite the barriers that have been erected.

Part Two: Halachah and Aggadah

To what holy war would Reuven Kimelman commit us? To what God does Reuven Kimelman pray in this paper? Reuven Kimelman is a political theorist. He informs us in the first line of his paper that his discussion of war is a "test case for any political theory of checks and balances" (1). He is interested, in other words, in government, more specifically, in the "ethical deployment of power" (1).

But his political theory is anchored in limit and restriction. As he writes:

> A consistent thread weaves its way from biblical ordinance through medieval reflection to modern practice, as noted by exponents throughout the ages. Just because an army is legitimately repelling an aggressor does not allow it to wreak havoc with civilian life. The warrior is the enemy, not the noncombatant civilian. A just war does not justify unjust acts.[4]

Reuven Kimelman is a servant of military action tempered by morality, of strength tempered by wisdom, in short, of right reason as it has been
expressed throughout a long history in our culture, some time ago in Europe
in the figure of the Christian soldier, but more recently in the writing of nineteenth century German philosophy, and especially that of Immanuel Kant.

Reuven Kimelman would have us look reasonably at warfare. He wants to
argue, to spell out thematically, the Talmudic, rabbinic distinction between
mandatory and discretionary warfare. He wants to show us that even in the
most mandatory of conditions, there is in the rabbinic conception of warfare
always a secular, humanist component at work, always an awareness of the
face of the other individual, and as a result of the personal. But such personal
exception in the context in which he has presented it only proves the rule. If
his position is not finally Jewish in the manner articulated by Martin Buber
or Emmanuel Levinas, and certainly not Christian in the manner articulated
by René Girard, it is because it is finally a species—whatever other alignments
it makes within the Jewish tradition—of secular humanism as articulated
by Kant and grounded in reason and a reasonable limit-based approach to
power, values, and historical reality.

Coming before us, in other words, in a conference on violence and institution anchored in Girard's thought (and, for me at least, in Jewish prophetic
thought, of which I take Girard's thought to be in part, at least, an expression), Reuven Kimelman would wage a holy war against us on behalf of the
gods of Platonic and Kantian reason. And the question of what to do about
it is a serious one.

In considering this question, I am reminded of the anecdote told, the
midrash told, in the aggadic material in Shabbat 30 of the Talmud about
Rabbi Hillel, when he was approached by someone who claimed to want to
know something about Torah. "Teach me the whole of Torah while standing
on one foot," the individual requested of him. Hillel, of course, understood
immediately that the pretended request was in fact a form of attack. The
Torah that can be taught during the duration that I am able to stand on one
foot, he knew quite well, is not Torah. And he understood moreover why
when the request-maker came earlier in the day before Hillel's more orthodox colleague—Shammai—his more orthodox colleague shooed him out of
the synagogue, the text tells us, with a "builder's cubit." (It's comforting to
know that the Orthodox Rabbis of two thousand years ago used the same

disciplinary methods as the Rabbis who taught Hebrew school in America in the 1950s!) Shammai did not have time for this kind of nonsense; he had other things to do. Hillel, who is said to represent the more liberal wing of ancient rabbinic response, also perceived the only slightly concealed aggressiveness of the question, but he decided to entertain the man anyway, perhaps to utilize the occasion as a teaching opportunity. And what he said to him succinctly, of course, was, as no doubt many of you know: "What you don't want done to you, don't do to me. That is the whole of Torah. The rest is commentary. Go and learn it."

What is the connection of this ancient story of Hillel and Shammai to our current dilemma? It might appear to you that I am suggesting that if Rabbi Hillel can engage an individual who, in the guise of an innocent inquiry would in fact attack him and attack Judaism, then it seems to me that we can certainly engage someone whom we have invited here, and who has at least accepted to come here in the spirit of genuine inquiry to display his wares before us, even if he hasn't yet begun to engage us.

But the comparison is not entirely apt. Professor Kimelman is hardly a novice to Jewish study. He may be the leading academic Talmudist in the country. In fact, it is his status as an academic Talmudist that connects him to this anecdote. For in many ways, the paper he has read represents the tradition of Hillel's more orthodox colleague Shammai, that is to say, the tradition of orthodox legalistic literalist Jewish reading, and the alternative position that I have offered thus far could well be described as the position of Hillel, the position that is concerned less with the literal doctrinal assertions of Torah or Talmud than with the scriptural contexts in which such literalist assertions are constructed.

And so perhaps it is time we drop the humorous facade that Professor Kimelman is waging a holy war against us and take up the real issues that I see dividing us. Is Professor Kimelman arguing a Shammaian position to my Hillelian position? In this connection, I would offer basically two kinds of comments. The first and primary comment has to do with reading, with non-literal reading, and specifically non-literal reading of Talmud. And the second has to do with the specifics of Reuven Kimelman's paper.

There is a confusion of history with text in Reuven Kimelman's essay. Professor Kimelman argues the difference between mandatory and discretionary warfare as if the Rabbis were arguing such a distinction politically, historically, morally, or in some other abstract fashion. But it is never clear that the Rabbis in their Talmudic discourses were offering any commentary whatsoever on what actually happened—politically, historically, morally, or otherwise, except as what actually happened passed through scripture. Let me say that again. It is never clear that the Rabbis were offering any commentary whatsoever on what actually happened—politically, historically, morally, or otherwise, except as what actually happened passed through scripture. It is never even clear that the Rabbis thought they *knew* what actually happened, let alone that they were commenting on it. What they *were* commenting on, what they were constructing, was always (is always, as we continue to read them) a text, a bit of scripture, and scripture as the Rabbis say in *Yoma*, is always a matter of reading and praying, never of sacrifice. It is always a matter of texts, never of history, unless it be of the history of precisely such textual or scriptural strategies.

On the other hand, the text is not arbitrary. Having asserted that it is a text or scripture that we read and not history, we are obligated to ask more specifically the function of that text or of scriptural reading. Is scripture neutral, for example? Do we read purely for the sake of demonstrating the textual or constructed nature of our representations? Here is where we might say structuralism and poststructuralism failed. Having demonstrated the textuality of all cultural constructions (of historical, anthropological, linguistic, psychoanalytical, philosophical claims), poststructuralism, for example, forgot to take the second step of asking the function of such textual construction, of investigating what kind of textual interpretation it was and what end it served. And thus the poststructuralist project got stuck in its own tracks and became what we might call a "fetishism of beginnings."

I would like to suggest to you that this question must be asked, that the answer is that scripture in Judaism is never neutral, and in particular that the ancient scriptural and Talmudic text is an ethical text, one to which we have given the name "prophetic," a name that we are not, of course, the first to apply. A prophetic text as I define it is one that recognizes the dramas in which human beings are involved and shows us the end of those dramas in order that we may choose to go there or not, a text that has, as Martin Buber likes to characterize it, a conditional or "if-then" structure, even if it appears to speak to us apodictically and oracularly. What the text does not show us, in other words, is what is—either what appears to be but is not, or what really is as opposed to what only seems to be, or any other version of representation or ontological conception). Buber calls such a text (no doubt thinking of Moses) a "stammering text," and that characterization seems apt. As in the case of the stammerer, we do not step in and say where the stammerer is going, even if we would like to think that we know where the stammerer is going. We respect the right of the stammerer to stammer, to not get there, to fail, to display weaknesses, James Alison might say.

In the specific context of Reuven Kimelman's paper, what we are concerned with is the reading of Talmud and through Talmud of Torah, not of historical reality or of rabbinical commentary on historical reality. Between the year 70 of the Common Era and 1948 there was no state, and so war was never a sacrificial institutional act. What the Rabbis are talking about is scripture. It is always a debate over scriptural interpretation. The distinction between mandatory and discretionary warfare already presupposes a sacrificial crisis in the Girardian sense, and in the hands of the Rabbis it is always already an interpretive act. The question is never whether a given war is or is not mandatory, but what does it mean in a scriptural context to say as much; how does saying as much function scripturally, which is to say, in the vocabulary I have used to characterize it, prophetically?

Part Three: The Talmudic Two-Step

I will conclude with an example. Joshua's invasion of Canaan is often taken as the very model of mandatory wars, because God is said to have mandated it explicitly. If Joshua's invasion of Canaan is not mandatory, what is? (I remember an extended discussion with Norbert Lohfink several years ago, in 1983, at the conference in Rene Girard's honor at Cerisy-la-Salle, on this point.)[5]

I want to turn to look at this question of Joshua's war in Canaan by looking at part of Reuven Kimelman's text. If you consult your copy of the text we will do a little close reading here. It's the passage that begins as follows:

> God commanded Moses to make war on Sihon, as it is said, "Engage him in battle" (Deuteronomy 2:24), but he did not do so. Instead he sent messengers . . . to Sihon . . . with an offer of peace (Deuteronomy 2:26). God

said to him: "I command you to make war with him, but instead you began with peace: by your life, I shall confirm your decision. Every war upon which Israel enters shall begin with an offer of peace."[6]

What we have here, it seems to me, is a wonderful little midrashic account with which we can begin to introduce a Girardian, and perhaps even a prophetic, analysis. It seems to me that there are four facts that we have to deal with in this particular text: (1) God commanded Moses to make war on Sihon; As it is said, "engage him in battle." (2) Moses "did not do so." (3) God said to him "I command you to make war with him" [i.e., Sihon], but instead you do something else, "you begin with peace." (4) "By your life, I shall confirm your decision." It seems to me what we have here is a brilliant textual moment, one that is subject to all the kinds of mimetic analysis that we love so much in this context.

That is to say, clearly, the question of the passage is, why does God confirm Moses's decision not to engage the enemy in battle straightaway, and in particular, why does He confirm it "by [Moses's] life?" I have talked elsewhere in print about the life of Moses and the way in which that life may be described as a move away from retributive justice and toward restorative justice.[7] The life of Moses begins with Moses seeing an Egyptian beating an Israelite. Moses intervenes and kills the Egyptian, and his intervention actually causes things to go from bad to worse because the next day two Israelites are fighting and they say: "Are you going to do to us the same thing you did to the other guy?" Soon news of the event spreads throughout the kingdom and Moses is forced to leave the land. So the mimesis leads in that case to expulsion and exile.

Later on in the same story, God says to Moses, "I have seen the suffering of my people, and I want you to charge in there and bring those suffering Israelites out of bondage." Moses hears, in other words, from God's own lips this time, so to speak, the same kind of narrative appeal to which he responded so precipitously before when he charged in and rescued the Israelite from the Egyptian.

But now, instead of doing what he did previously, Moses has a new response. He poses the questions that it never occurred to him to pose on the earlier occasion, namely, "Who am I to do it?" And "I cannot speak." And so forth. And God deconstructs each of his questions at each moment he offers them. "You have a brother, don't you? He can talk. You have an arm, don't you? Take it out. See, it has turned leprous. Now put it back. See, it has turned back into healthy flesh. Do you have a staff? Put it on the ground. See, it has turned into a snake. Now, pick it up again. See, it has turned back into a staff." And so forth.

All these verbal games, all these midrashic exchanges taking place between God and Moses, turn out to be ways of getting Moses to pose the questions he failed to pose previously. So that when he finally does return to Egypt, he does so not with a mind to rout the Egyptians (as he might well have done if he were still the same man as before). Rather he now goes in and says to the Pharaoh politely: "Please, sir, let my people go; let them worship as they wish to worship." He speaks politely, allowing the consequences to fall where they may. In that way, the episode becomes, among other things, an account of how a restorative justice emerges from a situation that began as a scene of retributive justice.

So, returning to our passage, it seems to me there is something that is readable here that could give us the beginning of the basis for discussion of the issues we have raised. Moses in the course of his "life" has learned to read commandment. He has learned that when God says do this or do that, or I have commanded you to do this or do that, he is *not necessarily to do* it, that he must hear God's commandments prophetically, that he must learn to hear God's commandments sometimes "in quotation marks," so to speak, as the future of the path he is traveling, but not a future he is necessarily to pursue, as what he might do if he were someone else, and if he were simply to continue in that alternative identity, but as what he should perhaps *not* do given who he is and in the circumstances in which he finds himself, that he can, in short, question God midrashically, and in some circumstances God will affirm that questioning of explicit commandment as the proper response to commandment, that sometimes, as the Rabbis say in *Baba Metzia*, "we are not to listen to heavenly voices."

And this prophetic interpretation of commandment offers us a foundation—especially since the above scriptural passage invokes other scriptural passages through the phrase "by your life"—for scriptural reading in general, for understanding this text not in terms of historical reality, nor in terms of any literal account whatsoever, but rather in terms of the overall scriptural context from which these texts derive.

And thereby we may rescue the text of Reuven Kimelman for a Girardian conference. Having begun by characterizing Reuven Kimelman's paper
as a military assault, we conclude by suggesting the ways in which it offers
us resources for prophetic scriptural reading. My criticism of Reuven Kimelman's paper is not that it is Shammaian while my own is Hillelian, but that
neither position taken alone is sufficiently Talmudic, that the goal of Talmudic interpretation is to move precisely from one to the other, from a Shammaian legalistic position first to a Hillelian prophetic position after, and that
such a one-way, two-step movement (and only such a one-way, two-step diachronic or sequential movement) constitutes Talmudic reading as distinct
from either perspective taken independently of the other. Far from accusing
Professor Kimelman of not being sufficiently Girardian or sufficiently prophetic (why, after all, *should* he be? he has not chosen those modes as his own
and has come here in good faith to offer us what he does do), I am suggesting
rather that neither of us (as I have thus far characterized our positions) is
sufficiently Talmudic, since neither the abstract halachic formulation of a
distinction between mandatory and discretionary warfare nor an aggadic
prophetic reading of their scriptural context alone is sufficiently Talmudic
(which is the mode both of us have chosen). To read Talmudically is to recognize from the position of Shammai that the position of Hillel is *necessarily* to
follow, and concomitantly to recognize from the position of Hillel that the
position of Shammai is its necessary prior foundation.

As Moses could reform his life in contradistinction to God's express
commandment, and then God could affirm Moses's action, so the action
commanded of us is to be similarly construed. Torah offers us the future of
the path we are following. If we continue to follow the course we are on,
here is the result: we will go to war. But by means of his experience, Moses
learned the necessity in certain circumstances of not doing that, of hearing
commandment in some circumstances as what not to do, as what will accrue
only if one continues mindlessly and idolatrously to pursue one's prior itinerary. To fetishize the Talmud as saying uniquely this or that, as offering a singularly defined course or set of distinctions, independently of the scriptural
circumstances from which it derives, is to fall prey to the very dangers Torah
and Talmud are describing. The only way out of that conclusion, for the Rabbis, is to read and pray: to read commandment as the future of the path one

is traveling and to sue for peace, to ask politely that one's people be free to worship as they choose.

It may be that wars will, in fact, continue, and there is certainly no guarantee that our pleas for peace will be successful. It may even be that wars will follow inevitably from our efforts at peace. But external historical fact does not invalidate the commandment: namely, in certain circumstances, to suspend, at least initially, commandment itself, even the commandment to make war upon our perceived enemy, and to substitute instead an offer of peace, to move, in other words, from an academic sacrificial distinction between mandatory and discretionary warfare (or from a distinction between Reuven Kimelman and myself) to the substitution instead of aggadic reading and a halachic prayer.

Let us give the last word to Reuven Kimelman who points out for us that in the case of Canaan, the action of Moses with Sihon set a precedent.

> Since Joshua is said to have extended such an offer to the Canaanites, and Numbers 27:21 points out Joshua's need for applying to the priestly Urim and Tumim to assess the chances of victory, it is evident that also divinely-commanded wars are predicated on overtures of peace as well as on positive assessments of the outcome.[8]

Commandment commits us to a "Thou must" which takes no account of a "Thou can."[9] The ethical imperative of the text enjoins us to the assumption of an infinite responsibility for the other human being. It is in that Talmudic spirit that I urge us to read scripture halachically and aggadically, that I affirm the necessity of Reuven Kimelman's legalistic reading of Torah and Talmud, and having done that, that I urge him then to read the texts that he reads prophetically, to engage René Girard's work on violence and the sacrificial (and other writers like Martin Buber, Franz Rosenzweig, and Emmanuel Levinas) as an expression of the Jewish prophetic tradition that the Rabbis felt to be so important.

Discussion[10]

James Alison opened the discussion by asking why the rabbis in the eleventh and thirteenth centuries were talking about this matter. Kimelman replied (with Goodhart's agreement) that Talmudic reflection, though it may have some reference to "reality," was not primarily reducible to the social-political conditions of the people doing the thinking, that it is primarily reflection upon reflection upon reflection of texts, plus interpretation and commentary.

David Vanderhooft asked about the apparent dichotomy of text versus history. Goodhart noted that there is always *some* correspondence. Talmudic interpretation doesn't violate history, but doesn't depend upon it either. Kimelman noted that although real events occur, history as an account of those events exists in the mind of the perceiver. Unless you are God, he noted, there can't be an argument between what actually happened (which only God can know) and how it is perceived. There's no such thing as history that has not been constructed through a text.

Robert Hamerton-Kelly then initiated an extended discussion with Kimelman. He began by trying to get Kimelman to adopt a practical ethical position regarding contemporary Israel and the extremist violence occurring within its boundaries. While indicating his ethical disapproval of the extremist violence from all sources, Kimelman maintained that this example too was an illustration of his basic position, namely, that it was a situation of different traditions regarding text-based arguments. In the course of this discussion, he also illustrated not only how the Jewish traditions managed to deal with embarrassingly violent biblical texts by finding ways to de-absolutize, limit, or relativize them, but also pointed out how the strong—dominant, he would claim—tradition of Talmudic interpretation had an amazingly strong trajectory in the direction of limiting violence.

When Hamerton-Kelly insisted that we are dealing here not just with textual interpretations, but living historical interpretations, Kimelman was able to point out that, even here, the radical extremists, to the extent that they were Jews, tried to base their argument and their practical legitimizing of violence on a text. Their favorite texts are those (such as Deuteronomy 25:17–19 and 1 Samuel 15:1–35) that command the eradication of the

Amalekites, thus turning Amalek into a metaphor for a people desiring the total annihilation of the Jews. However, in modern history, the only ones who can "live up" to this metaphor, Kimelman contended, are the Nazis of 1943 when Hitler commanded that trains continue to be assigned to bringing Jews to Auschwitz rather than to bringing much-needed help to the then retreating German forces on the Russian front. This response seemed to answer the apparent objection that Kimelman was attempting to deal only with texts and not with reality.

Vern Redekop then proposed putting this whole discussion into the perspective of the grand Girardian scheme and how, within the perspective of that scheme, destructive mimetic violence is dealt with either by scapegoating or by introducing a teaching that tries to get beyond scapegoating and limiting it. That, precisely, is what Kimelman has shown Torah (and Talmudic interpretation) to have been doing, Redekop noted. Then recalling his own work on the death penalty in relation to the Bible, Redekop reported that his research confirmed that the direction of the Torah is toward limiting the violence. He thanked Kimelman for pointing out that the tradition of Talmudic interpretation he has been expounding has been doing that in spades. Kimelman at that point recalled his own earlier studies on nonviolence. The first step in countering violence is to recognize and counteract the tendency to demonize the enemy, he said. The second step, then, in the Jewish tradition, is to fight texts with texts. Kimelman took this occasion to "demythologize" the common scholarly misunderstandings about "holy war" that have been popularized in his view by Gerhard von Rad and followed by most Protestant scholarship.

Goodhart took this occasion to amplify Kimelman's position that the Jewish way is to fight texts with texts. He also elaborated a bit more the remark he made in his formal response to Kimelman's paper, a remark that he felt might have been misunderstood as a criticism of Kimelman's appearing to espouse a position of Realpolitik to the neglect of the prophetic tradition. He noted that this current debate/discussion, although not planned that way, has turned out to be a striking illustration of precisely how Judaism works. To a certain extent, we have performed Judaism, here in this very debate, he said. Our engagement today, both in the seeming "argument" between Kimelman's position and my own, and in the seeming opposition in this "discussion" between the text-based arguments that both he and Kimelman were defending and the Realpolitik that some of questioners were proposing, has been a debate between one interpretation and another. Kimelman added to this observation a comment about the inadequacies of the "purely" prophetic tradition, that it often doesn't go beyond muckraking power and those in power. The ethical tradition, he asserted, is not fulfilling its responsibility if it only attacks power.

Britt Johnston expressed some disagreement with what he understood to be Goodhart's earlier criticism that Kimelman disregarded the prophetic tradition, suggesting that there was much that was "prophetic" in what Kimelman was doing, especially by at least implicitly raising the question: Why and from where does Judaism have and get this impulse to limit violence? Kimelman allowed that he was unable to answer this directly, and then expounded a bit more the challenges that Judaism faces in actually going about its task. It is the challenge of beginning from (1) a biblical tradition that allows for capital punishment and, while (2) still preserving the authority of that tradition, and yet nevertheless (3) still finding ways to limit its violence. One does that by fighting texts with texts, he said. Then he added: "The question is: How do you make that a real tradition?" Goodhart allowed that it may be difficult to say precisely where the urge toward limitation originates but that such a process of increasingly sharp distinction-making nonetheless constitutes its makeup, an example of which we have witnessed here today, and that the rabbis sometimes characterized in Talmudic discussions with the Hebrew word that was so odd to English-speaking people's ears—the word *pilpul*.

In a brief intervention, René Girard cautioned against the danger that so strong a text-based approach might not end up being fair to, or might not be giving proper due to the actual people who are real victims (e.g., the real people, the real experiences behind the laments of the Psalms). Kimelman responded by pointing out how extraordinary is the strong Talmudic tradition of the critique of Moses for killing the Egyptian. A brief exchange between Goodhart and Bob Hall highlighted the contrasting tendencies between a Jewish tradition bent on limiting violence, even legitimate legal violence, and an American legal tradition with its apparently primary strategy of attempting to identify the guilty party.

The discussion concluded with Kimelman recounting the intriguing Talmudic discussion regarding how to stone a condemned man, a discussion, he reminded his audience, less the document of an actual episode or instructions regarding how to go about doing it, than one more occasion for dismantling the tendency toward violence in such a situation. The procedure, he asserted, is to throw him out of a building. The discussion is about the floor from which to do it in order to have it be effective and still as painless as possible, all the while still also preserving as much as possible the dignity of the condemned man's body. One of the biblical texts quoted to support the solution (namely, to proceed from the second floor) was, interestingly enough, he pointed out, "Love thy neighbor as thyself."

The Self and Other People

Reading Conflict Resolution and Reconciliation
with René Girard and Emmanuel Levinas

Emmanuel Levinas . . . talks of the defenseless face of the other which
shows itself to us in a way we can't avoid. When we recognize this face, it
makes us a captive. This face is the face of the scapegoat, the victim, helpless
and without possibility of escape.

—Roel Kaptein[1]

Part One: Conflict Resolution, Girard,
and Levinas

One of the "hot" topics in conflict resolution studies over the past thirty
years or so has been the introduction of the idea of reconciliation.[2] The
idea behind it is that the resolution of conflict remains temporary as long
as we focus exclusively upon the symptomatic issues at hand and that only
if we step back and look more broadly at the people involved and the larger
contexts in which they live and work can it be made permanent—and thus
something like reconciliation becomes possible. In this expanding contextual
understanding, the work of René Girard has assumed special importance.

Why? Girard posits that all culture operates in effect as a management system for mimetic desire, a system sustained by what he calls the scapegoat mechanism, a system in which a victim arbitrarily chosen and sacrificially removed from the community in a veritable lynching is understood to be at the origin of all social distinction, founded as such distinction is upon the difference between the sacred and violence. The sacred and violence for Girard are one and the same. The sacred is violence effectively removed from the community, and violence is the sacred deviated from its segregated transcendent status and come down into the city to wreak havoc among its citizenry. If the system is effectively maintained, the originating violence is reenacted periodically in the form of commemorative ritual, and the result is the regeneration of the sacred. If the system is not maintained, the result is violence, which is to say, difference gone wrong, distinction gone awry, asserted in the extreme in its inefficacy. Untouched by the outside world, archaic communities, as Girard tells the story, sustained their existence for thousands of years within this cycle of difference, difference gone wrong (or sacrificial crisis), paroxysmal exclusionary behavior (or surrogate victimage), and new differentiation (and commemorative reenactment). With the advent of the "modern" world some twenty-five hundred years ago (and for whatever reason), these sacrificial systems were threatened and the ones that survived were the ones that effectively developed a means of living more or less without sacrificial victims in the traditional sense.

It is not hard to imagine how or why conflict resolution theorists would be interested in these ideas and identify in this account of sacrificial violence and its mechanism a useful model.

Here, for example, is how Roel Kaptein explains Girard:

Our culture increasingly gives us the impression that we are atomized individuals, responsible for and to ourselves and free to do what we want. Inevitably in this situation, everybody and everything else become tools which we can use to reach our own goals. Others get in the way between us and our goals.

When we see other people scapegoating and blaming others, we despise it. However, in despising and loathing it we actually prove that we are not free of it ourselves. Instead we show that we know all about it. Nevertheless, we continue to scapegoat and blame others, over and over again, without ever acknowledging what we are doing. Even while we are doing it, we remain absolutely certain that we ourselves are not scapegoating. We are sure that we are simply right!

Given this situation, everything which is in this enchiridion, indeed even everything which we learn from the gospel can be used to play the game of scapegoating, the game of culture, better. We can become even cleverer hypocrites, thinking ourselves superior. There is only one possibility of escape from this cycle; to recognize the scapegoating mechanism operating through us. We know that time and again we are made scapegoats ourselves. We fight to escape this predicament by scapegoating others. The alternative, a wholly different possibility, is to find the freedom to let it be. We can stop the fighting and so be free at last.

How do we go about this? How can we find a way to this possibility? Emmanuel Levinas, the great Jewish thinker, talks of the defenseless face of the other which shows itself to us in a way we can't avoid. When we recognize this face, it makes us a captive. This face is the face of the scapegoat, the victim, helpless and without possibility of escape. When we see this face, it shows us ourselves and our helplessness. We can only bow and serve.

In this way, the gospels ask us to look at Jesus, who shows us who we are, bringing us to the place we must find in order to find new life, freedom. It is the place we fear most, that of the scapegoat.[3]

Using Girard's ideas as a basis for his analysis, Kaptein asks the inevitable question: How do we go about finding a way out of this sacrificial crisis? This is an important move on Kaptein's part, and it highlights a very important feature of Girard's ideas, a feature often missed by a good many of the individuals who currently use Girard's ideas: namely, that there is no implied remedy. There is no ethical consequence to be gleaned from Girard's analysis, other than to end the violence, to *refuser la violence*.

Why do so many researchers think there is a "Girardian" solution to sacrificial violence? For two reasons, I would suggest. First, because Girard gives great weight to the exposé of sacrificial violence offered in the Jewish and Christian scriptural texts. The Christian Gospel is not the only place for Girard that it shows up (it show up first in Hebrew scripture—and especially the prophetic texts—and somewhat later in Greek tragedy hundreds of years before it does in the Gospel) but it is one of the key places, and, in any event, the place where, in his view, its analysis is "completed." If Girard gives so much weight to the Christian reading of these matters, it must be, these researchers reason, because Girard finds the Christian reading an acceptable one *in toto* and endorses its fundamental postulates.

But there is a second reason researchers easily move from a descriptive account to a prescriptive one. Girard himself has declared publicly that he is a practicing Christian, a member in good standing of the Roman Catholic Church, and Girardianism, therefore, these researchers argue, must be a Christian intellectual phenomenon. It is not unreasonable that fellow Christians (especially fellow Catholics) should surmise that Girard's view is specifically a Catholic one.

In fact, however, it is not. It is not a Christian view—Catholic or Protestant. It is not a Jewish view. It is not the view of ancient Greek tragedy (in the hands of Aeschylus, Sophocles, or Euripides), any more than it is the view of the ancient writers of the Hindu, Buddhist, or Islamic scriptures. And yet at the same time it is undoubtedly related to all of these orientations (and perhaps others we have not mentioned). It may even be the province of all of the so-called revealed religions—if we understand these orientations in a broad enough historical context. Girardianism as an intellectual movement—wherever Girard himself found it and to whatever moral consequences it leads him personally—is an understanding shared in part or as a whole by all of the above interpretative structures whether these structures have been used as the basis for systems of religious practice or not.

How is Girardianism not one of these orientations, and yet how does it nonetheless participate within the domain in which they constitute interpretative structures? It is not these views because it is not an ethical system. Girard has spared no pains to assert that he is not writing theology—of any kind—although his work has indeed been profitably compared with that of anthropologically oriented theologians like Karl Rahner and Bernard Lonergan.[4] He is not attempting to derive knowledge about the divine from within any one of these systems with an eye toward discerning what to do about it, what code of behavior to adopt on its basis. Girardianism is not a version of preaching, although, again, the knowledge of the sacrificial mechanism he offers has been usefully incorporated into the orientation of readers whose avowed aim is preaching.[5]

On the other hand, like each of these orientations, Girardian thinking is an interpretative system. As Girard understands the process, what he is doing is offering a reading, specifically the reading that he feels first Judaism and later Christianity offers of archaic cultures. Part of the limitation of our own customary perspective on these matters may be our thinking that traditional scriptural texts are only (or even primarily) scripts for religious practice. It may be that in order to understand a thinker like René Girard we need to expand our conception of both "the religious" and of "religious scripture," and recognize the extent to which scriptural writing, like the writing we have identified for the past two hundred years in European culture as the "literary," participates in the deepest and most thorough-going questioning available to us.[6]

Does that mean that in order to participate in a Girardian perspective one needs of necessity at least to share his reverence for Jewish and Christian interpretative readings? Again, not necessarily. Girard has asserted that his reading is a "scientific hypothesis" and indeed his claim has been taken very seriously by a number of researchers interested, for example, in the phenomena of mirror neurons.[7] We may identify a Girardian reading of archaic cultures, even one he identifies with Judaism and Christianity, as rigorously scientific without subscribing to any of the currently reigning religious or scientific views, views that may, in fact, only extend the representational understanding of these matters we have inherited from Platonic and Aristotelian philosophy. In my own work, I have tried to identify Girard's perspective as a species of prophetic thinking, as aligned with the "the prophetic" following the intuition of Martin Buber and Franz Rosenzweig in this endeavor—who see in it the interpretative structure "behind" the great prophetic writers of the ancient sixth century in Hebrew-speaking communities.[8] But my identification (or, more precisely, my use of Buber's and Rosenzweig's identification) is no more sacrosanct than any of the others.

Roel Kaptein is keenly aware of this state of affairs. Girardianism, like Greek tragedy, leads us to the door of the ethical by providing the critique of the sacrificial on which it is necessarily to be based, but does not—by constitution cannot—take us through that door. To do that we need another orientation. Kaptein finds that additional orientation in Emmanuel Levinas and, in particular, in the "defenseless" face of the other individual.[9] The face of the other individual, to which we are bound as a captive or hostage to a hostage taker, is the face of the victim, the face of the scapegoat, the face of the one we have blamed unjustly for the violence we ourselves have committed (whether the individual who bears that face has committed any violence or not). The face of the other individual is the face of the figure in Isaiah 53 who, "although he had done no violence," is counted among the evildoers, and whose punishment (or "stripes") "heals us" and leads us to proclaim in complete misunderstanding (and denial of our own responsibility) that "God or the Lord has caused this to happen to him."[10]

Roel Kaptein is a Christian so, like Girard, he interprets Girard's ideas about imitative desire and scapegoating in preeminently Christian terms. "In this way, the gospels ask us to look at Jesus, who shows us who we are, bringing us to the place we must find in order to find new life, freedom. It is the place we fear most, that of the scapegoat."[11] Jesus for him, we may say, is a "knowing Levinasian," bringing us to the place where we may find escape from these sacrificial trials, the place which is also at the origin of our fear, and thus for Kaptein of conflict. For Roel Kaptein, these remarks as prefatory to the book that follows offer a way of opening the door, not just to the temporary resolutions of conflicting agendas, but to more enduring reconciliatory ones.

Other conflict resolution theorists within the Girardian fold have made similar moves. Vern Neufeld Redekop, for example, similarly picks up on the importance of the work of Levinas for a Girardian approach to conflict resolution. Here is Redekop on Levinas:

> Emmanuel Levinas contrasts the concepts of totality and infinity. Totality is an approach to life in which the core of one's being—one's inner life, one's identity—can be grasped and controlled. Within each of us, however, is a vast, infinite universe of thought, feeling, spirit, memory, aspiration, and a host of other factors. The human face is the exterior manifestation of this infinite *interiority*, but it is in the *exteriority* of the face of the Other through which the fullness of humanity is encountered. Communication—using language in face-to-face interaction—is the bridge between Self and Other.[12]

Redekop takes things a bit further than Kaptein. He situates Levinas within the phenomenological setting in which Levinas's work specifically arises. Levinas's postulation occurs in the course of his meditation on traditional understandings of self and other, a reevaluation of traditional understandings of the constitution of identity in context of subjects and objects and, in particular, the role of the ethical. In *Totality and Infinity*, for example, Levinas's first major publication (written in 1961, the same year—as Benoît Chantre astutely points out—as Girard's "Romantic Lie and Novelistic Truth"), Levinas argues that traditional subjectivity has curiously excluded the category of the moral and that if we are not to be "duped" by the morality we are offered in the wake of Kantian analysis—a consciousness that is distinguishable from conscience—we will need to rethink subjectivity accordingly. In phenomenology, as in Jewish understanding, Levinas will argue, "ethics is an optics."[13] There is no non-ethical realm. The ethical is already in place once the sensory is activated. The ethical is built in to our very encounter with the other individual, although our traditional renderings of that ontological encounter have failed to observe that ethical conditioning. And the "human face" for Levinas (as Redekop notes) is the place where in customary encounters this obligation originates, the gateway or opening through which the infinite passes, so to speak. To the extent that we can take stock of this occurrence of the "infinite within the finite," and give up the veritable warfare to which the ontological totalizing analyses constructed in the wake of Hegel and Kant commits us, we may be able to move beyond the conflicts seeking resolutions in which we most commonly find ourselves. More specifically, to the extent that we can shift our familiar understanding of self and others, and use language in a way that owns what Levinas calls the *dire* before the *dit*, the "to say" before the "said," we may gain some headway in face-to-face interactions and move toward constructing a "bridge" over troubled ontological waters.

It is toward a clarification of the four ideas coming from Levinas and dominating the above passage that I would like to move in the essay that follows. The ideas of totality (and concomitantly of the infinite), of the face as an opening of gateway, of the Other (or the neighbor or the other individual), and of language or communication as a distinction between the *dire* and the *dit* are central to Levinas's conception of things. Levinas uses these ideas with great precision within the analysis he undertakes, and it behooves us to do the same in using them as intellectual tools. In looking more closely at Levinas's work in this way, we may provide a complement to a Girardian understanding of these matters and advance conflict resolution theorizing a bit, edging it a little closer to an ethical account of human behavior and thereby to its stated goal of reconciliation.

Part Two: Totality, the Face, the Other, and Language

"Totality" as Levinas uses the word is a reference to Hegel, and, in particular, what Franz Rosenzweig calls Hegel's "philosophy of the all" or "philosophy of the whole."[14] In *The Phenomenology of Spirit*, for example, Hegel set out to trace the history of the absolute in Western culture, a history beginning in ancient Greece and concluding, literally, in Hegel's time amidst the sounds of the French Revolution that he heard outside his window as he was writing its final passages.[15] Its content, in his view, was consciousness and its burgeoning awareness of both itself (and thus the subject or "self-consciousness") and its objects. Dissatisfied with this account as just one more treatment of God, the world, or mankind for its exclusivity (one that in Hegel's case simply emphasizes the last), Rosenzweig sets out to do something different: to trace the relations between these three philosophic nodes in terms he labels creation, revelation, and redemption as three modalities of the "infinite within the finite."[16]

The idea is decisive for Levinas who finds in it a new non-representational understanding of temporality and combines Rosenzweig's insight with an account of the infinite he finds in Descartes.[17] Levinas's project is nothing less than a reconstruction of subjectivity itself. We traditionally define subjectivity in terms of self and other. We start out in the domain of the familiar and the same. We venture out through sensory experience (and the enjoyment it confers upon us) until we bump up against the other, at which point we begin our return journey to our point of origin. Upon reaching home, we recount our round-trip journey as a narrative of self-formation, confident that we have fully elaborated the self, the other, and the identity they construct for us.

Levinas's account introduces important conceptual changes. Firstly, the self that feels satisfactorily defined by the journey's conclusion differs in the first place from the agency who began in the realm of the familiar, an agency Levinas names the "self-same." Secondly, what this earlier agency encounters as a limit and names the "other" (to distinguish it from itself) is more complicated than suspected. The other hides another foreigner to the self-same, another or second other, the real other individual also making the same journey and yet radically separated from our metaphysical protagonist by an exteriority or alterity that is non-traversable.

Finally, when the traveler returns to the "home" he thought he left, he finds himself in effect in a "no-man's land." Far from "round-trip," the journey has proved singularly "one-way," and he now identifies for himself, in context of a new internal experience of the Other, an unlimited responsibility he can no more shirk than he can shirk his own death. For all its pretense, the ego, and its account of this egoic journey, has been shattered, and far from free or in control of its experience and its encounters, the ego finds itself hostage to the other individual and to a responsibility that had been conferred upon it before the journey began, a responsibility from which, in fact, its real freedom turns out to be delimited.

The key to this breach of totality and our conceptualization of the movement beyond is the infinite and its accessibility through the face. The infinite for Levinas is the "more within the less," the "container within the contained." And Levinas often refers to "the infinite" borrowing Rosenzweig's conceptualization of the "infinite within the finite": not the finite within the infinite, nor the finite plus the infinite, but, more precisely, the infinite *within* the finite.[18]

Why is this definition important? Because this is where traditionally we have located the divine. The divine in Levinas has traditionally been presented to us at a remove of radical externality, radical alterity, unlimited separation—for example, in the medieval definition of God as "a circle whose center is everywhere and whose circumference is nowhere."[19] And yet what our traveler encounters, first in the other that is not an other, then in the same that is not the same, is that the infinite separation is to be found "closer to home."

Where? In the face. The face, *le visage*, is in Levinas's conception the gateway through which the infinite passes. What allows us to escape totality, to pass beyond and open onto the infinite, is the face. The face, for Levinas, is a passageway, an opening. It is not an object, or a manifestation, or a form of any kind. If we had to delimit the face, Levinas says, we would have to say that the face is nakedness itself, defenselessness itself, utter vulnerability, a "passivity more passive than the opposite of active." It is the speaking of the commandments, or, more precisely, of all the commandments as one commandment in particular, the speaking of the "Thou shalt not kill." The face is the *dire*, the "to say" (or "saying") as opposed to the said (which is that from which systems of signs are derived). It is "signifyingness itself," Levinas tells us.[20]

And in its wake, we are held captive. We are its hostages, no more free to walk away from it than we are free to have the other individual die in our place. Why? Because to walk away from the other individual, to reject the face of the Other, is to walk away from consciousness itself, and from everything consciousness entails.

There are thus finally for Levinas two others in phenomenological discussion: the non-self which stands in contrast to everything I identify as mine, and the other individual who is also doing that. French has two different words for these two very different conceptions. *L'autre* refers to the other pure and simple, whatever falls into that category, whatever is not mine. *L'autrui*, on the other hand, refers to the neighbor, the other individual standing next to me or in front of me who is doing roughly the same that I am doing—for example, making self-other distinctions. It is customary in writing about Levinas to render the first as simply "the other" and to say in the case of the second "the other individual," "the neighbor," or to write is as "the Other" with a capital "O."

And mention of the other individual leads us to language or communication. Language as communication is decidedly not for Levinas a system of signs. Rather it is welcome, hospitality, an openness to the orphan, the widow, the poor, in short, the disenfranchised of all species. As in the case of the face, Levinas distinguishes in language what has already been said from what is in the process of being said, what is still open—infinitely so—to what transpires before us.

◆   ◆   ◆

How does this discussion impact the discussion we have been having vis-à-vis conflict resolution read in connection with Girard and Levinas? René Girard's thinking offers us the best account available of the sacrificial and its mechanism. It is an account that has long been available to us, Girard insists, long before he expressed it: in Greek tragedy, for example; in Hebrew scripture; and especially in Christian scripture. But his account does not tell us what to do about it. There is no morality attached to Girard's ideas, however Christian his references turn out to be, and however Christian he himself is personally.

For an account of the ethical dimensions of the crisis, we must turn elsewhere—in this case to the thought of Emmanuel Levinas. And Levinas does not disappoint on that score. If conflict resolution theory seeks ways of describing a shift in orientation that allow for a redefinition of self, ways of reconstructing our conceptualization of identity so that what currently generates conflict finds a less conflictual home within it, Levinas would appear to fill the bill. His entire project is a new account of subjectivity, a movement away from one grounded in consciousness (and which posits a moral faculty as distinguishable from other non-moral faculties as we have learned from Kant and Hegel) to one grounded in our infinite obligation to the other individual (accessible in this instance via the face and language) in which the entire fabric of consciousness is moral and in which ethics is an optics, a way of seeing, a vision that focuses upon the other individual before me in my face-to-face encounter without limiting that gaze to formal manifestations.

There is one hitch, however, and this point is as important for Levinas studies as the non-theological nature of Girard's ideas is for Girardian studies. What Levinas offers is a descriptive ethical orientation, not a prescriptive one. His account of ethical consciousness is no more of a "remedy" to the sacrificial crisis than Girard's account is. What he offers that Girardian theory does not offer is an account in full of ethical dimensions of our dilemma: namely, our infinite responsibility for others, the fact that our relation to others passes already through the ethical not as an add-on or supplementary feature but as its very fabric. How we instrumentalize that responsibility, how we enact justice, for example, in the context in which a third person appears and my infinite responsibility to the other is doubled (since it remains in effect for each of the others facing me) is still open to discussion. Indeed, it may be that from both Girardian and Levinasian perspectives that is what our scriptural texts are all about, how we enact these sacrificial mechanisms and these ethical obligations in this or that situation in which we happen to find ourselves, situations in which the customary way of doing things would lead to disaster.

◆   ◆   ◆

An anecdote might help to amplify these distinctions. When I met Levinas for the first (and only) time in summer of 1994, the woman who lived in the apartment down the hall from his on rue Michel-Ange (I was later to learn) came to the door from within his apartment to greet me. After introducing herself, she introduced Emmanuel and Raïssa Levinas. "Permit me to introduce Monsieur and Madame Levinas," she said to me (in French), "I am the neighbor." "Indeed," I reflected to myself. "I have heard a great deal about you!" And as I entered his home after the introductions, and we were walking to the area of the room where our discussions would take place, Levinas said to me (in French), "I have been thinking that hospitality, the welcome, politeness, is everything."

The welcome—of the orphan, the widow, the poor, the disenfranchised of all stripes—is the key to all of it. The face of the victim in Girard's understanding and Levinas's. Do we not have in that welcoming gesture—as the ancient prophetic texts teach us—the pathway to all conflict resolution?

Part Three: Conclusions for Conflict Resolution

The story goes that King Solomon was brought in to adjudicate between two women with rival claims to a human life—a young baby who was also in the room. The two women have been part of the profession of prostitutes and have each had babies. The woman first to speak claims that the other woman had a baby (as she herself did), that the baby (of the other woman) died during the night, and that the other woman then switched the living child with the deceased one and now claims that the living child (born in fact of the first woman) is her own and has been stolen from her. The second speaker—the second woman—tells a similar story. Yes, they both had babies. Yes, one of the babies died during the night. But, in fact, the baby who died during the night was the child of the first woman who now blames the mishap upon her colleague and would steal her own rightful living child whom she has placed before the king.

Solomon is faced with a dilemma. If he credits the first woman's story, then justice may or may not be served. If the living baby (placed before them) is the child of the first woman, and he awards the child to the first speaker, then indeed the rightful mother has reclaimed her child. Whatever grief has inspired the second woman to steal the child of the first is separable from the fact that the living child is born from the body of the first woman. But what if the woman is lying? What if, indeed, what the second woman says is true, and the child before them is truly the child of the second speaker, a child the first woman lost during the night to death? Then in awarding the child to the first speaker he will have given the child to the mother whose child has died and participated in the theft of the living child from its rightful living mother.

Consideration in this instance of the truth, in short, of the empirical truth, would not seem a judicious path to justice. It may yield justice. But it may as well participate in its opposite. If ever there was a situation in which conflict resolution theory would be of assistance, this would seem to be one.

What does Solomon do? He redefines what counts as the "mother." The "mother" —whether empirically accurate or not—is the one who would sacrifice herself for the life of the child. The mother is the individual who would assume infinite responsibility for the other individual, for the other's responsibility, for the other's death. How is that determined? The king orders that the child be cut in half, that the child be treated as property, as an object. One woman is satisfied with that solution. The other is not. And Solomon now has his answer. He awards the child to the one who relinquishes her claim to the child for fear that it would cost the child its life.

What has taken place? Solomon has read the situation prophetically. The child could come indeed from either woman. And barring the introduction of testimony of witnesses there is no way of knowing which one is speaking accurately. The best candidate for the child's future well-being— which is all that is really of concern here given the ambiguity of all other considerations—will have to be decided on another basis. And Solomon makes a decision: it is the woman who can think prophetically, who can see where the road is leading—in this case to the death of the living child—and can act on that basis. If laying claim to the child results in the child's death, in insisting either upon my right or the empirical truth of the matter results in the death of the child, then my right and the empirical truth must themselves be abandoned for the sake of the child's life. A new theory of sacrifice must be adopted. Only in such a way can justice be served, a justice based not upon the empirical truth exclusively (although that truth is considered), or even upon the juridical rights of one individual over another exclusively (although those rights are also to be considered) but upon human life itself and my infinite responsibility for it, my responsibility, that is to say, to shoulder on earth the responsibilities of God, to shoulder the "otherwise than being," the otherwise than the ontological warfare in which since the nineteenth century our subjectivity conditions us to be embroiled.

It is to such responsibility that both the work of René Girard and Emmanuel Levinas lead us, a responsibility to which Girard points us in his book on Dostoyevsky written shortly after the publication of *Romantic Lie*, and to which Levinas will point us in the second major volume of his phenomenological enterprise (written in 1974).[21] It is a responsibility to which neither Girard nor Levinas lay originary claim since in their view both Jewish and Christian traditions (among other traditions) already refer us to such responsibility throughout, and to which I would like to suggest in the present essay that conflict resolution theorists, following the examples of Roel Kaptein and Vern Redekop, would be well-advised to pay significant heed.

From the Sacred to the Holy

René Girard, Emmanuel Levinas, and Substitution

Subjectivity is from the first substitution offered in place of another, but before the distinction between freedom and nonfreedom. Not a victim offering itself in his place, which would suppose there is a reserved region of subjective will behind the subjectivity of substitution. It is the null-place in which inspiration by the other is also expiation for the other, the psyche by which consciousness itself would come to signify. . . . Substitution is not the psychological event of compassion or intropathy in general, but makes possible the paradoxical psychological possibilities of putting oneself in the place of another. The subjectivity of the subject, as being subject to everything, is a pre-originary susceptibility, before all freedom and outside of every present. It is accused in uneasiness or the unconditionality of the accusative, in the "here I am" (*me voici*) which is obedience to the glory of the Infinite that orders me to the other. "Each of us is guilty before everyone for everyone, and I more than the others," writes Dostoyevsky in *Brothers Karamazov*. The subjectivity of the subject is persecution and martyrdom.

—Emmanuel Levinas[1]

Responsibility for the other, in its antecedence to my freedom, . . . an exposure [to the other] without holding back . . . is the frankness . . . of saying

... offering itself even in suffering. Substitution, at the limit of being, ends up in saying, in the giving of signs, ... But this saying remains, in its activity, a passivity, more passive than all passivity, for it is a sacrifice without reserve, without holding back, and in this non-voluntary—the sacrifice of a hostage designated who has not chosen himself to be hostage, but possibly elected by the Good, in an involuntary election not assumed by the elected one. For the Good cannot enter into a present nor be put into a representation. But, being Good, it redeems the violence of its alterity, even if the subject has to suffer through the augmentation of this ever more demanding violence.

—Emmanuel Levinas[2]

It is as though persecution by another were at the bottom of solidarity with another.

—Emmanuel Levinas[3]

All the transfers of feeling, with which the theorists of original war and egoism explain the birth of generosity (it is, however, not certain that war was at the beginning, before the altars), would not succeed in being fixed in the ego if it were not with its whole being, or rather with its whole disinterestedness, subjected not, like matter, to a category, but to the unlimited accusative of persecution. The self, a hostage, is already substituted for the others.

—Emmanuel Levinas[4]

Rabbinical thought states the extent of responsibility: "... to the point of being delivered over to stoning and insults" on the part of the very one for whom the responsible one answers. (Cf. Rashi's *Commentary* on Numbers 12:12 which here follows the ancient tradition of Siphri.)

—Emmanuel Levinas[5]

The position of victims [*la position des victimes*] in a world in disorder, which is to say, a world where the good does not triumph, is suffering. It reveals a God who, renouncing all helpful manifestation, appeals to the full maturity of the integrally responsible man. . . . The suffering of the

just individual for a justice which is without triumph is lived concretely as
Judaism. Israel—historic and carnal—becomes again a religious category.

—Emmanuel Levinas[6]

Prologue

I want to begin with this quote from Levinas, from the preface to the second
(augmented) edition of *De Dieu qui vient à l'idée* (Paris: Vrin, 1986) which
appeared no later than 1986:

> This work, which attempts to find the traces of the coming of God to mind
> [*la venue de Dieu à l'idée*], of his descent upon our lips and his inscription
> in books, limits itself to the point at which, thanks to the upwelling of
> the human within being, there can be an interruption or suspension of the
> impenitent perseverance of being in its being, that of universal inter-ested-
> ness, and consequently of the struggle of all against all. This interruption
> or dis-inter-estedness is produced in human beings responding for their
> fellow man who, as another person, is a stranger to them. Such a responsi-
> bility is the response to the imperative of gratuitous love, which comes to
> me from the face of another where abandonment and the election tied to
> his uniqueness signify simultaneously; this is the order of being-for-the-
> other or of holiness [*sainteté*] as the source of every value.[7]

Here, in the second preface to *De Dieu qui vient à l'idée* (which makes
it one of the last texts Levinas writes), Levinas reflects upon his intention in
the book that follows (that he has elsewhere described as part of a sequence
that begins with *Totality and Infinity* and *Otherwise Than Being*).[8] This book,
he tells us, is limited to describing the point at which a certain "interruption"
or "suspension" of being occurs. He is impressed by this interruption as a
break with the *conatus essendi*, the famous "persistence in being" with which
he has been struggling since encountering the idea in Heidegger as a student
some fifty years earlier, a being here imagined as he described warfare at the
outset of *Totality and Infinity*, namely, as the struggle of "all against all." It
is a being that he has since (in *Otherwise Than Being*) come to understand

precisely as inter-estedness, which is to say, a being-in-the-world that is also a being interred or being buried in the world. And thus the interruption or suspension of the ontological perseverance in such a world (a suspension of course recalling and rejecting Kierkegaard's famous suspension of the ethical), insofar as it is thus precisely a "dis-inter-estedness" (and thus also an echo and criticism of Kant's discussion of the moral imperative), a gesture of "dis-interring" or unearthing the human from being, that leads us to a responsibility for the other individual, a responsibility defined as a response to a commandment or imperative coming to us from the face of the other individual, a responsibility that comprises an "answerabilty" (a responsibility "for" although not necessarily a responsibility "to"), and that responds to a commandment for gratuitous love. It comes from a face that has known abandonment (or exclusion or assignation or accusation) tied to his election or uniqueness (or being singled out), and it participates in what Levinas calls holiness or saintliness as the foundation for all possible value.

It does not require an especially careful or subtle reader to recognize in this transition from the war of all against all (echoed in the totalitarian thinking of Hegel) to saintliness or holiness (as the source of all value) the same passage that René Girard describes in his many books as the movement from the sacrificial or sacred violence to the refusal of violence that Girard identifies in his latest work with the holy.[9] In Girard, the dynamics of the sacred and the sacrificial in its relation to violence and the mechanism of exclusionary behavior and the surrogate victim are described a little more fully than they are in Levinas. And in Levinas the dynamics of the ethical in its relation to responsibility, answerability, gratuitous love, "dis-interestedness," are described a little more fully than they are in Girard. But the end points of both writers would seem, I would suggest, fundamentally the same. They are both in the process of describing the passage from the sacred to the saintly or holy.

In the essay that follows, I would like to expand upon that commonality of design and in particular focus upon what I take to be its center: namely, substitution. If the end points are the same, and we wish to see the same movement take place, we could well imagine that the central structure in one case would be cognate with the central structure in the other. I want to suggest that substitution comprises precisely that cognate structure.

I will start by describing the idea of substitution in Girard's work, and then turn to describe it in Levinas's work. Finally, I will ask about the implications of such an "interdisciplinary" reading for both writers and perhaps for the variety of disciplines they engage, disciplines that may not be limited to philosophy and anthropology, but may open us to literary reading and readings from within religious studies.

Part One: Girard, the Sacred, and Substitution

At the root of René Girard's work are three ideas: mimetic desire, the relation between the sacred and violence (vis-à-vis sacrifice and the scapegoat mechanism), and the role of Hebrew and Christian scriptures in bringing to light this understanding.

In *Mensonge romantique et vérité romanesque* (1961), Girard first proposed that desire is imitative. Reading the tradition of the great European novel, from Cervantes, to Stendhal, Flaubert, Dostoyevsky, and Proust, Girard noticed that desire in the books of these writers is never perceived as issuing from the object but always revealed as proceeding *selon l'autre*, that one chooses one's desires not according to the needs of the subject, nor according to the exigencies of the object, but rather in accord with a third party that one has designated as one's "mediator" or "model." Moreover, that imitative or mimetic or mediated desire almost always issues in conflict. And finally, that the writers of these books have themselves been trapped within the prison house of this "metaphysical" desire and its consequences, and the great novel is in fact the story of his (or her) emancipation from its constraints, a liberation from sickness or illness that Girard identifies in the final chapter as a kind of resurrection and often the consequence of the writer's deathbed insight and imagined in specifically Christian terms.

Following *Mensonge romantique*, one might have expected that Girard would continue to show the strategic presence of triangular desire in other literary contexts. But he began reading Greek tragedy—Sophocles's *Oedipus Tyrannus*, Euripides's *The Bacchae*, among others—and wondering to what extent the religions and cultures we have inherited from the ancients retained traces of still older structures that were currently in crisis, and to what extent archaic communities in general were able to manage this imitative or mimetic desire and its violent consequences in ways that escaped us.

In *La violence et le sacré* (1972), he proposed his second major thesis, that culture itself may be ordered sacrificially, that all cultures on the planet may constitute, among other things, elaborate management systems for the control of appropriated desires through rituals that originate in the mechanisms of sacrificial expulsion and lynching.

The dominant assumption of French ethnology of the time was Durkheimian and his major interlocutors in anthropology were Marcel Mauss and Claude Lévi-Strauss. If we regard culture as a set of distinctions or differences, and accept the idea that all cultures on the planet distinguish between the sacred and the profane (as articulated, for example, by a writer like Mircea Eliade), then Girard argues that the sacred and the violence are one and the same. The sacred is violence that has been kept out of the city, sequestered in its outermost regions, cordoned off, so to speak, and violence is the sacred that has escaped from its sequestered and outlawed condition and runs amok within city limits. The distinction between the two, he offers, is established and maintained by sacrificial ritual that derives from (and continues to be organized by) a mechanism of collection expulsion or surrogate victimage to which we attach the Biblical word or concept of "scapegoating."

How so? Systems of difference break down. They do so either naturally or accidentally, either through periods of attrition and wear and tear (in ways that echo the laws of inertia in thermodynamics), or as the consequence of invasion or attack from without (or within). And when they do, the very structures of difference that once assisted and remedied the problem at hand now compound and exacerbate it. Two figures that were once distinguishable now give way to the reciprocal violence of enemy twins. One minute Oedipus welcomes Teiresias as the savior of the city who will help solve the Theban plague, and the next they are at each other's throats, each accusing the other of having started the generalized miasma. Difference itself has become none other than violence as it comes to be asserted in the extreme, invoked in a context in which it is no longer efficacious, and in which the remedy has become itself the poison or the good gone wrong.

Left unchecked in Girard's view, this violence will quickly issue in what political scientists like Hobbes describe as "the war of all against all" and at that moment a very strange thing occurs. As the pitch or frenzy of mutual accusation and counter accusation approaches a paroxysm, and the set of differentiated human beings becomes a set of human doubles, the enemy twin of each can instantaneously become the enemy twin of all. The most arbitrary and insignificant of differences—hair color, skin color, stature, the fact that one is present or absent—can quickly become absolute. William Faulkner illustrates this strange transformation in a story in which a black man is suddenly sought out and killed because he is a black man when some "good ole boys" happen to be standing around a barber shop and the discussion turns to the recent alleged rape of a white woman.[10]

Once that happens, once the war of all against all turns uncontrollably into the war of all against one, a curious result obtains. If the project is carried through to completion and the arbitrary victim is destroyed, peace returns. Just as suddenly as it began, the violence ends. And the community postulates that the victim must have been the god in disguise all along, and that next year the same drama should be reenacted in order to derive from it some of its beneficial effects. Ritual commemoration will reproduce both the "sacrificial crisis" (the breakdown of differences) and its resolution (the collective victimage or scapegoating) up to a point. Dionysos came down among the Cadmeans and, posing as a stranger within the city, stirred up all the frenzy of the *bacchantes* that issued in his rending or *sparagmos* (in the figure of Pentheus). Next year we will reproduce these Dionysian rites in the hope of encouraging these Apollonian effects.

Girard's thesis is that something like this double communal drama originates all ritual and religion in communities ethnologists designate as primitive or archaic, functioning for them as something like what linguists would call a real referent. Drawing upon themes (like the scapegoat) from Frazer and the Cambridge anthropologists, Girard finds social structure to derive not from superstition and the imaginary (which is where these nineteenth century thinkers locate its origins) but in the sustaining of real social relations. And drawing upon Freud's theses regarding murder and sacrifice at the foundation of social organization (for example, in the "primal hordes"), Girard proposes for these ideas a more mainstream context, as the basis for all social difference or distinction. If we haven't recognized this sacrificial crisis to this point, if we can view Euripides's staging of the Dionysian drama without being undone by it, it is because we remain protected in some way from its deleterious effects. That "way," in Girard's view, is the Jewish and Christian scripture which systematically exposes such sacrificial origins and thereby poses for us our modern dilemma: namely, how to live anti-sacrificially, how to refuse violence. In *Des choses cachées depuis la fondation du monde*, Girard suggests that first Judaism and then Christianity reveals for us these origins in the wake of which we continue to live.

Thus, substitution plays a key role in Girard's thinking, and there are some five or six different senses in which it operates. In the first case, as we have seen above the war of all against all is replaced by the war of all against one. But immediately upon its conclusion follows the second. In the second, the ritual commemoration is imagined. In place of enacting the original substitution, we will reenact every year a limited version of it in order to preserve its benefits. Taken together these two, the surrogate victimage and its ritual duplication constitute what Girard calls the "double substitution" at the heart of his system.

But circumstances may arise in which a victim for one reason or another no longer works or is no longer available, and another victim must be substituted. Sometimes it happens that, for whatever reason, the ritual victim, the victim who stands in for the original victim, needs to be changed. The cow that we substituted for the original victim needs to be replaced now in turn by a bird, or even by a non-animal form, a cake, for example. This replacement would constitute a third possible substitution. The system would still be in relative working order, but this would be one way the system would compensate for the changing conditions and still maintain itself.

Again, for whatever reason, it may happen that no victim may satisfy and the culture survives in a state of something like permanent sacrificial crisis. Suddenly, it happens that the clash of mutually exclusive cultural systems or a change in the elemental or meteorological conditions in which a community persists unexpectedly alter and no victim is now able to satisfy. The system goes into a kind of tailspin, a more or less perpetual state of sacrificial crisis. This is the condition in which, for example, we find Greek tragedy. The sacrificial system remains more or less in place. The play concludes with an endorsement of the mythic system. But in the course of the play, the end of that myth and the sacrificial system for which it stands in—their very efficacy—has been challenged. One cannot realistically imagine an alternative system taking over. But one can foresee, if only by prophetic perception, so to speak, that if things continue as they are, the day will come when the question asked by the Chorus in the second *stasimon* of Sophocles's most famous play, "*ti dei me choreuein*?" ("Why must I dance?"), will be a realistic one. This situation could readily and accurately be described as a fourth substitution.

And finally, at some point, the idea of a "sacrifice to end all sacrifices" may appear. And if the crisis continues beyond this point, one begins not just to imagine such alternative sacrificial (or even post-sacrificial) arrangements, but to try them out. Our modern political systems would appear to be a function of such developments, perhaps deriving from a cultural perception that the end of sacrifice is in sight. Evolving discernibly from sacrificial origins, modern politics, with its foundation in the idea of a single unit (or multiple units) retaining legitimate use of violence, may be said to be "halfway" between archaic sacrifice and a genuinely post sacrificial system.[11]

Or, alternatively, other substitutes to the ancient sacrificial system are suddenly imaginable. Platonic thinking in the fourth century before our era, for example, and one century after Greek tragedy has vanished from the scene as an original production, appears as a possible formulation of such a post-sacrificial or alternative sacrificial arrangement. As such, it could well appear to qualify as a fifth substitution.

What about learning to live without sacrifice, as Judaism proposes? "After the fall of the Second Temple and the end of the sacrifice," the Rabbis are proverbially cited as saying, "we pray and read." What about the "sacrifice to end all sacrifices" that Christianity proposes? It is clearly a step beyond Greek tragedy. The idea of a post-sacrificial or anti-sacrificial reading is clearly not part of the Greek tragic mode. As such, it too would qualify at least as a fifth substitution. On the other hand, it may even exceed the political alternative. The political may be beyond the archaic sacrificial. But it is clearly not beyond any and all sacrificial systems. Governments concentrate or monopolize the use of legitimate violence in their own hands—at least within the Western political tradition. But that sacrificial deployment continues. As such, the Christian post-sacrificial gesture could be seen either as another version of the fifth substitution or perhaps as constituting itself a sixth substitution.

These are the substitutions about which Girardians speak and some of the questions commonly asked. What about the work of Emmanuel Levinas in this connection? Is there a relation in Levinas to substitution?

Part Two: Levinas, Subjectivity, and Substitution

Substitution, I would argue, is, in fact, at the heart of Levinas's project. In a very real sense, substitution *is* his project.

How so? All of Levinas's philosophic writing is about the reconstitution of subjectivity. The conception of subjectivity or self-construction he inherits from Kant, Hegel, and the German idealist philosophers—principally Husserl and Heidegger—is consciousness-based. I am the subject of consciousness before objects of knowledge. The project is ego driven; I operate in complete freedom. I pursue my goal as philosophers since Plato have done—through reason and decision-making. The result is knowledge, identity, self, and the truth of being and discourse. I thematize myself, objects or things around me, and others as so many subjects (or objects) of my inquiry. Moreover, I do so within a conception of time or temporality understood as Aristotle understood it: with rigidly distinguishable boundaries among its component parts designating a discrete past, present, and future.

But then Levinas encounters Buber, Rosenzweig, Marcel, and others and this account of subjectivity is rendered partial. Why? Primarily because it leaves out the ethical. Kant's moralizing, Hegel's totalizing, Heidegger's ontologizing are all problematic in Levinas's view. Kant's moralizing always goes by way of the universal, the category, what "everyone should do"—in short, the third party. But the ethical, Levinas understands, is dyadic, two-party, and precedes all triadic or third party considerations—the political, the juridical, the social, cultural, or religious (in addition, of course, to the categorical and the universal). Hegel's totalizing is similarly categorical but in addition excludes the infinite that Kant at least retains. Hegel's *Phenomenology* tells the story of the absolute spirit as a young Geist. And Heidegger's "fundamental ontology," for all its initial excitement (following fast chronologically upon Husserl's research), and all the advances in idealist philosophy it promises, finally reduces the "all" no less to being. The ontological adventure is no less round-trip than that of the others, not much of an adventure, really, since it always returns to the same, to the point from which the agency, the freely roaming ipseity, set out. To the extent that the trip is an adventure, it is more like the journey of Homer's Odysseus than like the one-way trip of the biblical Abraham, who leaves home never to return.

Kant's implicit exclusion of the ethical by transcendentalizing it, in other words, Hegel's explicit exclusion by secularizing it within an historical narrative, Heidegger's reduction of the ethical by the substitution of the ontological for it as "first philosophy" are equally inadequate from Levinas's perspective, who will opt instead for Buber's distinguishing of the I-Thou from the I-it, and Rosenzweig's critique of the all in Hegel and the history of philosophy. The ethical precedes the ontological as first philosophy, for Levinas. It is not to be excluded implicitly as a mystical category or as the secondary and derived result of more primary human interactions or excluded explicitly in favor of more highly touted and warring totalitarian powers.

In its place, he will articulate a new subjectivity he would develop in three distinct stages.

For example, in *De l'existence aux existents* (1946), which was published shortly after the Second World War and which still bears the traces of his wartime prison experience, Levinas distinguishes between the something about which Heidegger speaks and a nothingness which he finds too restrictive.

> Let us imagine all beings, things and persons, reverting to nothingness. One cannot put this return to nothingness outside of all events. But what of this nothingness itself? Something would happen, if only night and the silence of nothingness. The indeterminateness of this "something is happening" is not the indeterminateness of a subject and does not refer to a substantive. Like the third person pronoun in the impersonal form of a verb, it designates not the uncertainly known author of the action, but the characteristic of this action itself which somehow has no author. This impersonal, anonymous, yet inextinguishable "consummation" of being, which murmurs in the depths of nothingness itself we shall designate by the term *there is*. The *there is*, inasmuch as it resists a personal form, is "being in general." . . . The anonymous current of being invades, submerges every subject, person or thing. The subject-object distinction by which we approach existents is not the starting point for a meditation which broaches being in general.
>
> We could say that the night is the very experience of the *there is*, if the term experience were not inapplicable to a situation which involves the total exclusion of light.[12]

In the face of this *il y a* or "there is," one imagines subjectivity, Levinas says, as a going and coming he names a "hypostasis," by which he means literally the positing or positioning of oneself outside of oneself and the return to oneself from that outside (he will later characterize this movement as a losing and finding—as an *anamnesis*). Although the discussion of the *il y a* remains the centerpiece of this early book (and he will never again give it the kind of extended treatment he gives it here), it remains fundamentally unchanged for him. Responsibility as a critique of ontology, as "dis-inter-estedness," continues responding to the *il y a*.

But it is in *Totalité et infini* (1961) and *Autrement qu'être ou au-déla de l'essence* (1972) that he takes full stock of that hypostatic structure. In the first book, *Totalité et infini*, he describes going out. The ego agent, the ipseity, the self-same, the oneself, or simply the self, proceeds out through the elemental, through dwelling and labor, through enjoyment and signification, and finally approaches the other individual: a relation with the other being encountered through the other's face (*le visage*). The face, in this context, is vulnerability, utter defenselessness, nudity or nakedness, exposure, a freestanding independent signifying unit that says "Thou shalt not kill."

And this encounter with alterity, after the prior encounter in being with the material world, shelter and provision, self-indulgence, and perception, opens that agency beyond totality to the infinite. What is "the infinite"? A term Levinas finds in Descartes, he uses it to express the more within the less, the container within the contained. The face in this context is the "infinite within the finite," a gateway or opening or entry point to the beyond of being, to radical exteriority or externality, to radical otherness, an otherness that escapes the "allergy" to alterity that the projective economy of the freely roaming ego would establish. One discovers, for example, in the erotic the potential that may issue in an ethical relation—in fecundity, for example—although the erotic remains distinct from the ethical per se. And, in fact, in the first book, the ethical obtains only insofar as one takes stock of what Levinas calls "radical alterity"—the other individual doing the same thing I am doing, a being glimpsed through a face that is not an object of vision.

In the second book, *Autrement qu'être ou au-déla de l'essence*, Levinas describes what could be characterized as the "return trip." One proceeds from the other individual back toward the same, a trip that could well appear simply a reversal of what the self-same has already experienced. But unexpectedly, the traveler overshoots the mark. Intending to return home, he finds him- or herself on the "hither side of home," beyond the starting point. And there he finds himself lodged within an unexpected obligation: infinite or unlimited responsibility for the other individual; a responsibility even greater than that, since it is in effect three responsibilities in one: responsibility for the other, responsibility for the other's responsibility, responsibility for the other's death. The responsibility of the subject in this context can only be compared, Levinas argues, in its depth and scope, to the psychic dimensions of maternity and gestation, the other in the same.

Tracing the encounter with the other in retrograde fashion, he now unearths, in a manner not unlike an archeologist, several distinct steps or strata. Responsibility for him, as a critique of the ontological (manifest as the ego, the elementary, dwelling and work, enjoyment, sensibility, the face, and so forth) is described as "dis-inter-ested." Now he will describe in turn each of seven prior conditions that have shaped that encounter, each corresponding to the regions he has already traversed (see the diagram).

He begins with the face. The face is now understood as pure "signifying-ness," freestanding auto-signification, presentation rather than representation. The face is saying (or the "to say") rather than the said, the *dire* rather than the *dit*. Such saying turns out to be rooted in proximity, the nearness of the other individual doing the speaking, contact, touch, or caress with that individual (as opposed to palpitation). Such proximity is in turn rooted in obsession, the impossibility of putting by, the impossibility of stopping or evading, a constancy or ceaselessness that we may say is more constant than the opposite of interruptive. That obsession in its own turn will show up rooted in passivity, a passivity or bearing or suffering, Levinas describes, as more passive than the opposite of active, a radical abiding or assumability that stands before the opposition of active to passive.

And that passivity is itself rooted in "an-archy." An-archy is used here in the Greek sense of being without qualities, or "qualitylessness," an *anarche* or unruliness or "principle-lessness" that precedes the opposition of rule or principle to chaos. Such anarchy will turn out in its own context rooted in substitution, in a one for the other, or a gestation of the other in the same, the veritable psyche, or subjectivity itself. And such substitution is encountered finally in persecution: in accusation, assignation, wound, trauma, the status of being a hostage, of an I that is in the accusative before being in the nominative.

LEVINASIAN SUBJECTIVITY: HYPOSTASIS

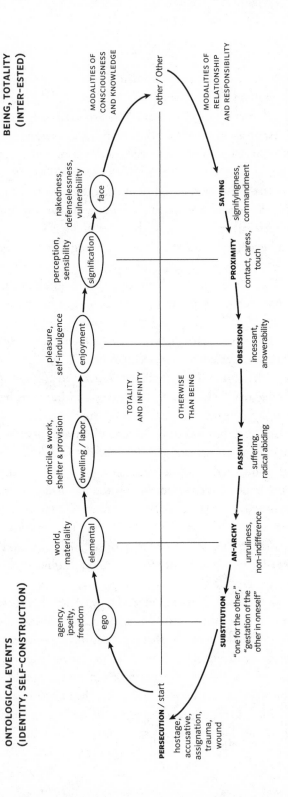

ONTOLOGICAL EVENTS
(IDENTITY, SELF-CONSTRUCTION)

BEING, TOTALITY
(INTER-ESTED)

MODALITIES OF CONSCIOUSNESS AND KNOWLEDGE

other / Other

MODALITIES OF RELATIONSHIP AND RESPONSIBILITY

nakedness, defenselessness, vulnerability — face

perception, sensibility — signification

pleasure, self-indulgence — enjoyment

domicile & work, shelter & provision — dwelling / labor

world, materiality — elemental

agency, ipseity, freedom — ego

SAYING
signifyingness, commandment

PROXIMITY
contact, caress, touch

OBSESSION
incessant, answerability

PASSIVITY
suffering, radical abiding

AN-ARCHY
unruliness, non-indifference

SUBSTITUTION
"one for the other," "gestation of the other in oneself"

TOTALITY AND INFINITY

OTHERWISE THAN BEING

PERSECUTION / start
hostage, accusative, assignation, trauma, wound

GROUND OF BEING
(CONDITIONS)

ETHICAL, INFINITE
(DIS-INTER-ESTED)

And all of these enabling conditions are versions of responsibility. Saying is responsibility as the "thou shalt not kill." Proximity is responsibility as "alongsidedness" or accompaniment, the "I will be there with you" of Biblical fame (in the discussion of the name of God in Exodus 3:12–14), as "dis-inter-estedness" proper. Obsession is responsibility as "the unstoppable," ceaselessness, an incessant answerability. Passivity is responsibility as radical abiding or suffering. Anarchy is responsibility as non-indifference. Substitution is responsibility as the one for the other. Persecution is responsibility as the status of a hostage.

And all correlate, in clockwise direction, in Levinas's schema, with the trip out. Saying correlates with the face, proximity with sensibility, obsession with enjoyment, passivity with work and dwelling, anarchy with the elemental, substitution with the ego, and persecution with home or the starting point.

What exactly does all of this mean? The several conditions from which responsibility for the other individual issue construct for Levinas a heteronomy in place of an autonomy, a subjectivity based upon relationship and responsibility rather than one based upon the freedom of ego, willfulness, and consciousness.

On what is that responsibility itself based? How does it come about? If we accept that all of these founding conditions—saying, proximity, obsession, passivity, an-archy, substitution, persecution—remain versions of responsibility, where does responsibility come from? It responds, of course, we know, to the *il y a*, the ground zero of being, the site of the disaster or horror, the anonymous rustling of being in general. But what makes responsibility an adequate response to the *il y a* rather than, say, something else? Why is responsibility better, for example, than radical egoism?

And secondly—and here is where we approach an answer to our second question above—how does it relate to Girard's work?

The key to both questions—what is the origin of responsibility and how does it relate to Girardian thinking—I suggest, are the last two terms of this series: substitution and persecution. The answer is a substitution founded in particular upon persecution; a responsibility founded upon a substitution founded in turn upon a persecution. It is in uncovering the origin of that persecution that we shall perceive the origins of responsibility and the connection between Girard's thinking and Levinas's.

Part Three: The Sacrificial and the Ethical, Victimage and Subjectivity

Girard's thinking is centered upon the idea of substitution. It describes for him the logic of archaic communities. It describes their transformation. It even describes their breakdown and the attempts to solve the problems those breakdowns occasion. Levinas's thinking is similarly anchored in substitution. It is not an exaggeration to say that for Levinas the psyche, subjectivity, *is* substitution. It is substitution that comprises its fundamental structure, the one for the other, the other in oneself. The gestational idea of loving the other as oneself is not a comparison in Levinas; it is a structural requirement. It is how the system is built and sustained.

When I made a presentation of some of these ideas some years ago at the North American Levinas Society meeting in Seattle (in 2008), an organization that my students founded from my graduate Levinas seminar at Purdue, Georges Hansel kindly offered a response. "It is not the same substitution that you are talking about," he said. And he, of course, was right. Substitution in René Girard's work is the logic of the social. Substitution in Levinas's, on the other hand, is an individual logic, the logic of the ethical insofar as the ethical is a two-party affair, insofar as the ethical precedes the political. Apples and oranges, it would appear. How do we get from one conception to the other? From the social logic to the individual logic?

The answer, it seems to me, which becomes more apparent in comparing Levinas's thought to Girard's than in considering either thinker alone, is that individual subjectivity in Levinas is the appropriation of the position of the victim René Girard would describe as the lynchpin to the exclusionary mechanism. Between the one and the many, Levinas chooses the one that stands for the many. Levinas's subjectivity of substitution and persecution is the appropriation of the Girardian voice of the victim. Substitution, we have said, is at the root of the psyche, of "one for the other." "I am *for* the other" because "I *am* the other." We are dealing, in this case, with a heteronomy, not an autonomy. Loving the other as myself is a structural determinant, not a convenient comparison. And the key to that substitution is persecution; the condition of being a hostage, a wound, assignation, accusation, or trauma. I am always in the accusative before I am in the nominative. But it is in the context of victimage, of the social mechanism of exclusion, that has also ironically served as its structural foundation that we encounter the individual at all.

Persecution, which is at the root of Levinasian substitution, is also the foundation for Girardian substitution in the modern world. Persecution is the good gone wrong, the sacrificial gone wrong. Persecution is victimage. The Levinasian substitution at the root of the ethical and responsibility and the Girardian substitution at the root of the sacrificial and violence in the modern world are one and the same.

Let me clarify one point upon which there may remain (or arise) some confusion—because I can already see Georges Hansel moving around in his seat as I speak. The subjectivity of substitution that is founded on persecution is not simply the subjectivity of a victim which, as Levinas says in my first epigraph, "would suppose there is a reserved region of subjective will behind the subjectivity of substitution." In speaking of the nether region of the ethical before the ontological, Levinas is careful to construct a vocabulary that avoids the language of being. Thus, passivity is a passivity more passive than the opposite of active, or an-archy is conceptualized, in our paraphrase (which is modeled on Levinas's discussion of passivity), as prior to the opposition of rule or principle and its lack, an unruliness, we may say, more unruly than the opposite of ruly or principled. What I am suggesting is that persecution of which Levinas speaks and the substitution it founds is not the subjectivity of the victim (which would be one more version of self-consciousness) but the position of the victim (or the "position of victims," to use a phrase from a later epigraph), the condition in which the victim discovers him- or herself to be a victim, the built-in dimensions or "conditionality" given in advance in which the victim of a sacrificial scapegoating exclusionary social process comes to understand his or her situation, his or her circumstances. "It is," as Levinas says, "the null-place in which inspiration by the other is also expiation for the other, the psyche by which consciousness itself would come to signify." It is this "pre-originary" condition which we would dub "the position of the victim" or "the voice of the victim."

How so? How does Levinas achieve that equation? How does the situation of victimage—between persecuted and persecutor—issue in the subjectivity of the victim? The answer, I suggest, is to be found within the texts of the Hebrew prophets, in the texts supporting welcome and hospitality to the widowed, the orphaned, the stranger, the poor, in short, the dispossessed of every imaginable stripe, ideas that have informed his texts from *Totality and Infinity* on. "You were yourself a stranger in a strange land," the prophet says (that the Lord says), and Levinas endorses that idea throughout.

There is no place here to develop more precisely how the linkage is made, either within the prophetic texts (or, indeed, throughout the Hebrew Bible), between the face as the infinite within the finite and the face as infinite responsibility for the other individual, or between victimage and subjectivity at large, between persecuting behavior and the appropriation of the voice of the persecuted as the model for subjectivity. Suffice it to say for the moment that it is discernibly the perspective of the victim to which Levinas is drawn and for which notions like persecutor, hostage status, accusation, the I who is situated in the accusative case prior to the nominative, assignation, wound, and trauma offer us a convenient index.

The prophetic texts, in other words, occupy for Levinas, as they do for many Jews of his generation, a privileged place.[13] In many ways, the texts of the Hebrew scripture were "written" by the writers of the prophetic texts, since their primary concerns would seem on plentiful display in earlier scriptural passages (Second Isaiah, for example, is often said to reflect the views of these Biblicists as a comparison of Second Isaiah to the Book of Job might readily show). The effects of the collapse of the first Temple in Jerusalem (in 586–87 BCE) can hardly be overestimated. A pre-sixth century Temple-centered scribal Judaism, about which we know relatively little, suddenly found itself in direct contest with a more portable text-centered diasporic Judaism and two fundamentally opposed interest groups were formed: a conservative faction that would return to the ways before the catastrophe (and succeeded, in fact, in rebuilding the Temple), and a more progressive liberal faction that would reconceive Judaism as a text-centered enterprise.[14] In many ways the two groups that emerge as opposed some centuries later—the Sadducees and the Pharisees—point back to these two earlier distinct orientations.

But how the information comes to us, how the linkage is made and transmitted, is another matter. Once we are given the linkage, between the face as the infinite within the finite and face as responsibility, for example, Levinas can elaborate the connection. He can give us the seven versions of responsibility that free us from our allergy to radical otherness, built in to

a subjectivity based on consciousness or self-consciousness. He can show us
how the ethical precedes the ontological, that the ethical is to be defined by
infinite responsibility for the other individual, and that at the root of that
infinite responsibility is a substitution founded in persecution.

Is there anything similar in René Girard's work? In fact, we can show
that Girardian thinking about Christianity also comes directly from the
Hebrew prophets. "The Prophet" for Jesus, par excellence, is Isaiah. And the
key text of Girard's reading of Christianity is the text on the "stoning of the
prophets."

> You say that had you been there, you would not have done that [namely,
> stoned the prophets]. But don't you see [the prophet continues] that in
> saying as much, in distancing yourself from those who stoned the prophets,
> you do the same thing once again. You put yourself at a sacred or sacrificial
> distance from those who stoned the prophets, which is precisely what
> stoning the prophets was about in the first place. You "stone the prophets"
> once again and this time right in front of us. And what's more, you do it
> in my name, [Jesus says (Girard says)]. And even more than that, you will,
> in fact, do the same to me for saying so to you, for telling you the truth of
> your own violence.

Historical Christianity for Girard, in *Des choses cachées depuis la fondation du
monde*, is the long history of that denunciation and neo-sacrificial repetition
of scapegoat victimage, a taking stock of the stoning of the prophets in such
a way that repeats the stoning of the prophets, in full view of the texts of the
Hebraic prophets in which such sacrificial, anti-sacrificial, and neo-sacrificial
behavior was already on full display, and what the writers of those books,
as well as the actors within them—prophets, like Isaiah, for example—were
observing being practiced around them.

There is no space in the present very limited context to develop this
argument here. As in the case of Levinas, we can only allude to it and set
it aside for later elaboration. Suffice it to say for the moment that Girard's
thought in my own estimation is entirely consonant with the thought of the
Hebrew prophets regarding sacrifice, scapegoating, and the role they play
in the formation of societies just as much as Levinas's thought is entirely
consonant with the prophets regarding the ethical premises of living life as a

witness to the Lord (as advocated in Second Isaiah). If Girard's thought takes up the sacred charge—what good are all your sacrifices?—Levinas's thought takes up the ethical remedy to the situation (or at least one ethical remedy): the appropriation of the position of the victim by everyone. Subjectivity, whether considered as deriving from the confessional practices surrounding the exercise of self-examination taken up by the Roman Catholic churches in the early centuries of the modern era or considered as deriving from nineteenth century secular philosophic sources, remains grounded in the voice of the victim. For Levinas, subjectivity itself is already substitution, radical susceptivity. Founded upon the ethical, an ethical which is, in turn, a matter of responsibility, responsibility understood as the "one for the other," or more precisely, the "other in me," subjectivity in Levinas is gestational, the literal embodiment of "loving the other as oneself."

The ethical for Levinas, in other words, is not a category of subjectivity—as it is for a thinker like Kant—but thoroughly infuses subjectivity. In the Heideggerian vocabulary, formulated somewhere between being and nothingness, responsibility is a response to the *il y a*. Responsibility alone meets the *il y a* on its own terms. And subjectivity is an extension of that responsibility, its very fabric, as it were. The ethical is simply another way of describing that infinite responsibility to which I am summoned for the other individual. My subjectivity, my internalization of "the one for the other," is my response to "the other in me." It is my answerability for the other, and it is not a voluntary one. It is "built in" to the possibility of me being me. I am given as the other's "redeemer" so to speak, as this concept is used, for example, in the Book of Ruth. "Take me for him," subjectivity says, as Yehuda says to his father Ya'akov, with regard to his son Benjamin. I am his substitute.

On the other hand, that same subjectivity (constituted as it is by ethical responsibility) is also said to be precisely a response to persecution. I am not in the nominative case but the accusative, always already a response to assignation, violation, transgression or violence. Why? From what sources does such violence derive? The source is never given in Levinas, although the filiation with violence is clear. Putting Levinas's thought next to Girard's, the answer seems evident. I have internalized the subjectivity of the victim within myself, indeed, *as* myself. The victim of the sacrificial is henceforth the position from which I necessarily speak. Heidegger's fundamental ontology may turn out less fundamental than the ethical.

Part Four: From the Sacred to the Holy

What are the implications of thinking this way? Seeing substitution as critical to both, and seeing that substitution linked in both cases to sacrificial victimage and persecution answers all kinds of questions for both Girardians and Levinasians.

For Girardians, it gives the theory an ethical component where none existed before. The Girardian understanding of the sacrificial has no predetermined ethical component or ethical consequence. Perhaps because Girard himself remains a committed Christian, or perhaps for other reasons, his thinking has often been confused with Christianity as if it is, in fact, an extension of Roman Catholicism, a version of Augustinian thinking.

Let me speak as clearly as I can on this point. Girardianism is not Christianity, or any version of Christianity, in any of its forms, although the thinking that animates Girard's readings of Christian texts—and especially the Evangelical text—is very much a part of Girardianism.

Girardianism reads the texts of Jewish scripture and the texts of Christian scripture as articulating truths about the sacrificial (and to some extent about the mimetic nature of desire and its dynamics). But it is not interchangeable in any manner with a Christian ethical position. The most we are able to say of an ethical nature after Girard's analysis of the sacrificial in archaic culture (and of our own position since then in a kind of perpetual sacrificial crisis) is *"il faut refuser la violence"* ("we must refuse violence"). We must read and understand "anti-sacrificially."

And that is fine, we may add; we can certainly endorse the importance of reading anti-sacrificially. The ancient rabbis say as much. But what exactly does that entail? How specifically does one do that?

One example for Girard (and Girardians) has been literary writers. In fact, before the last chapter of *Mensonge romantique et vérité romanesque*, one might well have anticipated that Girard would turn out, like so many other literary readers, to put literature in the central and governing position.

Part of the attraction for me, in fact, as an English major in an American university, to Girard's readings of the great European novel—Cervantes, Stendhal, Flaubert, Proust, Dostoyevsky—and of Greek tragedy—in the hands of Sophocles, and before him Aeschylus, and after him Euripides—was,

I confess, the inordinate value Girard seemed to have invested in these literary productions. And if I later turned to Jewish writing in his shadow—to scriptural, Talmudic, midrashic, mystical, and the later Rabbinic traditions of commentary—it was inevitably because I saw in this Jewish writing and in Rabbinic thought in general the same anti-sacrificial perspectives, the same "literary" perspectives, that Girard identified in European literature and in Greek tragedy.

But Girard did not, in fact, continue as a reader of literary works, as we all know, and took the alternative route of following the authors of such literary writings to their own origins. He pursued the anthropological path and asked instead "how did we get into this mess that we call mimetic desire and imitative rivalry?" And the answer at which he arrived was stunning. We got into this mess, he argued, through a "sacrificial crisis" that operated at the heart of all cultures on the planet but that in cultures other than our own—those we identify as archaic cultures—were efficaciously organized around sacrificial expulsion, around scapegoating or lynching of a collective victim (and the way ritual commemoration derived from that distinction between sacrifice and violence, a distinction or separation we recognize as difference itself), while in ours that distinction between sacrifice and violence had broken down and the distinction between the sacred and the profane, or the sacred and violence, was not able to be maintained.

And that anthropological path led him to a religious studies one. If it is true, he pondered, that the archaic sacrificial is no longer efficacious as an organizing structure for modern culture, and we find ourselves in a kind of runaway sacrificial crisis characterized by runaway mimetic appropriation and its consequence (i.e., conflict), then how is it we are able to speak about this crisis and not be destroyed by it (since one of the postulates he uncovered was that the system remains effective only so far as it is unconscious)? If all cultures on the planet operate sacrificially, and sacrificial organization depends upon an unconsciousness on the part of the participants (no lynchers say we are acting sacrificially against an arbitrary victim), how is it that we in our culture are able to talk about it?

And the answer at which he arrived was, of course, the now familiar one to Girardians: the Christian revelation, the scriptural testimony and subsequent theoretical (and theological) elaboration regarding the birth, ministry, and death of a young Jewish rabbi.

But Christianity is not the necessary or inevitable consequence of Girardian thinking. Christianity may be one possible outcome of Girardian thinking, but it is by no means the only one. And it may not even be, after all is said and done, the most prominent one in a wider cultural perspective. When future ages look back upon our own, and discern the importance of Girard's analysis of the sacrificial for posterity (as Michel Serres predicts they will), it may not be the ethical consequence prescribed by Christianity that gets linked to his thinking.[15]

Christianity is, of course, undoubtedly the path Girard took personally. And it would probably be fair to say that historically among our contemporaries, for that reason among others, it has to this point attracted the largest body of readers from within the Christian community. There are probably more Christian readers of Girard than there are readers of his work in academia—in English departments, or in anthropology departments—or outside of religious groups, although that may say more about American life than either Girardian thinking, academia, or extra-university intellectual life. And apart from myself, there are comparatively few readers of Girard among Jews. But the Christian revelation is by no means the exclusive path along which one is necessarily led after understanding Girard's analysis of the sacrificial and the mimetic. One can sustain a Girardian reading of the sacrificial and the mimetic, I submit, and remain a Christian, a Hindu, a Buddhist, a Muslim, or a Jew.

In fact, another path may be the thought of Emmanuel Levinas. For Levinasians, the union of Girard's sacrificial analysis with Levinas's ethical analysis gives the ethical a political extension; anti-sacrificial scapegoat politics; the question of justice, the question of the third, is not only messianic, but anti-sacrificial, a matter of reading, and a matter of teaching.

And that extension, understanding subjectivity as the appropriation of the position of the sacrificial victim, opens the door to understanding the long-standing mystery of the relation in Levinas between philosophy and Judaism. It resolves the opposition between the philosophic Levinas and the confessional Levinas and answers the question of the origin of responsibility, substitution, persecution, and the like.

How so? By those who are against connecting the two (largely the philosophers), that relation has been understood as two largely distinct, if parallel, courses. Levinas is a Jewish individual and he is a philosopher. As a

Jew he says certain things; as a philosopher he says certain things. But by no means have those two things necessarily been the same things.

By those who are for connecting the two, on the other hand (and very often the advocates of these positions have been Jewish), the work has been understood as a project in translation. He is translating Hebrew thought into Greek, into the language of the university, the language of reason. He is primarily Jewish, this perspective maintains. It is not as if he has split his allegiances into two separate but equal camps. And Judaism, in this view, has already understood all that philosophy would attempt to think out (even though Judaism has been relegated to the margins by philosophy, mistaken as an example of religious particularism). But Levinas has taken upon himself the task of explaining Judaism to philosophically primed ears. Not unlike Maimonides in that regard, this view would see him as an expositor of a thought native to his sensibility before a foreign audience with whom he finds himself for one reason or another engaged. Not unlike translation in Benjamin's vocabulary, he articulates the same thing in a foreign context.

In other words, Levinas asserts (and nothing we say would challenge that assertion) that the two paths the West has undertaken (the Biblical and the philosophic), and the two paths that he has taken in his personal and professional life, are indeed parallel up to a certain point. Levinas never invokes a Biblical passage to prove a philosophic argument. At the same time, Levinas's overall project, if we may describe his life's work in that fashion (which is, after all, how he describes it), is one of translation, a translation from the Hebrew into Greek, of the language of the ancient scriptural writers into the language of the university and the philosophers, from Plato and Aristotle to Kant and Hegel.

Understanding Levinas as reformulating our traditional understanding of subjectivity as ethical throughout, taking that ethical foundation specifically as a substitution for the other individual before me, and identifying that ethical substitution as an appropriation within the social or political context of the position of the sacrificial victim, we suddenly demystify the relation between the two.

Philosophy has never been neutral. From the outset, it has been an exclusion of ritual, an exclusion of sacrifice and all that is associated with religious observance from the mainstream of intellectual seriousness. Part of a humanist cultural movement that somewhat earlier assumed the form of the "Protagorean Enlightenment" in the ancient Greek fifth century, Plato's philosophic project took it upon itself to think all from the point of view of truth, being, and the idea.

Thus, philosophy has never been parallel to, convergent with, or divergent from, the path of Judaism, for Levinas. Rather, philosophy has always been an extension of prophetic thinking for Levinas (whose own access to the prophetic has always been through Judaism). Philosophy since the nineteenth century has been an attempt to refuse its relationship to victimage, to regard itself as neutral, arbitrary with regard to its makeup. If the consequences of philosophy may remain highly charged (think the role of Marxism in social change), the makeup, from this perspective, is not. Constituting subjectivity as a matter of subject and object (with myself as subject of consciousness before objects of knowledge), and the other as either a figment of my projective imagination (limited by my perception of the object or my perception of the subject), or as another individual doing the same thing I am doing (i.e., constituting subjects and objects of his knowledge and consciousness), I have in either case effectively excluded the ethical from my calculation. I have relegated it to the sidelines, rendered it an adjunct to my discussion of relations with other self-consciousnesses doing the same thing I am doing.

There are not two paths, in other words, either parallel or joined at the beginning or end, but one. They are one and the same path throughout, articulated within a different vocabulary and different degrees of awareness of its own resources, Levinas would teach us. Philosophy, from a Levinasian perspective—and this is the theme of *De Dieu qui vient à l'idée* which he identifies as his fourth major philosophic work—is no less an articulation of the importance of encountering the face of God in the other individual than Judaism is, although within the confines of Platonism one is not permitted to say as much. Judaism is no less an articulation of the infinite responsibility I have for the other individual than philosophy is. One path is colored with Greek lettering derived from Plato, the other with Hebrew lettering derived from the Rabbis.

◆   ◆   ◆

What are the implications for the disciplines of such flagrant interdisciplinarity?

What is the consequence of joining the thought of these two thinkers in this fashion? We gain for each an account of the passage from the sacred to the holy.

The sacred for Girard is everything he identifies with the sacrificial and its violent breakdown and reconstitution (or failure to reconstitute) in the sacrificial crisis. The holy would then be the move toward ownership of infinite responsibility for and hostage status before the other, an infinite I may very well experience as a version of the divine.

How would this account square with mimetic desire or what Girard (and the Girardians) have called the "mimetic hypothesis"? They are, in my view, entirely compatible. Loving the other literally as myself, understanding myself as the other individual in me in the Levinasian mode, I find my own mediator or model through the infinite, which is to say, through the divine, through non-deviated transcendence. Humbling myself infinitely before the other individual, I discover on my own shoulders all the responsibilities of God. This is the position that all the great novelists that Girard describes finally assume. The literary in this regard has turned out to be an ethical position after all.

Likewise, the holy for Levinas is everything that he would identify with the ethical—infinite responsibility for the other individual, hostage status before the other individual, responsibilities that extend to being for the other, for the other's responsibilities, and for the other's death. And the sacred would now be the conditioning premises that have brought me to, or occasioned, this subjectivity, that has occasioned the *il y a* to which my responsibility, configured as hypostasis, as verb becoming substance or thing, constitutes a response.

How would this account square with Judaism, which occupies for Levinas the place of the before in modern subjectivity? Precisely as the anti-sacrificial, as the law of anti-idolatry in which idolatry is understood as the moment when the sacrificial and the violent have become indistinguishable from each other, an anti-idolatry that even extends to the law of anti-idolatry itself, a law that especially applies in that latter case since in that eventuality there is no external authority to which one can appeal.

As we attempt to understand our relations to the elemental universe, to the social universe, and to the formation of our individuality and singularity in context of both of these, it is good to have two such powerful thinkers contribute to these inquiries in such complementary a fashion. How does joining the thinking of each thinker to the other in the way we are proposing change things? It allows, I would argue, each body of thought to complete itself.

Levinasian subjectivity is an appropriation of the position of the Girardian sacrificial victim, the persecuted one Girard would describe as the sacrificial victim. What Girard would describe as the victim, Levinas takes as the foundation for the subject, for modern subjectivity.

The analysis of the anti-sacrificial in Girard finds its ethical extension in the Levinasian understanding of the subject as hostage to the other individual through infinite responsibility for that other individual. Infinite responsibility for the other individual is the way that the anti-sacrificial shows up in modern life.

Subjectivity in the way that Levinas describes it, and the thinking through the position of the victim in the way that Girard describes it, are one and the same.

Epilogue

It is rare in France to glimpse the possibility such an interdisciplinary perspective. But if we reflect back on French thought of the last fifty years, is it not interdisciplinary to the core? Claude Lévi-Strauss in anthropology and structural linguistics, Jacques Lacan in psychoanalysis and structural linguistics, Roland Barthes in semiology and cultural studies, Jacques Derrida in philosophy, literary study, anthropological, religious, and linguistic study, Michel Foucault in philosophy, historical studies, and archeological studies—do not all of these writers in all of these disciplines transgress conventional boundaries? Are we really doing any more than they were doing? And are not all genuinely new and truly generative perspectives likely to do the same, indeed, perhaps even required to do the same, if they are to engender an audience receptive to their research?

Levinas's analysis of the ethical completes the Girardian analysis of the sacrificial along just the lines that Girard would suggest. He does so precisely by taking a culture of runaway victimage and hostage-taking and making it the foundation for subjectivity itself. And Girard's analysis of the sacrificial completes the Levinasian analysis of the ethical along just the lines that

Levinas would require—as a kind of "prequel," to use an American neologism. He does so by offering an account of the primitive sacred, the sacrificial mechanism at the heart of all culture and all community that precedes and conditions our own, in a manner that complements Levinas's analysis of the ethical.

A great deal more, of course, remains to be said on this topic. What I have undertaken in this preliminary report is the attempt at finding a place for each thinker in the thought of the other. The place for Girardian thinking in the thought of Levinas is in relation to the notion of substitution—understood in Levinasian terms as founded in persecution and as a consequence of one's status as a hostage before the Other individual before whom (and for whom), nonetheless, one remains infinitely responsible. Specifically, it is as the appropriation of the position of the sacrificial victim as the basis for subjectivity, a position Levinas finds in the texts of the Hebrew prophets. And the place for Levinasian thinking in the thought of René Girard is in relation to the ethical consequence of the notion of substitution which is embedded in the persecutory structure of the sacrificial mechanism pursued in context of the modern world. Specifically, it is as a modality for refusing violence, a sacrificial violence Girard personally comes to understand through Christian readings of the texts of the Hebrew prophets but that opens for us a Jewish reading to a wider audience.

It will remain for future researchers to walk through the doors that we in this conference, and I myself in this paper, have opened here today.

Back to the Future

The Prophetic and the Apocalyptic in Jewish and Christian Settings

Prologue

It has often been said that Judaism is about prophetic thinking and Christianity about apocalyptic thinking, and there is, of course, much truth to that claim. But if Judaism reads prophetically, I would maintain, it does so necessarily in the wake of disaster: in order to understand the steps leading up to it, and to foresee new ones lest one fall prey to them accidentally. And that if Christianity reads apocalyptically, it too is disaster-based and already premised upon prophetic understandings of both what has passed and what is coming down the road.

In other words, that the two, in short, are "entangled" as one might say today in the parlance of contemporary theoretical physics, two sides of the same interpretative coin. The apocalyptic is a reading from within the prophetic, a special case of the prophetic, in which devastation is the expected outcome of the dramas underway. The same understanding of the prophetic is operative in each of these cases, which may be expressed by the following formulation. The prophetic, we may say, is the recognition of the dramas in which human beings are engaged and the naming in advance of the end of those dramas in order that human beings may choose whether to go there

229

or not. Defining the two in this fashion sets them diametrically at odds with more popular accounts in which they are opposed as distinct species of prediction or fortune-telling. The word "prophetic" is often invoked, for example, in popular discussions to designate in retrospect an idea or event that first occurred in the past but now appears fulfilled by some other present occurrence. And the word "apocalyptic" is similarly invoked to speak about some catastrophic future occurrence forecast at a prior time and that now seems to have taken place in accord with that earlier prediction—often in a rhetorical framework of "I told you so," and as a means of chastising those who did not pay sufficient heed to that alleged warning.

What is at stake in what we are suggesting, on the other hand, is never what will inevitably, or unavoidably, come to pass but rather what will follow necessarily should the drama underway continue to its natural and forgone conclusion, a conclusion always generally known in advance and never in any doubt. The prophetic, and the apocalyptic as a species of the prophetic, is a return to a genuinely futural orientation, a future that is authentically open, that is inevitable should the dramas it designates play themselves through to their expected outcomes, but that need not do so, that have the capacity not to be played out. People can choose to follow them to their conclusion, but can equally choose not to do so should some other drama prove more attractive and better serve the circumstances at hand.

Now, there are many parts to this formulation of the prophetic I have offered you—which is in the first place essentially a "Greek" definition rather than a Hebraic or a Christian one—and a great deal more to be said about each part than can be developed here. But my purpose in setting this definition before you today, in this context, as an interpretative construction shared at a profound level by both Jewish and Christian readers, is that it appears to be plentifully in evidence in René Girard's last book, *Achever Clausewitz*, or, as it is rendered in English, *Battling to the End*.[1]

Part One: Girard

Girard's book is nominally a book-length conversation about the unfinished treatise of the nineteenth century Prussian military officer, Carl Von Clausewitz, which has come down to us with the title of *On War*. This is a treatise in which the author, in somewhat of a rational Aristotelian fashion, attempts to develop the principles of warfare as he understood them within the Napoleonic era in which he wrote and fought. What fascinates Girard about this book, and indeed what attracted him to it in the first place, is the writer's treatment in particular of reciprocity or "reciprocal action" which the author claims appears to have a life of its own once it starts, and, as such, to exceed the more commonly known Clausewitzean idea that war is "the continuation of politics by other means." Indeed, the treatment of reciprocity Girard finds in the books leads him to reverse that more familiar principle and to argue that in context of the book we have, politics is in fact an extension of warfare pursued in a slightly less intense context, a position which brings Girard in proximity to that of Michel Foucault, who famously makes something of the same claim in his lectures in the College de France and elsewhere, albeit to very different theoretical ends.[2]

But the real thrust of Girard's view is larger. For Girard wants to claim that Clausewitz's discovery of this runaway principle of violent reciprocity at the beginning of the nineteenth century is, in effect, a Biblical reading, a recognition and confirmation of the ancient prophetic reading of the Christian scriptural book of the apocalypse, namely, the Book of Revelation.

In other words, in Girard's view, the ancient Christian writers already recognized the dramas in which they and their Jewish and Christian contemporaries were engaged and were naming in advance of the end of those dramas in order to decide whether to proceed unimpeded to those ends. Clausewitz was simply registering, in Girard's view, whether unconsciously or not on Clausewitz's part, the unexpected fulfillment of such prophetic accounts.

In the following quotation, for example, Girard defines the appreciation of such coming disaster as "prescience."

> Christianity is the only religion that has foreseen its own failure. This prescience is known as the apocalypse. Indeed, it is in the apocalyptic texts that the word of God is most forceful, repudiating mistakes that are entirely the fault of humans, who are less and less inclined to acknowledge the mechanisms of their violence. The longer we persist in our error, the stronger God's voice will emerge from the devastation. This is why no one wants to read the apocalyptic texts that abound in the Synoptic Gospels

and Pauline Epistles. This is also why no one wants to recognize that these texts rise up before us because we have disregarded Revelation. Once in history *the truth about the identity of all humans* was spoken, and no one wanted to hear it; instead we hang ever more frantically onto our false differences.

Two world wars, the invention of the atomic bomb, several genocides, and an imminent ecological disaster have not sufficed to convince humanity, and Christians above all, that the apocalyptic texts might not be predictions but certainly do concern the disaster that is underway. What needs to be done to get them a hearing?[3]

"[T]he apocalyptic texts might not be predictions but certainly do concern the disaster that is underway." The whole of what we want to say is contained in those words. In the face of "disaster," we cling to "false differences." We misread the ancient texts as predictions and fail to see them as "prescient"—a profound reading of the very crises we are in the process of enacting, crises about the ownership of our own violence and its mechanisms, and mechanisms that derive, Girard explains elsewhere, from the very sacrificial structures that at other times have formed the basis for the genesis of the sacred.

Now what interests me here before you today is how Jewish this understanding remains, both Girard's understanding of the ancient (and modern) texts, and the understanding internal to the Book of Revelation in particular.

To demonstrate that idea, I want to turn in the remainder of my paper to Jewish conceptualizations of the prophetic.

Part Two: Buber

Martin Buber, Franz Rosenzweig, Gershom Scholem, Abraham Joshua Heschel, Emmanuel Levinas, Yehezkel Kaufmann, Michael Fishbane, and a multitude of others have all expatiated extensively upon prophetic thinking in the Rabbinic tradition, indeed, of the Rabbinical tradition as an example of prophetic thinking. Sometimes that thinking shows up as the prophetic tradition explicitly as it does in the case of Buber.[4] Other times it shows up in discussions of messianic thinking—which is another version from a

Jewish perspective of end-of-time thinking—as it does more commonly in the work of Gershom Scholem.⁵ But in all cases it is a matter of diachrony or diachronic thinking, of thinking toward a future orientation rather than any sort of synchronic construction. For present purposes, I will concentrate initially upon two texts in this connection: Buber's "Prophetic, Apocalyptic, and the Historical Hour" and "The Dialogue between Heaven and Earth."⁶ Then I will turn to one of the most famous texts of the scriptural canon, the Book of Isaiah (which in many ways originates this discussion) in order to ask what precisely a Jewish reading of that famous scriptural passage offers our more general understanding of the prophetic and the apocalyptic in these larger Jewish and Christian studies contexts. And finally I will return to ask about the status of Girardian thinking in this context.

◆ ◆ ◆

In the two texts cited above, Buber distinguishes fairly radically between the prophetic and the apocalyptic. The prophetic derives for him quite simply from the writing of the Hebrew prophets: Isaiah, Jeremiah, Ezekiel, and the like. "What good are all your sacrifices?" the prophet asks repeatedly, throughout what is commonly called First Isaiah. If you keep on going this way, in the way you have been acting, if you keep moving along the road you have been traveling, disaster is the inevitable result.

The prophetic, in other words, for Buber is an "if/then" structure. It may look like fortune-telling. It may have that appearance. You may think that the words are saying what will inevitably happen. But in fact there is always a hidden clause at work: if you do not give up the way in which you have been acting.

A good example is the Book of Jonah. "Forty days more and Ninevah will be destroyed," Yonah ben Amittai proclaims. If you continue your evil ways, if you continue doing what it is you have been doing, then here is what will happen. But if you give it up, if you give up that path, then suddenly everything changes. Who knows but God may relent of the destruction he has planned for you and put aside such terrifying designs. The people, of course, in the case of the Book of Jonah, do repent and their repentance is of an unprecedented nature. And if Yonah is unhappy with that repentance and God's giving up of his planned destruction, it is not because Yonah has not known that God is a compassionate God, full of mercy as well as justice (indeed, as he says, he has known that), but for reasons of a more personal nature, reasons from which the book appears to take some distance and upon which it offers some criticism.

The apocalyptic, on the other hand, for Buber is another matter entirely. It is almost mythic in structure. It begins in the present and justifies that present retrospectively, in an almost etiological fashion, as the fulfillment of earlier predictions. For Buber the apocalyptic approach is represented most fully by the originally joint Book of Nehemiah and Book of Ezra. The catastrophe occurred because you have done something wrong, the people are told, because you have sinned in some way that made God angry. You brought all this on yourself, the writers seem to say.

A good example of the poverty of this perspective in Buber's view is the Book of Job. The opening of the book of Job is about myth. *Ha-satan* and God plot Job's difficulties to satisfy a bet between them. The behavior of the friends at the human level parallels this position. You must have done something wrong. Evil comes only from evil. If evil is the result, evil is also the cause. But I am innocent, Job protests, in what Buber regards as the third major movement of the book. From divine play with human fate to flippant formulaic responses of well-meaning but naïve friends, Job protests his innocence. I have done nothing to bring this about. And for Buber the lesson available in this reading process turned into a site of instruction is completed only when we hear from God Himself that the answer to human suffering is creation, a creational principle we may only glimpse in the present context but which nonetheless orders everything.

We may not understand how creation answers human suffering, Buber admits. We may need to introduce Jewish ideas such as anti-idolatry to do so, ideas more plentifully on display in the Book of Isaiah, for example, for the answer to become evident (we recall that Job from the Rabbis' point of view in the midrashim is regarded as "not Jewish"). But the instruction in any event is scripted in advance: from myth, to formulaic responses, to protestations of human suffering, to creation, the path for Buber is clear. The apocalyptic is but one step along the way and in the view of the friends as in the minds of the author of the Book of Ezra and Nehemiah—in Buber's view—it has been perverted out of all proportion. It has been taken as a counter logic to the prophetic as a whole of which it is, in fact, only a part and, in fact, a small one.

But it may be that we need to turn elsewhere in scriptural texts to iden-tify instances where the apocalyptic is given a more positive and robust treat-ment. In the Book of Isaiah, for example, the modality of the apocalyptic is given considerably more status and, in fact, identified with the prophetic perspective itself in the first thirty-nine chapters. Let us turn, then, to Isaiah, and in conclusion we will return to Girard and larger Jewish and Christian usages of it.

Part Three: Isaiah

The Book of Isaiah is traditionally regarded as made up of two parts. Chap-ters 1 through 39 are said to constitute the various Isaiahan takes on the days leading up to the fall of Jerusalem said to occur in 586 or 587 BCE. And chapters 40 through 66 are said to constitute a post-exilic perspective, the writings gathered under the rubric of the Isaiahan school once the unthink-able has occurred. Sometimes the last eleven chapters, 56 to 66, are identified as a third division supplementing these two but that idea is by no means universally accepted.

It is hard for us today to imagine just how disruptive that event (or series of events) in 586–87 BCE was to the Hebrew psyche. It was the incommen-surate par excellence, the un-sayable or unimaginable itself. How could one conceive the possibility—let alone the reality—that the Temple at Jerusalem could be overrun? That after generations of independence the community would be forced to live under the thumb of foreign powers thousands of miles from the regions in which they are raised? It inaugurated an entirely new mindset, a mindset with which, I would suggest, we are still grappling, a mindset that dislodged itself from the stable physical cultural manifesta-tions in which other cultures of the region found their solace (think of Egypt or Babylon or Sumeria) and developed a view of the text as homeland.[7] If I have recourse on occasion to the idea that the Holocaust is not entirely new, that disaster has been lurking behind Scripture for as long as there has been Scripture, that Scripture as a whole is a kind of "book of destruction" (to use Geoffrey Hartman's phrase), or the "Writing of the Disaster" (to use Blanchot's), l'écriture du désastre, the writing or notation of (or from) the destruction, it is to this series of events that I refer.

The Book of Isaiah is thus in many ways the proof text of Jewish scriptural writing. It is the veritable origin of the text, the text being written while the writings we know as Scripture were being gathered and constituted.

And it is from the constructed two parts of this book, First Isaiah and Second (or Deutero-) Isaiah, that I would suggest the concomitant notions of the prophetic and the apocalyptic may effectively be distinguished. The Book of Isaiah is unquestionably prophetic throughout. Its language is the same language used in the Book of Job—"where were you when I created the Heaven and the earth?" "Did you lock in the sea with doors?"—minus the discussion of anti-idolatry, which is what is missing from its more famous counterpart. In the first part of Isaiah, the future of the road they are traveling is articulated: here is the consequence of your actions. And in the second part the future of the path they are pursuing is again articulated, although the end of the path they are traveling is conceived there somewhat differently.

But since in both cases the future is conceived in somewhat dire terms, we could qualify both perspectives equally as apocalyptic. What good are all your sacrifices, the prophet cries out. They will only end in destruction. They do nothing to forestall that destruction they were designed to thwart and, in fact, given the time you take pursuing these wasteful activities they take away energy and resources that could otherwise be used to divert that impending disaster.

In part two the circumstances are no less dire. The prophet's theme here is comfort—"comfort, comfort my people, says the LORD," says the prophet. But before that redemptive moment, much that is unsettling is likely to occur. The servant of YHWH, the servant of the LORD, Israel, the house of Ya'akov, the community of those who have owned their election, their infinite responsibility for other individuals, which is to say, those who have chosen to live in accord with the commandments, with the instruction or teaching handed down by our beloved teacher, Moses Rabbeinu, will undergo great hardships.

If we consider the servant—the family of Ya'akov, Israel—in the manner of a single man, then the drama is clear. It has several parts. We will throw him out, exclude him from our community. But it will really be our sins to which in effect he will be bearing witness. Since in fact he will have done no violence, his exclusion will only come to serve as a teaching tool, reminding us of our own violence. It will serve to unite us since by his stripes will we be healed. It is hard not to think of a young Rabbi from the town of Nazareth several hundred years later being highly impressed by these ideas and taking upon himself to illustrate them, making them his life's project as it were, Torah incarnate, so to speak. The word of God made flesh.

In this context at least then, the prophetic and the apocalyptic are one and the same. Jews read the anti-sacrificial perspective of First Isaiah and the redemptive structure of the coming Kingdom of YHWH in consequence of having already suffered "double" for their sins. They will therefore, not unlike like Job, merit "double back" at the moment of their redemption, the moment when the one who redeems you, who stands as surety for you (as described in the Book of Ruth), answers for you when your number is called. And Christians similarly read the anti-sacrificial perspective of First Isaiah and the coming (and trying) fate of Israel or Jacob, of the servant of the LORD in the final days. The Jewish prophetic de-emphasizes the coming disaster (or the recent past disaster) for an emphasis upon the changes still capable of being made, and the Christian apocalyptic mode emphasizes those dire consequences of our current behavior de-emphasizing what may be done in the interim. The two perspectives remain nonetheless dual approaches to the same fundamental orientation. The Christian reads from within the Jewish perspective and not about it, even if at times it fails to recognize that Jewish prophetic apocalyptic perspective as its own, and mistakenly identifies Jews (and Judaism) as foreign to its own internal program.

And even if at times it adopts the midrashic perspective that the Isaiahan servant of the LORD is the literal son of God, and reads from within that perspective prophetic midrashic view.

Part Four: Strong and Weak Readings

The prophetic and the apocalyptic, in other words, in both their Judaic and Christian settings, have both a weak and a strong sense. The weak Judaic sense of the prophetic is a matter of prediction or fortune-telling, for example, the way the Rabbis sometimes read Joseph's dreams. Joseph dreams that they were binding sheaves in the field and that his sheaves stood up and those of the others bowed down to it. The rabbis read the dreams as predictive of Joseph's ascendancy in Egypt when he will serve as right-hand man of

Pharaoh and the distributor of their daily bread. The weak Judaic sense of the apocalyptic is reflected in Buber's explanation of the Book of Ezra / Book of Nehemiah or parts of the Book of Job where you must have done something wrong to bring this about.

Concomitantly, the weak Christian sense of the prophetic is sometimes invoked by Christians reading Hebraic writing. Isaiah 52–53, for example, is famously read as predicting the coming of Jesus five hundred years later. And the weak Christian sense of the apocalyptic is invoked in reading the Book of Revelation not as an account of Christianity (or its future "failure," to use Girard's words) but as literal predictions of end-of-time events yet to take place.

But there is also a strong Judaic sense of the prophetic. The Joseph story, for example, may be read as the record of the desires of the father enacted in the behavior of the children—both Joseph and his brothers and the violent and sacrificial dynamics in which they become engaged—rather than anything to do with Egypt. And there is a strong Judaic apocalyptic mode although Buber seems not to have much use for it. "Forty days more and Ninevah will be destroyed" is undoubtedly prophetic language. But it is also apocalyptic language. It is about the coming disaster, the crisis forecasted to occur should we continue behaving as we have been. And the anti-sacrificial language of the major prophets is nothing else if not forecasts of a coming destruction should the contemporary and repeated warnings not be heeded.

And a strong Christian sense of the prophetic is evident in the Gospel—for example, Jesus in John 8: here is where your accusations are leading, rocks on the shore of the sea which are fragments of the blood of exclusionary behavior. In bringing the woman before me, a woman caught in the shame of adultery, do you not do the same thing that she did? And are you not subject by Talmudic law to the same punishment for not stopping her from committing it? And are you not attacking me in doing so, accusing me of betraying the Mosaic law if I do not enforce this violent consequence? Rather than counterattack, however, Jesus literally removes himself from the line of fire. He stirs the rocks with his finger, as if to say: here is the future of stoning, countless acts of violence. Here is language the covenant speaks, descendants as numerous as stars in the sky or grains of sand along the shores of the sea. This is where your violence leads. And if they don't get it, he stands up and says, "Okay, he who is without sin, let him be the first to cast a stone," repeating exactly the same lesson. They already know by Talmudic law (since they have brought the woman to him as a group) that there must always be two witnesses to any act of violence, and that first-person confession is never acceptable (so that there needs to be two witnesses other than themselves). Therefore, if they nominate themselves in response, they already transgress the law they say they invoke. Nor is the woman free of the danger of such transgression, for he never says to her "you are innocent" (indeed he never challenges their assertion of her guilt) but rather "go and sin no more."

And there is, finally, a strong Christian sense of the apocalyptic: a reading of the Book of Revelation as an account of what's coming down the road rather than any mysterious figures from science fiction or fantasy, an account of the future of the revelation developed in the letters and the texts of the synoptic Gospels.[8]

It is, in fact, I would argue, that trouble is born when weak and strong senses are set in opposition to each other, whether within Judaism and Christianity or between them.

Why should one view be considered weak and the other strong? Why should reading Isaiah 52–53 as predictive of the specific person of Jesus be weak, while reading the same passage as reflective of the dramas afoot in Second Isaiah (in the previous songs of the servant of YHWH, for example, transformed midrashically into the drama of a single individual)—even if Jesus would subsequently appropriate such dramas as a script for his own life—be considered strong?

To some extent, of course, I am echoing here the distinction Walter Benjamin makes regarding a "weak messianic power" in his famous "Theses on the Philosophy of History" although in a different context and to different ends.[9]

To respond at length would require a more thorough development than I can undertake here. Suffice it to say for the present that there appear to be four criteria at work: predictivity, retrospectivity, freedom, and fulfillment.

Let us take one example included above: the interpretation of Isaiah 52–53 as the prediction of the coming of Jesus specifically five hundred years later. What is wrong with that reading? It appears odd in the first place as an historical prediction. How would people of the time of Second Isaiah (in the immediately postexilic moment in Babylon or Jerusalem) know in advance that five hundred years later (in the time of the end of the Second Temple) an individual would come along named Jesus from the city of Nazareth whose experiences would duplicate the dramas sketched in Isaiah 52–53?

In fact, of course, they wouldn't. Saying so is equivalent to saying in 2012 that in the year 2512, Blubbety-Blub will come along and it is Blubbety-Blub to whom the text refers in 2012. The determination is made retrospectively, not prospectively, and that retrospectivity is substituted for the prospectivity desired in and attributed to the 2012 account. The 2012 account is designated subsequently as predictive but in fact it is both more than predictive and not predictive enough. It is more than predictive since it is, in fact, based on what historically will take place (since it has, in fact, already taken place). But it is also not predictive enough, and too limited in its scope, since it excludes all other possible candidates for the messianic agency it identifies. What if another figure five hundred years after Blubberty-Blub should come along and reorganize everything once again? How does the 2012 account know that the 2512 appearance is the unique appearance of such a figure, a singular messianic event? And on what basis does it excludes other figures who have come along after 2012 but prior to 2512, others who, in retrospect of 2512, have come to count as "false" messianic or prophetic figures?

What, then, would a prophetic account of the same text look like? It would be a genuinely prospective reading. It would begin in the present—2012—and forecast on the basis of known diachronic cultural patterns the inevitable conclusion of the dramas that are afoot. Its determinations would be absolute since they would be the dramas in which the culture has traditionally and continually participates. But they would also be infinitely open and free since those dramas—and therefore those endings—need not be invoked or, if invoked, need not be completed. Other dramas may intervene and other conclusions may obtain this time around. If the ending foreseen should in fact come about, then that ending fulfills the prediction only to the extent that it satisfies it, rather than completes it once and for all. And the possibility (indeed, the necessity) of new fulfillments at some time in the future remain open.

Prospective rather than retrospective, absolute and specific rather than sketchy and relative, free rather than determined and constricted, and fulfilling though not completing once and for all, such prophetic reading would proceed above all contextually. It would read in terms of the texts, languages, cultural dramas, and practices already afoot in the circumstances to which it is assigned. In the above example, it would read in accord with the proto-Rabbinic Jewish cultural milieus of the ancient sixth century, a reading that I have tried to suggest Jesus himself later chooses as his adoptive path, just as others around him choose other perspectives from the surrounding Jewish culture.

Why then is the weak reading important? Why is weak prophetic reading not just a false reading and able to be dismissed as such? Because it introduces the terms that are genuinely important, although without setting them in the right relationship to each other. It gives you the terms that need to be brought into relation, even if it gets wrong what that relationship should be.

Weak reading retains, in short, the structure of myth that serves above all and primarily the community from which it derives and for which it works as a narcissistic projective defense and etiological justification of the current situation rather than the open and freedom-based structure of the prophetic as we have tried to describe it.

Which brings us back to the work of René Girard.

Epilogue

René Girard reads in *Battling to the End* from a strong apocalyptic sense which shares with the strong prophetic sense in both Judaism and Christianity fundamental affinities. Within Christianity, those affinities derive from a young rabbi in Nazareth who is indisputably Jewish and at the same time indisputably at the center of Christian thinking, a young rabbi whose own personal affinities seem to have derived from a prophetic voice he identifies simply as "the prophet" in which prophetic and apocalyptic senses are fairly indistinguishable from each other.

Girard's reading of Clausewitz, then, as stumbling upon an understanding of reciprocity that conforms to the deepest prophetic insights of Christian scripture (which in turn conforms to the deepest prophetic insights of the writing that some six centuries earlier founded the text-centered thinking and practice from which the rabbinic perspective contemporary with Christian writers derived) opens new doors for us. It ushers in a new appreciation for Judaism, for Christianity, for the prophetic, for the apocalyptic, and for their interaction (in weak and strong varieties) throughout the history of Western Europe in which the dynamics of mimetic behavior, sacrificial violence, and their exposure in the religious texts of our culture (that Girard describes so compellingly) play themselves out.

It is to that history of the mimetic, the sacrificial, and their violent conflation in context of Biblical scripture and their prophetic and apocalyptic understanding that I would suggest Girardian research of the future might—dare I say "profitably"?—be oriented.

Conclusions

Reading René Girard

To what purpose is the multitude of your sacrifices unto Me? saith the
LORD. . . .

—Isaiah 1:11

. . . we did esteem him stricken, smitten of God, and afflicted. But he was
wounded because of our transgressions; he was crushed because of our
iniquities: the chastisement of our welfare was upon him, and with his
stripes we were healed. . . . he was cut off out of the land of the living,
for the transgression of my people to whom the stroke was due. And they
made his grave with the wicked, . . . although he had done no violence,
neither was any deceit in his mouth . . . .

—Isaiah 53:4–9

On the 15th of April in 2011, in a symposium on "René Girard and
World Religions," conducted at the University of California at
Berkeley, I delivered a paper on the topic of "Judaism and the Exodus from Archaic Religion." The planning for the meeting was unique in a
number of ways. Girardians had for a long time gathered to share ideas and

meet new people from other disciplines and theoretical orientations. And on a number of occasions smaller groups had gathered more or less spontaneously—often at the annual meeting of the AAR/SBL. For a few years already Girard's personal attendance at these meetings had become more sporadic. But in this one, we were handpicked, for reasons that were not entirely clear at first, and we were assigned specific tasks. And although the meeting was held in Berkeley—"next door," so to speak, to Girard's hometown of Stanford—Girard was not, in fact, invited.

No doubt, if Girard had shown up at the door of the conference, he would not have been denied entrance, and many of us took the opportunity to visit him at his home. But the intent of the organizers, Wolfgang Palaver and Richard Schenk, was clearly to do something different: to stand back, to assess the range and scope of René Girard's work in at least one arena in particular, that of world religions. The nominal occasion was the publication of an English translation of *Le sacrifice*.[1] I seized the opportunity to explore not just Girard's big three ideas, or the relation of Judaism to Christianity vis-à-vis Girard (both of which I had done before), but to try something new myself: namely, to speak about Girard's personal structure of mediation, and to do so, moreover, in ways that echoed its subject matter.

Let me do the same here. Throughout this book, I have tried to discuss the intellectual movement known increasingly in the disciplines as "Girardianism." I have suggested that its fundamental symbolic code is Biblical thinking. I have elaborated its origins in Greek tragic writing or scriptural writing by suggesting that it is all really a literary or midrashic plot. And I have attempted to draw the ethical and prophetic consequences of such a literary scriptural argument. I have, in short, performed the four levels that the medieval rabbis often identified as *pshat*, *remez*, *derash*, and *sod*: the rhetorical or historical, the symbolic, the midrashic, and the prophetic, the reading method summarized in the anagram PaRDeS.

Does this gesture succeed in turning our text into a site of instruction in a way that it would describe the scriptures or great literary texts as doing? Let me reproduce here the text more or less as I wrote it for the occasion in April of 2011, and let me advise the reader to hear it as much as possible as if you were there when I delivered it.

Prologue

We are coming upon the week when in Judaism we tell the story in the Book of Exodus of the passage from Egypt to the desert where the people led by Moses will gather at the "foot of the mountain" in Rashi's translation (*b'tachtiyt hahar* in Exodus 19:17)—some say beneath the mountain—ready to receive the *aseret hadibrot*, the ten utterances or commandments. What has always been of special interest to me in the *seder* (that Jews hold in the diaspora on the first and second night of Pesach or Passover) is the extent to which we are asked (when we read the story in the Haggadah) to respond as if we ourselves were there in Egypt when these events occurred, to describe these events that occurred "when we were in Egypt" rather than events described in a fictional scriptural text, to act, in other words, as if the text is a performative, as if in reading it or saying it we are doing something rather than just invoking it as if the act of reading is a scene or a site of instruction.

All of Judaism, I would like to suggest to you, is a site of instruction. Perhaps all of Christianity as well. If we push this idea to the extreme, perhaps all of the world's "revealed religions" are sites of instruction, places or loci where what is being taught inside is being enacted outside, where the outside is in fact an extension of the inside rather than its representation. That may be, in my view, the most important lesson to be garnered from today's conference on "René Girard and World Religions."

Part One: Judaism and the Exodus

It is not without good reason that the theme of exodus and the religious practice known historically and on the contemporary scene as Judaism have long been associated with each other. Judaism is nothing if not the exodus from archaic religion, the systematic removal of its practitioners from all traces of the behavior that in the communities from which they have come have led them into difficulty. The name for this exodus is the law of anti-idolatry, the recognition of the moment at which the sacrificial and violence—to use the Girardian vocabulary—have become indistinguishable from each other, when the way out is also the way back in, when all efforts to remove oneself from the sacrificial crisis are the very efforts that ensure its uninterrupted continuation. The law of anti-idolatry recognizes this moment precisely (and not unexpectedly) as "idolatry," as the moment of the confusion of the divine with the human, the substitution of what is not God for God. Judaism has arrived at this assessment from within the logic of what I have called—and I am not the first one to do so—the prophetic, which is to say, the recognition of the dramas in which human beings are engaged and the naming in advance of the end of those dramas in order that they may decide whether to proceed to that end or not, or, to use a less Greek and more Hebraic structure, an "if / then" structure, a structure recognizable, for example, in the Book of Jonah. "Forty days more, and Ninevah will be destroyed," the reluctant prophet is admonished to proclaim. And we are to understand by that proclamation not that God may change his mind, or that such is the inevitable outcome of your behavior no matter what you do, but rather *if* you do not change your evil ways, if you continue down the path you have been traveling, then here is what will happen. On the other hand, if you change your ways, if you give up the destructive path you are on, *then* who knows what creative possibilities may occur; God may relent the planned destruction he has in mind for you and you may not, in fact, be destroyed. The logic of the prophetic appeared in Judaism around the time of the overrunning of the Temple in Jerusalem by the Babylonians in 586 before the common era—before the collapse, during the exile, and during the return (in 530 under the aegis of the Persian empire) and the building of the Second Temple during the subsequent century—and is reflected most famously in texts like those of Isaiah and Jeremiah. It is within the context of this prophetic Judaism—and not the cultic sacrificial practices that opposed it internally—that Rabbinic Judaism and the Judaism of the classical Rabbis emerged (after the destruction of the Second Temple). And it is within the context of this prophetic Rabbinic thinking that the law of anti-idolatry came to be formulated, and with its formulation, to reread the entire tradition: the sacrificial priestly cult (known historically in the first century of the modern era as the Sadducees), the literary, historical, legal, and autobiographical narratives (known collectively as Chumash or "five books of Moses"), the prophetic texts proper, and everything else that went into the subsequent writings.

Judaism teaches classical rabbinic thinking. Classical thinking is prophetic thinking. And the manifestation of this prophetic thinking is the law of anti-idolatry, the exodus from the surrounding cultural communities that we designate today as archaic. Judaism is already "Girardianism before the fact," so to speak, a systemic anti-sacrificial critique built in to the very fabric of the religious orientation preceding Christianity. So what, then, has this seeming "Johnny-come-lately" to add to classical Judaism? What has this post-Holocaust thinker and the extraordinary body of work he has compiled over the last fifty years—from *Mensonge romantique* in 1961 to *Achever Clausewitz* in 2010 and 2011 which, I take it, will be his last new book—to add to this ancient classical Judaic body of prophetic scriptural writing?

A great deal, I would like to argue. What Girard does for us, which no other thinker on the contemporary scene does for us, is make explicit the prophetic sacrificial critique, or tragic prophetic critique, at the root of classical post-exilic Judaism, and therefore (since Christianity is an extension of this particular Judaism) at the root of Christianity. Girard's three big ideas— mimetic desire, the logic of the sacrificial, and the scapegoat mechanism, the exposure of all of this in Christian scriptural writings—are the articulation of that to which Judaism is already above all and primarily a response, a response, that is to say, constructed along the ethical lines that a thinker like Emmanuel Levinas has articulated as infinite responsibility for the other individual, for other members of the community in which we happen to be living. Girard articulates the core of the crisis, the collapse of the sacrificial structuration that he, along with Judaism and Christianity, see as the motor force behind all cultures worldwide, and Judaism, and later Christianity, articulate and refine the ethical possibilities that derive from this prophetic anti-sacrificial critique.

In order to demonstrate what I mean, to give you a concrete example of it, in context of a recent book published in France in 2003 (and published in translation in this country just a few weeks ago), I want to turn to a passage of *Le sacrifice*.[2] In that book, more so than in any other to my knowledge, Girard undertakes to place his theories regarding sacrifice within the context of the world's revealed religions other than Judaism and Christianity, in particular those of the Vedic tradition and others of the Indian subcontinent. In my final sections, I will return to this idea that I have begun to develop, that Girard articulates the sacrificial crisis behind Judaism.

Part Two: The Frazerians and the Durkheimians

The nineteenth century had two very different ways of viewing sacrifice, both forms of dismissal. On the one hand, it was viewed within the province of superstition. This view is that of Sir James Frazer and those around him in England who congregated to his insights—the "Cambridge anthropologists" or "Cambridge ritualists"—Gilbert Murray, Jane Ellen Harrison, and Francis Cornford, among others. In *The Golden Bough*, Frazer laid out an entire panorama of rites, customs, and behaviors of primitive peoples, all of whom were deemed childlike in their inspiration, and not to be taken seriously in comparison to the reason-governed institutions populating the modern English and European cultural scene.

On the other hand, starting with Emile Durkheim, and later pursued at the turn of the century by Marcel Mauss, and more recently by Claude Lévi-Strauss, an understanding was formulated that founded itself upon pure differences, systematic oppositions. From this point of view, primitive peoples and modern European peoples were considered to be operating on an equal playing field, so to speak, solving the problems that all cultures faced albeit in different ways. This later tradition, it may be observed, was probably as much reflective of French culture as the former was of English culture, the hyper-Cartesianism of the latter school echoing, in its opposition (and by its prizing of opposition) the importance assigned to an appreciation of the quaint and eccentric in cultural life by the former.

But from a Girardian point of view, both rejected sacrifice as a reality. Surprisingly, in Girard's view, Freud alone notices something real in the sacrificial; something murderous and distinctly exclusionary in its import when he writes about the primal horde in *Totem and Taboo* (and later again in *Moses and Monotheism*). This is somewhat surprising for Girard since in his more mainstream writings Freud relegated all such behaviors to the psychological category of illusion (although in the case of Freud personal illusion prevails over social illusion). The English version thus served to bolster cultural supersessionism and triumphalism, a secular version of the old religious idea, while the French position supported an ecumenism and cultural relativism that could be seen as its inverse.

In the middle of these formalist and interpretative readings, Girard inserts mimetic desire. The mimetic hypothesis explains ritual behavior on the level of real human relations (unlike the explanation of the Frazerians for whom it is one more species of the imaginary), and offers a reading of enigmatic phenomena like sacrifice (which can appear at one moment as the cause of all the worst violence in the community and at another as its salvation), a phenomenon that in the purview of the French formalists is reducible to purely formal categories. The Bible and the Christian scriptural tradition make their appearance in Girard's scenario as the source of the understanding of culture's foundational and generative sacrificial mechanisms. Like the Frazerians, Girard takes seriously the idea of sacrifice (although for him it operates in both the primitive universe and modern universe, and for him it operates at the level of "real" social exchange rather than simply the imaginary), and like the Durkheimians, Girard reads sacrifice systematically and structurally (although he gives it a generative understanding in relation to the category of the sacred). Both the reality of sacrificial behaviors and their systematic importance in culture remain, however, for him the legacy of Jewish and Christian scriptural writings.

Part Three: The Bible, the Gospels, and the Vedic Texts

How so? The Bible and the Gospels reveal the mechanism of mimesis and sacrifice and that revelation undoes their efficacy. And this revelation (and consequence of repudiation) is present in other cultural writings as well: for example, in the Vedic Indian scriptures.

> One thus finds in the Bible and the Gospels the explanation of the sacrificial process. . . . The revelation and repudiation of sacrifice go hand in hand, and all of this is found, up to a certain point, in the Vedanta and in the Buddhist refusal of sacrifices.
>
> By recognizing that the Vedic tradition can also lead to a revelation that discredits sacrifice, mimetic theory locates within sacrifice itself a paradoxical power of quiet reflection that leads, in the long run, to the eclipse of this violent institution that is, nevertheless, fundamental for the development of humanity. (xi–xii)

Later in the same book, Girard suggests that the Vedic texts are also anti-sacrificial.

> We will not have time to complete our study, but I cannot conclude these
> lectures without mentioning certain developments essential to our theme,
> even if we are unable to treat them at great length. They have to do of
> course—my audience suspects it—with the presence of an anti-sacrificial
> and even nonsacrificial inspiration in the most advanced parts of the
> Vedic tradition, those which announce the great Indian mysticism of the
> Upanishads, as well as those which, leaving India, ultimately give rise to
> Buddhism. (87–88)

The existence of these "anti-sacrificial and even nonsacrificial" texts in
the Vedic tradition, in fact, leads Girard to question the purported superiority of Western knowledge over other traditions in a new way. "Far from
unduly privileging the Western tradition and awarding it a monopoly on the
knowledge and repudiation of blood sacrifice," Girard notes, "mimetic analysis recognizes the comparable but never truly identical traits in the Indian
tradition" (xii).

And after comparing the appearance of the Vedic texts to the appearance of the texts of the Hebrew prophets in Israel (Micah for example), he
concludes:

> In the end, the two texts, the Vedic and the Biblical, formulate the same
> critique of sacrifice which is presented to divert men from violence but
> actually encourages it. There is the same understanding on both sides, but
> in India it is expressed in an ironic and satirical fashion. (83)

The "same critique of sacrifice." In other words, ethnocentrism is a mistake. The nineteenth century anthropological thinkers who saw the West as
superior before a superstition driven and myth-driven universe in archaic
culture were rationalizing their own cultural egos, projecting the narcissistic
image they saw in the mirror rather than making independent, realistic, and
verifiable claims about the nature of the structure of planetary communities.
But so is anti-ethnocentrism, the dogmatic and intolerant anti-dogmatism
that arose in response to such ethnocentrism and assumed in the late

twentieth century, under the banner of "deconstruction" in Girard's view, alternative prominence, ironically, a new dogmatism, an intolerant and triumphalist regard for ethnocentric cultures. And the same for the inverse. If absolute differences among cultures are not to be rewarded (whether positive or negative), neither are absolute identicalities, as if culture were a system of pure differences, and all cultures as participated in a kind of planetary soup or *bouillabaisse*, a universal humanism or ecumenism spanning the full range of mathematical options.

The only viable approach, in Girard's view, is the one the scriptural texts of both traditions teach: both the Biblical and Gospel, on one side, and the Vedic on the other. Mimetic analysis teaches that the Vedic is "comparable" if not identical to Western approaches, the "same critique of sacrifice," as the prophetic critique from which the Hebrew Bible, the Israelitic scriptural texts, have emerged.

But that idea has unexpected consequences. For if the Vedic texts are comparable, the "same critique" of sacrifice, a number of conclusions follow.

The first is that we now understand in a new way what it means to say that Girard is not a theologian but an anthropologist. Whatever the dynamics of his personal faith, whatever Girard's individual religious orientation, "Girardianism" as an intellectual movement is a scientific hypothesis, a theory of the origins and ongoing structure of human community in the ancient and modern universe. The "mimetic hypothesis" is a hypothesis, a view to be verified or counter-verified, revealed as intellectually useful and powerful, or revealed as flawed and partial in its usefulness. If the Vedic is "comparable" to the Christian and to the post-exilic Hebraic, then neither the Judaic nor the Christian can be primary, superior to all the rest.

But there is a second consequence and it is more tricky. If the Vedic texts are comparable, the "same critique" of sacrifice, what does that say about our own Jewish and/or Christian orientation? What does it say, for example, about God? Or about the Christian scriptural revelation of the truth of sacrificial violence?

Let me elaborate. Girard claims that the Christian Gospel is a reading of primitive archaic religion. He says that his reading of sacrifice and of the mimetic hypothesis is not original with him but that he is just finding it within the scriptural writings, that the theory of sacrifice as the origin and ongoing motor structure of human community is an anthropological perspective he has located in the scriptural writings. It is not entirely surprising, then, that his understanding of the Gospel has been compared to that of Karl Rahner and Bernard Lonergan.

How does he know that? He finds it there and it is effective. He can show it, demonstrate its presence in passages like Jesus's "reference to the stone that the builders rejected," or John the Baptist's reference to the "lamb of God."[3] And the proof is in the proverbial pudding. The theory works. Cultural life is an elaborate management machine for the control of mimetic desire in order that its work get done. Sacrifice ensures its survival and regenerates its distinctions at moments of its breakdown through the identification of an arbitrarily chosen sacrificial victim. Violence is kept removed from the city as the sacred, segregated, sequestered, and commemorative ritual repetition keeps the process in check. The theory and its four stages (the effective operation of differences, the sacrificial crisis and "undifferentiation," the scapegoating mechanism and its engendering of a difference to end all differences, and ritual commemoration of the whole process up to a point) explain all we need to explain. It is a better explanation than others that have been proposed.

And its appearance in scripture—which suggests that it is no longer effective—allows us to pose a new problem: How do we go on in a universe in which sacrifice no longer works (or no longer works with the efficacy of bygone days), the problem of the ethical.

But how does Girard know it does not come from elsewhere? For example, from Judaism? What if, in other words, Christian scripture derives necessarily from Jewish scripture? If we ask "Where does Christian scripture come from?" we get ourselves quickly into a tight corner. We get answers like the Church fathers—Augustine, Origen, Ambrose, other writers of the early Church who collected and decided what Gospels would count as the key four. Or we turn to the Gospel writers—Matthew, Mark, Luke, John. Or to the apostles: Peter, for example, and especially Paul. Or, ultimately, we invoke the inspiration of Jesus himself. The apostles, the writers of the Gospels, the subsequent Church fathers (east and west) emulate Jesus himself.

Let us, for the sake of argument, accept all of these answers. Let us say, the Church fathers are emulating Gospel writers or the Apostles or Paul or others preceding them. And let us say that these earlier generations of writers are getting the insights that populate their writings from Jesus himself.

Where does Jesus get it? Do we not have to say either that he gets it by direct divine intervention (or divine origin), or that he gets it from the Jewish community in which he learned and grew from childhood on?

And what if we do say he gets it from God, the God whom he identifies as his father and whose firstborn male son he is by virtue of Christian theology? What are we to make of the fact that what he gets from God turns out to be exactly what Judaism is saying? In other words, even if he gets it from God, and even we accept that he gets it from God, by divine intervention or divine origin, then what God says to him in effect is that Jews are right. If everything that comes out of his mouth, everything that Jesus says, is absolutely compatible with the way in which we have been describing Judaism, the Judaic position, the law of anti-idolatry, the midrashic deconstruction of all positions that would posit themselves within the mythic and sacrificial system, does it matter if he gets that understanding from God or from Judaism? For all intents and purposes they are one and the same.

And if René Girard then comes along in the latter half of the twentieth century (and first decade of the twenty-first) and finds within that Christian perspective the foundation for his own theories, are we not led, after all is said and done, to an unexpected conclusion: namely, that Girard and Girardianism are Jewish?

Part Four: Judaism and Girardianism

In the spirit of Passover, which is upon us in a few days, we are suddenly prompted to ask: Why is this conference different from all other conferences in which Girardians gather? And the answer is suddenly apparent. All other conferences have been "for" René Girard. This conference is "about" René Girard.

What would it mean to say that Girard is a Jewish thinker, that Girard (or, more precisely, his work) participates, not in spite of but precisely through its affiliation with Christian scriptural insights, in the tradition of Hebraic prophetic thinking?

To say that René Girard is a Jewish thinker is a characterization that at first glance beggars description. Although Girard has enormous respect for Judaism, he has very little professional interest in Judaism proper, either in the ancient Rabbis (except for passing references made by some continental thinkers like Emmanuel Levinas), or in liturgical practice of Judaism in either its ancient or modern incarnations. It is simply not his topic.

And yet I want to make the claim that Girard's work is fundamentally Jewish, that it is Jewish not in spite of its relation to Christianity but because of it, that what his thinking discovers through Christianity is its Jewish strain, a strain or line of thought he gets not in spite of the Jewish origin of its founder but because of that origin, a founder, Jesus of Nazareth, for whom Judaism is, and in particular prophetic Judaism is, the be-all and end-all of religious thinking. Finally, if Girard, or Girardianism, is to be afforded a place in the series of strategies mounting a critique of religions, it is above all because of its affinities to Jewish thinking, and through Judaism to the prophetic structure of which it is a reflection.

In what sense then is he Jewish?

Girard is Jewish insofar as he is writing from the point of view of Jesus and Jesus is writing (teaching, speaking) from the point of view of Judaism. Girard elaborates the dynamics Judaism identifies as the pre-Judaic dynamics, the dynamics to which Judaism is already a response: the dynamics of sacrificial violence and scapegoating, the anti-sacrificial dynamics that rose to the surface in Isaiah 1–39 but especially in 40–65. Isaiah is the proof text for Jesus as it is for Judaism at large. And he does what all the Rabbis do: enact the text, live "a life of Torah," perform the text in a manner that is known as oral tradition or oral Torah.[4]

There are many ideas in this compact set of assertions and no time to expand them in any but the most elliptical manner. The argument I am making has in effect four prongs or planks.

One, Girard's mediator is Jesus. Thus Girard says repeatedly he is not a theologian. He is not. He reads Jesus as Jesus reads, just as when he turns to Greek tragedy, he reads not from the point of view of any critical position but from the text itself, as it identifies a coherent "tragic prophetic" reading. He reads "before" the theologians who come along later in the process.

Two, Jesus's mediator is Isaiah. Isaiah is the text in context of which Jesus actively structures his life and ministry. Isaiah is not just one more text for Jesus. It is one of the—if not in fact "the"—text for him, as Isaiah is not just one prophet among others but "The Prophet." There are others: the Joseph story, in which the one expelled becomes the right hand man of Pharaoh who dispenses the daily grain, and the *akeidah*, in which the one to be sacrificed emerges from the sacrificial altar and the place of that event is memorialized as *yiru-shalem* which becomes Jerusalem. But Isaiah is the key text.

Three, Isaiah is the "proof text" in the foundation of Judaism, the text that along with a few others reflects the climate in which the ancient texts were assembled. Isaiah (especially Deutero-Isaiah) is part of the community immediately preceding the catastrophe of 587, during the exile, and immediately following the return. Its language echoes the language in the latter half of the Book of Job and examines all the themes engaged by the Book of Job: namely, the mythic thinking of the Adversary; the institutional thinking of the friends; the social justice thinking of Job; and the creation-centered thinking of the divine. It includes all we recognize through Girard as the critique of the sacrificial: namely, the anti-sacrificial as a program, the scapegoat mechanism (with its innocent victim of community violence whose "stripes" heal the community) as the expression of its failure, anti-idolatry as the solution, and creation and suffering (or social injustice) as its themes.

Four, Jesus responds to this text in a way that is characteristic of the Rabbis of his time—the Rabbis of the Talmudic tractates, for example. He takes the act of reading the text (or, more properly, studying the text—which the Rabbis say is equivalent to doing all of the commandments) as a site of instruction. And in particular he takes his body and his life as a "teaching tool" with regard to it. "I am going to live a 'life of Torah'" he says, in effect, as it has not been lived to this point. He constructs his life to perform the text, to enact it, to display it in a particularly spectacular fashion as a means of teaching it. He sacrifices his life, in effect, to the text, to Torah, to Jewish instruction. Enacting the text of Isaiah, taking it as his own life story, Jesus makes not only reading but his own life into a site of instruction.

As a consequence, we understand René Girard's reading in a new way. Girard's appropriation of Jesus, of Jesus's appropriation of Isaiah's, of Isaiah's reading of the anti-sacrificial and the anti-idolatrous, is the appropriation of a prophetic Jewish reading. Girard articulates what is at the core of Isaiah's reading of Judaism, which is at the core of Jesus's reading, which is thus at the core of Judaism itself.[5]

Thus the long tradition that perceives Isaiah 52–53 as foretelling the history of Jesus has it both profoundly right and profoundly wrong. It is right because it recognizes the link between that narrative and the life of Jesus.

But it is wrong because it reverses the priority. In the shadow of this Jewish text, a text at the heart of his tradition, Jesus takes on the project of living it, takes it on as his own. He could have done otherwise. He chooses to give his life to make this Jewish text alive for others. As such, the fortune-telling reading of 52:13 to 53:12 that identifies a historical prediction about an event six hundred years down the line, is wrong in another sense. It is just such a historical reading that Jesus rejects. What Jesus opposes in choosing to enact the text (rather than see it as a remote intellectual formulation that he reads from the outside and over which he has no control) is just such a reading that divorces the text from history, that separates it from human choice and sacrificial drama. The fortune-telling reading is wrong not because it is literal, but because it is not literal enough, because it is, in fact, a ground level metaphorical reading, one that wrests control of the text and its experience away from the community it reflects. Judaic readers, like Jesus, undertake to read the text in a way that recognizes the continuity between the inside and the outside, the duplication of the inside in the outside or more precisely "as" the outside.

Does the interpretation I am proposing—of Girard, or of Jesus, or of Isaiah and its relation to Judaism, or of Jesus and his relation to the reading of texts—challenge transcendental understandings of Jesus? In fact, I would suggest rather that it strengthens them. Jesus is only effectively transcendent if he is at the same time also fully human, if his message appears within and as a reflection of the community into which he is born.

Epilogue

Born on December 25, 1923, René Noel Girard, iconoclastic son of Avignon, reads the Gospel as the Gospel reads, namely, through its central figure, Jesus of Nazareth, who reads, we have suggested, Jewishly, and in particular through Isaiah, and in a performative manner the rabbis would recognize as oral Torah.

The exodus from archaic societies is at the heart of what Judaism is doing—in the face of which it develops the link between creation and suffering known as anti-idolatry which it takes as the law of the universe—is at the heart of René Girard's work as it is the heart of the work or ministry of

Jesus of Nazareth who is his model or mentor or mediator. Whether or not the rabbis have perceived the prophetic anti-sacrificial reading at the heart of Torah, and whether or not the Christian Church fathers have perceived this prophetic anti-sacrificial reading of Jesus at the heart of the Gospel, is another matter, another discussion for another time.

Suffice it to say for the present that Judaism, Jesus, Christianity, and Girard's thought about the scapegoat mechanism and the innocent victim, the victim innocent of all the crimes of which he has been charged—above all, of being the one responsible for all the violence—are profoundly linked. Any understanding of Judaism, Christianity, Jesus, or Girardian thinking that eschews this linkage is bound to be partial.

To read Judaism as exodus from archaic religion is to read Girard as expressing insight buried within Judaism, insights from which Judaism emerged. If we accept Girard's analysis as accurate for the understanding of world religions and world culture (and I do), and if we take seriously his claim that his insights come specifically from Christian scripture (and I accept that claim as well), then the Jewish understanding of Girard has to be that Jesus gets it from Judaism: that Jesus is "Girardianism before the fact," and, to the extent that Jesus's view is a legitimate expression of Judaism (and I think it is), that Judaism is "Girardianism before the fact."

This is not a conclusion we might have predicted. But it is one to which we must be committed, I would suggest, if we are to take the texts before us seriously, both the scriptural texts and the secular texts, a prospect that, however daunting, may yield unexpected rewards.

Notes

An Introduction to Girardian Reading

1. The three books are *Sacrificing Commentary: Reading the End of Literature* (Baltimore: Johns Hopkins University Press, 1996), *For René Girard: Essays in Friendship and Truth* (East Lansing: Michigan State University Press, 2000), coedited with Thomas Ryba, James Williams, and Jørgen Jørgensen, and *Sacrifice, Scripture, and Substitution: Readings in Ancient Judaism and Christianity* (South Bend, IN: Notre Dame University Press, 2010), coedited with Ann Astell.

2. "Discussion" is my translation of "Débat," a conversation that originally appeared in Paul Dumouchel, ed. *Violence et vérité autour de René Girard*, Colloque de Cerisy (Paris: Éditions Grasset et Fasquelle, 1985), 84–89. For the texts of others see René Girard, "Response," in Willard M. Swartley, ed., *Violence Renounced: René Girard, Biblical Studies and Peacemaking* (Telford, PA: Pandora Press, 2000), 308–20. Raymund Schwager, "A Reply to Sandor Goodhart," tr. B. Palaver, first appeared as "A Jewish-Christian Dialogue," in Wolfgang Palaver, ed., *Bulletin of the Colloquium on Violence and Religion* 7 (October 1994): 12 (hereafter *Bulletin of COV&R*); Józef Niewiadomski, "A Reply to Sandor Goodhart," tr. B. Palaver, first appeared in "A Jewish-Christian Dialogue," in Wolfgang Palaver, ed., *Bulletin of COV&R* 7 (October 1994): 12; R. Schwager, "A Second Reply to Sandor Goodhart," first appeared in "A Jewish-Christian Dialogue III," in W. Palaver, ed., *Bulletin of COV&R* 9 (October 1995): 12; Charles Mabee, "A New Grammar for Jewish-Christian Dialogue: The Prophetic Vortex of the Common Scriptures," first appeared in W. Palaver, ed., *Bulletin of COV&R* 8 (March 1995): 4; and Hans Jensen, "Nature, Bible, Priestly Theology: A Reply to Sandor Goodhart and Charles Mabee," first appeared in W. Palaver, ed., *Bulletin of COV&R* 8 (March 1995): 4.

3. The proceedings of the conference planned by Paul Dumouchel and Jean-Pierre Dupuy was published as Paul Dumouchel, ed. *Violence et vérité* (1985). Among the Americans associated with Girard's work at the time and also attending the conference were Eric Gans, Andrew Feenberg,

Tobin Siebers, Paisley Livingston, and Terrel Butler. Girard's handful of students also included Andrew McKenna, Eugenio Donato, and Josué Harari.

4. The book on the novel was *Mensonge romantique et vérité romanesque* (Paris: Grasset, 1961), tr. Yvonne Freccero, as *Deceit, Desire, and the Novel* (Baltimore: Johns Hopkins University Press, 1965). *Violence and the Sacred* was published as *La violence et le sacré* (Paris: Grasset, 1972), tr. Patrick Gregory, as *Violence and the Sacred* (Baltimore: Johns Hopkins University Press, 1977). For his essays on Oedipus in Greek tragedy, see Mark Anspach, *Oedipus Unbound: Selected Writings on Rivalry and Desire* (Stanford, CA: Stanford University Press, 2004), and for his essay on Euripides, see René Girard, "Dionysus and the Violent Genesis of the Sacred," tr. Sandor Goodhart, *boundary 2* 5, no. 2 (Winter 1977): 487–505.

5. It appeared in *Violence et vérité* (1985), 69–83. English versions of the essay were subsequently reproduced in *To Honor René Girard* (Saratoga, CA: Anma Libri, 1986), 85–111, and *Violence and Truth* (London: Athlone Press, 1987), 53–74, although without the discussion that followed in the original French. For that text see Dumouchel, *Violence et vérité* (1985), 84–89, and my translation in "'I Am Joseph.'"

6. See *Deceit, Desire, and the Novel* (1965) and *Violence and the Sacred* (1972).

7. See *Des choses cachées depuis la fondation du monde* (Paris: Grasset, 1978); tr. Stephen Bann and Michael Metteer as *Things Hidden since the Foundation of the World* (Stanford, CA: Stanford University Press, 1987).

8. See "Discussion avec René Girard," *Esprit* 429 (November 1973): 528–63, and "Les malédictions contre les Pharisiens," *Bulletin du Centre Protestant d'Études* (Genève, 1975): 5–29. In *Things Hidden*, he had written, for example: "I believe it is possible to demonstrate that historical Christianity took on a persecutory character as a result of the sacrificial reading of the Passion and the Redemption" (225).

9. See Rebecca Adams and René Girard, "Violence, Difference, Sacrifice: A Conversation with René Girard," *Religion and Literature*, 25, no. 2 (Summer 1993): 9–33.

10. See *The Scapegoat* (Baltimore: Johns Hopkins University Press, 1986), tr. Yvonne Freccero, of *Le bouc émissaire* (Paris: Grasset, 1982); *Job, the Victim of his People* (Stanford, CA: Stanford University Press, 1987), tr. Yvonne Freccero, of *La route antique des hommes pervers* (Paris: Grasset, 1985); and *I See Satan Fall Like Lightning* (Maryknoll, NY: Orbis, 2001), tr. James G. Williams, of *Je vois Satan tomber comme l'éclair* (Paris: Grasset, 1999).

11. Cf. René Girard, *Quand ces choses commenceront: Entretiens avec Michel Treguer* (Paris: Arléa, 1994), 195: "Crowds of avant-gardists may parse my works, but my true Christian readers are not wrong—Father Schwager, Father Lohfink, the late von Balthazar, Father Corbin, Father Alison, and others still." The precise relationship of Schwager to Girard's work—and especially his influence over it—will no doubt be newly examined once the letters exchanged between them are published in a volume currently in preparation.

12. The key book on this discussion is Paul Dumouchel's recent *Le sacrifice inutile* (Paris: Flammarion, 2012); a translation from Michigan State University Press is forthcoming.

13. *Sacrifice*, tr. David Dawson (East Lansing: Michigan State University Press, 2011).

14. René Girard and Emmanuel Levinas both cite this idea. For the origin of this quote, see Dostoyevsky's *The Brothers Karamazov* on "The Russian Monk" (book VI, chapter 3).

15. See "The Science of the Concrete," in *The Savage Mind* (Chicago: The University of Chicago Press, 1966), 3–33.

16. See Bruce Ward, "Giving Voice to Isaac: The Sacrificial Victim in Kafka's Trial," *Shofar* 22, no. 2 (Winter 2004): 64–84. See also my commentary on this distinction in "Excluding Judaism," *Shofar* 22, no. 2 (Winter 2004): 1–8.

17. See Michel Serres's essay, on the occasion of the induction of Girard into the French Academy, in *For René Girard: Essays in Friendship and in Truth* (East Lansing: Michigan State University Press, 2008), 1–17.

18. See "The Times They Are A-Changin'" in note 19.

19. The verse continues: "Come writers and critics / Who prophesize with your pen / And keep your eyes wide / The chance won't come again / And don't speak too soon / For the wheel's still in spin / And there's no tellin' who / That it's namin' / For the loser now / Will be later to win / For the times they are a-changin'. // Come senators, congressmen / Please heed the call / Don't stand in the doorway / Don't block up the hall / For he that gets hurt / Will be he who has stalled / There's a battle outside / And it is ragin' / It'll soon shake your windows / And rattle your walls / For the times they are a-changin'. // Come mothers and fathers / Throughout the land / And don't criticize / What you can't understand / Your sons and your daughters / Are beyond your command / Your old road is / Rapidly agin' / Please get out of the new one / If you can't lend your hand / For the times they are a-changin'. / The line it is drawn / The curse it is cast / The slow one now / Will later be fast / As the present now / Will later be past / The order is / Rapidly fadin' / And the first one now / Will later be last / For the times they are a-changin'." See Bob Dylan, "The Times They Are A-Changin'" in *Bob Dylan—Lyrics: 1962–2001* (New York: Simon and Schuster, 2004), 81–82.

20. Primo Levi, *I sommersi e i salvati* (Torino: Giulio Einaudi, 1986). The customary English translation is "The Drowned and the Saved." See *The Drowned and the Saved* (New York: Vintage, 1989). But the Italian words maintain a distinction between those who are saved (or rescued) and those who remain immersed in the turbulence of the waters.

21. "Literature in Secret," in *The Gift of Death, Second Edition, and Literature in Secret* (Chicago: University of Chicago Press, 2008), 150, tr. David Wills, of *Donner la mort* (Paris: Éditions Galilée, 1999), 199. Derrida writes: "Dieu pardonne à Noé, seulement à lui, aux siens et à un couple d'animaux de chaque espèce. Mais en limitant de façon aussi terrible sa grâce, il châtie et détruit toute autre vie sur terre. Or il procède à ce pangénocide à peu près absolu pour châtier un mal et dans l'élan du regret pour un mal qu'il a en somme commis lui-même : avoir créé des hommes qui ont le mal au cœur. Comme s'il ne pardonnait pas les hommes et les vivants de sa propre faute, du mal qu'ils ont en eux, à savoir le désir, alors qu'il a commis, lui, la faute de le mettre en eux. Comme si en somme, du même coup, il ne se pardonnait pas lui-même le méfait, le mal fait de sa création, à savoir le désir de l'homme" (199).

22. How seriously are we permitted to take this commentary? Have we at last "found out" Derrida's position, exposed his secret battle as he says that literature is buried as a secret within scripture, namely, a struggle with a God whom he is unable to forgive? Or is this one more staging of a textual reading, a battle with the father not unlike the battle with the father in Kafka's case (or Kierkegaard's battle with others in his life), a drama that is also his subject matter, in this essay and associated texts? Or somehow all of these?

23. "Oh, God said to Abraham, 'Kill me a son' / Abe says, 'Man you must be puttin' me on' / God say, 'No,' Abe say 'What?' / God say 'You can do what you want Abe, but / The next time you see me comin' you better run' / Well Abe says, 'Where do you want this killin' done?' / God says, 'Out on Highway 61.'" See Bob Dylan, "Highway 61 Revisited" in *Bob Dylan—Lyrics: 1962–2001* (New York: Simon and Schuster, 2004), 178.

"I Am Joseph": Judaism, Anti-Idolatry, and the Prophetic Law

An earlier version of this essay first appeared in *To Honor René Girard*, 10th Anniversary Volume of the *Stanford French Review* 10, no. 1–3 (1986): 85–111, edited by Alphonse Juilland, and then again, shortly afterward, in *Violence and Truth: On the Work of René Girard*, edited by Paul Dumouchel (London: Athlone Press, 1987), 53–74. It constitutes a slightly revised version of the English original of "'Je suis Joseph': René Girard et la loi prophétique," tr. Paul Dumouchel, for his edited volume of the 1983 Cerisy proceedings, *Violence et vérité* (1985), 69–83, which was first delivered, in an abbreviated form, at the Colloque at Cerisy-la-Salle in 1983 in Normandy, France, and followed by a "Débat" (see "Discussion" in this essay). The earlier version was further revised and published as chapter 3 of *Sacrificing Commentary* (1996). This essay remains the sole text of mine in this volume that appeared previously in book form under my name. I include it here because it offers an overview to Girardian thinking for new readers and because it constitutes the historical origin of my ongoing engagement with Raymund Schwager and Józef Niewiadomski of the Innsbruck school, and others within their orbit (like Norbert Lohfink). I have retained the notes to the 1996 version and updated slightly the text citations.

1. *Le parasite* (Paris: Grasset, 1980), 219. "He is Jewish and therefore understands what he must understand by his milieu and his culture, that sacrifice must be stopped, that there must be a substitute" (my translation). An English translation by Lawrence R. Schehr appeared as *The Parasite* (Baltimore: Johns Hopkins University Press, 1982).

2. Eric Gans, "Pour un esthétique triangulaire," *Esprit* 429 (November 1973): 581.

3. For early bibliographies of Girard's writings and the critical response, see Michel Deguy and Jean-Pierre Dupuy, eds. *René Girard et la problème du mal* (Paris: Grasset, 1982), 315–33, and Juilland, ed., *To Honor René Girard* (1986), iii–xxxii. For another early collection, see Dumouchel, *Violence et vérité* (1985). For subsequent applications of Girard's ideas in psychoanalysis and psychiatry, see Mikkel Borch-Jacobsen, *The Freudian Subject*, tr. Catherine Porter (Stanford, CA: Stanford University Press, 1988), and Jean-Michel Oughourlian, *The Puppet of Desire*, tr. Eugene Webb (Stanford, CA: Stanford University Press, 1991). For readings of Girard's work in context of the Christian Bible and theology, see Raymund Schwager, *Must There Be Scapegoats?* (San Francisco: Harper and Row, 1987), Norbert Lohfink, *Gewalt und Gewaltlosigkeit im Alten Testament* (Freiburg, Germany: Herder, 1983), and James G. Williams, *The Bible, Violence, and the Sacred* (San Francisco: Harper and Row, 1991). For a book-length study of the relation of Girard's work to deconstruction, see Andrew McKenna, *Violence and Difference: Girard, Derrida, and Deconstruction* (Urbana: University of Illinois Press, 1991). See also Robert Hamerton-Kelly, *Violent Origins: Walter Burkert, René Girard and Jonathan Z. Smith on Ritual Killing and Cultural Formation* (Stanford, CA: Stanford University Press, 1987) for a discussion of Girard's work by anthropologists and scientists of religion, and Paisley Livingston, *Models of Desire: René Girard and the Psychology of Mimesis* (Baltimore: Johns Hopkins University Press, 1992), for discussions within the physical sciences. For a short biographical sketch and other books on Girard's work, see Sandor Goodhart, "Biblical Theory and Criticism, 2: Modern Criticism," in Michael Groden and Martin Kreiswirth, eds., *The Johns Hopkins Guide to Literary Theory and Criticism* (Baltimore: Johns Hopkins University Press, 1993), 84–89, and Sandor Goodhart, "René Girard," in Groden and Kreiswirth, *The Johns Hopkins Guide* (1993), 355–56. Finally, for the most up-to-date bibliography of primary and secondary sources for Girard's work, see Dietmar Regensburger's "Bibliography of Literature on the Mimetic Theory of René Girard" at http://www.uibk.ac.at/theol/cover/girard/mimetic_theory.html.

4. See Paul Dumouchel and Jean-Pierre Dupuy, *L'enfer des choses* (Paris: Seuil, 1979), Ilya Prigogine

and Isabelle Stengers, *Order Out of Chaos: Man's New Dialogue with Nature* (New York: Bantam Books, 1984), and Jean-Pierre Dupuy, *Ordre et désordres* (Paris: Seuil, 1982).

5. See Dumouchel, *Violence et vérité* (1985). A conference on the work of Girard, Michel Serres, and Ilya Prigogine was held at the University of Texas at Austin in 1980. Another on "Disorder and Order" centered more focally on the work of Girard and the "mimetic hypothesis" was held at Stanford University in 1981. The proceedings were published as Paisley Livingston, ed., *Disorder and Order* (Saratoga, CA: Anma Libri, 1984). A conference on "auto-organization" in the human and natural sciences took place in 1981 and its proceedings appeared as Paul Dumouchel and Jean-Pierre Dupuy, eds., *L'auto-organisation: De la physique au politique* (Paris: Seuil, 1983). A conference on "Vengeance" took place at Stanford University in 1988. For the past twenty years or so there have been yearly meetings of the "Colloquium on Violence and Religion" (hereafter COV&R) and additional meetings at the joint annual convention of the American Academy of Religion and the Society of Biblical Literature. The colloquium produces a newsletter with information about Girard's work and, since 1995, a journal devoted entirely to Girard's work and research associated with it, *Contagion: Journal of Violence, Mimesis, and Culture*. A highly personal account of his experiences of Girard and the history of COV&R is offered by James G. Williams in *Girardians: The Colloquium on Violence and Religion, 1990–2010* (Vienna, Austria: LIT Verlag, 2012). Girard was admitted into the French Academy on December 7, 2005.

6. Girard, *Mensonge romantique* (1961), translated as *Deceit, Desire, and the Novel* (1966).

7. See *La violence* (1972), translated as *Violence and the Sacred* (1977).

8. *Des choses cachées* (1978), translated as *Things Hidden* (1987), and *Le bouc émissaire* (1982), translated as *The Scapegoat* (1986).

9. For further discussion of Girard's views on the Christian Gospel, see "Discussion avec René Girard" in *Esprit* 429 (November 1973): 528–63, and "Les malédictions contre les pharisiens et la révélation évangélique," *Bulletin du Centre Protestant d'Études* 27 (1975): 5–29.

10. "Nouveau prophétisme" was a phrase used, for example, in the eighties by commentators in France to negatively characterize the work of the "nouveaux philosophes."

11. On the shift away from essentialistic conceptualizations in philosophy and literary criticism, see Emmanuel Levinas, *Otherwise than Being, or, Beyond Essence* (Pittsburgh, PA: Duquesne University Press, 1998), Paul de Man, *Blindness and Insight* (New York: Oxford University Press, 1971), and Stanley Fish, *Is There a Text in This Class* (Cambridge, MA: Harvard University Press, 1980).

12. The theme of the "tiers exclu" is persistent in Michel Serres's work. See, for example, his early book on communication, *Hermès Tome I. La Communication* (Paris: Les Éditions de Minuit, 1968), 41, portions of which were translated as *Hermes: Literature, Science, Philosophy* (Baltimore: Johns Hopkins University Press, 1982); and his book on the foundations of Rome, *Rome: Le livre des fondations* (Paris: Grasset, 1983), 169, tr. Felicia McCarren, as *Rome: The Book of Foundations* (Stanford, CA: Stanford University Press, 1991). It is interesting that in English we say "excluded middle," whereas in French one says "tiers exclu" ("excluded third"). It is as if in each linguistic context we have domesticated the notion to read either as a middle or as a third, excluding commonly their conjunction—that the "tiers exclu" is at once between the communicants (a middle) and outside of them (a third).

13. Little has been done, to my knowledge, on this interesting aspect of Girardian thinking concerning the inefficacy of sacrificial structuration at the moment of the appearance of Greek humanism, Judaism, and in general, modern cultural forms.

14. On the centrality of the notion of anti-idolatry to Hebraic religion, see Yehezkel Kaufmann, *The Religion of Israel*, tr. Moshe Greenberg (New York: Schocken, 1972). On the notion of the prophetic, see also Martin Buber, *On the Bible* (New York: Schocken, 1982). For a penetrating account of the criticism of idolatry in non-Jewish writing, see John Freccero, "The Fig-Tree and the Laurel: Petrarch's Poetics," *Diacritics* 5 (1975): 34–40.

15. For a discussion of the way in which the "secondary" or interpretative texts of Jewish tradition extend Torah, see Susan Handelman, *The Slayers of Moses* (Albany: SUNY Press, 1982), 38, and Emmanuel Levinas, *L'au delà du verset* (Paris: Minuit, 1982), 7, tr. Gary Mole, as *Beyond the Verse: Talmudic Readings and Lectures* (Bloomington: Indiana University Press, 1994). The standard authority, in the English-speaking world, for discussions of Jewish spirituality and mysticism, is, of course, Gershom Scholem. See, for example, Scholem, *Major Trends in Jewish Mysticism* (New York: Schocken, 1972) and *Kabbalah* (New York: Meridian, 1978). On interpretation in the Jewish tradition, see also Michael Fishbane, "Jewish Biblical Exegesis: Presuppositions and Principles," in Frederick Greenspahn, ed., *Scripture in the Jewish and Christian Traditions: Authority, Interpretation, Relevance* (Nashville, TN: Parthenon, 1982), 91–110; *Biblical Interpretation in Ancient Israel* (Oxford, UK: Clarendon, 1985); and *The Garments of Torah: Essays in Biblical Hermeneutics* (Bloomington: Indiana University Press, 1989).

16. *The Holy Scriptures According to the Masoretic Text: A New Translation* (Philadelphia: The Jewish Publication Society of America, 1917). The specific commandment against idolatry has often been taken to be the second: "Thou shalt not make unto thee a graven image" (Ex. 20:4). The first commandment has been taken, on the other hand, as the statement of Hebraic monotheism. It may be, however, that by virtue of the second commandment we may understand the first as the law of anti-idolatry ("Thou shalt have only an external God, no internal Gods"). The reading, then, of the first as a statement of monotheism would reflect already an exclusion of the second and in general of the diachronic or prophetic context in which the first appears, the only context, in fact, in which such a list of commandments can be read as a text or narrative. For a collection in English of older rabbinic commentaries upon the biblical text, see A. C. Feuer and N. Scherman, *Aseres Hadibros/The Ten Commandments* (Brooklyn, NY: Mesorah, 1981). On the shift away from viewing the Hebrew Bible as concerned with monotheism as opposed to polytheism and toward viewing it as opposed to paganism, see Bernard-Henri Lévy, *The Testament of God*, tr. George Holoch (Baltimore: Johns Hopkins University Press, 1985). For a fuller discussion of the interpretive issues raised in counting commandments, see Sandor Goodhart, "Reading the Ten Commandments. Torah, Interpretation, and the Name of God," in *Sacrificing Commentary* (Baltimore: Johns Hopkins University Press, 1996), 122–38.

17. The importance of the work of Emmanuel Levinas to this discussion—and in general to the notion of the exteriority of transcendence—cannot be overestimated. See, for example, Levinas, *Totality and Infinity: An Essay on Exteriority* (Pittsburgh, PA: Duquesne University Press, 1969) and *Otherwise than Being* (1998). For Levinas's writing on Judaism, see *Difficult Freedom: Essays on Judaism* (Baltimore: Johns Hopkins University Press, 1990), *Nine Talmudic Studies* (Bloomington: Indiana University Press, 1993), *In the Time of the Nations* (Bloomington: Indiana University Press, 1994), *Beyond the Verse* (Bloomington: Indiana University Press, 1994), *New Talmudic Readings* (Pittsburgh, PA: Duquesne University Press, 1999), among other works. The work of Maurice Blanchot in this connection is also important. See *The Book to Come* (Stanford, CA: Stanford University Press, 2003), *The Space of Literature* (Lincoln: University of Nebraska, 1982), *The Work of Fire* (Stanford, CA: Stanford University Press, 1995), *The Gaze of Orpheus and Other Literary Essays* (Barrytown, NY: Station Hill Press, 1981), and *The Infinite Conversation* (Minneapolis: University of Minnesota, 1992). For an application of some of these ideas within a political context, see Lévy, *Barbarism with a Human Face* (New York: Harper and Row, 1979). For other important accounts of Judaism, see André Neher, *The Prophetic Existence* (South

Brunswick, NJ: A. S. Barnes, 1969), *L'existence juive* (Paris: Seuil, 1962), and André Chouraqui, *Histoire de judaïsme* (Paris: Presses Universitaires de France, 1964).

18. The phrase was used by Foucault to characterize Blanchot's work. See Foucault, "La pensée du dehors," *Critique* 229 (1966): 523–46. For a profound meditation on the themes of exodus, exile, and the desert in Dante, see Giuseppe Mazzotta, *Dante, Poet of the Desert* (Princeton, NJ: Princeton University Press, 1979).

19. The text of Exodus is from Rabbi J. H. Hertz, *The Pentateuch and the Haftorahs*, 2nd ed. (London: Soncino, 1979). See also Everett Fox's translation in *The Five Books of Moses: Genesis, Exodus, Leviticus, Numbers, Deuteronomy* (New York: Schocken, 1995). For other important editions of Torah and its commentaries, see Robert Alter, *The Five Books of Moses* (New York: Norton, 2008), Adele Berlin, et al., *The Jewish Study Bible* (New York: Oxford University Press, 2004), Arthur Cohen, *The Soncino Chumash* (London: The Soncino Press, 1979), and A. B. Isaiah and B. Sharfman, *The Pentateuch and Rashi's Commentary* (Brooklyn: S. S. & R., 1949). On Genesis alone, see also the monumental six volume ArtScroll edition of Meir Zlotowitz and Nosson Sherman, *Bereishis/Genesis,* 6 vols., Artscroll Tanakh Series (Brooklyn: Mesorah Publications, 1977–1981).

20. Cf. Ex. 3:10: "Come now therefore, and I will send thee unto Pharaoh, that Thou mayest bring forth My people the children of Israel out of Egypt."

21. Cf. Ex. 3:13: "And Moses said unto God: 'Behold, when I come unto the children of Israel, and shall say unto them: The God of your fathers hath sent me unto you; and they shall say to me: What is His name? what shall I say unto them'"?

22. Cf. Ex. 3:14–15: "And God said unto Moses: 'I AM THAT I AM'; and He said: 'Thus shalt thou say unto the children of Israel: I AM hath sent me unto you.' And God said moreover unto Moses: 'Thus shalt thou say unto the children of Israel: The LORD, the God of your fathers, the God of Abraham, the God of Isaac, and the God of Jacob, hath sent me unto you; this is My name for ever, and this is My memorial unto all generations.'"

23. For a similar account of the name of God, see Buber, *On the Bible* (1982), 80–82. For further commentary, see Levinas, *L'Au-delà du verset* (1982), 143–57, and Jacques Derrida, *La Carte Postale* (Paris: Flammarion, 1980), 179.

24. See, for example, Scholem, *Kabbalah* (1978), 282–303.

25. Cf. Ex. 3:10–12: "'Come now therefore, and I will send thee unto Pharaoh, that Thou mayest bring forth My people the children of Israel out of Egypt.' And Moses said unto God: 'Who am I, that I should go unto Pharaoh, and that I should bring forth the children of Israel out of Egypt?' And He said: 'Certainly I will be with thee.'"

26. Rashi, the medieval French biblical exegete, and the foremost among commentators of the later rabbinic tradition, draws our attention to this possibility—with the subtlety displayed by so many Toradic commentators. He notes that in the later passage, while the word *'imach* ("with you") does not literally recur, we are entitled to include it. See Isaiah and Sharfman, *The Pentateuch and Rashi's Commentary* (1949), 23.

27. "Being with" or "being there with" is a better translation than "being." Buber notes that there is no abstract presence in the Hebrew. See Buber, *On the Bible* (1982), 44–62. For a translation in English of Genesis and Exodus in accord with the principles embodied in the famous translation of Buber and Rosenzweig of Torah into German, see Fox, *Five Books of Moses* (1995). For a discussion of these translation matters, see Martin Buber and Franz Rosenzweig, *Scripture and Translation* (Bloomington: Indiana University Press, 1994).

28. Such a notion—that the Torah itself may be understood as a covenant—has led non-Jewish historical scholars of the Bible to see the "Old Testament" as structured around the notion of covenant. See, for example, Walther Eichrodt, *Theology of the Old Testament*, 2 vols., tr. J. A. Baker (Philadelphia, PA: Westminster Press, 1961). For a more personal account of covenant in the "Old Testament" and the Christian Gospel from a Catholic perspective, see J. Bishop, *The Covenant: A Reading* (Springfield, IL: Templegate, 1982).

29. It is customary within Orthodox synagogues for women to sit segregated from the men.

30. Zlotowitz, *Bereishis/Genesis*, vol. 5 (1980), 1613.

31. On the prophetic interpretation of dreams among older commentators, see Zlotowitz, *Bereishis/Genesis*, vol. 5 (1980), 1620.

32. E. A. Speiser, for example, in his prestigious edition of Genesis in the Anchor Bible Series, summarizes this long and persistent tradition of biblical criticism in which scholars have divided up the text into distinctive compositional sources—a "J" document, an "E" document, and so on—in accordance with the various words employed for the naming of divinity. See Speiser, *Genesis* (Garden City, NY: Doubleday, 1964). My own interest—as I hope is clear in this essay—is not to challenge this important work, but to ask a different question: namely, by what principle of coherence can these admittedly diverse and heterogeneous materials be seen as "going together," a principle to whose unifying power the very fervor with which we pursue an interest in heterogeneity in the text may offer ample testimony? On the shift away from traditional historical concerns to a closer reading of narrative and poetic detail, the groundbreaking book, of course, is Robert Alter's *The Art of Biblical Narrative* (New York: Basic Books, 1981). It is Alter, for example, who takes Speiser to task over just such issues. Whatever the potential pitfalls of an organicist approach—namely, that it be developed at the expense of historicism—Alter's book is profoundly exciting. He allows us to envision a new biblical criticism as yet in its infancy that would cull the insights of both formalism and historicism (eschewing the limitations of each) into a critical position that is something like that of the Bible itself.

33. Jacob's blessing of the sons of Joseph is itself an interesting moment in context of our presentation. Instead of blessing Manassah (Joseph's first-born) with his right hand, and Ephraim with his left (as tradition would dictate), Jacob crosses his hands and blesses Manassah with his left hand and Ephraim with his right. He does this, he tells Joseph, because Manassah's younger brother "shall be greater than he" (48:19). Is Jacob continuing the sacrificial reading of his earlier days, favoring the younger son, the gesture that set the whole drama into motion (and, perhaps, because he recalls his own position as second-born)? Or does his gesture here reflect an anti-sacrificial position, one perhaps that he has learned from the events that have transpired? Such a view would recognize at once that Manassah is first-born and that Ephraim must not be slighted, a view that contrasts with the rigid distinction between Cain and Abel at the other end of the first book of Torah. Malbim, one of medieval Rabbis commonly anthologized in interpretations of scriptural passages, suggests that Jacob placed his left hand above the right, thereby blessing Manassah with the hand that was on top and Ephraim with the right, refusing to some extent, that is, to distinguish between them. What seems clear, in any event, is that the text of Jacob's blessing of the sons, like the Joseph story proper, and like Jacob's hands within that text (and not to mention the hands or texts of the commentators), superimposes one view upon the other. Jacob has "wisely directed his hands," Rashi tells us in his interpretation of this passage. For all these commentaries, see Zlotowitz, *Bereishis/Genesis* (1981), 2110. I thank Holli Levitsky, of Loyola Marymount College, for drawing my attention to this passage in context of the above argument.

34. Scholem, *Major Trends in Jewish Mysticism* (1972), 141–42.

35. Serres, *Le parasite* (1980), 219, from which the epigraph is drawn. An English translation of this

book reads: "He is a Jew, and thus he understands what he must understand in his milieu and his culture, that the sacrifice must be stopped, that there must be a substitute"(see Serres, *The Parasite* [1982], 164). The differences between "He is a Jew" as a translation of "*Il est juif*" and "the sacrifice" as a translation of "*le sacrifice*" in this context are noteworthy.

36. "Discussion" is my translation of "Débat," a conversation that originally appeared in Paul Dumouchel, ed. *Violence et vérité* (1985), 84–89. The account was written (and the event moderated) by Paul Dumouchel. Participants included Joseph-Marie Crispin, Jean-Pierre Dupuy, Jean-Claude Durbant, René Girard, Sandor Goodhart, Rena Krebs, Pierre Lantz, Norbert Lohfink, and Raymund Schwager.

A Jewish-Christian Dialogue

This chapter collects nine short passages from the COV&R *Bulletin* in which the following dialogue took place. The opening section, Raymund Schwager's "Reply to Sandor Goodhart," tr. B. Palaver, and Józef Niewiadomski's "Reply to Sandor Goodhart," tr. B. Palaver, first appeared in "A Jewish-Christian Dialogue" in Wolfgang Palaver, ed., *Bulletin of the Colloquium on Violence and Religion* 7 (October 1994): 11–12. My "Reply to Father Raymund Schwager and Józef Niewiadomski" first appeared in "A Jewish-Christian Dialogue II" in Wolfgang Palaver, ed., *Bulletin of COV&R* 8 (March 1995): 12–13. Raymund Schwager's "Second Reply to Sandor Goodhart" first appeared in "A Jewish-Christian Dialogue III," in Wolfgang Palaver, ed., *Bulletin of COV&R* 9 (October 1995): 12. My "Second Reply to Raymund Schwager" first appeared in "A Jewish-Christian Dialogue IV" in Wolfgang Palaver, ed., *Bulletin of COV&R* 10 (March 1996): 10–12. "The Prophetic Tradition as a Basis for Jewish-Christian Dialogue" is the abstract of a paper delivered at the COV&R conference in Chicago, November 18, 1994, at Loyola University. It first appeared in Wolfgang Palaver, ed., *Bulletin of COV&R* 8 (March 1995): 4. Charles Mabee's "A New Grammar for Jewish-Christian Dialogue: The Prophetic Vortex of the Common Scriptures" first appeared in Wolfgang Palaver, ed., *Bulletin of COV&R* 8 (March 1995): 4. Hans Jensen's "Nature, Bible, Priestly Theology: A Reply to Sandor Goodhart and Charles Mabee" first appeared in Wolfgang Palaver, ed., *Bulletin of COV&R* 8 (March 1995): 4.

1. Trans. by B. Palaver.

2. Trans. by B. Palaver.

3. Bulletin No. 8, page 12.

4. "Violence, Difference, Sacrifice: A Conversation with René Girard," *Religion & Literature* 25, no. 2 (1993): 13–14.

5. Trans. by Elisabeth Thurner.

al lo-chamas 'asah (Although He Had Done No Violence): René Girard and the Innocent Victim

"'*al lo-chamas asah*' (Although He Had Done No Violence): Isaiah 52–53, René Girard, and the Innocent Victim," was originally published in Willard M. Swartley, ed., *Violence Renounced: René Girard, Biblical Studies, and Peacemaking* (Telford, PA: Pandora Press, 2000), 200–17.

1. René Girard, *Deceit, Desire, and the Novel* (1965), originally published as *Mensonge romantique* (1961).

2. René Girard, *Violence and the Sacred* (1977). See, for example, Hayden White's essay, "Ethnological Lie and Mythical Truth," *Diacritics* 8, no. 1 (1978), 2–9.

3. For an example of the kind of heated controversy to which discussion of Girard's work has given way, See Robert G. Hamerton-Kelly's *Sacred Violence: Paul's Hermeneutic of the Cross* (Philadelphia, PA: Fortress Press, 1993) and articles edited by Ted Peters in *Dialog* 32, no. 4 (Fall 1993) under the title "Paul and Luther: A Debate over Sacred Violence," 247–88, in which Hamerton-Kelly restates his view and is answered by Krister Stendahl, Hayim Goren Perelmuter, David Frederickson, René Girard, and Gerhard O. Forde. For another response by a Pauline scholar, see Daniel Boyarin's review of Hamerton-Kelly's book in his article "The Subversion of the Jews: Moses' Veil and the Hermeneutics of Supersession," *Diacritics* 23, no. 2 (Summer 1993): 16–35, as well as his book *A Radical Jew: Paul and the Politics of Identity* (Berkeley: University of California Press, 1994).

4. See René Girard, *Bulletin du Centre Protestant d'Études* (Genève, 1975), 5–29.

5. René Girard, *Quand ces choses commenceront: Entretiens avec Michel Treguer* (Paris: Arléa, 1994), 118–19. An English translation, *When These Things Begin*, was published by Michigan State University Press in 2014.

6. My translation.

7. *The Holy Scriptures: A New Translation* (Philadelphia, PA: Jewish Publication Society of America, 1917), 543–44.

8. For the Jewish tradition, see Rabbi A. J. Rosenberg, *The Book of Isaiah*, vol. 2 (New York: The Judaica Press, 1983). For the Christian tradition, see the Anchor Bible series volume, John McKenzie, *Second Isaiah* (New York: Doubleday and Company, Inc., 1979).

9. Cf. Isaiah, 40:1–2.

10. Christian exegete Norbert Lohfink has written about the possibility of a double revelation from a Christian perspective. See Norbert Lohfink, *The Covenant Never Revoked: Biblical Reflections on Christian-Jewish Dialogue*, trans. John Scullion (New York: Paulist Press, 1991).

11. Michel Foucault seems to have been working on this problem at the moment of his death. See *The History of Sexuality*, vol. 2, *The Use of Pleasure* (London: Penguin, 1992), and vol. 3, *The Care of the Self* (London: Penguin, 1994). See also Foucault's lectures on St. Augustine and confession discussed in J. Joyce Schuld's *Foucault and Augustine: Reconsidering Power and Love* (South Bend, IN: University of Notre Dame Press, 2013).

Response by René Girard and Reply to René Girard

"Response by René Girard" was originally published in Willard M. Swartley, ed., *Violence Renounced: René Girard, Biblical Studies and Peacemaking* (Telford, PA: Pandora Press, 2000), 308–20. "Reply to René Girard" is an amplified version of "We Will Cling Fast to Your Torah: A Response to René Girard's Reply to *Violence Renounced*," in Paul Bellan-Boyer, ed., *Bulletin of COV&R* 19 (November 2000), 14–17.

1. Isaiah 52:2–3, *The Holy Scriptures* (Philadelphia, Pa: Jewish Publication Society of America, 1917), 543.

2. See René Girard, "Response," in Swartley, ed., *Violence Renounced*, 308–20.

3. *Bava Metzia* 59A–59B. See for example Adin Steinsaltz, ed., *The Talmud*, vol. 3, *Tractate Bava Metzia*, part 3 (New York: Random House, 1990), 235–37.

4. For a compendium of such aggadic materials, see Hayim Nahman Bialik and Yehoshua Hana Ravnitzky, eds., *The Book of Legends*, tr. William G. Braude (New York: Schocken, 1992).

5. See Swartley (2000), 200–17.

6. See Swartley (2000), 308–20.

7. See *Je vois Satan* (2000), 197, my translation.

8. See James G. Williams, *The Girard Reader* (New York: Crossroads Publishing Company, 1996), 280.

9. See *The Star of Redemption*, tr. William W. Hallo (Notre Dame, IN: University of Notre Dame Press, 1985).

10. *Things Hidden* (1987), 235, originally *Des choses cachées* (1978).

The End of Sacrifice: Reading René Girard and the Hebrew Bible

"The End of Sacrifice: Reading René Girard and the Hebrew Bible" appeared in *Contagion: Journal of Violence Mimesis and Culture* 14 (2007): 59–78.

1. René Girard was inducted into the French Academy on December 15, 2005.

2. Everett Fox, ed., *The Five Books of Moses: Genesis, Exodus, Leviticus, Numbers, Deuteronomy* (New York: Schocken Books, 1995), 21. Unless otherwise indicated, all citations from the Hebrew Bible in this chapter are from this edition.

3. See, for example, Levinas, *Totality and Infinity: An Essay on Exteriority*, tr. Alphonso Lingis (Pittsburgh, PA.: Duquesne University Press, 1969).

4. This aggadic material is drawn from the legendary work of Hayim Nahman Bialik and Yehoshua Hana Ravnitsky. See Bialik and Ravnitsky, eds., *The Book of Legends/Sefer Ha-Aggadah: Legends from the Talmud and Midrash*, tr. William G. Braude (New York: Schocken, 1992), 15, para 60. Bracketed comments are those of the translator.

5. Bialik and Ravnitsky, *The Book of Legends*, 15, para 60. The first bracketed comment is that of Leon Nemoy, a former editor of the Yale Judaica series. The second is from William Braude.

6. See for example William Gesenius's *A Hebrew and English Lexicon of the Old Testament* (London: Oxford University Press, 1951), tr. Francis Brown, S. R. Driver, and Charles Briggs (hereafter BDB), 61. BDB in fact explicitly cites the occurrence of *ishah* in Genesis 2.23 as derivative of the third meaning of *insh*.

7. For a view of the ethical as my infinite responsibility for the other individual, see Emmanuel Levinas, *Otherwise than Being, or, Beyond Essence*, tr. Alphonso Lingis (Pittsburgh, PA: Duquesne University Press, 1998).

8. For a development of this view, see Emmanuel Levinas, "Useless Suffering," in *Entre Nous: Thinking-of-the-Other*, tr. Michael B. Smith (New York: Columbia University Press, 1998), 91–101.

From Sacrificial Violence to Responsibility: The Education of Moses in Exodus 2–4

"From Sacrificial Violence to Responsibility: The Education of Moses in *Exodus 2–4*" first appeared in *Contagion: A Journal of Violence, Mimesis, and Culture* 6 (Spring 1999): 12–31.

1. Cited in W. Günther Plaut, *The Torah: A Modern Commentary* (New York: Union of American Hebrew Congregations, 1981), 383.

2. See, for example, Eric Havelock, *Preface to Plato* (Cambridge, MA: Belknap Press, 1963).

3. See, for example, Walter Ong, *Literacy and Orality* (New York: New York University Press, 1975).

4. Sandor Goodhart, *Sacrificing Commentary: Reading the End of Literature* (Baltimore: Johns Hopkins University Press, 1996), 261.

5. The word *Tanakh* is an anagram of the words used to name the three books that comprise it (*Torah, Ktuvim*, and *Nevi'im*).

6. See "Biblical Humanism" in Martin Buber, *On the Bible: Eighteen Studies*, ed. Nahum Glatzer (New York: Schocken, 1982), 211–16.

7. Ibid., 212.

8. Ibid., 214.

9. Emmanuel Levinas, *Difficult Freedom: Essays on Judaism*, tr. Seán Hand (Baltimore, Johns Hopkins University Press, 1990), 275.

10. Levinas, *Difficult Freedom* (1990), 268.

11. Levinas, *Difficult Freedom* (1990), 273–76. The original French title of this essay, "Pour un humanisme hébraïque," appeared in 1956 and was republished in *Difficile liberté: Essais sur le judaïsme* (Paris: Albin Michel, 1983), 350–54.

12. J. H. Hertz, ed. *The Pentateuch and the Haftorahs*, 2nd ed. (London: Soncino Press, 1979), 294–95. All subsequent references to the Hebrew text or English translation are from this book.

13. God considered creating the universe of justice alone, the midrash goes, and turned to the angels for their thoughts about the plan. The universe would not survive Your justice for even five minutes, they said to the Holy One. So God proposed creating the universe of mercy. Human beings would not survive each other for even five minutes, was the angels' reply this time. Therefore, God created the universe of both justice and mercy.

Reading Religion, Literature, and the End of Desire: *Mensonge romantique et vérité romanesque* at Fifty

"Reading Religion, Literature, and the End of Desire: *Mensonge romantique et vérité romanesque* at Fifty," appeared in *Religion and Literature* 43, no. 3 (Autumn 2011): 150–58.

1. Cesáreo Bandera's *Mimesis conflictiva: Ficción literaria y violencia en Cervantes y Calderon* was published in 1975 (Madrid: Gredos). See, more recently, *The Sacred Game: The Role of the Sacred in the Genesis of Modern Literature* (University Park: Pennsylvania State University Press, 1994), and *The Humble Story of Don Quixote: Reflections on the Birth of the Modern Novel* (Washington, DC: Catholic University of America Press, 2006).

2. "What stirs lyrical poets to their finest flights," the passage continues, "is neither the delight of the senses, nor the fruitful contentment of the settled couple; not the satisfaction of love but its *passion*. And passion means suffering. There we have the fundamental fact" (Denis de Rougemont, *Love in the Western World* [Princeton, NJ: Princeton University Press, 1983], 15).

3. See *Quand ces choses commenceront: Entretiens avec Michel Tregeur* (Paris: Arléa, 1994), 192–95 (Michigan State University Press published an English translation of this, *When These Things Begin: Conversations with Michel Treguer*, in 2014), and Girard's interview with Williams in *The Girard Reader* (New York: Crossroad, 1996), 262–88. See also *Evolution and Conversion* (London: Continuum, 2007). In a paper read before a meeting of the journal *Christianity and Literature* he says much the same thing. For that paper, see *Mimesis and Theory* (Stanford, CA: Stanford University Press, 2008), 263–73.

4. *Violence and the Sacred* was originally intended to conclude with a chapter on Christianity. But the book had become so large by that point and Girard had so much to say that he decided to reserve consideration of Christianity for a separate volume. *Things Hidden* (1978) became the opportunity to develop that latter set of reflections.

5. *Deceit, Desire, and the Novel: Self and Other in Literary Structure*, tr. Yvonne Freccero (Baltimore: Johns Hopkins University Press, 1966), 2.

6. The so-called French invasion took place. Lévi-Strauss, Barthes, Lacan, Derrida, and Foucault, among others, claimed center stage in critical theory for the next twenty-five years—a move encouraged in part by Girard himself, who was instrumental (with Richard Macksey) in bringing a number of these individuals to the 1966 conference at Johns Hopkins University, "The Languages of Criticism and the Sciences of Man," and later to SUNY Buffalo.

7. Cf. Levinas's essay, "A Religion of Adults," (in *Difficult Freedom*) and Girard's remark in *Battling to the End*: "Christ will have tried to bring humanity into adulthood but humanity will have refused. I am using the future perfect on purpose because there is a deep failure in all this" (East Lansing: Michigan State University Press, 2010), 118.

"Nothing Extenuate": Love, Jealousy, and Reading in Shakespeare's *Othello*

Thanks to Benoît Chantre and ARM (Association Recherches Mimétiques) for organizing this seminar, and to Trevor Merrill for conducting it.

"'Nothing Extenuate': Love, Jealousy, and Reading in Shakespeare's *Othello*" was delivered at a conference in Paris at the Sorbonne on Girard's book on Shakespeare on November 10, 2012.

1. The conference was later published as *The Structuralist Controversy*, eds. Richard Macksey and Eugenio Donato (Baltimore: Johns Hopkins University Press, 1970).

2. See *Shakespeare's Festive Comedy: A Study of Dramatic Form and Its Relation to Social Custom* (Princeton, NJ: Princeton University Press, 1959).

3. The movie, distributed by Warner Brothers (1935), was directed by William Dieterle and Max Reinhardt, also starred James Cagney (as Bottom), Joe E. Brown (as Flute), Olivia de Havilland (as Hermia), and Dick Powell (as Lysander). Girard gives an alternate account in *Evolution and Conversion* where he reports that it was the Royal Shakespeare Company production. See René Girard with Pierpaolo Antonello and Joao Cezar de Castro Rocha, *Evolution and Conversion: Dialogues on the Origins of Culture* (London: Continuum, 2007).

4. See *A Theater of Envy: Williams Shakespeare* (New York: Oxford), 1991. Girard wrote eight chapters out of thirty-eight on *A Midsummer Night's Dream* (chapter 3–8, 19, and 27).

5. *To Double Business Bound* was written in English but to my knowledge never appeared in French.

6. See *A Theater of Envy: William Shakespeare* (London: St. Augustine's Press, 2004).

7. "Everything and Nothing": "No one has ever been so many men as this man. . . . History adds that before or after dying he found himself in the presence of God and told Him: 'I who have been so many men in vain want to be one and myself.' The voice of the Lord answered from a whirlwind: 'Neither am I anyone; I have dreamt the world as you dreamt your work, my Shakespeare, and among the forms in my dream are you, who like myself are many and no one'" (*Labyrinths*, ed. James E. Irby and Donald A. Yates [New York: New Directions Books, 1964], 249]).

8. The play confirms all five of these senses. She is lodged there on the bed ("I know not where he lodges," the Clown says in III.4.8, "and for me to devise a lodging / and say he lies here or he lies there, were to lie in mine own throat"). She lay prostrate across the bed ("there's millions now alive," Iago says in IV.1.68, "that nightly lie in those unproper beds"). She has been attacked for allegedly lying sexually with Cassio ("Lie with her! lie on her!" Othello notes in IV.1.35, "We say lie on her, when they belie her. Lie with her! that's fulsome"). She has been accused of telling falsehoods about the act, of lying about it ("for me to devise a lodging," the Clown says at III.4.8, "and say he lies here or he lies there, were to lie in mine own throat"). And her condition is mortal ("Minion, your dear lies dead," Othello says to Desdemona, when he thinks he learns of the death of Cassio in V.1.33; or Iago refers to Rodrigo, who has been killed by Cassio, as "He that lies slain here" in V.1.102).

9. Edward Pechter gathers these stories from the stage history of the play in *Othello and Interpretative Traditions* (Iowa City: University of Iowa Press, 1999), 11–30.

10. See the introduction to the New Arden edition of the play, *Othello: The Arden Shakespeare*, 3rd ed., ed. by E. A. J. Honigmann (London: Thomas Nelson and Sons, Ltd., 1997), 1–102.

11. *Othello*, V.ii.340–56.

12. Eliot's remarks on *Othello* occur in "Shakespeare and the Stoicism of Seneca," reproduced in *Selected Essays* (New York: Harcourt Brace, 1950), 107–20.

13. Leslie Fiedler, *The Stranger in Shakespeare* (New York: Stein and Day, 1972).

14. *Othello: A New Variorum Edition of Shakespeare*, 10th ed., ed. by Horace Howard Furnace (Philadelphia, PA: J. P. Lippincott, 1886), 302–7.

15. "*Ō ploute kai turanni kai teknē teknēs / hyperpherousa tō poluzēlō biō*" (380–81) ("O wealth, and empire, and skill surpassing skill in life's keen rivalries"). See Sir Richard Jebb, *Sophocles: The Plays and Fragments, Part I* (Cambridge, UK: Cambridge University Press, 1902), 60–61.

Reading Halachically and Aggadically: A Response to Reuven Kimelman

"Reading Halachically and Aggadically: A Response to Reuven Kimelman" appeared in Robert Daly, ed., *Contagion: Journal of Violence Mimesis and Culture* 9 (Spring 2002): 64–76.

1. Reuven Kimelman's paper was published as "Working Warfare and Its Restrictions in the Jewish Tradition," *Contagion* 9 (Spring 2002): 43–63.

2. Kimelman, "Working Warfare," 57.

3. Lillian Dykes constructed and distributed a pin for us to wear that said "No Scapegoats!"

4. Kimelman, "Working Warfare," 55.

5. For a record of the proceedings of this conference, see Paul Dumouchel, ed., *Violence et vérité, autour de René Girard: Colloque de Cerisy* (Paris: Éditions Grasset et Fasquelle, 1985). For

a portion of my discussion with Norbert Lohfink about the "textuality" of scripture, see "Discussion" at the end of "'I Am Joseph.'"

6. Kimelman, "Working Warfare," 55–56.

7. "From Sacrificial Violence to Responsibility: The Education of Moses in Exodus 2–4," *Contagion: Journal of Violence, Mimesis, and Culture* 6 (Spring 1999): 12–31 (see "From Sacrificial Violence to Responsibility" in this volume).

8. Kimelman, "Working Warfare," 56.

9. On the notion of commandment as a "a Thou-must which takes no account of a Thou-can," see Levinas's essay, "Revelation in the Jewish Tradition," in Seán Hand's *The Levinas Reader*, tr. S. Richmond (London: Basil Blackwell, 1989), 190–210.

10. This discussion, written by Robert Daly, followed the presentation of my paper in Robert Daly, ed., *Contagion: Journal of Violence Mimesis and Culture* 9 (Spring 2002): 77–79. I have edited Daly's printed discussion slightly to conform to my own recollection of the exchange. Interventions were made by James Alison, Reuven Kimelman, Sandor Goodhart, David Vanderhooft, Robert Hamerton-Kelly, Vern Redekop, Britt Johnston, René Girard, and Bob Hall.

The Self and Other People: Reading Conflict Resolution and Reconciliation with René Girard and Emmanuel Levinas

"The Self and Other People: Reading Conflict Resolution and Reconciliation with René Girard and Emmanuel Levinas," *Journal of Philosophy: A Cross Disciplinary Inquiry* 7, no. 16 (Fall 2011): 14–25.

1. Roel Kaptein, *On the Way of Freedom* (Dublin: The Columbia Press, 1993), 12.

2. See, for example, the volume of Yaacov Bar-Siman-Tov, ed., *From Conflict Resolution to Reconciliation* (New York: Oxford University Press, 2004) on this idea. "In its simplest form," Bar-Siman-Tov writes, "reconciliation means restoring friendship and harmony between the rival sides after conflict resolution, or transforming relations of hostility and resentment to friendly and harmonious ones" (4).

3. Kaptein, *On the Way of Freedom*, 12. Nearly thirty years ago, at a conference held in Cerisy-la-Salle in 1983 in honor of René Girard, I first met Roel Kaptein. We took to each other immediately and I spent a wonderful afternoon wandering the French countryside with him and another member of his religious community, Aat van Rhijn. We continued to meet at COV&R conferences and to share insights about scapegoating and mimetic desire. His untimely death in 1996 of brain cancer cut short the life of an extraordinary human being whose work in peacemaking and conflict resolution in the broadest terms was only beginning to be more widely known. I dedicate this essay to his memory.

4. See, for example, Robert Daly's volume on the COV&R conference of 2000 in *Contagion* 9 (Spring 2002) which took place at Boston College in which the relation of the five "revealed" religions to Girardian thinking were addressed.

5. See, for example, Paul Nuechterlein's "Girard lectionary" (http://www.girardianlectionary.net/) or the website on "preaching peace" developed by Michael Hardin and Anthony Bartlett (http://www.preachingpeace.org/).

6. Jacques Derrida offers this insight in an essay translated recently (although obscured to some extent from public view previously) entitled "La littérature au secret" (which would have to be

translated, if taken literally, as something like "Literature Put into Solitary Confinement"). The theme of his essay is his analysis of Biblical scripture. See *The Gift of Death, Second Edition, and Literature in Secret*, tr. David Wills (Chicago: University of Chicago Press, 2008).

7. The work of Jean-Pierre Dupuy should be cited in this context, as should the work of Scott R. Garrels on "mirror neurons." See, for example, his essay "Imitation, Mirror Neurons, and Mimetic Desire: Convergence between the Mimetic Theory of René Girard and Empirical Research on Imitation," *Contagion* 12–13 (2005–2006): 47–86. See also Garrels, ed., *Mimesis and Science: Empirical Research on Imitation and the Mimetic Theory of Culture and Religion* (East Lansing: Michigan State University Press, 2011).

8. In that regard, my identification is shared by Charles Mabee. See, for example, his essay, "A New Approach to the Christian-Jewish Dialogue," in Deborah Ellens, Marvin Sweeney, Michael Floyd, and Wonil Kim, eds., *Reading the Hebrew Bible for a New Millennium: Form, Concept, and Theological Perspective*, vol. 1 (Harrisburg, PA: Trinity Press International, 2000), 321–27.

9. Kaptein, *On the Way of Freedom*, 12.

10. Isaiah 53:10: "But the LORD chose to crush him."

11. Kaptein, *On the Way of Freedom*, 12.

12. Vern Neufeld Redekop, *From Violence to Blessing* (Toronto: Novalis, 2002), 148. The subtitle of Redekop's book, *How an Understanding of Deep-Rooted Conflict Can Open Paths to Reconciliation*, echoes the work of John W. Burton, work that Redekop credits with the theoretical underpinnings of this idea. See Burton's *Resolving Deep-Rooted Conflicts* (Lanham, MD: University Press of America, 1987); *Deviance, Terrorism and War* (Oxford: Martin Robertson, 1979); *Conflict: Human Needs Theory* (New York: St. Martin's Press, 1990); and *Conflict: Resolution and Prevention* (New York: St. Martin's Press, 1990). See also Burton and Frank Dukes, eds., *Conflict: Readings in Management and Resolution* (New York: St Martin's Press, 1990). Redekop's volume also contains a useful bibliography of conflict resolution theory.

13. *Mensonge romantique et vérité romanesque* (Paris: Grasset, 1961) is the original title of Girard's book, published in English as *Deceit, Desire, and the Novel*, tr. Yvonne Freccero (Baltimore: Johns Hopkins University Press, 1965). Benoît Chantre makes that point in his conversation with Girard in *Achever Clausewitz* and again in the postface to the second edition. See *Achever Clausewitz: Entretiens avec Benoît Chantre* (Paris: Flammarion, 2011). Levinas's sentence has appeared in numerous essays. See, for example, "A Religion of Adults" in *Difficult Freedom: Essays on Judaism*, tr. Seán Hand (Baltimore: Johns Hopkins University Press, 1990), 11–23. The particular phrase to which we refer, "ethics is an optics," occurs, for example, in the original *Difficile liberté* (Paris: Albin Michel, 1983) on page 33: L'éthique n'est pas le corollaire de la vision de Dieu, elle est cette vision même. L'éthique est une optique ("Ethics is not the corollary of the vision of God, it is that vision. Ethics is an optics," my translation).

14. See, for example, *The Star of Redemption*, tr. Barbara E. Galli (Madison: University of Wisconsin Press, 2005), chapter 1.

15. It was Alexandre Kojève who first pointed out how literally Hegel thought he was hearing the end of history. See his *Introduction to the Reading of Hegel* (Ithaca, NY: Cornell University Press, 1980).

16. Rosenzweig speaks about his ideas in the opening chapter to *The Star of Redemption*, a work, Levinas famously says, is too omnipresent in his own book to cite.

17. See, for example, Levinas's foreword to Stéphane Mosès's book on Rosenzweig, *System and*

Revelation: The Philosophy of Franz Rosenzweig, tr. Catherine Tihanyi (Detroit: Wayne State University Press, 1992), 13–22.

18. In a public interview at the American Academy of Religion, Jacques Derrida was asked directly about this idea and responded that he could not accept it. An account of that exchange was published in Yvonne Sherwood and Kevin Hart, eds., *Derrida and Religion: Other Testaments* (New York: Routledge, 2004), 27–52.

19. Georges Poulet, *The Metamorphoses of the Circle*, tr. Carley Dawson and Eliott Coleman (Baltimore: Johns Hopkins University Press, 1967). The reference to this common idea occurs throughout Poulet's book.

20. *Otherwise than Being, or, Beyond Essence*, tr. Alphonso Lingis (Pittsburgh, PA: Duquesne University Press, 1998), 142.

21. See Girard, *Du double à l'unité* (Paris: Plon, 1963), tr. James G. Williams, as *Resurrection from the Underground: Feodor Dostoevsky* (New York: Crossroad, 1997), and Levinas, *Autrement qu'être: ou, au délà de l'essence* (Paris: Livre de Poche, 2004), tr. Alphonso Lingis, as *Otherwise than Being, or, Beyond Essence* (Pittsburgh, PA: Duquesne University Press, 1998).

From the Sacred to the Holy: René Girard, Emmanuel Levinas, and Substitution

I thank Benoît Chantre for working through these ideas with me.

1. Levinas, *Otherwise than Being, or, Beyond Essence*, tr. Alphonso Lingis (Pittsburgh, PA: Duquesne University Press, 1998), 145–46.

2. Levinas, *Otherwise Than Being*, 15.

3. Levinas, *Otherwise Than Being*, 102.

4. Levinas, *Otherwise Than Being*, 118.

5. Levinas, *Otherwise Than Being*, 192n24.

6. Levinas, *Difficult Freedom. Essays on Judaism*, tr. Seán Hand (Baltimore: Johns Hopkins University Press, 1990), 191.

7. See Emmanuel Levinas, *Of God Who Comes to Mind*, tr. Bettina Bergo (Stanford, CA: Stanford University Press, 1998), ix.

8. See "Preface to the German Edition of *Totality and Infinity*" in *Entre Nous: On Thinking-of-the-Other* (New York: Columbia University Press, 1998), 197.

9. For example, in *Achever Clausewitz*, tr. Mary Baker, *Battling to the End: Conversations with Benoît Chantre* (East Lansing: Michigan State University Press, 2009). See the second edition of this book edited by Benoît Chantre (Paris: Flammarion, 2008).

10. See "Dry September" (1931). The trigger seems to be the barber's insistence that the man didn't do it.

11. For a recent analysis along these lines, see Paul Dumouchel, *Le sacrifice inutile: Essai sur la violence politique* (Paris: Flammarion, 2012).

12. Levinas, Emmanuel, *Existence and Existents*, tr. Alphonso Lingis (Pittsburgh, PA: Duquesne University, 2001), 57–58.

13. On the idea of the importance of prophetic thinking for this and subsequent generations of Jews, see Pierre Bouretz, *Witness for the Future: Philosophy and Messianism*, tr. Michael B. Smith (Baltimore: Johns Hopkins University Press, 2010). The book includes chapters on Cohen, Rosenzweig, Benjamin, Scholem, Buber, Bloch, Strauss, Jonas, and Levinas. One could imagine expanding the list to Kafka, Jabès, Jankélévitz, and Derrida.

14. On this idea, see George Steiner, "Our Homeland, The Text" in *Salmagundi* 66 (Winter–Spring 1985): 4–25.

15. See Michel Serres's essay, on the occasion of the induction of Girard into the French Academy, in *For René Girard: Essays in Friendship and in Truth* (East Lansing: Michigan State University Press, 2008), 1–17.

Back to the Future: The Prophetic and the Apocalyptic in Jewish and Christian Settings

"Back to the Future: The Prophetic and the Apocalyptic in Jewish and Christian Settings" was delivered at the Colloquium on Violence and Religion conference in Tokyo, Japan, July 5–8, 2012. I thank Thomas Ryba, my colleague at Purdue, for suggesting this reference to the popular movie series.

1. *Achever Clausewitz* (Paris: Carnets Nord, 2007), tr. Mary Baker, *Battling to the End: Conversations with Benoît Chantre* (East Lansing: Michigan State University Press, 2009).

2. See, for example, Michel Foucault, *Society Must Be Defended: Lectures at the College de France, 1975–1976* (New York: Picador, 2003), 15.

3. Girard, *Battling*, x.

4. See, for example, Martin Buber, *The Prophetic Faith* (New York: Collier, 1985).

5. See Gershom Scholem, *The Messianic Idea in Judaism, and Other Essays on Jewish Spirituality* (New York: Schocken, 1995).

6. See Buber, *On the Bible: Eighteen Studies*, edited by Nahum Glatzer, with an introduction by Harold Bloom (New York: Schocken, 1982), 172–87, and Buber, *On Judaism*, edited by Nahum Glatzer (New York: Schocken, 1967), 214–25.

7. See George Steiner's essay "Our Homeland, the Text," *Salmagundi* 66 (Winter-Spring 1985), 4–25.

8. Charles Mabee is developing what seems to me a brilliant prophetic reading of the four horsemen, which in my view is indistinguishable from the strong apocalyptic reading.

9. See "Theses on the Philosophy of History" in *Illuminations*, ed. Hannah Arendt (New York: Schocken, 1969), 253–64.

Conclusions: Reading René Girard

1. (Paris: Bibliothèque nationale de France, 2003), tr. Matthew Pattillo and David Dawson, as *Sacrifice* (East Lansing: Michigan State University Press, 2011).

2. All page references in this chapter are to the English edition.

3. *Sacrifice*, xi.

4. My colleague, Charles Mabee, would argue that the figure in the text we know as Jesus is Paul's creation so that it would be Paul who identifies Jesus with Isaiah, and Paul, who would certainly be aware of the common Rabbinic practice of "oral Torah," of reading Torah in such a way that recognizes the site of reading as a site of instruction, who would identify Jesus as reading in such a way. Although I am not in a position to evaluate this view theologically or historically, it seems to me that Mabee's view is entirely compatible with the view expressed in this paper and adds an additional (and welcome) layer of complexity to it.

5. Here is one text from Isaiah 1:4–13 on the anti-sacrificial: "4 Ah sinful nation, a people laden with iniquity, a seed of evil-doers, children that deal corruptly; they have forsaken the LORD, they have condemned the Holy One of Israel, they are turned away backward. . . . 11 To what purpose is the multitude of your sacrifices unto Me? saith the LORD; I am full of the burnt-offerings of rams, and the fat of fed beasts; and I delight not in the blood of bullocks, or of lambs, or of he-goats. . . . 13 Bring no more vain oblations; it is an offering of abomination unto Me; new moon and sabbath, the holding of convocations—I cannot endure iniquity along with the solemn assembly."

And here is another on the scapegoat: Isaiah 52:13–53:12: "13 Behold, My servant shall prosper, he shall be exalted and lifted up, and shall be very high. 14 According as many were appalled at thee—so marred was his visage unlike that of a man, and his form unlike that of the sons of men—15 So shall he startle many nations, kings shall shut their mouths because of him; for that which had not been told them shall they see, and that which they had not heard shall they perceive. 53:1 'Who would have believed our report? And to whom hath the arm of the LORD been revealed? 2 For he shot up right forth as a sapling, and as a root out of a dry ground; he had no form nor comeliness, that we should look upon him, nor beauty that we should delight in him. 3 He was despised, and forsaken of men, a man of pains, and acquainted with disease, and as one from whom men hide their face: he was despised, and we esteemed him not. 4 Surely our diseases he did bear, and our pains he carried; whereas we did esteem him stricken, smitten of God, and afflicted. 5 But he was wounded because of our transgressions, he was crushed because of our iniquities: the chastisement of our welfare was upon him, and with his stripes we were healed. 6 All we like sheep did go astray, we turned everyone to his own way; and the LORD hath made to light on him the iniquity of us all. 7 He was oppressed, though he humbled himself and opened not his mouth; as a lamb that is led to the slaughter, and as a sheep that before her shearers is dumb; yea, he opened not his mouth. 8 By oppression and judgment he was taken away, and with his generation who did reason? for he was cut off out of the land of the living, for the transgression of my people to whom the stroke was due. 9 And they made his grave with the wicked, and with the rich his tomb; although he had done no violence, neither was any deceit in his mouth.' 10 Yet it pleased the LORD to crush him by disease; to see if his soul would offer itself in restitution, that he might see his seed, prolong his days, and that the purpose of the LORD might prosper by his hand: 11 Of the travail of his soul he shall see to the full, even My servant, who by his knowledge did justify the Righteous One to the many, and their iniquities he did bear. 12 Therefore will I divide him a portion among the great, and he shall divide the spoil with the mighty; because he bared his soul unto death, and was numbered with the transgressors; yet he bore the sin of many, and made intercession for the transgressors."

Bibliography

Adams, Rebecca, and René Girard. "Violence, Difference, Sacrifice: A Conversation with René Girard." *Religion and Literature* 25.2 (Summer 1993): 9–33.

"Albert Camus—Banquet Speech." *Nobelprize.org.* http://www.nobelprize.org/nobel_prizes/literature/laureates/1957/camus-speech.html.

Alter, Robert. *The Art of Biblical Narrative.* New York: Basic Books, 1981.

———. *The Five Books of Moses.* New York: Norton, 2008.

Arendt, Hannah, ed. *Illuminations.* New York: Schocken, 1969.

Astell, Ann W., and Sandor Goodhart, eds. *Sacrifice, Scripture, and Substitution: Readings in Ancient Judaism and Christianity.* Notre Dame, IN: University of Notre Dame Press, 2010.

Bandera, Cesáreo. *Mimesis conflictiva: Ficción literaria y violencia en Cervantes y Calderon.* Madrid: Gredos, 1975.

———. *The Humble Story of Don Quixote: Reflections on the Birth of the Modern Novel.* Washington, DC: Catholic University of America Press, 2006.

———. *A Refuge of Lies: Reflections on Faith and Fiction.* East Lansing: Michigan State University Press, 2013.

———. *The Sacred Game: The Role of the Sacred in the Genesis of Modern Literature.* University Park: Pennsylvania State University Press, 1994.

Barber, C. L. *Shakespeare's Festive Comedy: A Study of Dramatic Form and Its Relation to Social Custom.* Princeton, NJ: Princeton University Press, 1959.

Bar-Siman-Tov, Yaacov, ed. *From Conflict Resolution to Reconciliation*. New York: Oxford University Press, 2004.

Bellan-Boyer, Paul, ed. *Bulletin of the Colloquium on Violence and Religion* 19 (November 2000).

Benjamin, Walter. "Theses on the Philosophy of History." In Arendt (1969), 253–64.

Berlin, Adele, et al. *The Jewish Study Bible*. New York: Oxford University Press, 2004.

Bialik, Hayim Nahman, and Yehoshua Hana Ravnitsky, eds. *The Book of Legends/Sefer Ha-Aggadah: Legends from the Talmud and Midrash*. Tr. William G. Braude. New York: Schocken, 1992.

Bishop, Jonathan. *The Covenant: A Reading*. Springfield, IL: Templegate, 1982.

Blanchot, Maurice. *The Book to Come*. Stanford, CA: Stanford University Press, 2003.

——. *The Gaze of Orpheus and Other Literary Essays*. Barrytown, NY: Station Hill Press, 1981.

——. *The Infinite Conversation*. Minneapolis: University of Minnesota, 1992.

——. *The Space of Literature*. Lincoln: University of Nebraska, 1982.

——. *The Work of Fire*. Stanford, CA: Stanford University Press, 1995.

Borch-Jacobsen, Mikkel. *The Freudian Subject*. Tr. Catherine Porter. Stanford, CA: Stanford University Press, 1988.

Borges, Jorge Luis. "Everything and Nothing." In Borges (1964), 248–249.

——. *Labyrinths*. Ed. Donald Yates and James E. Irby. New York: New Directions, 1964.

Bouretz, Pierre. *Witness for the Future: Philosophy and Messianism*. Tr. Michael B. Smith. Baltimore: Johns Hopkins University Press, 2010.

Boyarin, Daniel. *A Radical Jew: Paul and the Politics of Identity*. Berkeley: University of California Press, 1994.

——. "The Subversion of the Jews: Moses' Veil and the Hermeneutics of Supersession." *Diacritics* 23.2 (Summer 1993): 16–35.

Buber, Martin. "Biblical Humanism." In Buber (1982), 211–216.

——. *On Judaism*. Ed. Nahum Glatzer. New York: Schocken, 1967.

——. *On the Bible: Eighteen Studies*. Ed. Nahum Glatzer. New York: Schocken, 1982.

——. *The Prophetic Faith*. New York: Collier, 1985.

Buber, Martin, and Franz Rosenzweig. *Scripture and Translation*. Bloomington: Indiana University Press, 1994.

Burke, Kenneth. "*Othello*: An Essay to Illustrate a Method." In Newstok (2007), 65–100.

Burton, John. *Conflict: Human Needs Theory*. New York: St. Martin's Press, 1990.

——. *Conflict: Resolution and Prevention*. New York: St. Martin's Press, 1990.

——. *Deviance, Terrorism, and War*. Oxford: Martin Robertson, 1979.

——. *Resolving Deep-Rooted Conflicts*. Lanham University Press of America, 1987.

Burton, John, and Frank Dukes, eds. *Conflict: Readings in Management and Resolution*. New York: St. Martin's Press, 1990.

Chouraqui, André. *Histoire de judaïsme*. Paris: Presses Universitaires de France, 1964.

Cohen, Arthur. *The Soncino Chumash*. London: The Soncino Press, 1979.

Daly, Robert, ed. *Contagion: Journal of Violence Mimesis and Culture* 9 (Spring 2002).

de Man, Paul. *Blindness and Insight*. New York: Oxford University Press, 1971.

Derrida, Jacques. *La Carte Postale*. Paris: Flammarion, 1980.

———. "Literature in Secret." In Derrida (2008), 117–158.

———. *The Gift of Death, Second Edition, and Literature in Secret*. Tr. David Wills. Chicago: University of Chicago Press, 2008.

Donato, Eugenio, and Richard Macksey, eds. *The Structuralist Controversy: The Languages of Criticism and the Sciences of Man*. Baltimore: Johns Hopkins University Press, 1970.

Dostoyevsky, Fyodor. *The Brothers Karamazov*. Tr. Constance Garnett. Ed. Ralph Matlaw. New York: Norton, 1976.

Deguy, Michel, and Jean-Pierre Dupuy, eds. *René Girard et la problème du mal*. Paris: Grasset, 1982.

Dumouchel, Paul. *Le sacrifice inutile: Essai sur la violence politique*. Paris: Flammarion, 2012.

Dumouchel, Paul, ed. "Discussion." Tr. Sandor Goodhart. In Dumouchel (1985), 84–89.

———. *Violence and Truth: On the Work of René Girard*. London: Athlone Press, 1987.

———. *Violence and Truth: On the Work of René Girard*. Stanford, CA: Stanford University Press, 1988.

———. *Violence et vérité, autour de René Girard: Colloque de Cerisy*. Paris: Edition Grasset et Fasquelle, 1985.

Dumouchel, Paul, and Jean-Pierre Dupuy. *L'enfer des choses*. Paris: Seuil, 1979.

Dumouchel, Paul, and Jean-Pierre Dupuy, eds. *L'auto-organisation: De la physique au politique*. Paris: Seuil, 1983.

Dupuy, Jean-Pierre. *Ordre et désordres*. Paris: Seuil, 1982.

Duran, Robert. "Editor's Introduction: Literature as Theory." In Girard (2008), xi–xxvi.

Dylan, Bob. "Highway 61 Revisited." In *Bob Dylan—Lyrics: 1962–2001*. New York: Simon and Schuster, 2004, 178.

———. "The Times They Are A-Changin'." In *Bob Dylan—Lyrics: 1962–2001*. New York: Simon and Schuster, 2004, 81–82.

Eichrodt, Walther. *Theology of the Old Testament*. Tr. J. A. Baker. 2 vols. Philadelphia, PA: Westminster Press, 1961.

Eliade, Mircea. *The Sacred and the Profane: The Nature of Religion*. New York: Harcourt, 1987.

Eliot, T. S. "Shakespeare and the Stoicism of Seneca." *Selected Essays*. New York: Harcourt, 1950, 107–20.

Ellens, Deborah, M. Sweeney, M. Floyd, and W. Kim, eds. *Reading the Hebrew Bible for a New Millennium: Form, Concept, and Theological Perspective*. Harrisburg, PA: Trinity Press International, 2000.

Faulkner, William. "Dry September." *Scribner's Magazine* 90.1 (January 1931): 49–56.

Feuer, A. C., and Nosson Scherman. *Aseres Hadibros/The Ten Commandments*. Brooklyn, NY: Mesorah, 1981.

Fiedler, Leslie. *The Stranger in Shakespeare*. New York: Stein and Day, 1972.

Fish, Stanley. *Is There a Text in This Class*. Cambridge, MA: Harvard University Press, 1980.

Fishbane, Michael. *Biblical Interpretation in Ancient Israel*. Oxford, UK: Clarendon, 1985.

———. "Jewish Biblical Exegesis: Presuppositions and Principles." In Greenspahn (1982), 91–110.

———. *The Garments of Torah: Essays in Biblical Hermeneutics*. Bloomington: Indiana University Press, 1989.

Foucault, Michel. "La pensée du dehors." *Critique* 229 (1966): 523–46.

———. *Society Must Be Defended: Lectures at the College de France, 1975–1976*. New York: Picador, 2003, 15.

———. *The Care of the Self*. London: Penguin, 1994.

———. *The History of Sexuality*. Vol. 2, *The Use of Pleasure*. London: Penguin, 1992.

Fox, Everett, ed. *The Five Books of Moses. Genesis, Exodus, Leviticus, Numbers, Deuteronomy*. New York: Schocken, 1995.

Frazer, James George. *The Golden Bough: A Study in Magic and Religion*. 12 vols. London: Macmillan, 1906–15.

Freccero, John. "The Fig-Tree and the Laurel: Petrarch's Poetics." *Diacritics* 5 (1975): 34–40.

Freud, Sigmund. *The Interpretation of Dreams*. Tr. James Strachey. New York: Avon, 1965.

———. *Moses and Monotheism*. Tr. Catherine Jones. New York: Random House, 1955.

———. *Totem and Taboo*. Tr. James Strachey. New York: W. W. Norton, 1950.

Frye, Northrop. *Anatomy of Criticism*. Princeton: Princeton University Press, 1966.

Gans, Eric. "Pour un esthétique triangulaire." *Esprit* 429 (November 1973): 581.

Garrels, Scott R. "Imitation, Mirror Neurons, and Mimetic Desire: Convergence between the Mimetic Theory of René Girard and Empirical Research on Imitation." *Contagion* 12–13 (2005–2006): 47–86.

Garrels, Scott, R. ed., *Mimesis and Science: Empirical Research on Imitation and the Mimetic Theory of Culture and Religion*. East Lansing: Michigan State University Press, 2011.

Gaultier, Jules de. *Le bovarysme*. Paris: Mercure de France, 1921.

Gesenius,William. *Hebrew and English Lexicon of the Old Testament*. Tr. Francis Brown, S. R. Driver, and Charles Briggs. London: Oxford University Press, 1951.

Giraldi, Giovanni Battista. *Hecatommithi (One Hundred Stories)*. Tr. Joseph Satin. In Satin (1966), 430–439.

Girard, René. *Achever Clausewitz. Entretiens avec Benoît Chantre*. Paris: Carnets Nord, 2007.

———. *Achever Clausewitz: En collaboration avec Benoît Chantre*. Paris: Flammarion, 2011.

———. *A Theater of Envy: William Shakespeare*. London: St. Augustine's Press, 2004.

———. *A Theater of Envy: William Shakespeare*. New York: Oxford, 1991.

———. *Battling to the End: Conversations with Benoît Chantre.* Tr. Mary Baker. East Lansing: Michigan State University Press, 2010.

———. *Deceit, Desire, and the Novel.* Tr. Yvonne Freccero. Baltimore: Johns Hopkins University Press, 1965.

———. *Des choses cachées depuis la fondation du monde.* Paris: Grasset, 1978.

———. "Dionysus and the Violent Genesis of the Sacred." Tr. Sandor Goodhart. *boundary 2* 5.2 (Winter 1977): 487–505.

———. "Discussion avec René Girard." *Esprit* 429 (November 1973): 528–63.

———. *Du double à l'unité.* Paris: Plon, 1963.

———. *Evolution and Conversion: Dialogues on the Origins of Culture.* With Pierpaolo Antonello and Joao Cezar de Castro Rocha. London: Continuum, 2007.

———. *I See Satan Fall Like Lightning.* Tr. James G. Williams. Maryknoll, NY: Orbis, 2001.

———. *Je vois Satan tomber comme l'éclair.* Paris: Grasset, 1999.

———. *Job, the Victim of his People.* Tr. Yvonne Freccero. Stanford, CA: Stanford University Press, 1987.

———. *La route antique des hommes pervers.* Paris: Grasset, 1985.

———. *La violence et le sacré.* Paris: Grasset, 1972.

———. *Le bouc émissaire.* Paris: Grasset, 1982.

———. *Le sacrifice.* Paris: Bibliothèque nationale de France, 2003.

———. "Les malédictions contre les pharisiens et la révélation évangélique." *Bulletin du Centre Protestant d'Études* 27 (Geneva: CPE, 1975): 5–29.

———. *Mensonge romantique et vérité romanesque.* Paris: Grasset, 1961.

———. *Mimesis and Theory: Essays on Literature and Criticism, 1953–2005.* Stanford, CA: Stanford University Press, 2008.

———. *Oedipus Unbound: Selected Writings on Rivalry and Desire.* Ed. Mark Anspach. Stanford, CA: Stanford University Press, 2004.

———. *Quand ces choses commenceront: Entretiens avec Michel Treguer.* Paris: Arléa, 1994.

———. "Response by René Girard." In Swartley (2000), 308–20.

———. *Resurrection from the Underground: Feodor Dostoevsky.* Tr. James G. Williams. New York: Crossroad, 1997.

———. *Sacrifice.* Tr. Matthew Pattillo and David Dawson. East Lansing: Michigan State University Press, 2011.

———. *Shakespeare: Les feux de l'envie.* Tr. Bernard Vincent. Paris: Grasset et Fasquelle, 1990.

———. *The Scapegoat.* Tr. Yvonne Freccero. Baltimore: Johns Hopkins University Press, 1986.

———. *Things Hidden since the Foundation of the World.* Tr. Stephen Bann and Michael Metteer. Stanford, CA: Stanford University Press, 1987.

———. *Violence and the Sacred.* Tr. Patrick Gregory. Baltimore: Johns Hopkins University Press, 1977.

Goldmann, Lucien. *Towards a Sociology of the Novel*. Tr. Alan Sheridan. London: Tavistock, 1975.

Goodhart, Sandor. "'*al lo-chamas asah*' (Although He Had Done No Violence): Isaiah 52–53, René Girard, and the Innocent Victim." In Swartley (2000), 200–217.

———. "Biblical Theory and Criticism, 2: Modern Criticism." In Groden and Kreiswirth (1993), 84–89.

———. "Excluding Judaism." *Shofar* 22.2 (Winter 2004): 1–8.

———. "From Sacrificial Violence to Responsibility: The Education of Moses in *Exodus 2–4*." *Contagion: A Journal of Violence, Mimesis, and Culture* 6 (Spring 1999): 12–31.

———. "'I Am Joseph': Judaism, Anti-Idolatry, and the Prophetic Law." In Dumouchel (1988), 53–74.

———. "'I Am Joseph': Judaism, Anti-Idolatry, and the Prophetic Law." In Goodhart (1996), 99–121.

———. "'I Am Joseph': Judaism, Anti-Idolatry, and the Prophetic Law." *To Honor René Girard*. Ed. Alphonse Juilland. *Stanford French Review* 10.1–3 (1986): 85–111.

———. "Isaiah 52–53, René Girard, and the Innocent Victim." In Palaver (1994), 12.

———. "'Je suis Joseph': René Girard et la loi prophétique." Tr. Paul Dumouchel. In Dumouchel (1985), 69–83.

———. "Reading Halachically and Aggadically: A Response to Reuven Kimelman." In Daly (Spring 2002), 64–76.

———. "Reading Religion, Literature, and the End of Desire: *Mensonge romantique et vérité romanesque* at Fifty." *Religion and Literature* 43.3 (Autumn 2011): 150–58.

———. "Reading the Ten Commandments. Torah, Interpretation, and the Name of God." In Goodhart (1996), 122–38.

———. "René Girard." In Groden and Kreiswirth (1993), 355–56.

———. "Reply to Father Raymund Schwager and Józef Niewiadomski." In Palaver (March 1995), 12–13.

———. "Reply to René Girard." Modified from "We Will Cling Fast to Your Torah: A Response to René Girard's Reply to *Violence Renounced*." See Bellan-Boyer (November 2000), 14–17.

———. *Sacrificing Commentary: Reading the End of Literature*. Baltimore: Johns Hopkins University Press, 1996.

———. "Second Reply to Raymund Schwager." In Palaver (1996), 10–12.

———. "The End of Sacrifice: Reading René Girard and the Hebrew Bible." *Contagion: Journal of Violence Mimesis and Culture* 14 (2007): 59–78.

———. "The Prophetic Tradition as a Basis for Jewish-Christian Dialogue." In Palaver (March 1995), 4.

———. "The Self and Other People: Reading Conflict Resolution and Reconciliation with René Girard and Emmanuel Levinas." *Journal of Philosophy: A Cross Disciplinary Inquiry* 7.16 (Fall 2011): 14–25.

———. "We Will Cling Fast to Your Torah: A Response to René Girard's Reply to *Violence Renounced*." In Bellan-Boyer (November 2000), 14–17.

Goodhart, Sandor, Jørgen Jørgensen, Thomas Ryba, James G. Williams, eds. *For René Girard: Essays in Friendship and Truth*. East Lansing: Michigan State University Press, 2009.

Greenspahn, Frederick, ed. *Scripture in the Jewish and Christian Traditions: Authority, Interpretation, Relevance*. Nashville, TN: Parthenon, 1982.

Groden, Michael, Martin Kreiswirth, and Imre Szeman, eds. *The Johns Hopkins Guide to Literary Theory and Criticism*. Baltimore, MD: Johns Hopkins University Press, 1993.

Hamerton-Kelly, Robert G. *Sacred Violence: Paul's Hermeneutic of the Cross*. Philadelphia, PA: Fortress Press, 1993.

———. *Violent Origins: Walter Burkert, René Girard, and Jonathan Z. Smith on Ritual Killing and Cultural Formation*. Stanford, CA: Stanford University Press, 1987.

Hand, Seán, ed. *The Levinas Reader*. London: Basil Blackwell, 1989.

Handelman, Susan. *The Slayers of Moses*. Albany: SUNY Press, 1982.

Hartman, Geoffrey H. "Midrash as Law and Literature." In Hartman and O'Hara (2004), 205–222.

———. "The Struggle for the Text." In Hartman and Budick (1986), 3–18.

Hartman, Geoffrey H. and Daniel T. O'Hara, eds. *The Geoffrey Hartman Reader*. New York: Fordham University Press, 2004.

Hartman, Geoffrey H. and Sanford Budick, eds. *Midrash and Literature*. New Haven, CT: Yale University Press, 1986.

Havelock, Eric. *Preface to Plato*. Cambridge, MA: Belknap Press, 1963.

Hegel, Georg Wilhelm Friedrich. *Phenomenology of Mind*. Tr. J. B. Baillie. New York: Harper and Row, 1967.

Heidegger, Martin. *Being and Time*. Tr. John Macquarrie and Edward Robinson. New York: Harper, 1962.

Hertz, J.H. Rabbi, ed. *The Pentateuch and the Haftorahs. Hebrew Text, English Translation, and Commentary*. London: Soncino Press, 1979.

Heschel, Abraham J. *The Prophets*. New York: Harper, 2001.

Holy Scriptures According to the Masoretic Text: A New Translation, The. Philadelphia, PA: Jewish Publication Society of America, 1917.

Husserl, Edmund. *Logical Investigations*. Tr. J. N. Findlay. 2 vols. London: Routledge, 1970.

Isaiah, A. B., and B. Sharfman, *The Pentateuch and Rashi's Commentary: A Linear Translation in English*. Brooklyn: S. S. and R., 1949.

Jebb, Sir Richard. *Sophocles: The Plays and Fragments, Part I*. Cambridge, UK: Cambridge University Press, 1902, 60–61.

Jensen, Hans. "Nature, Bible, Priestly Theology: A Reply to Sandor Goodhart and Charles Mabee." In Palaver (March 1995), 4.

Johnsen, William A. *Violence and Modernism: Ibsen, Joyce, and Woolf*. Gainesville: University Press of Florida, 2003.

Juilland, Alphonse, ed. "Bibliography." *To Honor René Girard. Stanford French Review* 10.1–3 (1986): iii–xxxii.

Kaptein, Roel. *On the Way of Freedom*. Dublin: The Columbia Press, 1993.

Kaufmann, Yehezkel. *The Religion of Israel*. Tr. Moshe Greenberg. New York: Schocken, 1972.

Kimelman, Reuven, "Working Warfare and Its Restrictions in the Jewish Tradition." *Contagion* 9 (Spring 2002): 43–63.

Kojève, Alexandre. *Introduction to the Reading of Hegel*. Ithaca, NY: Cornell University Press, 1980.

Lacan, Jacques. "Of Structure as an Inmixing of an Otherness Prerequisite to Any Subject Whatever." In Donato and Macksey (1970), 186–200.

Lapide, Pinchas. *The Resurrection of Jesus: A Jewish Perspective*. Tr. Wilhem C. Linss. Eugene, OR: Wipf and Stock, 2002.

Levi, Primo. *I Sommersi e i Salvati*. Torino: Giulio Einaudi, 1986.

———. *The Drowned and the Saved*. Tr. Raymond Rosenthal. New York: Vintage, 1989.

Levinas, Emmanuel. "A Religion of Adults." In Levinas (1990), 11–23.

———. *Autrement qu'être: ou, au délà de l'essence*. Paris: Livre de Poche, 2004.

———. *Beyond the Verse: Talmudic Readings and Lectures*. Tr. Gary Mole. Bloomington: Indiana University Press, 1994.

———. *Difficile liberté: Essais sur le judaïsme*. Paris: Albin Michel, 1983.

———. *Difficult Freedom. Essays on Judaism*. Tr. Seán Hand. Baltimore: Johns Hopkins University Press, 1990.

———. *Entre Nous: On Thinking-of-the-Other*. Tr. Michael B. Smith. New York: Columbia University Press, 1998.

———. *Existence and Existents*. Tr. Alphonso Lingis. Pittsburgh, PA: Duquesne University, 2001.

———. "Forward." In Mosès (1992), 13–22.

———. *In the Time of the Nations*. Tr. Michael B. Smith. Bloomington: Indiana University Press, 1994.

———. *L'au delà du verset*. Paris: Minuit, 1982.

———. *New Talmudic Readings*. Tr. Richard A Cohen. Pittsburgh, PA: Duquesne University Press, 1999.

———. *Nine Talmudic Studies*. Tr. Annette Aronowicz. Bloomington: Indiana University Press, 1993.

———. *Of God Who Comes to Mind*. Tr. Bettina Bergo. Stanford, CA: Stanford University Press, 1998.

———. *Otherwise than Being, or, Beyond Essence*. Tr. Alphonso Lingis. Pittsburgh, PA: Duquesne University Press, 1998.

———. "Pour un humanisme hébraique." In Levinas (1983), 350–54.

———. "Preface to the German Edition of *Totality and Infinity*." In Levinas (*Entre Nous*, 1998), 197–200.

———. "Revelation in the Jewish Tradition." In Hand (1989), 190–210.

———. *Totality and Infinity: An Essay on Exteriority*. Tr. Alphonso Lingis. Pittsburgh, PA.: Duquesne University Press, 1969.

———. "Useless Suffering." In Levinas (*Entre Nous*, 1998), 91–101.

Lévi-Strauss, Claude. "The Science of the Concrete." In *The Savage Mind*. Chicago: University of Chicago Press, 1966, 3–33.

Lévy, Bernard-Henri. *Barbarism with a Human Face*. Tr. George Holoch. New York: Harper and Row, 1979.

———. *The Testament of God*. Tr. George Holoch. Baltimore: Johns Hopkins University Press, 1985.

Livingston, Paisley. *Models of Desire: René Girard and the Psychology of Mimesis*. Baltimore: Johns Hopkins University Press, 1992.

Livingston, Paisley, ed. *Disorder and Order*. Saratoga, CA: Anma Libri, 1984.

Lohfink, Norbert. *Gewalt und Gewaltlosigkeit im Alten Testament*. Freiburg, Germany: Herder, 1983.

———. *The Covenant Never Revoked: Biblical Reflections on Christian-Jewish Dialogue*. Tr. John Scullion. New York: Paulist Press, 1991.

Mabee, Charles. "A New Approach to the Christian-Jewish Dialogue." In Ellens, Sweeney, Floyd, and Kim (2000), 321–27.

———. "A New Grammar for Jewish-Christian Dialogue: The Prophetic Vortex of the Common Scriptures." In Palaver (March 1995), 4.

Mazzotta, Giuseppe. *Dante, Poet of the Desert*. Princeton, NJ: Princeton University Press, 1979.

McKenna, Andrew. *Violence and Difference: Girard, Derrida, and Deconstruction*. Urbana: University of Illinois Press, 1991.

McKenzie, John. *Second Isaiah*. New York: Doubleday, 1979.

Miller, Arthur. *Death of a Salesman*. New York: Viking Press, 1949.

Mosès, Stéphane. *System and Revelation: The Philosophy of Franz Rosenzweig*. Tr. Catherine Tihanyi. Detroit: Wayne State University Press, 1992.

Neher, André. *L'existence juive*. Paris: Seuil, 1962.

———. *The Prophetic Existence*. South Brunswick, NJ: A. S. Barnes, 1969.

Newstok, Scott L., ed. *Kenneth Burke on Shakespeare*. West Lafayette, IN: Parlor Press. 2007.

Niewiadomski, Józef. "A Reply to Sandor Goodhart." Tr. B. Palaver. In Palaver (1994), 11–12.

Ong, Walter. *Literacy and Orality*. New York: New York University Press, 1975.

Oughourlian, Jean-Michel. *The Puppet of Desire*. Tr. Eugene Webb. Stanford, CA: Stanford University Press, 1991.

Palaver, Wolfgang, ed. "A Jewish-Christian Dialogue." *Bulletin of the Colloquium on Violence and Religion* 7 (October 1994): 11–12.

———. "A Jewish-Christian Dialogue II." *Bulletin of the Colloquium on Violence and Religion* 8 (March 1995): 12–13.

———. "A Jewish-Christian Dialogue III." *Bulletin of the Colloquium on Violence and Religion* 9 (October 1995): 12.

———. "A Jewish-Christian Dialogue IV." *Bulletin of the Colloquium on Violence and Religion* 10 (March 1996): 10–12.

Pechter, Edward. *Othello and Interpretative Traditions*. Iowa City: University of Iowa Press, 1999, 11–30.

Peters, Ted, ed. "Paul and Luther: A Debate over Sacred Violence." *Dialog* 32.4 (Fall 1993): 47–88.

Plaut, W. Günther. *The Torah: A Modern Commentary*. New York: Union of American Hebrew Congregations, 1981.

Poulet, Georges. *The Metamorphoses of the Circle*. Tr. Carley Dawson and Eliott Coleman. Baltimore: Johns Hopkins University Press, 1967.

Prigogine, Ilya, and Isabelle Stengers. *Order out of Chaos: Man's New Dialogue with Nature*. New York: Bantam Books, 1984.

Rad, Gerhard von. *Holy War in Ancient Israel*. Eugene, OR: Wipf and Stock, 2000.

Redekop, Vern Neufeld. *From Violence to Blessing*. Toronto: Novalis, 2002.

Regensburger, Dietmar. "Bibliography of Literature on the Mimetic Theory of René Girard." http://www.uibk.ac.at/theol/cover/girard/bibliography.html.

Rosenberg, Rabbi A. J. *The Book of Isaiah*. Vol. 2. New York: The Judaica Press, 1983.

Rosenzweig, Franz. *The Star of Redemption*. Tr. Barbara E. Galli. Madison: University of Wisconsin Press, 2005.

———. *The Star of Redemption*. Tr. William W. Hallo. Notre Dame, IN: University of Notre Dame Press, 1985.

Rougemont, Denis de. *Love in the Western World*. Princeton, NJ: Princeton University Press, 1983.

Satin, Joseph. *Shakespeare and His Sources*. New York: Houghton Mifflin, 1966.

Scheler, Max. *Ressentiment*. Ed. Lewis A. Coser. Tr. William W. Holdheim. New York: Schocken, 1972.

Scholem, Gershom. *Kabbalah*. New York: Meridian, 1978.

———. *Major Trends in Jewish Mysticism*. New York: Schocken, 1972.

———. *The Messianic Idea in Judaism, and Other Essays on Jewish Spirituality*. New York: Schocken, 1995.

Schuld, Joyce. *Foucault and Augustine: Reconsidering Power and Love*. South Bend, IN: University of Notre Dame Press, 2013.

Schwager, Raymund. "A Reply to Sandor Goodhart." Tr. B. Palaver. In Palaver (1994), 12.

———. "A Second Reply to Sandor Goodhart." In Palaver (October 1995), 12.

———. *Must There Be Scapegoats?* San Francisco: Harper and Row, 1987.

Serres, Michel. *Hermes: Literature, Science, Philosophy*. Baltimore: Johns Hopkins University Press, 1982.

———. *Hermès Tome I. La Communication*. Paris: Les Éditions de Minuit, 1968.

———. *Le parasite*. Paris: Grasset, 1980.

———. "Receiving René Girard into the Académie Française." Tr. William A. Johnsen and Andrew McKenna. In Goodhart, Jørgensen, Ryba, and Williams (2009), 1–17.

———. *Rome: Le livre des fondations*. Paris: Grasset, 1983.

———. *Rome: The Book of Foundations*. Tr. Felicia McCarren. Stanford, CA: Stanford University Press, 1991.

———. *The Parasite*. Tr. Lawrence R. Schehr. Baltimore: Johns Hopkins University Press, 1982.

Shakespeare, William. *A Midsummer Night's Dream*. Dir. William Dieterle. Burbank, CA: Warner Bros. Entertainment, 1935.

———. *Othello: A New Variorum Edition of Shakespeare*. Ed. Horace Howard Furnace. Philadelphia, PA: J. P. Lippincott, 1886.

———. *Othello: The Arden Shakespeare*. Ed. E. A. J. Honigmann. London: Thomas Nelson and Sons, 1997.

Sherwood, Yvonne, and Kevin Hart, eds. *Derrida and Religion: Other Testaments*. New York: Routledge, 2004.

Speiser, E. A. *Genesis*. Anchor Bible Series. Garden City, NY: Doubleday, 1964.

Steiner, George. "Our Homeland, the Text." *Salmagundi* 66 (Winter–Spring 1985): 4–25.

Steinsaltz, Adin, ed. *The Talmud*. Vol. 3. *Tractate Bava Metzia*. Part 3. New York: Random House, 1990.

Swartley, Willard M., ed. *Violence Renounced: René Girard, Biblical Studies, and Peacemaking*. Telford, PA: Pandora Press, 2000.

Ward, Bruce. "Giving Voice to Isaac: The Sacrificial Victim in Kafka's Trial." *Shofar* 22.2 (Winter 2004): 64–84.

White, Hayden. "Ethnological 'Lie' and Mythical 'Truth.'" *Diacritics* 8.1 (1978): 2–9.

Williams, James G. *Girardians: The Colloquium on Violence and Religion, 1990–2010*. Vienna, Austria: LIT Verlag, 2012.

———. *The Bible, Violence, and the Sacred*. San Francisco: Harper and Row, 1991.

———. *The Girard Reader*. New York: Crossroads Publishing Company, 1996.

Zlotowitz, Meir, and Nosson Sherman. *Bereishis/Genesis*. 6 vols. Artscroll Tanakh Series. Brooklyn, NY: Mesorah Publications, 1977–1981.

Index